CPA
REVIEW GUIDE

CPA
REVIEW GUIDE

Jay Ballantine
University of Colorado - Boulder

Prentice Hall, Upper Saddle River, NJ 07458

Acquisitions editor: *Linda Schreiber*
Associate editor: *Kristen R. Imperatore*
Project editor and cover design: *Theresa Festa*
Manufacturer: *Quebecor Printing Group*

Printed in the United States of America

10 9 8 7 6 5 4 3 2

ISBN 0-13-085909-5

Prentice-Hall International (UK) Limited, *London*
Prentice-Hall of Australia Pty. Limited, *Sydney*
Prentice-Hall Canada Inc., *Toronto*
Prentice-Hall Hispanoamericana, S.A., *Mexico*
Prentice-Hall of India Private Limited, *New Delhi*
Prentice-Hall of Japan, Inc., *Tokyo*
Prentice-Hall (Singapore) Pte Ltd
Editora Prentice-Hall do Brasil, Ltda., *Rio de Janeiro*

TABLE OF CONTENTS

Preface

Chapter   Title

DEDICATION

To Timmy Tinkham, for all her help, hard work, support, and
suggestions in connection with this project and
all that she brings and gives to life itself

HOW TO USE THIS CPA REVIEW IN CONJUNCTION WITH THE TEXT

This CPA Review Guide is designed to be used along with *Contemporary Business Law, Third Edition*, as you prepare for the CPA examination. By using a CPA review guide which is specifically coordinated with the text you have already studied from, you get maximum benefit in your CPA exam preparation from the work you have already done in your business law course. Advantages of this system include:

- An outline format keyed into a text with which you are already familiar.

- Additional detail in CPA exam subject areas not covered by the text.

- Ability to reinforce your study of legal rules by reference to numerous text examples.

- An outline which is more concise because the text is available to fill in the gaps.

Each chapter in this CPA Review Guide corresponds to a single chapter in the text, except for the first four chapters. The corresponding chapter from the text is indicated on the page headings throughout this book. The CPA Review Guide usually, though not always, presents the material in the same order that it is presented in the chapter. This allows you to reinforce your review of the rules with examples, many of which you will remember as soon as you start to read them, thus saving time. Each chapter contains several components.

CHAPTER COMPONENTS

1. *Overview*. The overview gives an overall picture of the area of law covered in the chapter. Candidates often are so focused on memorizing detailed rules that they fail to grasp overall concepts.
2. *Outline*. The outline is the primary presentation of the subject matter which must be mastered to succeed on the CPA exam.
3. *Exam Tips*. The exam tips give further explanations of complex areas or highlight areas that can be confused with one another.
4. *Likely Exam Topics*. These are topics that have been heavily tested on past exams. There are no certainties regarding future exam coverage, and now that the CPA exam is only partially disclosed, it might become harder to predict topic areas. The official AICPA Content Specifications on the next page illustrate the broad subject areas from which questions can be drawn.
5. *Key Terms*. Candidates should be familiar with all the terms listed. The list is generally in the same order as the items appear, in bold type, in the outline.
6. *Practice Questions*. Most of the questions are from past CPA exams. The answers to the essay questions are the unofficial answers provided by the AICPA, except for the essay questions written by the author. The explanations for the multiple choice questions and other objective format questions are written by the author. The questions from past exams are identified by exam date and question number.

AICPA CONTENT SPECIFICATIONS OUTLINE (as of August 1999))

I.   **Professional and Legal Responsibilities (15%)**
   A. Code of professional conduct.
   B. Proficiency, independence, and due care.
   C. Responsibilities in other professional services.
   D. Disciplinary systems imposed by the profession and state regulatory bodies.
   E. Common law liability to clients and third parties.
   F. Federal statutory liability.
   G. Privileged communications and confidentiality.
   H. Responsibilities of CPAs in business and industry, and in the public sector.

II.   **Business Organizations (20%)**
   A. Agency.
      1. Formation and termination.
      2. Duties of agents and principals.
      3. Liabilities and authority of agents and principals.
   B. Partnership, joint ventures, and other unincorporated associations.
      1. Formation, operation, and termination.
      2. Liabilities and authority of partners and owners.
   C. Corporations.
      1. Formation and operation.
      2. Stockholders, directors, and officers.
      3. Financial structure, capital, and distributions.
      4. Reorganization and dissolution.
   D. Estates and trusts.
      1. Formation, operation, and termination.
      2. Allocation between principal and income.
      3. Fiduciary responsibilities.
      4. Distributions.

III. **Contracts (10%)**
   A. Formation.
   B. Performance.
   C. Third-party assignments.
   D. Discharge, breach, and remedies.

IV.   **Debtor-Creditor Relationships (10%)**
   A. Rights, duties, and liabilities of debtors and creditors.
   B. Rights, duties, and liabilities of guarantors.
   C. Bankruptcy.   [continued on next page]

AICPA Content Specifications Outline (cont.)

V.   Government Regulation of Business (15%)
    A. Federal securities acts.
    B. Employment regulation.
    C. Environmental regulation.

VI.   Uniform Commercial Code (20%)
    A. Negotiable instruments.
    B. Sales.
    C. Secured transactions.
    D. Documents of title.

VII.   Property (10%)
    A. Real property including insurance.
    B. Personal property including bailments and computer technology rights.

Suggested publications to study--business law and professional responsibilities

AICPA Code of Professional Conduct
AICPA Statements on Auditing Standards dealing explicitly with proficiency,
    independence, and due care
AICPA Statement on Standards for Consulting Services
AICPA Statements on Responsibilities in Personal Financial Planning Practice
Books covering business law, auditing, and accounting

FORMAT AND GRADING OF THE CPA EXAM

- The CPA exam is a two-day exam consisting of four parts. The business law section is three hours long and consists of three kinds of questions, multiple choice, other objective format, and essay.
- The exam is given twice a year, an Wednesday and Thursday of the first week of May and the first week of November.
- The passing score on each section is 75 out of 100, but this is not based on a straight percentage. There is a complex "curving" and normalizing process applied to the raw scores.
- The essay questions are hand-graded by professors, practicing CPAs, and attorneys who grade only one question and thereby become an expert on that question. This makes it impossible for a candidate to pull a "snow job" in an essay.
- There is a review and regrading process with extra steps for exams with scores just below the passing score.
- Five percent of the score is based on writing ability. It is crucial that candidates with weak writing skills improve them prior to the exam, and that all candidates remember to use all their writing skills to their fullest.

- Grading is based on awarding points for correct answers, or in the case of essays, for correct aspects of the answer. There is no penalty for incorrect answers. Thus candidates should answer all questions, even if the candidate can only guess.
- On essay questions, even a very weak or incomplete answer will likely earn some points. Candidates should allocate some time to all questions rather than spend too much time trying to make the answer to one question the best in the nation.
- Current information about the CPA exam can be found at the website for the American Institute of Certified Public Accountants at www.aicpa.org.

GENERAL BUSINESS LAW STUDY SUGGESTIONS.

- Mastering business law requires that you be able to do several things. You must know, mainly through memorization, a large number of legal rules. You must also be able to determine which rule applies to a given factual situation, and be able to apply that rule to the particular facts. To illustrate:
  1. You must **know the legal rules and principles** of the law, for example:
     - What are the elements of fraud?
     - What are the primary provisions of the Securities Exchange Act of 1934?
     - What are the real defenses to payment of a negotiable instrument?
  2. You must be able to **identify which legal rules or principles are applicable in a given factual situation**, for example:
     - Where a party to a contract claims to have received less than that party bargained for, you must quickly recognize that this could involve issues of fraud or breach of warranty.
     - In a debtor/creditor situation where there is only one creditor and there is a question whether this creditor can enforce a security interest, you must quickly recognize that *attachment*, not perfection, is at issue.
  3. You must be able to **apply the legal rules or principles to the particular factual situation**, for example:
     - With fraud, you must determine whether the statement, "This car will make it to California," is a false statement of a material fact in the particular situation of the question.
     - To determine whether the warranty of fitness for a particular purpose applies, you must examine the facts and determine whether the seller knew of the purpose for which the buyer was acquiring the goods.
     - If attachment of a security interest is the issue, you must examine the facts and determine whether this has occurred.

- On the day of the exam you should know the rules and principles (No. 1 above) so well that you can instantly recall them. You simply cannot afford to waste precious exam time trying to remember, for example, which implied warranties apply to merchants only, and which apply to all sellers. You must know this thoroughly when you walk into the exam. That will allow you to spend your time at the exam on the second two steps.

- Much of the business law material lends itself to studying with a partner and asking one another questions. It is easy to overestimate your preparedness in the business law area. Your ability to answer your study partner's questions can be a good preparedness measure.
- Most CPA exam essay questions are structured such that there is a single correct outcome. Many cases discussed in business law courses and on exams are questions where the application of the rule could have different outcomes.
- When working practice questions, you should simulate exam conditions. Most important is to force yourself to answer a question rather than peek back at the outline. It will develop your skill to answer questions when you are not sure of the answer, a skill even the best-prepared candidate needs.
- Consider having an English instructor critique a couple of your answers to essay questions. Write the essay under exam conditions, and also give a copy of the unofficial AICPA answer to the person doing the critique.

SUGGESTIONS FOR TAKING THE EXAM

All Questions

- Draw diagrams to understand complex fact situations. You should almost always do this when there are more than two parties. For example, agency questions will generally involve at least three parties. Also, where there is a series of events over a period of time, a diagram can help you understand the sequence of events.
- Before trying to determine the outcome of a factual situation, state to yourself the applicable legal rule(s) involved. It is all too easy to allow the facts to influence your answer. For example, in a fraud case, you should remind yourself of all the fraud requirements. Then, only if all those elements are present, do you conclude that fraud is present. This will prevent you from concluding that there is fraud based solely on the sleaziness or unfairness of the defendant's behavior.

Multiple Choice Questions

- Read the essay questions before doing the multiple choice questions, and mark multiple choice questions which could provide hints or ideas for the essay solutions.
- Be aware of the format of your answer sheet, as there are several different patterns used.
- If the question's structure allows, try to answer the question before reading the answer choices.
- Answer all questions as you work them, even the ones you are not sure of and plan to look at again. If you forget to go back or run out of time, you will at least have a chance of getting it correct.
- Do not take too long on any one question.
- Do not let extremely tough or bizarre questions rattle your concentration or self-confidence. They will be tough or bizarre for everyone. Every exam has a few trial questions that are not graded.
- You should usually not change your answer unless you are sure that your new answer is correct, for example, when you misread the question the first time, or suddenly remember the applicable rule.
- You will never have two identical answer choices. If two choices are similar, either they are both incorrect or there is a small difference that makes one correct and the other incorrect.

Other Objective Format Questions

- These questions take many forms, but they are generally multiple choice or true/false questions in various formats.
- Be sure to read the instructions carefully on these to learn all the requirements and limitations, such as whether answer choices can be used more than once, or a question can have multiple answers.

Essay Questions

- Answer essay questions by first stating your conclusion. Then state the legal rule or rules applicable to the situation. Lastly, explain how the facts fit the rule and lead to your conclusion. Note that the statement of the rule will often involve stating the general rule followed by stating an exception which applies in the particular question.
- Be careful using pronoun references. There are often many parties, thus it is better to refer to each by name or role in the question, such as "seller" or "agent," rather than merely using "he" or "she." Questions sometimes use names of parties to indicate their roles. For example, a buyer's name might begin with the letter "B" and the seller's name with the letter "S."
- Outline your answer before beginning to write. This has several benefits. It will help organize your answer. You might get a point or two for items in the outline if your actual essay is weak. An outline will also force you to think through your analysis to the conclusion before you begin writing. This will reduce the likelihood of getting to the end of an essay, only to realize that you have reached an incorrect conclusion. Even though it will take a minute or two to prepare the outline, it will allow you to write a better essay more quickly.
- Although you should prepare an outline, your essay should be written in essay format using complete sentences only. The only deviation is that you might be able to list the elements required in a particular case. Thus it would be acceptable to list out the elements of fraud. Otherwise, you should use complete sentences.
- Make sure that all points of your outline make it into your essay. Although the graders might give you some credit for material in your outline, you cannot count on this. Make sure that everything you have to say is in your essay.
- Answer only the specific question or questions posed. In many essay questions, there might be legal issues present which you are not asked to discuss. Discuss only what is asked, although you might take a sentence or two to relate to other issues. For example, in a question asking whether fraud is present, if you conclude that not all of the elements are present, you might mention the possibility of a mutual mistake being present.
- Remember that CPA exam essay questions usually have only one correct outcome.
- If time permits, after you have written your essay, go back and reread the question and immediately read your answer. As you do so, check to see if your essay actually responds to the questions posed, if it is clear and concise, and if your conclusions are adequately supported in your analysis.

SUGGESTIONS FOR AROUND EXAM DAY

The following suggestions are largely common sense, but they are also ideas and tips which can be forgotten or overlooked in the stressful and sometimes crazed period just before the CPA exam. These are merely suggestions, and only you can decide if they are right for you.

- **Get on an Early Schedule**. If you are cramming in the days before the exam, get up early to study rather than staying up late. You will likely have difficulty getting to sleep on the night before the exam. Even under the best of circumstances, if you have been staying up until 2:00 a.m., you will have difficulty getting to sleep if you suddenly try to go to sleep several hours earlier. If, on the other hand, you have been going to bed at 10:00, even taking an extra hour getting to fall sleep will still allow a reasonably good night's sleep.
- **Get Some Exercise**. Whether or not you usually exercise, getting some exercise around the exam will make you more tired physically, which will help you sleep better. It will also reduce stress. Of course, the goal is not to beat yourself into the ground--leave that to the CPA exam.
- **No First-Day Post-Mortems**. After the first day, do not talk about the exam with others who are taking it. It is all too easy to focus on items missed. These "post-mortem" conversations may discourage or depress you as you think about all those answers that other people provided and that you didn't. In reality, your answers were probably at least as good, if not better, than those of the other candidates. Resist the temptation to discuss the exam! Once the entire exam is over, you can have these conversations if you really want to. On Wednesday evening, your only concern should be to do your best on day two. Even after day two, there is not much point to such discussions, but at least then they won't adversely affect your performance on the exam. At that point, they'll only adversely affect your mental health until you get your results.
- **Make Plans for a Relaxing Wednesday Night**. Arrange to relax on Wednesday night. Limit any studying to cursory review because you are exhausted from your first day, and your brain is nearly full anyway. Consider arranging, in advance, a dinner out with friends, none of whom is taking the CPA exam. There can be many negative aspects of spending an evening with others who are taking the exam, including contagious fear and panic.
- **Have a Backup Plan to Reach the Exam Site**. Give yourself extra time and make backup plans to get to the exam on the big days. This includes a second alarm or friend to ensure that you do not oversleep. It should also include an alternate means to get to the exam site if your car decides to not start for the first time ever. Leave early enough so that if there is an unexpected delay, you have time to spare. Consider staying walking distance from the exam. Even if not needed, these precautions will give you less to worry about the night before. If practical, drive to the exam site ahead of time so you will not be trying to find it for the first time on exam day.
- **Choose Your Hotel Carefully**. If the exam is being given at a hotel, consider staying at a nearby hotel rather than the hotel where the exam is given. This will give you a change of scenery and get you away from many of the other stressed-out candidates.
- **Dress in Layers**. You should be ready for any temperature at the exam site.

CHAPTER 1
BASIC LEGAL CONCEPTS

OVERVIEW

Most of the material in the first chapter is not specifically tested on the CPA exam. However, the CPA exam assumes a knowledge of most of these concepts. In addition, knowledge of these topics will help in understanding many of the specific subjects which are tested, and can help you respond better to essay questions by using terms and discussing general concepts correctly. CPA exam candidates can be very focused on individual rules while not understanding general legal principles. Because of this chapter's introductory nature, it contains only an outline and does not contain the features of the other chapters. Most of the material in this chapter can be found in the first couple of chapters of *Contemporary Business Law* or other business law texts. There are two primary purposes for providing the material in this first chapter. First, it provides some general concepts and an overview of the general context in which many of the specific rules operate. Second, it introduces some general terminology which candidates often misunderstand.

OUTLINE

I. **Sources of Law.**
   A. <u>General Concepts</u>. Law comes from many sources. The material covered on the CPA exam comes primarily from the following:
   B. <u>Common Law</u>. **Common law** is the body of past court decisions which is used in deciding later cases. These earlier decisions are sometimes referred to as **precedent**. Common law is often referred to as judge-made law and covers situations where there are no statutes. Common law is also used to interpret a statute which is unclear. For example, contracts covering services and the sale of real property are covered by common law. Much of the common law today originated in England because the United States courts originally followed English common law. The connection has become less direct over time as the body of United States common law has become more extensive. Despite this, courts still occasionally look to past English decisions in deciding a current case.
   C. <u>Statutes</u>. Statutes are laws enacted by Congress or by state legislatures. In many areas of the law, state statutes differ little from state to state.
      1. *Uniform Laws*. There are a number of uniform state laws such as the Uniform Commercial Code. These are substantially similar state statutes which have been adopted by some or all of the states. Many were originally drafted by the American Law Institute, a group of legal scholars and practitioners. The drafted model statute is then available to be adopted by the legislature of each of the states. The Uniform Commercial Code is an example of a uniform law.
      2. *Federal v. State*. Most of the statutory law covering business is at the state level. Certain areas, such as bankruptcy and securities regulation, are covered primarily by federal statutes.

D. <u>Regulations</u>. Regulations are usually authorized by a statute and are issued by the agency given authority by the statute to do so. For example, the Occupational Safety and Health Administration (OSHA) issues regulations addressing workplace safety, and the Internal Revenue Service issues regulations addressing the tax laws. Regulations often provide more detailed requirements for a statute. For example, a tax statute might require that records be kept to support a particular tax deduction and related regulations could provide more detail on the exact type and extent of records required.

II. Basic Legal Concepts.

A. <u>Civil v. Criminal Lawsuits</u>.

1. *Criminal Suit*. A criminal suit involves action by the government against a party for engaging in prohibited conduct or for failing to complete a required act such as the filing of a tax return. A criminal case is based on the <u>conduct</u> of the defendant, and not on whether than conduct caused harm to anyone. Generally speaking, the remedy in a criminal case is punishment of some sort. If the defendant is an individual, the punishment is usually either a fine, imprisonment, or both. If the defendant is a business, the punishment is usually a fine because a business cannot be imprisoned.

2. *Civil Suit*. A civil suit involves action by a plaintiff seeking recovery from a defendant based on the defendant's wrongdoing. A civil case is based on the <u>injury</u> to the plaintiff caused by the defendant. Generally speaking, the remedy in a civil case is the recovery of money from the defendant to compensate the plaintiff for the loss caused by the defendant. In some cases, the defendant might be ordered to take some action or to refrain from some action, such as selling goods which violate a patent, in the future.

3. *Other Suits*. Some statutes today provide for recovery of civil penalties for certain conduct of defendants. These are civil cases where the remedy is punishment, making the case more like a criminal one. There are other special types of cases, such as those for bankruptcy, which are different from both criminal and civil cases.

B. <u>Parties in Lawsuits</u>.

1. *Parties in Civil Suits*. A civil suit is brought by a **plaintiff** who is usually seeking some sort of monetary recovery from a **defendant**.

2. *Parties in Criminal Suits*. The plaintiff in a criminal suit is the prosecutor, and the party charged with the crime is the defendant. The prosecutor is always the government, either the state or the federal government.

C. <u>Burden of Proof</u>. Generally, the plaintiff or prosecutor has the burden of proving the case. The degree to which the case must be proven is different for civil and criminal suits.

1. *Civil Suit*. In a civil suit, the plaintiff must prove her case by having the jury or judge believe that more than half the evidence in the case is in her favor. If the jury or judge believes the evidence is equally balanced or more than half on the defendant's side, the defendant wins. This is often referred to as the **preponderance of the evidence**. Stated differently, the plaintiff wins only if the jury or judge believes that the plaintiff's version is more likely correct than not correct.

2. *Criminal Suit*. In a criminal suit, the prosecutor must prove the case beyond a reasonable doubt. Thus, if a jury believes that the defendant is probably guilty, but also believes there is some reasonable doubt about the guilt, the jury must deliver a verdict of not guilty.

D. <u>Guilty or Liable</u>. Guilt is a term that generally applies only to criminal suits. Candidates often make statements such as "The party is guilty of breaching the contract." This is incorrect usage. This would be accurately stated, "The party has breached the contract and is therefore liable to pay damages to the nonbreaching party." In civil cases, the issue is generally whether or not the defendant is liable (usually for a payment) to the plaintiff, not whether or not the defendant is guilty. Guilt applies to crimes.

III.   Other General Concepts and Terminology.

A. <u>Courts of Law and Courts of Equity</u>. Courts of law were the original courts, with the courts of equity added (in England originally) because the limited remedies available in the courts of law sometimes led to unfair results. In many states, this distinction is primarily of historical interest today, although some remedies, such as certain contract remedies, are called **equitable remedies** because they originated in the equity courts.

B. <u>Parties' Roles Described by "or" and "ee."</u> There are many terms describing various parties in legal relationships such as employer and employee and donor and donee. Candidates often have difficulty with some of these concepts. The term ending in "or" (or sometimes "er") generally describes the person who owes something or does something toward a party described by the term ending in "ee." For example, an obligor owes a duty, or obligation, to an obligee. And an offeror makes an offer to an offeree.

C. <u>Operation of Law</u>. Something which happens **by operation of law** is something that happens automatically upon the occurrence of some other event. For example, an offer to form a contract terminates automatically, or by operation of law, if the offeror dies.

D. <u>Majority Rule</u>. Much of business law does not differ significantly from one state to another. Some aspects of business law, however, are quite different in some states compared to others. Where this is the case, the rule that applies in the majority of the jurisdictions is called the **majority rule**. Any rule followed by less than half of the jurisdictions is a minority rule. Jurisdictions include the states as well as Washington, D.C. and the territories such as the U.S. Virgin Islands.

E. <u>Difficulty of Proving a Case</u>. The CPA exam tests on the rules of law. Some of these rules cause candidates to question whether the requirements can be proven. The CPA exam tests the rules, and not the difficulty of proof. In the real world, a client's likelihood of proving his case is crucial in deciding whether or not to pursue a cause of action. But on the CPA exam, you must know what must be proven to win a particular type of case, or what the outcome is if the items given in a specific question are proven. Do not assume that the plaintiff will lose because she has a difficult case to prove. Questions usually focus on what must be proven, not on how difficult it might be to prove.

F. <u>Who Decides Issues</u>. Lawsuits can involve either disputes of fact (what happened) or disputes of law (what the law means, or how it should apply in a given circumstance). Disputes of law in all trials are decided by the judge. Disputes of fact are decided by the jury if there is one, otherwise they are also decided by the judge. Parties often choose not to have a jury trial for cost, expediency, and other reasons. In this guide and most business law texts, references to actions that "courts" might take, could refer to judges, juries, or both, depending on the context.

CHAPTER 2
CODE OF PROFESSIONAL CONDUCT AND CPA RESPONSIBILITIES

OVERVIEW

The **Code of Professional Conduct** (Code) is issued by the American Institute of Certified Public Accountants (**AICPA**). The Code sets conduct standards for CPAs. Some of the standards address mandatory conduct, others address prohibited conduct. The Code is based on CPAs being members of a profession, one aspect of which is self regulation. Candidates must be familiar with the Code, and the rules related to it. In studying the Code, candidates often find many of the provisions to be common sense. Candidates should focus on those sections which, to them, do not appear to be logical at first glance. There are some gaps in the numbering of the interpretations due to the deletion of prior interpretations. When coming across an exam question or situation for which the candidate cannot remember a specific applicable rule, the candidate should generally determine what would be necessary for the CPA to best serve the goals of competence, integrity, and (in audit engagements) independence.

OUTLINE

I. **Introduction.**
   A. <u>AICPA</u>. The American Institute of Certified Public Accountants is a not-for-profit organization which works for improvement of the profession of accounting. The AICPA writes and administers the CPA Exam. Members of the AICPA must abide by the Code of Professional Conduct (Code).
   B. <u>Applicability</u>. The Code applies to all professional services provided by members in public practice. The covered services include audits, special reports, compilations, reviews, engagements related to forecasts, etc. Only Rules 102 and 501 apply to members not in public practice.
   C. <u>Structure of Code</u>. The Code contains a series of general principles, followed by a series of rules. The Principles set out the general framework for the rules and can be viewed as a set of objectives for the Code. For the rules, there are related interpretations which further explain the rules. In addition, ethics rulings illustrate application of the rules to specific circumstances.
   D. <u>The Code as Part of the Profession</u>. One characteristic of a profession is the adoption of a voluntary code of conduct which recognizes the responsibility of the profession to the public.
   E. <u>Members</u>. The Code uses the term "member" to refer to CPAs who are members of the AICPA. The terms "member" and "CPA" will be used interchangeably in the discussion of the obligations under the Code.

II. **Principles of the Code of Professional Conduct.**
   A. <u>Article I--Responsibilities</u>. "In carrying out their responsibilities as professionals, members should exercise sensitive professional and moral judgments in all their activities."
   B. <u>Article II--Public Interest</u>. "Members should accept the obligation to act in a way that will serve the public interest, honor the public trust, and demonstrate commitment to the profession."

C. <u>Article III--Integrity</u>. "To maintain and broaden public confidence, members should perform all professional responsibilities with the highest sense of integrity."

D. <u>Article IV--Objectivity and Independence</u>. "A member should maintain objectivity and be free of conflicts of interest in discharging professional responsibilities. A member in public practice should be independent in fact and appearance when providing auditing and other attestation services."

E. <u>Article V--Due Care</u>. "A member should observe the profession's technical and ethical standards, strive continually to improve competence and the quality of services, and discharge professional responsibility to the best of the member's ability."

F. <u>Article VI--Scope and Nature of Services</u>. "A member in public practice should observe the Principles of the Code of Professional Conduct in determining the scope and nature of services to be provided."

III. **Rules of the Code of Professional Conduct.**

A. <u>Rule 101--Independence</u>. A member in public practice shall be **independent** in the performance of professional services as required by standards promulgated by bodies designated by the AICPA Council. Independence helps ensure that the auditor's opinion will not be improperly influenced and helps increase public confidence in the work of CPAs.

1. *Interpretation 101-1.* Independence is impaired if, at the time the opinion was given, the member or the member's firm:

   a. Owned a direct financial interest in the client. Any size of direct interest, or a commitment to obtain an interest, impairs independence.

   b. Owned an indirect <u>material</u> financial interest in the client. A mutual fund with holdings of the client's stock is an example of an indirect interest. **Exam tip #1.**

   c. Was a trustee or executor. Where the CPA is a trustee or executor, ownership by the trust or estate of any direct or a material indirect interest in the client impairs the independence of the CPA who is the trustee or executor.

   d. Had a joint investment. Any material joint investment with the client, including investments through partnerships, impair independence.

2. *Interpretation 101-2.* A former partner is not considered a member if the former partner does not actually participate, or appear to participate in the firm's business, and does not receive any retirement benefits other than ones fixed as to dates and amounts of payments. Inflation adjustments in retirement benefits would not cause the former partner to be considered a member. Amounts based on firm profits would make the retiree a member.

3. *Interpretation 101-3.* Performance of write-up services does not impair independence so long as the CPA does not:

   a. Consummate transactions,

   b. Prepare source documents, or

   c. Make changes in the client's data without the client's consent.

4. *Interpretation 101-4.* A CPA who is a director of a large nonprofit organization does not lose independence if:

   a. The position is honorary,

   b. It is identified as honorary on external materials, and

   c. The CPA does not vote and does not participate in management affairs.

5. *Interpretation 101-5.* The following loans from financial institutions do not impair independence so long as they were made under normal lending procedures:
   a. Loans existing as of January 1, 1992.
   b. Loans obtained by the CPA before the institution became a client.
   c. Loans originally obtained from an institution not requiring independence but which were later sold to one requiring independence.
   d. Loans obtained by the CPA prior to becoming a member of the firm requiring independence.
   e. Collateralized automobile loans and leases.
   f. Loans of the surrender value under an insurance policy.
   g. Borrowings fully collateralized by cash deposits.
   h. Credit cards and cash advances of $5,000 or less.
6. *Interpretation 101-6.* Litigation between the client and the CPA impairs independence in the following circumstances:
   a. The client actually initiates litigation alleging audit work deficiencies.
   b. The CPA actually initiates litigation alleging management fraud or deceit.
   c. The client threatens litigation alleging audit work deficiencies and the CPA believes it likely that the claim will be filed.
   Immaterial disputes unrelated to the performance of the audit, such as billing disputes, usually do not impair independence.
7. *Interpretation 101-8.* Financial interests in a nonclient who has a financial interest in a client can impair independence in some circumstances.
8. *Interpretation 101-9.* "Members" of a firm include all of the following:
   a. The firm, and its owners.
   b. Professional staff members participating in the engagement.
   c. All managerial employees in any office which performs a significant portion of the engagement.
   d. Spouse and other dependent relatives with respect to financial interest.
9. *Interpretation 101-12.* Material cooperative business arrangements can impair independence. The arrangement will not be considered a cooperative arrangement if all three of the following requirements are met:
   a. The firm's and client's participation are governed by different agreements.
   b. Neither the firm nor the client assumes any responsibility for the other.
   c. Neither party is an agent of the other.
10. *Unpaid Audit Fees.* Independence is impaired if any audit fees from prior years remain unpaid when the current year's report is issued.

B. Rule 102--Integrity and Objectivity. In the performance of any professional service, a member shall (a) maintain objectivity and integrity, (b) avoid conflicts of interest, and (c) not knowingly misrepresent facts or subordinate judgment. Resolving doubt in the client's favor in tax matters does not, by itself, impair integrity or objectivity. Objectivity toward one client might be impaired because of a relationship with another person, entity, product or service. If there is such a relationship which might be viewed as impairing objectivity, the work can be performed if the CPA believes the work can be performed with objectivity and the CPA gives the client disclosure and obtains consent. **Exam tip #2.**

C. Rule 201--General Standards. A member must comply with the following **general standards** in all engagements:
   1. *Undertake Only Engagements that the Member can Competently Complete.*
   2. *Exercise Due Professional Care.* This can require consultation with experts.
   3. *Obtain Sufficient Relevant Data.* The data should support the conclusions and recommendations.
   4. *Adequately Plan and Supervise Engagements.*
D. Rule 202--Compliance with Standards. A member who performs auditing, review, compilation, management consulting, tax, or other professional services shall comply with standards promulgated by bodies designated by Council. The designated bodies are:
   1. *Financial Accounting Standards Board.*
   2. *Government Accounting Standards Board.*
   3. *Auditing Standards Board.*
   4. *Accounting and Review Services Committee.*
   5. *Management Advisory Services Committee.*
E. Rule 203--Accounting Principles. Members cannot state that statements are in accordance with Generally Accepted Accounting Principles (GAAP) if they contain departures having a material effect on the financial statements taken as a whole, unless a departure from GAAP is necessary to prevent the statements from being misleading. When a departure is needed, the auditor's report must indicate the departure and why the statements would be misleading without the departure. Departures from GAAP might be needed to comply with new laws or for new types of business transactions.
F. Rule 301--Confidential Client Information. A member in public practice shall not disclose **confidential client information** without client consent. Client consent is not needed when the request for information is made by any of the following:
   1. *Enforceable Subpoena or Summons.*
   2. *AICPA Quality Review.*
   3. *Official Investigative or Disciplinary Body of the AICPA or State CPA Society.*
   In addition, a member may allow a prospective purchaser of her practice to review confidential client information without the client's consent, but should take precautions to prevent the further disclosure of the information.
G. Rule 302--Contingent Fees. Contingent fees are any fees determined on the basis of the specific result obtained, such as the amount of taxes due on a return. Fees fixed by courts or other judicial bodies are acceptable. Fees based on a tax amount in a judicial proceeding is acceptable, because the amount is determined by someone other than the CPA. **Exam tip #3.**
H. Rule 501--Acts Discreditable. A member shall not commit an act **discreditable** to the profession. The following are examples of discreditable acts:
   1. *Retention of Client Records.* Retention of client records after the client has demanded their return is discreditable. Papers prepared by the client for the CPA need not be returned, and the CPA can keep papers with information not on the client's books until fees are paid. **Exam tip #4.**
   2. *Major Crime.* Commission of a crime punishable by imprisonment for more than one year is discreditable.
   3. *Failure of the Member to File Any Required Personal Tax Return.*

   4. *Filing a False or Fraudulent Return for the Member or a Client.*
   5. *Revocation of the CPA's License by a Governmental Authority.*
   6. *Disclosure of CPA Exam Questions or Answers.*
I. Rule 502--Advertising. A member in public practice shall not seek to obtain clients by false, misleading, deceptive advertising or other means of solicittion. Types of prohibited advertising include advertising which:
   1. *Creates False or Unjustified Expectations.*
   2. *Implies the Ability to Influence a Court, Tribunal, or Regulatory Agency.*
   3. *Contains Urealistic Estimates of Fees.*
   4. *Contains Any Claim Likely to Mislead a Reasonable Person.*
J. Rule 503--Commissions and Referral Fees. A member in public practice shall not accept a commission for recommending any product or service to a client when the member or the member's firm also performs any of the following services for the same client:
   1. *An Audit or Review of a Financial Statement.*
   2. *A Compilation.* This applies only if the CPA is independent and reasonably expects a third party to rely on the statement or the compilation report.
   3. *An Examination of Prospective Financial Information.*
   Any commission or referral fee not prohibited by the above rules must be reported to the client. Any fee paid to obtain a client likewise must be reported to the client.
K. Rule 505--Form of Practice and Name. Members may practice under various forms of business organization, but may not use a misleading name.
   1. *Members of AICPA.* Membership in AICPA can be claimed only if all members of the firm are AICPA members.
   2. *Past Partners.* Use of past partners' names is acceptable.
   3. *One Partner Remaining.* Once there is only one member of the firm remaining, the partnership name can be used for only two more years.
   4. *Fictitious Names.* Fictitious names are acceptable.
   5. *Specialization.* A name indicating specialization is acceptable if not misleading.
L. Non-CPA Ownership of CPA Firms. Non-CPAs are now permitted to hold ownership interests in CPA firms under certain conditions:
   1. *Two Thirds Ownership Held by CPAs.* CPAs must hold at least two thirds of both voting rights and financial interests. The Non-CPA owners must have their own profession and not practice accounting.
   2. *CPA Must Have Ultimate Responsibility.* CPA owners must bear ultimate responsibility for the services covered by accounting, auditing, or compilation standards.
   3. *CPE Requirements.* Non-CPA owners must meet the same Continuing Professional Education (CPE) requirements as CPAs.
   4. *Baccalaureate Degree.* Non-CPA owners must have a baccalaureate degree.
   5. *Code of Professional Conduct.* Non-CPA owners must abide by the AICPA Code of Professional Conduct.

IV.   Responsibilities in Management Consulting Services.

  A. Generally. The Management Services Executive Committee of the AICPA issues Statements on Standards for Consulting Services.

    1. *CPA Develops the Findings.* In consulting services, the CPA develops the findings, conclusions, and recommendations presented. The nature of the services is determined solely by agreement between the CPA and the client.

    2. *For Use Solely by the Client.* A consulting engagement's findings, conclusions, or recommendations are generally only for the use and benefit of the client, and not for use by third parties.

    3. *Consulting Services for an Attest Client.* Independence must be maintained when providing consulting services to an attest client (generally an audit client). The mere fact of the performance of the consulting services does not impair independence. Independence is not required for other consulting clients, although objectivity is required.

  B. Types of Consulting Services.

    1. *Consultation.* This is a relatively short duration engagement such as commenting on a client-prepared business plan or recommending software for client investigation.

    2. *Advisory Services.* Examples include an operational review and improvement study, analysis of an accounting system and assistance with strategic planning.

    3. *Implementation Services.* These involve the CPA putting an action plan into effect, with examples including installing and supporting a computer system or executing steps to improve productivity.

    4. *Transaction Services.* These usually involve services with a specific client transaction, usually with a third party, and could include valuation services or litigation support services.

    5. *Staff and Other Support Services.* These involve providing staff and support services to perform tasks specified by the client. Examples include computer programming, bankruptcy trusteeship and controllership activities.

    6. *Product Services.* These involve providing a product and associated support services. Examples include the sale, delivery, installation, and implementation of training programs or computer software.

  C. Standards Applicable to Consulting Services:

    1. *General Standards of Rule 201.*
      a. Professional Competence.
      b. Use of Due Professional Care.
      c. Obtaining of Sufficient Relevant Data.
      d. Adequate Planning and Supervision.

    2. *Consulting Services Requirements of Rule 202.*
      a. Client Interest. The CPA must serve the client interest while maintaining integrity and objectivity.
      b. Understanding with Client. The CPA must obtain an oral or written understanding with the client about the responsibilities of the parties and the nature, scope and limitations of the services to be performed.
      c. Communication with Client. The CPA must inform the client of conflicts of interest, any reservations about the engagement, and significant findings of the engagement.

V. Responsibilities in Personal Financial Planning.

    A. <u>Generally</u>. **Personal financial planning engagements** are only those engagements that involve strategies and making recommendations to assist a client in defining and achieving personal financial planning goals.

    B. <u>Aspects of Financial Planning Engagements</u>.

        1. *Defining Engagement Objectives.*

        2. *Planning Specific Procedures Appropriate to the Engagement.*

        3. *Developing a Basis for Recommendations.*

        4. *Communicating Recommendations to the Client.*

        5. *Identifying Tasks for Taking Action on Planning Decisions.*

    C. <u>Additional Possible Aspects of Some Financial Planning Engagements</u>.

        1. *Assisting the Client to Take Action on Planning Decisions.*

        2. *Monitoring the Client's Progress in Achieving Goals.*

        3. *Updating Recommendations and Helping the Client Revise Planning Decisions.*

    D. <u>Rules from the Code of Conduct Applicable to Personal Financial Planning</u>.

        1. *Rule 102--Integrity and Objectivity.*

        2. *Rule 201--General Standards.* All four general standards apply.

        3. *Rule 301--Confidential Client Information.* Permission is needed for disclosure.

        4. *Rule 302--Contingent Fees.*

    E. <u>Other Considerations</u>.

        1. *Financial Statement Preparation.* If the engagement includes preparation of financial statements or projections, the CPA should consider the applicable provisions of AICPA pronouncements.

        2. *Engagement Letter.* The CPA should document her understanding of the scope of services to be provided and consider using an engagement letter.

        3. *Relevant Information.* The CPA should consider the client's goals, financial position, and available resources.

        4. *Written Recommendations.* Recommendations should ordinarily be in writing and include a summary of the client's goals, significant assumptions, and a description of any limitations on the work performed.

        5. *Not Responsible for Further Action.* Unless otherwise agreed, the CPA is not responsible for assisting the client in acting on planning decisions, monitoring the client's progress in achieving goals, or updating recommendations and revising planning decisions.

        6. *Implementation Engagement.* An implementation engagement involves assisting a client in acting on financial planning decisions.

VI.   Working Papers and Communications Privileges.

    A. <u>Working Papers</u>.

        1. *Definition.* The accountant's **working papers** include various types of written work prepared by a CPA to support the CPA's opinion or other conclusions.

        2. *Purposes.* Working papers are used to help determine and provide support for the opinion issued. An additional purpose is to provide a record of the type and extent of work that was done in the event of litigation or for other purposes.

3. *Items Included.* Working papers can include worksheets, compilations, summaries, analyses, schedules, notes, memoranda, and other communications. Working papers are distinguished from client records which might come into the CPA's possession during the course of the engagement.

4. *Ownership.* Working papers are the property of the CPA, although there are limits on what the CPA can do with them, described below. Client records remain the property of the client even when in the possession of the CPA.

5. *Limits on Working Paper Disclosure.* Although the CPA owns the working papers, the CPA has a duty to not allow improper disclosure of the confidential information contained in working papers. Generally the CPA cannot disclose the information in the working papers (by any means, including by transferring possession of the working papers themselves) to anyone without the consent of the client.

6. *When Working Paper Disclosure Is Allowed.* There are certain circumstances in which working papers can be shown to third parties without the client's consent.
   a. Subpoena. Client consent is not needed to show the working papers to a government agency or court pursuant to a valid subpoena.
   b. CPA Quality Review. Client consent is not needed to show the working papers to a CPA quality review panel.
   c. Surviving Partner. Client consent is not needed to give the working papers to a surviving partner of a deceased partner. **Exam tip #5.**

B. Privileged Communications.
   1. *Definition.* A **privileged communication** is any communication arising out of a confidential relationship which the law protects from being disclosed in a legal proceeding.
   2. *Source of Privilege.* Some privileges exist under common law, but many are created by statute, mostly at the state level. Many privileges are recognized in some states but not in others. There is no accountant-client privilege under state law.
   3. *Purpose.* Privileged communications laws exist to encourage clients to be able to fully disclose information to a professional without fear of the professional being required by a court to disclose the information. They encourage open discussion by the client of all aspects of the client's situation, both good and bad. With full information, the professional is best able to help the client. **Exam tip #6.**
   4. *Examples.* Common privileged communications include those between attorney and client, doctor and patient, therapist and client, husband and wife.
   5. *How the Privilege Works.* If the privilege exists, the holder of the privilege can prevent the other party to the communication from disclosing it, even in a court proceeding or pursuant to a subpoena. For example, if a client discussed legal matters with an attorney as part of an attorney-client relationship, the attorney cannot be forced to testify about the contents of that discussion without the consent of the client.
   6. *Privilege is Held by the Client.* In privileges arising from professional relationships, the privilege is held and controlled by the client only. Thus, the client can disclose the contents of any discussions or other communications with an attorney even if the attorney objects. A client might want to disclose the contents of such discussions as part of a malpractice suit against the attorney.

7. *Federal Law: No Accountant-Client Privilege.* Federal law does not recognize an accountant-client privilege, thus in a federal legal proceeding, a CPA can be forced to disclose the contents of communications, including working papers, without the consent of the client.

8. *State Law: Only a Few States Recognize the Accountant-Client Privilege.* The accountant-client privilege exists under state law only in the few states where it has been created by statute.

9. *Requirement for the Privilege to Apply.* In states with an accountant-client privilege, the privilege applies if the communication was part of a professional relationship intended to be confidential when the communication took place, and if the privilege has not been waived by the client. For example, the privilege would not apply to statements made to a CPA in a casual conversation at a cocktail party. **Exam tip #7.**

EXAM TIPS

1. A direct interest of any amount, even an immaterial amount, impairs independence. Do not be misled by a question where a CPA owns an immaterial amount of stock in a client. That ownership would impair independence.

2. Rule 102 applies to all services undertaken by members.

3. A contingent fee based on the tax due on a tax return is not acceptable, but a contingent fee based on the results of a tax audit or lawsuit is acceptable.

4. Candidates often confuse client records with the CPA's working papers. Be sure to know the rules for each, but also be sure to not inadvertently think of one when the question addresses the other.

5. Note that disclosure or transfer of working papers to the purchaser of the CPA's practice requires the consent of the client. The rationale is that the client should be able to control the disclosure to the purchaser of the practice, given that there is usually no preexisting relationship between the client and such a purchaser.

6. Even without a privilege, the CPA cannot voluntarily disclose confidential client information without the client's consent. Without a privilege, a court can compel the CPA to testify about communications with the client. Where there is a privilege, a court cannot compel the testimony.

7. Candidates should understand exactly how the accountant-client privilege works, and the fact that it can be waived only by the client. It is not designed to protect the CPA.

KEY CONCEPTS LIKELY TO BE TESTED ON THE CPA EXAM

1. Situations in which independence is impaired.
2. General Standards of Rule 201.
3. When confidential client information can and cannot be disclosed.
4. Acceptable forms of CPA firm names.
5. Which standards apply only to audit engagements and which apply to all engagements.
6. Consulting engagements and related responsibilities.
7. Accountant-client privilege, where it exists and how it works.

KEY TERMS

Code of Professional Conduct   General Standards   Personal Financial Planning
AICPA   Confidential Client Information   Working Papers
Independence   Discreditable Acts   Privileged Communication

MULTIPLE CHOICE QUESTIONS

1.   Law Nov 95 #1
According to the ethical standards of the profession, which of the following acts is generally prohibited?
A. Purchasing a product from a third party and reselling it to a client.
B. Writing a financial management newsletter promoted and sold by a publishing company.
C. Accepting a commission for recommending a product to an audit client.
D. Accepting engagements obtained through the efforts of third parties.

2.   Law Nov 95 #2
According to the ethical standards of the profession, which of the following acts is generally prohibited?
A. Issuing a modified report explaining a failure to follow a governmental regulatory agency's standards when conducting an attest service for a client.
B. Revealing confidential client information during a quality review of a professional practice by a team from the state CPA society.
C. Accepting a contingent fee for representing a client in an examination of the client's federal tax return by an IRS agent.
D. Retaining client records after an engagement is terminated prior to completion and the client has demanded their return.

3.   Law May 95 #1
According to the standards of the profession, which of the following circumstances will prevent a CPA performing audit engagements from being independent?
A. Obtaining a collateralized automobile loan from a financial institution client.
B. Litigation with a client relating to billing for consulting services for which the amount is immaterial.
C. Employment of the CPA's spouse as a client's internal auditor.
D. Acting as an honorary trustee for a not-for-profit organization client.

4.   Law May 93 #3
According to the standards of the profession, which of the following events would require a CPA performing a consulting services engagement for a nonaudit client to withdraw from the engagement?

I.   The CPA has a conflict of interest that is disclosed to the client and the client consents to the CPA continuing the engagement.
II. The CPA fails to obtain a written understanding from the client concerning the scope of the engagement.

A. I only.
B. II only.
C. Both I and II.
D. Neither I nor II.

5.   Law Nov 94 #3

To exercise due professional care, an auditor should

A. Critically review the judgment exercised by those assisting in the audit.
B. Examine all available corroborating evidence supporting management's assertions.
C. Design the audit to detect all instances of illegal acts.
D. Attain the proper balance of professional experience and formal education.

6.   Law Nov 94 #5

According to the professions's standards, which of the following is **not** required of a CPA performing a consulting engagement?

A. Complying with Statements on Standards for Consulting Services.
B. Obtaining an understanding of the nature, scope, and limitation of the engagement.
C. Supervising staff who are assigned to the engagement.
D. Maintaining independence from the client.

7.   Law Nov 94 #1

The profession's ethical standards most likely would be considered to have been violated when a CPA represents that specific consulting services will be performed for a stated fee and it is apparent at the time of the representation that the

A. Actual fee would be substantially higher.
B. Actual fee would be substantially lower than the fees charged by other CPAs for comparable services.
C. CPA would **not** be independent.
D. Fee was a competitive bid.

8.   Law May 94 #2

Which of the following reports may be issued only by an accountant who is independent of a client?

A. Standard report on an examination of a financial forecast.
B. Report on consulting services.
C. Compilation report on historical financial statements.
D. Compilation report on a financial projection.

9.   Law Nov 95 #4

According to the standards of the profession, which of the following activities would most likely **not** impair a CPA's independence?

A. Providing extensive advisory services for a client.
B. Contracting with a client to supervise the client's office personnel.
C. Signing a client's checks in emergency situations.
D. Accepting a luxurious gift from a client.

10.   Law May 94 #2

Which of the following statements best explains why the CPA profession has found it essential to promulgate ethical standards and to establish means for ensuring their observance?

A. A distinguishing mark of a profession is its acceptance of responsibility to the public.
B. A requirement for a profession is to establish ethical standards that stress primary responsibility to clients and colleagues.
C. Ethical standards that emphasize excellence in performance over material rewards establish a reputation for competence and character.
D. Vigorous enforcement of an established code of ethics is the best way to prevent unscrupulous acts.

ESSAY QUESTION (Estimated time -- 15 to 25 minutes)

Law R96 # 2(a)

Dredge Corp. engaged Crew, a CPA licensed by a state board of accountancy, to perform an audit of Dredge's financial statements so that Dredge could obtain a large capital improvement loan. During the Audit, Bold, Dredge's CFO, asked Crew to accept a consulting engagement to assist Dredge with the installation of a new computerized accounting system. Crew accepted the consulting engagement and performed it simultaneously with the audit.

While performing the audit, Crew discovered material misstatements in Dredge's financial statements resulting from management fraud committed by Bold. Crew notified Bold of the discovery and was told to disregard it or Crew would lose the consulting engagement. Believing that the consulting engagement would be lost, Crew intentionally did not notify Dredge's audit committee of the fraud, and rendered an unqualified opinion on Dredge's financial statements.

Dredge submitted to Ocean Bank the materially misstated financial statements together with Crew's auditor's report. Ocean relied on the opinion in agreeing to finance Dredge's capital improvement.

While performing the consulting engagement, Crew failed to discover that Dredge's new computerized accounting system had insufficient control procedures because Crew omitted steps in order to complete the engagement on time. The insufficient control procedures had allowed and were allowing employees to steal from the corporation.

As a result of Bold's fraud, Dredge defaulted on the Ocean loan and was petitioned into bankruptcy under Chapter 11 of the Federal Bankruptcy Code.

The following events resulted from the above situation:

- Dredge Corp. reported Crew's actions to the state board of accountancy that licensed Crew.
- Dredge Corp. Sued Crew for negligence in performing the consulting engagement.
- Ocean Bank sued Crew for common law fraud for giving an unqualified opinion on Dredge's financial statements.

Required:

a. 1. Determine whether or not Crew violated the profession's standards in the areas of independence (when accepting the engagements), due care, and acts discreditable to the profession, and give the reason for your conclusions.

2. State the action the state board of accountancy may take against Crew.

EXPLANATIONS TO MULTIPLE CHOICE QUESTIONS

1. C is the correct answer. A CPA cannot accept a commission for recommending a product or service to an audit client. Choice A describes an acceptable act because if the product is being sold to the client, the client is not relying on the CPA's expertise as in the case of a product recommendation. Accepting engagements though the efforts of third parties is common and is allowable.

2. D is the correct answer. It is an ethical violation to retain client records after the client has demanded their return. Do not confuse client records with working papers. Working papers are property of the CPA, although there are restrictions on the client's use of them. Choice B is incorrect because client consent is not needed to release information pursuant to a quality review. Choice C is incorrect because contingent fees are acceptable where the amount of taxes due is determined by a court or the IRS.

3. C is the correct answer. A CPA's spouse and dependent relatives are considered members of the firm for determining independence. The incorrect choices are all situations which the Code of Conduct considers as not impairing independence.

4. D is the correct answer. Because the ultimate user of a consulting engagement is the client, the client's consent to the conflict of interest allows the CPA to continue with the engagement. Note that an audit client's consent to a conflict of interest or independence would not allow the CPA to perform the engagement because the ultimate user of the financial statements is someone other than the client. Although a written engagement letter is preferable, it is not necessary. An oral understanding is sufficient.

5. A is the correct answer. This question seeks the steps that the auditor should take to achieve the general goal of exercising due professional care. The review of the audit staff's judgment will help achieve this. Choice B is incorrect because it is not necessary to examine all evidence. Choice D is an example of an item that is desirable, but does not achieve the specific goal sought in the question. This is a common type of wrong answer. It sounds like a good choice but does not answer the question asked. If two answers seem correct, reread the question and see if one more directly answers the particular question.

6. D is the correct answer. Independence is not required in consulting engagements, although objectivity is. The incorrect answer choices are all required in consulting engagements.

7. A is the correct answer. It is an ethical violation to give an estimated fee for services when it is known at the time that the estimate is given that the actual fee will probably be higher. Choice B is incorrect because it is acceptable for a CPA to charge a lower price for services than other CPAs. Choice C is incorrect because independence is not required for consulting engagements. Choice D is incorrect because competitive bidding for engagements is acceptable and quite common.

8. A is the correct answer. Independence is required for a standard report on a financial forecast because third parties will be relying on the auditor's opinion. Choices C and D are incorrect because independence is not needed for a compilation report because the CPA is not expressing an opinion for others to rely on.

9. A is the correct answer. Advisory services do not impair independence, so long as they are only advisory in nature and the CPA does not take on any management roles. Choices B and C are both management functions which would impair independence. This question is somewhat tricky. The use of the word "extensive" in the correct choice might make it appear that the advisory services would impair independence. It is the nature of the services, not the quantity, that is important. The use of the words "in emergency situations" in choice C might make it appear that the signing of checks would not impair independence. Engaging in management functions impairs independence, and the fact that it was done in an emergency situation does not change that. Be very careful with answer choices which try to make an acceptable situation appear unacceptable or vice versa.

10. A is the correct answer. One value of a profession is its responsibility to the public. Choice B is incorrect because the primary responsibility is broader than to only clients and colleagues. Choice D is incorrect because it is too narrowly focused. The ethical standards exist to meet the responsibility to the public, and not merely to prevent violations. Furthermore, statements like answer choice D are statements of opinion about which reasonable minds can differ. Such answer choices are seldom the correct answer on the CPA exam.

UNOFFICIAL AICPA ANSWER TO ESSAY QUESTION

Law R96 #2(a)

a. 1. Crew did not violate the profession's standards regarding independence when the engagements were accepted. A CPA may perform consulting services simultaneously with an audit engagement.

Crew violated the profession's standards in failing to perform the consulting engagement and the audit with due care. Crew acted without due care by failing to discover the insufficient control procedures because of omitting steps in the engagement and by issuing an unqualified opinion on the financial statements.

Crew committed acts discreditable to the profession by failing to notify Dredge's audit committee of the material misstatements contained in the financial statements, failing to disclose Bold's fraudulent activities, and profiting from withholding the information.

2. The state board of accountancy may permanently revoke Crew's license to practice or may suspend or restrict it for period of time. If suspended or restricted, Crew may be required to take additional CPE courses as a condition of reinstatement.

CHAPTER 3
CPA LEGAL LIABILITY TO CLIENTS AND THIRD PARTIES

OVERVIEW

CPAs can incur legal liability from a number of sources. This chapter discusses the types of liability that a CPA can be subject to, as well as the extent of that liability. CPA legal liability is complicated by the fact that often the party injured by the CPA was not in a contractual relationship with the CPA. In other words, if a CPA failed to detect material misstatements in a client's financial statements and issued an unqualified opinion, it is unlikely that the client would be the party who was injured. Most likely, creditors or investors who have no contractual relationship with the CPA would be the injured parties.

OUTLINE

I. Introduction.
   A. <u>Audits</u>. In an **audit engagement**, the CPA typically examines the financial statements and performs various tests in order to issue an opinion on whether the financial statements "fairly present" the actual financial results and position of the client. Various third parties, such as current creditors and investors as well as potential creditors and investors, rely on the statements and the auditor's opinion in making investing and credit extension decisions.
   B. <u>Third Party Often Suffers a Loss</u>. When a CPA makes a mistake, it is usually one of these third parties who loses money when a loan is not paid back or an investment loses money. A CPA's mistake often does not cause a loss to the client.

II. Breach of Contract.
   A. <u>Only Contractual Parties Can Recover</u>. Recovery for breach of contract can be made only by parties to the contract. Such parties are said to be in **privity of contract**. **Exam tip #1.**
   B. <u>Used Where Client Suffers a Loss</u>. A client would use breach of contract as a cause of action where the CPA's breach caused a loss to the client. For example, if the breaching CPA did not perform the services agreed to and the client had to pay a higher fee to another CPA to perform the services, the client could recover the difference in amount from the breaching CPA. Or if a CPA was late in issuing audited financial statements, thus causing a delay in getting a loan such that the interest rate was higher, the client could recover the increased interest costs caused by the CPA's delay.
   C. <u>General Contract Remedy Rules Apply</u>. The general principles for remedies and damages for breach of contract apply to contract disputes involving a CPA. These general rules are discussed in Chapter 10 of this guide.
   D. <u>Common Law Applies</u>. Contracts with CPAs generally involve services. Do not think of the financial statements as a good or product. As a service, the source of law is common law.

III. Fraud.
   A. <u>Similar to Other Fraud Cases</u>. A **fraud** case against a CPA is based on the same basic elements of fraud required to be proven in other fraud cases.

B. <u>Elements</u>. Fraud against a CPA requires proof of all of the following:
   1. *False Representation,*
   2. *Of a Material Fact,*
   3. *Made With Intent to Deceive,*
   4. *Relied on by the Plaintiff,*
   5. *In Circumstances Where the Reliance was Justified,* and
   6. *Causing Damages or Injury as a Result.*

   The third requirement is often defined in terms of knowledge of the falsity, also called **scienter**. These elements of fraud must all be present, and are explained in more detail in connection with contracts in Chapter 8 of this guide.
C. <u>Punitive Damages</u>. Punitive damages are damages intended to punish the CPA for the wrongful conduct and can be recovered in actual fraud cases.
D. <u>Constructive Fraud</u>. A **constructive fraud** case can be brought where the CPA has acted with **reckless disregard** of the truth or consequences of his actions. Such cases are sometimes classified as **gross negligence**.
E. <u>Privity of Contract Not Required</u>. In fraud cases, a CPA can be held liable to any foreseeable party who can prove all the elements of fraud.

IV. **Negligence.**
   A. <u>Generally</u>. **Negligence** is a widely used cause of action that applies in many situations. With respect to accountants, negligence can exist where the accountant has failed to use reasonable care, skill, knowledge, and judgment in performing accounting services.
   B. <u>Elements of Negligence</u>. To win a negligence case against a CPA, the plaintiff must prove all five of the following;
      1. *The CPA Owed a Duty to the Plaintiff,*
      2. *The CPA Breached That Duty,*
      3. *The Plaintiff Suffered an Injury,*
      4. *The CPA's Breach Was the Actual Cause of the Injury,* and
      5. *The Injury was a Foreseeable Consequence of the Breach (Proximate Causation).*
   C. <u>The Duty Owed</u>. A CPA owes a duty to use reasonable care, skill, knowledge, and judgment in the performance of services. This is measured against the standard of a reasonable accountant. This duty requires that the CPA follow generally accepted accounting principles and generally accepted auditing standards where applicable, as well as other applicable standards.
   D. <u>To Whom the Duty is Owed</u>. The crucial issue (discussed below) in many CPA negligence cases is the extent to which the duty to use reasonable care extends to third parties.

V. **Negligence Liability of CPAs to Third Parties.**
   A. <u>State Law--Three Standards</u>. Negligence liability of clients to parties other than the client, or third parties, is based on state law, and thus differs from state to state. Three general standards have been developed, with only one of these applying in a given state. **Exam tip #2.**
   B. *Ultramares* <u>Doctrine</u>. The name of the *Ultramares* **doctrine** comes from the 1931 court case that established it. The *Ultramares* doctrine provides that the CPA is liable to only a limited group of defendants.

1. *A Negligent CPA Is Liable to*:
   a. Contractual Parties. This generally is the client.
   b. Parties in a contract-like relationship. This would be a third party where the CPA knew the identity of the third party and the purpose for which the third party was to use the financial statements or other auditor's report.
2. *Most Favorable to the CPA*. The *Ultramares* doctrine is the most limited of the three standards, and thus the most favorable to CPAs.
3. *Minority Rule Today*. Today the *Ultramares* doctrine is followed in a minority of states.

C. Restatement Standard. The **Restatement (Second) of Torts** established a slightly broader CPA liability to third parties for negligence. The Restatement is a compilation of many aspects of tort law which courts often refer to and follow. Under the Restatement rule, the CPA is liable to all members of a limited class. Thus, if the CPA prepared financial statements to enable a client to get a bank loan, the CPA would be liable to any bank who suffered a loss due to the CPA's negligence. The limited class would be "banks."
1. *Foreseen Party*. Under the Restatement rule, the members of the limited class are often referred to as **foreseen parties**. Thus, if the CPA prepares financial statements for the client to use at Third National Bank, other banks would be foreseen parties. **Exam tip #3.**
2. *Majority Rule*. The Restatement rule is the **majority rule** which applies in a majority of the states today. **Exam tip #4.**

D. Foreseeability Standard. The broadest test for liability extends liability to any foreseeable user of the financial statements. Under the **foreseeability standard**, there is no requirement that the CPA have known of the client's intended use of the financial statements or auditor's report or the identity of the user. This, like *Ultramares*, is a minority rule.

E. Negligence Only. These tests apply to negligence cases only, not to fraud or contract cases.

VI.   Statutory Civil Liability Under the Securities Acts.

A. Generally. The securities acts impose civil liability on accountants for misstatements in financial statements that the accountant is associated with. The requirements for imposing liability are quite specific, and differ under the two primary acts. The securities acts are discussed in general in Chapter 24 of this guide.

B. Securities Act of 1933. The **Securities Act of 1933** requires certain disclosures in connection with an issuance of securities to the public. Financial statements must be included, and liability can be imposed on accountants associated with them.
1. *Section 11*. The liability of experts, which includes CPAs, is imposed in **Section 11** of the 1933 Act.
2. *Plaintiff Proof Requirements*. Plaintiffs in a Section 11 case must prove the existence of:
   a. Material Misstatement.
   b. Damages.
   The plaintiff need not prove causation or intent, usually making the plaintiff's case very easy to prove. The damages usually arise from a decline, including to zero, in the value of the securities purchased.
3. *Defenses*. If the plaintiff has been able to prove its case, the CPA then has a chance to try to prove the existence of a defense. The presence of any valid defense will result in the CPA winning the case and avoiding liability.

4. *Due Diligence Defense.* The **due diligence defense** is by far the most important defense in a Section 11 case. The breadth of the defense somewhat compensates for how little the plaintiff must prove. If the CPA can prove that he made a reasonable investigation and had reasonable grounds to believe the statements were not materially misstated, the CPA will avoid liability. **Exam tip #5.**
5. *Other Defenses.*
   a. Plaintiff knew of the misstatement when the security was purchased.
   b. The CPA followed generally accepted accounting principles and generally accepted auditing standards.
   c. The misstatement was not the cause of the loss.
6. *Burden of Proof.* The limited elements which a plaintiff must prove essentially shifts the burden of proof on many issues to the CPA. For example, in most other cases a plaintiff must prove causation, but in a Section 11 case, the plaintiff need not prove it. The defendant, however, has the opportunity to prove lack of causation as a defense.

C. <u>Securities Exchange Act of 1934</u>. The **Securities Exchange Act of 1934** requires most large publicly held corporations to file annual and quarterly reports, including financial statements. This act contains antifraud provisions which can impose liability on CPAs associated with financial statements which are part of the required reports.
   1. *Section 10(b) and Rule 10b-5.* Section 10b imposes liability for fraud in connection with the required reports and prohibits misstatements or omissions of material facts. The courts have implied a private (civil) cause of action to recover for losses caused by **Rule 10b-5** violations.
   2. *Plaintiff Proof Requirements.* Plaintiffs in a Rule 10b-5 case must prove:
      a. A misstatement or omission in the financial statements,
      b. Of a material fact,
      c. Made with knowledge of the misstatement or omission (scienter),
      d. Relied on by the plaintiff,
      e. In circumstances where the reliance was justified, and
      f. Causing damages or injury as a result.
      These are basically the elements of a fraud case because Rule 10b-5 is based on fraud.
   3. *Defenses Available.*
      a. The plaintiff knew of the misstatement when the security was purchased.
      b. The plaintiff did not rely on the misstatement.
      c. The misstatement was not the cause of the loss.
      d. The audit was performed with due care. This is somewhat similar to the due diligence defense. When used as a defense, it essentially negates the scienter requirement of the plaintiff's case.
   4. *Section 18(a) Liability.* The 1934 act also imposes civil liability for making false or misleading statements in any application, report, or document filed with the SEC. This would include a CPA making such a statement.

D. <u>Comparison of 1933 Act and 1934 Act Cases</u>. A plaintiff needs to prove much less with a 1933 Act case than with a 1934 Act case. The biggest difference is that scienter, or "evil intent" must be proven in a 1934 Act case. **Exam tip #6.**

E. <u>Situation Determines Which Case Can be Brought</u>. If the misstated financial statement was issued in connection with an offering of securities under the 1933 Act, a Section 11 case is the only option for a plaintiff. Likewise, if the misstated financial statement was issued in connection with a report required under the 1934 Act, a Rule 10b-5 case is the only option for a plaintiff.

VII.   Criminal Liability.
A. <u>Generally</u>. A few statutes impose criminal liability on CPAs. Criminal liability usually results in punishment in the form of fines or imprisonment.
B. <u>Securities Act of 1933 Violations</u>. CPAs can have criminal liability under the securities acts in addition to civil liability. CPAs can be liable for willful violations, such as purposely putting false information into a registration statement or conspiring with management in fraudulent activity. Violations can result in fines up to $10,000 or imprisonment for up to five years, or both.
C. <u>Securities Act of 1934 Violations</u>. The 1934 Act also imposes criminal liability for willful violations for making false or misleading statements, with fines up to $1 million or imprisonment for up to 10 years, or both.
D. <u>Racketeer Influenced and Corrupt Organizations Act (RICO)</u>. The **Racketeer Influenced and Corrupt Organizations Act** was originally intended to control organized crime. The statute is very broad, and covers fraud under the securities laws and mail fraud.
  1. *Criminal Liability.* A CPA associated with an organization which engages in a pattern of the prohibited conduct can be held criminally liable. A **pattern of racketeering** can exist with as few as two violations over a 10-year period.
  2. *Civil Liability.* In addition, a CPA can have civil liability for RICO violations, including treble (triple) damages.
E. <u>Tax Preparation Criminal Liability</u>. The Tax Reform Act of 1976 imposed a number of tax preparer criminal liability provisions which are discussed in the next chapter of this guide.

EXAM TIPS

1. Privity of contract issues are frequently tested on the CPA exam. To be in privity of contract with a party simply means to have an existing contractual relationship. Candidates should know which types of CPA liability require privity of contract and which do not.
2. Candidates must know the names and requirements of the three standards. Candidates need not know which standard applies in a particular state. Thus, a fact application question must tell you which standard applies if that makes a difference in the outcome of the situation.
3. Be sure to understand the difference in foreseen parties and foreseeable parties. The term "foreseen" is a particular term that applies only in this subject area on the CPA exam. The term "foreseeable" is a general term which applies in other areas of the law as well.
4. If a question asks what "generally" or "usually" applies in connection with CPA negligence liability to third parties, it is seeking the majority, or the Restatement, rule.
5. The due diligence defense can be tested under accountant liability or under the securities laws. It is important to know that it applies only to Section 11 liability under the 1933 Act.

6. Candidates must clearly know the differences in the requirements for cases under each of the securities acts. The securities acts are covered in more depth in Chapter 24 of this guide.

KEY CONCEPTS LIKELY TO BE TESTED ON THE CPA EXAM

1. CPA fraud including constructive fraud.
2. The requirements to prove a negligence case, including the standard to which a CPA is held.
3. The three tests for CPA liability for negligence to nonclients (third parties).
4. Determining to whom a CPA is liable, including privity issues.
5. Liability of CPAs under the 1933 and 1934 securities acts.

KEY TERMS

Audit Engagement	Negligence	Securities Act of 1933
Privity of Contract	*Ultramares* Doctrine	Section 11
Fraud	Restatement of Torts	Due Diligence Defense
Scienter	Foreseen Party .	Securities Exchange Act of 1934
Constructive Fraud	Majority Rule	Rule 10b-5
Reckless Disregard	Foreseeability Standard	Pattern of Racketeering
Gross Negligence	Racketeer Influenced and Corrupt Organizations Act	

MULTIPLE CHOICE QUESTIONS

1.   Law Nov 94 #10
Under common law, which of the following statements most accurately reflects the liability of a CPA who fraudulently gives an opinion on an audit of a client's financial statements?
A. The CPA is liable only to third parties in privity of contract with the CPA.
B. The CPA is liable only to known users of the financial statements.
C. The CPA probably is liable to any person who suffered a loss as a result of the fraud.
D. The CPA probably is liable to the client even if the client was aware of the fraud and did **not** rely on the opinion.

2.   Law Nov 91 #3
Ford & Co., CPAs, issued an unqualified opinion on Owens Corp.'s financial statements. Relying on these financial statements, Century Bank lent Owens $750,000. Ford was unaware that Century would receive a copy of the financial statements or that Owens would use them to obtain a loan. Owens defaulted on the loan.

To succeed in a common law fraud action against Ford, Century must prove, in addition to other elements, that Century was
A. Free from contributory negligence.
B. In privity of contract with Ford.
C. Justified in relying on the financial statements.
D. In privity of contract with Owens.

3.   Law Nov 95 #8
Under the "Ultramares" rule, to which of the following parties will an accountant be liable for negligence?

	Parties in Privity	Foreseen Parties
A.	Yes	Yes
B.	Yes	No
C.	No	Yes
D.	No	No

4.   Law May 93 #1
Sun Corp. approved a merger plan with Cord Corp. One of the determining factors in approving the merger was the financial statements of Cord that were audited by Frank & Co., CPAs. Sun had engaged Frank to audit Cord's financial statements. While performing the audit, Frank failed to discover certain irregularities that later caused Sun to suffer substantial losses. For Frank to be liable under common law negligence, Sun at a minimum must prove that Frank
A. Knew of the irregularities.
B. Failed to exercise due care.
C. Was grossly negligent.
D. Acted with scienter.

5.   Law May 93 #3
Which of the following elements, if present, would support a finding of constructive fraud on the part of a CPA?
A. Gross negligence in applying generally accepted auditing standards.
B. Ordinary negligence in applying generally accepted accounting principles.
C. Identified third party users.
D. Scienter.

6.   Law Nov 95 #11
Under the anti-fraud provisions of Section 10(b) of the Securities Exchange Act of 1934, a CPA may be liable if the CPA acted
A. Negligently.
B. With independence.
C. Without due diligence.
D. Without good faith.

7.   Law R97 #1
Which of the following statements is generally correct regarding the liability of a CPA who negligently gives an opinion on an audit of a client's financial statements?
A. The CPA is only liable to those third parties who are in privity of contract with the CPA.
B. The CPA is only liable to the client.
C. The CPA is liable to anyone in a class of third parties who the CPA knows will rely on the opinion.
D. The CPA is liable to all possible foreseeable users of the CPA's opinion.

8.   Law May 94 #10
Which of the following statements is correct with respect to ownership, possession, or access to a CPA firm's audit working papers?
A. Working papers may **never** be obtained by third parties unless the client consents.
B. Working papers are **not** transferable to a purchaser of a CPA practice unless the client consents.
C. Working papers are subject to the privileged communication rule which, in most jurisdictions, prevents any third-party access to the working papers.
D. Working papers are the client's exclusive property.

OTHER OBJECTIVE FORMAT QUESTION

Law May 94 #2 part A

Select the **best** answer for each item. Use a No. 2 pencil to blacken the appropriate ovals on the Objective Answer Sheet to indicate your answers. **Answer all items**. Your grade will be based on the total number of correct answers.

A. Items 1 through 6 are based on the following:

Under Section 11 of the Securities Act of 1933 and Section 10(b), Rule 10b-5 of the Securities Exchange Act of 1934, a CPA may be sued by a purchaser of registered securities.

Required:

   Items 1 through 6 relate to what a plaintiff who purchased securities must prove in a civil liability suit against a CPA. For each item determine whether the statement must be proven under Section 11 of the Securities Act of 1933, under Section 10(b), Rule 10b-5, or the Securities Exchange Act of 1934, both Acts, or neither Act, and blacken the corresponding oval on the Objective Answer Sheet.

* If the item must be proven **only** under Section 11 of the Securities Act of 1933, blacken **A** on the Objective Answer Sheet.
* If the item must be proven **only** under Section 10(b), Rule 10b-5, of the Securities Exchange Act of 1934, blacken **B** on the Objective Answer Sheet.
* If the item must be proven under **both** Acts, blacken **C** on the Objective Answer Sheet.
* If the item must be proven under **neither** of the Acts, blacken **D** on the Objective Answer Sheet.

Only Section 11	Only Section 10(b)	Both	Neither
A	B	C	D

The plaintiff security purchaser must allege or prove:

1. Material misstatements were included in a filed document.
2. A monetary loss occurred.
3. Lack of due diligence by the CPA.
4. Privity with the CPA.
5. Reliance on the document.
6. The CPA had scienter.

ESSAY QUESTION (Estimated time -- 15 to 20 minutes)

Law May 87 #3

Dill Corp. Was one of three major suppliers who sold raw materials to Fogg & Co. on credit. Dill became concerned over Fogg's ability to pay its debts. Payments had been consistently late and some checks had been returned, marked "insufficient funds." In addition, there were rumors concerning Fogg's solvency. Dill decided it would make no further sales to Fogg on credit unless it received a copy of Fogg's current, audited financial statements. It also required Fogg to assign its accounts receivable to Dill to provide security for the sales to Fogg on credit.

Clark & Wall, CPAs, was engaged by Fogg to perform an examination of Fogg's financial statements upon which they subsequently issued an unqualified opinion. Several months later, Fogg defaulted on its obligations to Dill. At this point Dill was owed $240,000 by Fogg. Subsequently, Dill discovered that only $60,000 of the accounts receivable that Fogg had assigned to Dill as collateral was collectible.

Dill has commenced a lawsuit against Clark & Wall. The complaint alleges that Dill has incurred a $180,000 loss as a result of negligent or fraudulent misrepresentations contained in the audited financial statements of Fogg. Specifically, it alleges negligence, gross negligence, and actual and/or constructive fraud on the part of Clark & Wall in the conduct of the audit and the issuance of an unqualified opinion.

State law applicable to this action follows the majority rule with respect to the accountant's liability to third parties for negligence. In addition, there is no applicable state statute which creates an accountant-client privilege. Dill demanded to be provided a copy of the Fogg workpapers from Clark & Wall who refused to comply with the request claiming that they are privileged documents. Clark & Wall has asserted that the entire action should be dismissed because Dill has no standing to sue the firm because of the absence of any contractual relationship with it, i.e., a lack of privity.

Required:

Answer the following, setting forth reasons for any conclusions stated.

a. Will Clark & Wall be able to avoid production of the Fogg workpapers based upon the assertion that they represent privileged communications?

b. What elements must be established by Dill to show negligence on the part of Clark & Wall?

c. What is the significance of compliance with GAAS in determining whether the audit was performed negligently?

d. What elements must be established by Dill to show actual or constructive fraud on the part of Clark & Wall?

EXPLANATIONS TO MULTIPLE CHOICE QUESTIONS

1. C is the correct answer. Liability for fraud extends to any reasonably foreseeable user of the financial statements. Choices A and B relate to negligence liability. Choice D is incorrect because reliance is one of the required elements of fraud. If any of the required fraud elements is missing, there is no liability.

2. C is the correct answer. In order to recover for fraud, the plaintiff must have relied on the fraudulent statements and that reliance must have been justifiable. This question is a good example of the importance of thoroughly knowing legal rules. In answering this question, as soon as fraud appears as the issue, the candidate should recall all the elements of fraud. If this is properly done, the candidate simply looks for the answer choice which states one of those elements. Note that the facts given in the first paragraph are not crucial to answering the question.

3. B is the correct answer. Under the *Ultramares* rule, a CPA has negligence liability only to parties in privity or a privity-like relationship. Remember that *Ultramares* is the minority rule.

4. B is the correct answer. Negligence is often defined as a failure to exercise due care. This can also be described as breaching a duty. Choice C is incorrect simply from a logic standpoint. It is illogical that one would be required to prove something worse than ordinary negligence in order to be able to prove ordinary negligence. Choices A and D are essentially the same because scienter means knowledge. Both are incorrect because negligence can occur inadvertently.

5. A is the correct answer. Constructive fraud can occur where there has been gross negligence or a reckless disregard for the truth. Choice D is wrong because although scienter is required to prove actual fraud, it is not required to prove constructive fraud.

6. D is the correct answer. This can be a difficult question because well-prepared candidates would look for scienter as a Section 10(b) requirement. Candidates who thoroughly know the requirements for a Rule 10(b) case could eliminate choices A, B, and C. Because it is impossible for good faith to exist if a CPA has knowledge of a misstatement, lack of good faith is another way of stating the scienter requirement.

7. C is the correct answer. This question asks about CPA negligence liability to third parties. The question does not explicitly state which of the three rules it seeks. The word "generally" in the question means that it seeks the majority rule which is the rule of the Restatement.

8. B is the correct answer. Candidates should be alert in questions addressing working papers or client records because it is easy to confuse them, even by candidates who understand the rules for each. The client might not want the purchaser of a practice to see the working papers, thus client consent is required for their transfer. C is incorrect because most states do not recognize an accountant-client privilege. Choice D is incorrect because the working papers are the property of the CPA, although the CPA's use and transfer of them is limited. Remember that a client can always demand the return of client records.

EXPLANATION TO OTHER OBJECTIVE FORMAT QUESTION

1. C is the correct answer. Without the misstatement, the CPA is not liable. Note that a material omission is considered a material misstatement.

2. C is the correct answer. Without a monetary loss, the plaintiff has no reason to recover.

3. D is the correct answer. This can be a tricky question. The due diligence defense applies in Section 11 cases, but it is a <u>defense</u>. This means that the plaintiff does not need to prove the absence of due diligence, rather the defendant has the opportunity to prove the presence of due diligence. Thus if the plaintiff in a Section 11 case can prove the two required elements of a material misstatement and a loss, the plaintiff wins unless the defendant can prove the presence of due diligence, or some other defense. Because of the plaintiff's greater proof requirements in a Section 10(b) case, the due diligence defense is not applicable. Proof of the required Section 10(b), Rule 10b-5 elements essentially negates the presence of due diligence.

4. D is the correct answer. The securities laws are designed to protect the general investing public, thus privity is not required for either cause of action.

5. B is the correct answer. Reliance does not need to be proven in a Section 11 case.

6. B is the correct answer. The scienter requirement makes a significant difference in the ease of proving a Section 11 case compared to proving a Section 10(b) case. Even an innocent misstatement will result in Section 11 liability (unless due diligence can be proven) whereas liability under Section 10(b) requires going beyond negligence and proving scienter. A Section 11 case requires the plaintiff to prove <u>less</u> than must be proven in a negligence case, whereas a Section 10(b) case requires proof of <u>more</u> (scienter) than is needed for negligence.

UNOFFICIAL AICPA ANSWER TO ESSAY QUESTION

Law May 87 #3

a. No. Since there is no accountant-client privilege recognized at common law and there is no applicable state statute which creates an accountant-client privilege, Clark & Wall will be required to produce its workpapers. Furthermore, the right to assert the accountant-client privilege generally rests with the client and not with the accountant.

b. The elements necessary to establish a cause of action for negligence against Clark & Wall are:

- A legal duty to protect the plaintiff (Dill) from unreasonable risk.
- A failure by the defendant (Clark & Wall) to perform or report on an engagement with the due care or competence expected of members of its profession.
- A causal relationship, i.e., that the failure to exercise due care resulted in the plaintiff's loss.
- Actual damage or loss resulting from the failure to exercise due care.

c. The primary standards against which the accountant's conduct will be tested are GAAS. Such standards are generally known as "the custom of the industry." Failure by Clark & Wall to meet the standards of the profession will undoubtedly result in a finding of negligence. However, meeting the standard of the profession will not be conclusive evidence that Clark & Wall was not negligent, although it is of significant evidentiary value.

d. The requirements to establish actual or constructive fraud on the part of Clark & Wall are:

1. A false representation of fact by the defendant (Clark & Wall).
2. For actual fraud, knowledge by the defendant (Clark & Wall) that the statement is false (scienter) or that the statement is made without belief that it is truthful. Constructive fraud may be inferred from gross negligence or a reckless disregard for the truth.
3. An intention to have the plaintiff (Dill) rely upon the false statement.
4. "Justifiable" reliance upon the false statement.
5. Damage resulting from said reliance.

Author's Note:

In part (b) above, the second bullet point of the negligence requirements is another way of describing the breach of the duty.

Note also that the unofficial answer did not explain the causation requirement in depth. It did not specifically mention the requirement for proximate causation or foreseeability. Be sure to include proximate causation or foreseeability. Its presence in an answer will not lower the score on the question, and could raise it.

Remember that evaluation of a CPA's conduct is based on GAAS, or generally accepted auditing standards, rather than generally accepted accounting principles (GAAP). This is because the primary focus is on the CPA's conduct, or how the audit was conducted, which is addressed by GAAS.

CHAPTER 4
CPA RESPONSIBILITIES IN TAX PRACTICE, PRIVATE INDUSTRY, AND THE PUBLIC SECTOR

OVERVIEW

This short chapter covers the responsibilities that CPAs have when working in tax practice, private industry, or the public sector. Although CPA certification is not required for many of these positions, AICPA members in such positions have certain responsibilities.

OUTLINE

I. Tax Practice Obligations.
  A. <u>Tax Return Preparation</u>.
    1. *Client Responsibility*. The client is ultimately responsible for all the information that is on the return or should be on the return.
      a. CPA Is Not an Auditor. In preparing a tax return, a CPA is not functioning as an auditor and is not required to verify amounts or estimates provided by the client.
      b. Must Investigate Suspicious Amounts. Although not required to verify any amounts, if a CPA suspects that an amount is incorrect, the CPA must investigate the amount. A suspicion based on information from any source must be investigated.
      c. Information From Another Client's Return. In determining if an amount provided by the current client is reasonable, the CPA must consider any relevant information from the returns of other clients. For example, assume that a CPA also prepared the tax return of a major customer of the current client and that some information from the customer's return cast doubt on the current client's stated sales amount. The CPA must investigate the stated sales amount of the current client based on the information known by the CPA from preparing the return of the current client's customer. **Exam tip #1.**
    2. *Negligence*. As with all services, a CPA should exercise reasonable care in tax return preparation. Reasonable care would usually include advising the client of the effects of elections and other options or choices available to reduce the tax paid.
    3. *Questions on the Return*. A CPA should make a reasonable effort to answer all questions on the return. A CPA can omit the answer (no explanation of the omission is necessary) to the question in any of the following circumstances:
      a. Information Unavailable. If the information is not readily available and the answer is not materially significant with respect to the tax liability or with respect to the taxable income or loss, the answer can be omitted.
      b. Question Unclear. If the meaning of the question is unclear, the answer can be omitted.
      c. Unreliable Information. If there is uncertainty about the reliability of the information needed to answer the question, the answer can be omitted.
    4. *Positions Taken on a Return*. A CPA should not recommend a tax position to a client unless there is reasonable support for the position taken.

a. Contrary to Treasury Department. It is possible for the reasonable support requirement to be met even if the position is contrary to that of the Internal Revenue Service (IRS).
b. Advice to Client. The client should be advised of the possibility of penalties connected with the recommended position.
c. Positions Without Reasonable Support. A CPA should not sign a return known to contain positions that do not meet the reasonable support requirement.

5. *Estimates*. A CPA may use the client's estimates of amounts if it is impractical to obtain the related actual amounts and the estimated amounts are reasonable. The CPA is not required to verify any estimates, but must investigate them further if the CPA suspects them to be incorrect.

6. *Error on Current Return*. If a CPA becomes aware of an error which causes the tax liability to be materially understated, the CPA should advise the client to either correct the error or report the error to the IRS. If the client refuses, the CPA should withdraw from the engagement.

7. *Error on Past Return*. If a CPA becomes aware of an error on a previously filed return, the CPA must promptly notify the client of the error and recommend action to be taken. The CPA is not required to inform the IRS of the error, and in fact cannot do so without the consent of the client. These requirements apply whether or not the CPA prepared the return containing the error.

8. *Failure to File Past Return*. If a CPA becomes aware that a client failed to file a return in the past, the CPA must take the same steps required for discovery of an error on a past return.

B. Other Tax Advice. When giving tax advice to a client, the following requirements apply.

1. *Positions Recommended*. The same requirements for positions taken in preparing a tax return apply to other tax advice given.

2. *Form of Recommendations*. There is no requirement that advice be in writing, but written advice is better, especially if the matter is complicated or unusual.

3. *Subsequent Events*. A CPA is generally not required to update advice previously given to a client because of later events. However, the CPA must update the advice if the CPA is helping the client implement the suggested actions or the CPA has otherwise agreed to update the advice.

II. Internal Revenue Code Tax Preparation Requirements.

A. Income Tax Preparer. The tax preparer rules apply only to **tax preparers**. A tax preparer is generally anyone who prepares a return for a fee or hires others to do so. A person would not be a tax preparer by providing typing or reproducing assistance, by preparing a return for a regular employer, or by preparing a return for a trust or estate for which she is a fiduciary.

B. No Minimum Qualifications. There are no minimum qualifications to work as a tax preparer.

C. Disregard of Rules and Regulations. Intentional or negligent disregard of rules and regulations can result in a $100 fine per return.

D. Willful Understatement of Tax Liability. A willful attempt to understate tax liability can result in a $500 fine per return.

E. Copies of Tax Return.
  1. *Copy to Taxpayer.* A preparer must provide the taxpayer with a copy of the return before or at the time the original is given to the taxpayer to be signed, otherwise a fine of $25 can result.
  2. *Copy Retained by Preparer.* A preparer must retain a copy of each return prepared until three years beyond the period covered by the return. Alternatively, the preparer may keep a list of all returns prepared, including taxpayer identification numbers, years, and types of returns.
F. Signature of Preparer. A preparer must provide a handwritten signature, identifying number and address on every return prepared, or face a $25 fine per return.
G. Negotiating Refund Checks. A preparer is subject to a $500 fine for negotiating a tax refund check of a taxpayer.
H. Disclosure of Confidential Information. Any disclosure of confidential information of a taxpayer can result in criminal penalties and civil liability to the taxpayer for any damages caused by the disclosure.
I. Employer-Preparers. Preparers who employ others to prepare returns must keep records of the name, identification number, and place of work of each person employed to prepare returns.

III. **Private Industry--Internal Auditing.**
  A. Definition. An **internal audit** is an audit performed by employees of the company.
  B. Characteristics.
    1. *Can Include Operational Auditing.* **Operational auditing** is directed at improving operational efficiencies and effectiveness. This is frequently part of an internal audit. CPAs can also be hired to do operational audits.
    2. *More Flexibility.* Because the results are used internally, internal audits can be tailored more specifically to the needs of the business. There is less flexibility when the business wants the external auditors to rely on the work of the internal auditors.
    3. *Other Purposes.* Internal audits can serve other purposes such as compliance with statutes requiring internal control.
  C. Certification. Internal auditors can get a CIA, or **Certified Internal Auditor** certification, instead of the CPA.
  D. Standards. The Institute of Internal Auditing has issued Standards for Professional Practice of Internal Auditing which address five areas.
    1. *Independence.* This is different in concept from AICPA independence because internal auditors are employees. The requirement is independence from the activity of part of the company being audited. Internal auditors frequently report to the board of directors or an audit committee.
    2. *Professional Proficiency.*
    3. *Scope of Work.* Internal auditors frequently perform operational auditing, can audit for internal control compliance, and can audit for adherence to policies and procedures.
    4. *Performance.* Includes proper planning and communication of results.
    5. *Management of the Internal Audit Function.* The internal audit function should be coordinated with the external audit. Internal audit work may be reviewed by external auditors, but internal audit work does not replace external audit work. **Exam tip #2.**

E. <u>Responsibility</u>. Internal auditors are responsible to management, rather than to financial statement users.

F. <u>Compliance Auditing by CPA</u>. A **compliance audit** is an audit to determine an organization's compliance with certain laws or other regulations. This can be performed by internal auditors, or by CPAs. If performed by a CPA, the CPA can issue an opinion based on the findings.

III. Governmental Auditing Responsibilities.

A. <u>Generally</u>. Governmental auditing requirements apply to audits of governmental units. These audits can be performed by government employees who are auditors or by CPAs.

B. <u>Compliance With AICPA and Government Auditing Standards</u>. When auditing governmental units, the CPA must comply with both governmental and AICPA auditing standards.

   1. *AICPA Generally Accepted Auditing Standards*. CPAs must follow all relevant generally accepted auditing standards.

   2. *Government Auditing Standards*. Government auditing standards are developed by the General Accounting Office (GAO). It is a violation of the AICPA Code of Conduct to not follow government auditing standards when auditing a governmental entity.

      a. Generally Follow GAAS. The government standards generally follow GAAS, but contain differences specific to government needs. There are requirements for testing compliance with laws, for example.

      b. Cover Financial Statement Audits. The government standards also provide guidance for whether financial statements fairly present the financial results and whether internal controls exist.

C. <u>Single Audit Act</u>. The **Single Audit Act** applies to state and local government units receiving federal funding and requires that a single audit be made to ensure compliance with all requirements of the various funding sources. This eliminates the duplicate work of separate audits for each funding agency. It applies to state and local governments receiving over $100,000 in funding in a fiscal year. The audit must report on internal control, compliance with laws and regulations including those related to eligibility for federal assistance. Congress has mandated other goals and requirements that must be reported on in the audit, such as civil rights violations.

EXAM TIPS

1. The CPA's use of information about one client to investigate an amount provided by a different client is not the same as disclosing confidential client information. This information simply triggers further investigation by the CPA and does not affect the requirement to not disclose confidential client information.

2. Be sure to understand that regardless of how much work is performed by the internal auditors, the external auditors have sole responsibility for the external audit. The external auditors might rely on the work of the internal auditors to reduce their own testing, but responsibility for gathering sufficient evidence is not shared with the internal auditors.

KEY CONCEPTS LIKELY TO BE TESTED ON THE CPA EXAM

1. The role of the tax preparer, including who is responsible for items on a tax return.
2. The requirements for a CPA to recommend a position to be taken on a tax return.
3. The CPA's obligation upon discovery of an error on a client's tax return.
4. The various Internal Revenue Code requirements for tax preparers.
5. The internal audit function and its relationship to the external audit.

KEY TERMS

Tax Preparer   Operational Audit   Compliance Audit
Internal Audit   Certified Internal Auditor   Single Audit Act

MULTIPLE CHOICE QUESTIONS

1.   Aud May 91 #56
When a CPA prepares a client's federal income tax return, the CPA has the responsibility to
A. Take a position of independent neutrality.
B. Argue the position of the Internal Revenue Service.
C. Be an advocate for the entity's realistically sustainable position.
D. Verify the data to be used in preparing the return.

2.   Aud May 85 #43
Where a reasonable basis exists for omission of an answer to an applicable question on a tax return
A. An explanation of the reason for the omission **need not be provided**.
B. A brief explanation of the reason for the omission should be provided.
C. The question should be marked as nonapplicable.
D. A note should be provided which states that the answer will be provided if the information is requested.

3.   Law Nov 94 #7
According to the profession's standards, which of the following statements is correct regarding the standards a CPA should follow when recommending tax return positions and preparing tax returns?
A. A CPA may recommend a position that the CPA concludes is frivolous as long as the position is adequately disclosed on the return.
B. A CPA may recommend a position in which the CPA has a good faith belief that the position has realistic possibility of being sustained if challenged.
C. A CPA will usually **not** advise the client of the potential penalty consequences of the recommended tax return position.
D. A CPA may sign a tax return as preparer knowing that the return takes a position that will not be sustained if challenged.

4.   Aud Nov 91 #15
Which of the following statements is correct
concerning a CPA's responsibility when the
CPA uses taxpayer estimates in preparing a
tax return?
A. Tax preparation requires the CPA to
   exercise judgment, but prohibits the
   CPA's use of estimates and
   approximations.
B. Use of taxpayer estimates in a tax return
   is prohibited unless they are specifically
   disclosed by the CPA.
C. When all facts relating to a transaction
   are **not** accurately known because
   records are missing, reasonable estimates
   made by the taxpayer of the missing data
   may be used by the CPA.
D. The CPA may prepare tax returns
   involving the use of taxpayer estimates
   even if it is practical to obtain exact data.

5.   Aud May 80 #22
In accordance with the AICPA Statements
On Responsibility in Tax Practice, if after
having provided tax advice to a client there
are legislative changes which affect the
advice provided, the CPA
A. Is obligated to notify the client of the
   change and the effect thereof.
B. Is obligated to notify the client of the
   change and the effect thereof if the client
   was not advised that the advice was
   based on existing laws which are subject
   to change.
C. Cannot be expected to notify the client of
   the change unless the obligation is
   specifically undertaken by agreement.
D. Cannot be expected to have knowledge
   of the change.

6.   Law Nov 95 #6
According to the standards of the profession,
which of the following sources of
information should a CPA consider before
signing a client's tax return?

I. Information actually known to the CPA
    from the tax return of another client.
II. Information provided by the client that
    appears to be correct based on the
    client's returns from prior years.

A. I only.
B. II only.
C. Both I and II.
D. Neither I nor II.

7.   Law Nov 95 #7
According to the standards of the profession,
which of the following statements is(are)
correct regarding the action to be taken by a
CPA who discovers an error in a client's
previously filed tax return?

I. Advise the client of the error and
    recommend the measures to be taken.
II. Withdraw from the professional
    relationship regardless of whether or not
    the client corrects the error.

A. I only.
B. II only.
C. Both I and II.
D. Neither I nor II.

8.   Author
The Single Audit Act applies to audits of
A. All state and local governments.
B. State and local governmental units
   receiving $100,000 or more per year in
   federal funding.
C. Corporations which are subject to the
   Securities Exchange Act of 1934.
D. Federal agencies which disburse grants.

ESSAY QUESTION (Estimated time -- 10 to 15 minutes)

Author

Pat has recently graduated with a degree in accounting and has been interviewing for jobs in CPA firms as an auditor. This type of position has been Pat's sole focus in the interviewing process. Upon a friend's recommendation, Pat applied for an internal auditor position. Pat's father has worked in a medium-sized business for many years and has had some dealings with the staff auditors from the firm which performs the financial statement audit. His job has not changed in years and he is unfamiliar with the work of an internal auditor.

Pat's father is curious about this position and would like to know more about internal auditors and how their work differs from that of an auditor from a CPA firm. He also wants this information because he thinks that perhaps his employer should consider hiring an internal auditor.

Required:

Draft a memorandum to Pat's father describing the internal audit function, the work of internal auditors, and if there are any standards that internal auditors must follow.

EXPLANATIONS TO MULTIPLE CHOICE QUESTIONS

1. C is the correct answer. A CPA may advocate a position which has a realistic chance of being upheld if challenged. Choice A is incorrect because independence is not required in tax work. Choice D is incorrect because the CPA is not functioning as an auditor when preparing a tax return.

2. A is the correct answer. When there is a reasonable basis for omitting the answer to a question, the answer can be omitted without the need to provide an explanation.

3. B is the correct answer. A CPA must have a good faith belief in the realistic possibility that a position will be upheld before the position can be recommended. The CPA need not believe that the position will probably, or more likely than not, be upheld, merely that there is a realistic possibility that it will be.

4. C is the correct answer. The use of estimates made by the taxpayer is acceptable if it is not practical to obtain the actual data. The disclosure that estimates were used is usually not required.

5. C is the correct answer. It is not reasonable to expect the CPA to notify clients, after representation has ended, of changes in tax laws. If the CPA has agreed to do this, then the CPA does have an obligation to do so. The question is a good example of a question where common sense can help lead to the correct answer. In analyzing whether the CPA must notify the client, the practical implications are so great that such a notification requirement would be unworkable. It might be impossible to notify certain clients, and there is the question of how long after the engagement the obligation would last. Such consideration should lead a candidate who does not know the answer to conclude that there must be no such notice requirement.

6. C is the correct answer. The CPA is required to consider information from various sources, including the return of another client. Many candidates are surprised at this requirement. Note that this is not a requirement to disclose the information on the other client's return, nor is it a requirement that the CPA examine the returns of other clients in a search for information relevant to the accuracy of the return of the current client. But CPAs often prepare returns of clients who have business relationships with one another, and if the information on one is inconsistent with that on the other, the CPA should use that information in deciding whether to sign the return.

7. A is the correct answer. The CPA is not working for the IRS and is not an enforcement officer. The client is responsible for deciding what action to take, and it is the CPA's obligation to advise the client of the error and to recommend a course of action. If the client does not follow the recommended course of action, the CPA should consider withdrawing. The CPA's obligations are the same whether the CPA or someone else originally prepared the return.

8. B is the correct answer. The act does not apply to a government unit receiving under $100,000.

EXPLANATION TO ESSAY QUESTION

Author

Internal auditors can perform many different functions, with the result that the job of the internal auditor can be quite different from one organization to another. Internal auditors are responsible to management. All external auditors have the same general goal of expressing an opinion on the financial statements whereas companies can use internal auditors for a variety of purposes.

Internal auditors can perform operational audits with the purpose of improving various operational efficiencies of the organization. In connection with this, they can also use the internal audit function to measure compliance with organizational policies.

Internal auditors can also provide assistance to the external auditors, and in so doing might be able to reduce the amount of work performed by the external auditors. In such a case, the external auditors will need to evaluate the effectiveness of the internal audit function in a particular organization in order to determine the extent to which they can rely on the internal auditors' work. One area where internal auditors can provide assistance, both to the external auditors and to their organization, is in evaluating internal controls. Internal auditors can also perform compliance audits to determine the organization's compliance with statutes and regulations.

Internal auditors can be certified either as a CPA or as a Certified Internal Auditor, or CIA. The Institute of Internal Auditing has issued standards for internal auditing covering five areas. The first of these is independence, which is different from the independence required of external auditors. Because internal auditors report within the organization, they cannot be independent of the organization. However, they should report to a person or department outside of the one being audited. Generally, the higher in the organization that the internal auditors report, the better from an independence standpoint.

Other standards address professional competency, the scope of work which internal auditors do, and how the internal auditors should perform their work. Lastly, standards address the management of the internal audit function and its coordination with the external auditors.

CHAPTER 5
THE NATURE AND CLASSIFICATION OF CONTRACTS

OVERVIEW

Contracts can be classified in a number of ways, such as by the method of formation or the nature of the subject matter. It is important to understand these classifications and the related terminology. One must also understand that common law governs contracts involving services or real property, while the Uniform Commercial Code governs contracts for the sale of goods. This chapter and the next five chapters will cover the common law contract rules, followed by three chapters on the Uniform Commercial Code. This chapter is introductory, with many concepts explained in later chapters.

OUTLINE

I. **Contract Basics.**
   A. Definition. One definition is "a promise or a set of promises for the breach of which the law gives a remedy or the performance of which the law in some way recognizes a duty."
   B. Elements. For a contract to be enforceable, four requirements must be met:
      1. *Agreement.* The parties must reach **agreement** through an offer and acceptance.
      2. *Consideration.* Each party must give **consideration** by suffering a bargained-for legal detriment.
      3. *Contractual Capacity.* The parties must have the legal **capacity** to enter into a contract.
      4. *Lawful Object.* To be valid, a contract must have a **lawful object**.
   C. Defenses. There are two general types of defenses to the enforcement of a contract.
      1. *Genuineness of Assent.* The agreement of the parties must be based on **genuine assent**, and not based on fraud, duress, etc.
      2. *Writing and Form.* Certain contracts must be in **writing** or in a specific form.
   D. Sources of Contract Law.
      1. *Common Law.* **Common law** is judge-made law, where court cases are decided based on prior cases known as precedent. Common law governs contracts for services or real property. The common law of contracts is state law; that law is similar in all states, but there are minor differences from state to state.
      2. *The Uniform Commercial Code.* The **Uniform Commercial Code (UCC)** is a model law which all states have enacted, with some variation, and some omissions. Article 2 of the UCC covers contracts for the sale of goods, and where different, the UCC supersedes common law for such contracts.
      3. *Restatement of the Law of Contracts.* The **Restatement** is a compilation of contract law, based on prevalent practices, in the opinion of the drafters. It is not binding law, but is often referred to and followed by judges.

II. **Classification of Contracts.** Contracts can be classified based on a number of characteristics.
   A. Bilateral and Unilateral. These refer to what the offeror seeks from the offeree in order to initially form a contract and affect when the contract actually comes into existence.

1. *Bilateral*. In a **bilateral** contract the offeror seeks a promise of performance from the offeree. For example, Bob says to Sam, "If you will promise to paint my house, I will pay you $5,000." This is an offer for a bilateral contract because Bob seeks a promise of performance in advance. If Sam makes the promise, Sam becomes obligated to perform. A bilateral contract has promises from two parties. A bilateral contract comes into existence as soon as the offeree's return promise is made. The offeror wants eventual performance of the promised act, but the promise is all that is needed to form the contract.

2. *Unilateral*. In a **unilateral** contract the offeror does not seek a promise of performance, but promises to pay <u>if</u> the offeree completes the action. For example, Bob says to Alice, "If you cut my grass while I am gone, I will pay you $40." Bob is not seeking an advance promise from Alice that she will cut the grass, but has promised that he will pay her if she actually cuts it. A unilateral contract has promises from only one party. A unilateral contract does not come into existence until the offeree completes the act. **Exam tip #1.**

B. <u>Express and Implied</u>. These terms also describe how a contract is formed.

   1. *Express*. Any contract based on the words of the parties is an **express** contract. The words can be either written or oral. **Exam tip #2.**

   2. *Implied-in-fact*. **Implied-in-fact** contracts are formed by the parties' conduct, rather than their words. Ordering food in a restaurant and pumping gas at a self serve station are examples. The recipient of the goods or services does not expressly promise to pay for them. Generally one party has taken some action to obtain goods or services from another, who then provides the goods or services with the expectation of being paid, and the recipient could have rejected the goods or services, but did not. The conduct implies an obligation to pay.

   3. *Objective Theory of Contracts*. Whether a contract has been formed, including implied-in-fact contracts, is based on an **objective** standard. This means that whether a contract was intended is based on the words and conduct of the parties and the surrounding circumstances. Thus that the actual intent of a restaurant patron to not pay for food ordered is ignored because a reasonable person would intend to pay for food ordered.

C. <u>Quasi-Contracts</u>. **Quasi contracts** are not actual contracts, but situations where the court can force a party to pay for a benefit received if it would be unfair for the person to not pay for it. They are also known as **implied-in-law** contracts. For example, if a homeowner saw a nursery employee mistakenly start to plant a tree in his yard and the homeowner said nothing to stop the nursery, the homeowner would have to pay under quasi-contract. Unlike the implied-in-fact situation, the homeowner did nothing to initiate the planting of the tree. If the homeowner discovered the tree only after the planting was complete, he would not be liable, but the nursery could remove it if doing so would not damage the homeowner. **Exam tip #3.**

D. <u>Formal and Informal</u>. **Formal** contracts are contracts which must have a particular form. Negotiable instruments and letters of credit are two common formal contracts. Any contract that does not require a particular form is an informal contract, even if very long and complicated. Most contracts are informal. The first four letters of "formal" are "form."

E. <u>Valid Contracts</u>. Contracts with all required elements present are **valid** and enforceable.

F. <u>Void Contracts</u>. **Void** contracts are contracts which have no legal effect and are considered nonexistent by the courts. Courts simply ignore void contracts and leave the parties where they are. Illegal contracts are an example of void contracts. **Exam tip #4.**

G. <u>Voidable Contracts</u>. Contracts where a party can avoid her obligations under a contract are **voidable**. Minors and fraud victims are two examples of persons who can avoid a contract.

H. <u>Unenforceable Contracts</u>. **Unenforceable** contracts are contracts which exist, but one party has a defense to its enforcement. The most common situation is where there is an oral contract which is required to be in writing under the Statute of Frauds. The contract exists, but the court will not enforce it if suit is brought. **Exam tip #5.**

I. <u>Executory and Executed Contracts</u>. These terms describe whether a contract has been completed. A contract becomes **executed** only when all parties have performed all their obligations under the contract; prior to that point, the contract is executory. If one party has fully performed but the other has not, the contract at that point is **executory**.

EXAM TIPS

1. Most contracts are bilateral. This is because most people want the certainty of a promise of performance. This is a fairly heavily tested area on the CPA exam. Remember to see if one party or both parties make promises. The word "promise" does not need to be used; any synonym such as "I agree" or "I will" is a promise by that party. A unilateral contract is not created until the actual performance of the requested act.

2. An oral contract can be an express contract. The words to make an express contract need not be in writing. Do not equate express contracts to written contracts.

3. Do not confuse implied-in-fact contracts, which are actual contracts, and implied-in-law contracts, which are not actual contracts. In the implied-in-fact situation, the recipient of goods or services has usually initiated the transaction, but the implied-in-law situation often follows from a mistake.

4. Void and voidable are commonly confused and frequently tested. Void contracts are void from the beginning, treated as nonexistent by the courts. Voidable contracts are <u>able</u> to be <u>voided</u> by one of the parties.

5. The legal effect of a void contract and an unenforceable contract is usually the same. The court will do nothing. For the CPA exam, though, candidates must know which term applies in a given situation.

KEY CONCEPTS LIKELY TO BE TESTED ON THE CPA EXAM

1. Knowledge of the source of applicable law, based on the contract subject matter. This often will not be asked explicitly, but the correct answer will require knowing whether common law or the UCC rule applies.

2. Classification of a contract as bilateral or unilateral based on a fact situation.

3. Classification and rules for implied-in-fact contracts and implied-in-law contracts.

4. Void and voidable contracts. Questions can test which contracts fall into each category, as well as the legal consequences of a contract falling into one of these categories.

5. Unenforceable contracts, which are usually oral contracts which should have been in writing.

6. Executory contracts, which are any contracts not yet fully performed by all parties.

KEY TERMS

Agreement
Consideration
Contractual Capacity
Lawful Object
Defenses
Genuineness of Assent
Writing Requirement
Common Law

Uniform Commercial Code
The Restatement
Bilateral
Unilateral
Express
Implied-in-fact
Objective Theory
Quasi Contract

Implied-in-law
Formal
Valid
Void
Voidable
Unenforceable
Executory
Executed

MULTIPLE CHOICE QUESTIONS

1.   Law Nov 79 #5
Which of the following represents the basic distinction between a bilateral contract and a unilateral contract?
A. Specific performance is available if the contract is unilateral but not if bilateral.
B. Only one promise is involved if the contract is unilateral but two if bilateral.
C. The Statute of Frauds applies to a bilateral contract but not to a unilateral contract.
D. Rights under a bilateral contract are assignable, whereas rights under a unilateral contract are not assignable.

2.   Author
A client contacted a lawyer to represent her in a legal dispute. The lawyer and the client reach agreement on the phone that the lawyer would handle the matter at a rate of $150 per hour. Which of the following is true?
A. They formed a formal contract because of the agreement that was reached.
B. They formed an implied-in-fact contract based on their conduct.
C. They formed an implied-in-law contract based on the services to be delivered.
D. They formed an express contract based on their phone conversation.

3.   Law Nov 81 #11
When a client accepts the services of an accountant without an agreement concerning payment, the result is
A. An implied-in-fact contract.
B. An implied-in-law contract.
C. An express contract.
D. No contract.

4.   Author
Mary agrees to pay John $1,000 to paint her garage. After John finishes the painting, but before he is paid, this contract is
A. Void.
B. Voidable.
C. Executory.
D. Executed.

5.   Author
Which of the following would be classified as a formal contract?
A. A negotiable promissory note to be repaid in 90 days.
B. A two year written employment contract.
C. A written contract for the purchase of real estate.
D. A CPA's liability insurance contract.

OTHER OBJECTIVE FORMAT QUESTION

Author

For each of the situations below, select as many terms from the list below which are known to be applicable based on the information given in the description. More than one term can be used in each situation, and any term can be selected more than once.

Terms:
A. Bilateral.
B. Unilateral.
C. Express.
D. Implied-in-fact.
E. Quasi contract.
F. Implied-in-law.
G. Void.
H. Voidable.
I. Unenforceable.
J. Executory.
K. Executed.

1. Ann said to Bob, "If you get a chance to cut down the dead tree in my yard this weekend, I will pay you $150." Bob cut the tree down on Saturday, but has not yet received payment from Ann. Bob and Ann are both adults, and neither is insane or was intoxicated when Ann made the statement to Bob.

   Letters corresponding to applicable terms:_____

2. Mark and Sue entered into a written agreement for Sue to buy Mark's house. Mark lied to Sue about termite infestation in the house, and the age of the roof on the house. He told Sue that there were no termites even though he knew that termites are active in the basement. He also told Sue that the roof was two years old, when he knew that it was actually nine years old. The closing has not yet been held, but Sue has discovered that Mark told these two lies.

   Letters corresponding to applicable terms:_____

3. Jim delivered his car to an automotive detail shop to have the interior of his car cleaned. He signed a work order calling for cleaning the interior at a cost of $75, paid in advance. As he stood across the street waiting for his wife to pick him up, he noticed an employee beginning to wash and wax the exterior of his car. Jim said nothing to anyone at the detail shop. When Jim picked up the car, the interior was cleaned, but he refused to pay for the exterior wash and wax.

   Letters corresponding to applicable terms for the interior cleaning:_____

   Letters corresponding to applicable terms for the exterior wash and wax:_____

EXPLANATIONS TO MULTIPLE CHOICE QUESTIONS

1. B is the correct answer. Unilateral and Bilateral refer to the number of parties who have made promises in a contract. It is the number of parties who have made at least one promise, which is important, not the number of promises. The incorrect choices do not describe the basic bilateral/unilateral distinction. They are all incorrect statements as well. Note that the incorrect answer choices are often correct statements which simply do not answer the specific question.

2. D is the correct answer. Because they have expressed the terms of the agreement in words, this is an express contract. The expression of words in an express contract can be either written or spoken. Choice A is incorrect because there is no particular form required for a contract covering legal services. Choices B and C are incorrect because as an express contract, it can be neither an implied-in-fact nor implied-in-law contract.

3. A is the correct answer. The conduct of accepting the services implies an agreement to pay for those services. In answering a question like this, one must assume the most likely set of facts, including that the client had in some way initially requested that the accountant perform the services, making this an implied-in-fact situation. Choice B is incorrect because implied-in-law contracts usually involve someone accepting a good or service that she did not request, and this question does not indicate that the client did not request the services.

4. C is the correct answer. Because at least one person, Mary in this case, has not fully performed, the contract is executory. Once Mary pays John, it will become executed. Nothing in the question indicates that the contract is either void or voidable.

5. A is the correct answer. There are only a few types of formal contracts. A formal contract is simply one which must be in a specific form to be valid. A contract does not become formal by its length, by the importance of the parties, or the length of time covered. The incorrect answer choices are all contracts which have no particular requirements as to form, thus they are informal.

EXPLANATION TO OTHER OBJECTIVE FORMAT QUESTION

1. B, C, and J are correct. This contract is unilateral because Ann seeks the completed act, not a promise, for the formation of the contract. Ann's words make this an express contract, and until Ann makes payment to Bob, it is executory because at least one person has not fully performed.

2. A, C, and H are correct. The written contract containing the promises to buy and sell make it bilateral and express. Mark's fraud committed toward Sue makes the contract voidable by Sue.

3. A, C, and K are correct for the interior cleaning. Both sides made promises in the signed work order, making for a bilateral express agreement. It is executed because both have fully performed. F is correct for the exterior wash and wax. There was no contract, but it would be unfair to allow Jim to not pay for the service because he could have easily corrected the situation.

CHAPTER 6
AGREEMENT AND CONSIDERATION

OVERVIEW

This chapter covers two of the four basic elements of contracts. The first is the agreement, or meeting of the minds, which contains the components of offer and acceptance. It takes both offer and acceptance to meet the agreement requirement. There are many detailed rules to determine whether a valid offer or acceptance has been made. The second requirement is that of consideration. Consideration is very confusing for many students, both in its basic rule and its exceptions.

OUTLINE

I. Agreement.
   A. <u>Offer and Acceptance</u>. These are the two basic components of an agreement. An **offeror** makes an **offer** to an **offeree** to form a contract. The offeror is the party who makes the offer, and the offeree is the person to whom it is made. The offeree then has the power of acceptance and can form a contract by accepting the offer.
   B. <u>Offer</u>. The offer is the proposal for the terms of a contract. In order to be effective, an offer must meet three requirements.
      1. *Objective Intent.* The offeror must have **objective intent** to be bound by the offer. Based on all the surrounding circumstances, this requirement is met if a reasonable person would conclude that the offeror truly intends to be bound by the terms of the "offer." For example, a driver whose new Cadillac has just broken down on the road, and gets out of his car screaming, "I hate this car, it is yours for $50," does not meet this requirement. A reasonable person would not think the driver really wants to sell the car for $50. Offers clearly made in jest, anger, or excitement do not meet this requirement. **Exam tip #1.**
      2. *Definiteness of Terms.* An offer must have a minimum level of **definiteness** in order to be valid. Vague offers such as, "I'll sell you lots of bananas for a great price," does not meet the requirement. Although courts are more willing today to imply "reasonable terms" where terms are missing, an offer usually needs to contain, at a minimum:
         a. Identification of the Parties.
         b. Identification of the Contract Subject Matter.
         c. The Consideration to be Paid.
         d. The Time of Performance.
      3. *Communication.* An offer must be **communicated** to the offeree in order to be effective. Generally, this means that the offer must be received by the offeree.
         a. Advertisements. Advertisements to sell goods or services are usually not offers, but are considered to be invitations to deal. Very specific advertisements can be offers, such as a car ad which lists an inventory stock number, or an ad that says the price is available only to the first five customers.

b. Rewards. Offers for rewards are usually considered offers for a unilateral contact; a promise to pay for a specific act, namely the return of the missing item. The communication requirement means that if someone returns a lost item without knowledge of a reward, that person is not entitled to the reward, because the offer had not been communicated to them prior to the performance of the act. There would be acceptance, and entitlement to the reward, only if the return of the item was done with knowledge of the reward.

c. Auctions. Auctions fit into two categories. In an **auction with reserve**, the seller is free to refuse all bids, including the high bid, thus the bids are offers and the acceptance occurs, if at all, when the item is declared sold. In an **auction without reserve**, the seller has made an offer to sell to the highest bidder, the bidders are the offerees, and the offer is accepted by being the highest bidder.

C. Duration and Termination of Offers. Once there is a valid offer, there often is an issue over how long the offer remains effective. An offer is effective until it is terminated or accepted. Offers can terminate by:

1. *Revocation by the Offeror.* **Revocation** occurs when the offeror makes an express statement revoking the offer, or does an act that is inconsistent with the offer, such as selling the item to someone else. Generally, revocation is effective only when notice of it is received by the offeree. Revocation cannot occur once there has been acceptance. A promise to hold open an offer for a period of time is generally revocable unless there is separate payment in an **option contract.** In an option contract the offeree pays the offeror to hold the offer open for a specified period of time, and the offeror cannot revoke the offer during that period. Absent an option contract, even when an offeror says, "You have until next Friday to accept," the offeror can revoke the offer any time prior to acceptance.

2. *Special Revocation Rule for Unilateral Offers.* Normally, the offeror can revoke an offer at any time until acceptance, which in the case of a unilateral offer occurs at the completion of the requested act. Strict application of this rule would allow the offeror to revoke the offer when the offeree has almost, but not quite, completed the act. To prevent this, the special rule for unilateral offers is that the offeror cannot revoke the offer once the offeree has started to perform the act, or has taken steps (such as acquiring the materials for a construction job) in preparation of performing the act.

3. *Rejection by the Offeree.* **Rejection** occurs when the offeree communicates to the offeror that the offeree does not want the offer. The rejection terminates the offer, thus there is no offer to accept if the offeree later changes his mind. For example, a painter says to Pam, "I will paint your house for $3,000," to which Pam replies, "I won't pay that much." Pam has rejected the offer, and any later statement to the painter that she is willing to pay $3,000 is a new offer, which the painter is free to accept or reject. **Exam tip #2.**

4. *Counteroffer by the Offeree.* A **counteroffer** is a combined rejection (terminating the original offer) and a new offer by the offeree, which reverses the roles of the offeree and the offeror.

5. *Destruction of the Contract Subject Matter.* If the subject matter of a contract is destroyed before an offer has been accepted, the offer terminates by operation of law.

6. *Death or Incompetency of the Offeree or Offeror.* Death of either, prior to acceptance, terminates the offer.

7. *Supervening Illegality.* If the proposed contract was legal when the offer was made, but has become illegal since then, such as due to the passage of a new statute, the offer terminates by operation of law due to this **supervening illegality**. **Exam tip #3.**

8. *Passage of Time.* Offers terminate, if they have not been accepted, at their stated termination time if there is one; otherwise they terminate after the passage of a reasonable time. What constitutes a reasonable time can differ considerably based on circumstances.

D. <u>Acceptance</u>. **Acceptance** is the manifestation by the offeree of assent to the terms of the offer. In bilateral contracts, acceptance occurs by making a return promise, and in unilateral contracts by performing the requested act. The moment of acceptance is the moment that a contract is formed. In addition:

1. *Offerees Only.* Only offerees are able to accept offers.

2. *Unequivocal.* The offeree's acceptance must be **unequivocal**. There has been no acceptance if the offeree indicates doubt or wavering in her acceptance.

3. *Mirror Image Rule.* The **mirror image rule** requires that a purported acceptance be identical in all respects to the offer, or it is not effective as an acceptance. This is true even if the language sounds like an acceptance. If someone offers to sell Ann a 31-inch TV for $599, and Ann responds by saying, "I accept your offer and will buy the 35-inch TV," this might sound like an acceptance, but is not because it is different than the offer. It is a counteroffer.

4. *Silence.* Generally silence is not acceptance, but there are exceptions:
   a. Offeree states that silence is acceptance, "I'll buy it if you don't hear back from me today."
   b. Prior agreement, such as music clubs where a selection is automatically sent each month unless the club is notified that the member does not want it.
   c. Prior dealings where automatic shipments are made at regular intervals.
   d. Offeree accepts benefits of goods or services, and could have rejected them, but did not and knows that the offeror expects to be compensated for them.

5. *Mailbox Rule.* The **mailbox rule** is that acceptances are effective the moment they are sent even if they never reach their destination. This rule can be modified by the terms of the offer itself stating that an acceptance is effective only when received. **Exam tip #4.**

II. **Consideration.** Consideration must be given by both parties to a contract. **Consideration** is something of legal value which is given in exchange for the promise of the other party. Consideration frequently takes the form of an amount paid, or a good or service delivered, but it can take other forms as well. **Exam tip # 5.**

A. <u>Legal Value</u>. Each party must suffer a **legal detriment**. The two common forms of legal detriment are giving up a legal right or taking on a new legal duty. A new legal duty might be an obligation to perform a service, and giving up a legal right might be forgoing using your tickets to an event by letting someone else use them, or agreeing with a neighbor to not build an otherwise legal addition on your home which would block their view of nearby mountains. In the common contract for the sale of goods, the seller gives up the goods, and the buyer gives up money for the purchase price.

B. <u>Bargained-For Exchange</u>. To meet the consideration requirement, the legal detriment of each party must have been **bargained for** and **given in exchange** for that of the other party.

C. <u>Monetary Value Not Important</u>. In determining if the consideration requirement is met, courts are not concerned about the value of the consideration, nor must the consideration given by one party be comparable in value to that given by the other party. So long as each party has suffered legal detriment of some sort, consideration is sufficient.

D. <u>Gift Promises</u>. A promise to make gift is a **gratuitous** promise and does not meet the consideration requirement if the recipient of the gift suffers no legal detriment. It is certainly acceptable to make gifts and promises of gifts, but courts will not force someone who has promised to make a gift to follow through on that promise, unless the recipient of the gift gave consideration in return.

E. <u>Option-to-Cancel Clauses</u>. An **option to cancel** might make it appear that one party has not suffered a legal detriment because there is no firm obligation. Such a contract does meet the consideration requirement so long as there was consideration paid for the option to cancel.

F. <u>Best Efforts Contracts</u>. The duty to apply one's **best efforts** to obtain a result, even though the party does not promise to achieve it, is sufficient to meet the consideration requirement.

G. <u>Common Situations Where Consideration Is Lacking</u>.

1. *Illusory Promises*. **Illusory promises** are statements that sound like a promise, but do not really create an obligation, such as, "I promise to sell you my car if I decide to get rid of it." This creates no legally enforceable obligation, thus is not consideration.

2. *Moral obligation*. Promises made based on a sense of **moral obligation**, such as love and affection, do not meet the consideration requirement, and are unenforceable.

3. *Past Consideration*. **Past consideration** exists if, at the time a promise is made, it is made based on something that the other party has done in the past The past action does not meet the consideration requirement for the new promise. If Pat arrived home and surprisingly sees that the neighbor has cut Pat's grass, a statement by Pat, "Thank you! In consideration of your cutting my grass, I'll feed your dog next week," is not supported by consideration from the neighbor because when the promise to feed the dog was made, the neighbor had already cut the grass. Past consideration is no consideration. **Exam tip #6.**

4. *Preexisting Duty*. A promise to do what one is already obligated to do is based on a **preexisting duty** is not consideration.

   a. Based on Office or Position Held. For example, a city firefighter and a homeowner with a burning house agree for the homeowner to pay the firefighter to put out the fire. The firefighter's promise does not meet the consideration requirement because the firefighter already had a duty, as a firefighter, to put out the fire.

   b. Based on a Preexisting Contract. If a roofer has agreed to replace a roof for a homeowner for $2,000 by May 18, a later agreement that the homeowner pay an extra amount in order to ensure that the job is finished on time is unenforceable because the roofer already was obligated to finish the job by May 18. If the homeowner's extra payment was to get the job finished sooner, the earlier completion date is a new obligation, and the roofer has given new consideration.

   c. Unforeseen Difficulties. Where unforseen difficulties arise in the performance of a contract, courts will enforce a modification even if it is not supported by consideration.

5. *Illegal Consideration*. A promise to refrain from an illegal act is based on **illegal consideration** and is not consideration. There was never a legal right to do the illegal act.

H. <u>Output and Requirements Contracts</u>. These contracts do meet the consideration requirement. An **output** contract is an agreement by a seller to sell the seller's entire output to a certain buyer, but frequently not obligating any minimum output level. A **requirements** contract obligates a buyer to purchase its entire requirements for an item from a particular seller. Although these contracts often obligate a party to nothing, they do limit the legal right to buy from or sell to other sources, and that limitation is a sufficient legal detriment.

I. <u>Accord and Satisfaction</u>. An **accord** is an agreement to settle a legitimate contract dispute and the **satisfaction** is the performance of the new settlement agreement. So long as the dispute is of an **unliquidated debt**, the accord and satisfaction meets the consideration requirement because each party has given up the right to enforce the original contract. An unliquidated debt is one where, in the circumstances, reasonable minds could differ as to the amount of the obligation. A **liquidated** debt is one where there is no legitimate dispute over the amount owed. An accord and satisfaction of a liquidated debt must contain new consideration.

J. <u>Promissory Estoppel</u>. **Promissory estoppel** is a doctrine where certain promises will be enforced even though they do not meet the consideration requirements. Generally, promissory estoppel is the last option that someone uses to try to get a promise enforced. It is an equitable remedy based on fairness. A promise not supported by consideration will be enforced if:
1. *The Promisor Made a Promise*;
2. *The Promisor Should Have Reasonably Expected the Promisee to Rely on the Promise*;
3. *The Promisee Actually Does Rely Substantially on the Promise*; and
4. *The Promisee Would Suffer Injustice if the Promise Were Not Enforced*.

These requirements are sometimes summarized as **detrimental reliance**. For example, if Sam promised Sally that he would give her his old car, and in relying on that promise Sally sold her car, Sally would be able to recover her loss. Her loss, because she could use the proceeds from her old car to get another, might be less than the value of the item promised to her. If Sally cannot prove all the elements of promissory estoppel, the promise would be treated as an unenforceable gratuitous promise.

EXAM TIPS

1. Objective intent is based on how a reasonable person would evaluate whether the offeror truly intended to make an offer. The offeror's own intent is not important here.
2. Candidates must clearly understand the difference between revocation and rejection. Revocation is the act of the offer**o**r in taking back the offer. Rejection is the act of the offer**e**e in saying that the offer is not wanted. Notice how the letter "e" and letter "o" go together here.
3. Supervening illegality occurs where the offer was legal when made, but then becomes illegal prior to acceptance. This should not be confused with the situation where an actual agreement is reached for an illegal contract (in Chapter 7 of this guide) or where the contract becomes illegal <u>after</u> acceptance has taken place (in Chapter 8 of this guide).
4. The mailbox rule is frequently tested. Acceptances (whether by mail, fax, etc.) are effective upon dispatch. Offers, rejections, counteroffers, and revocations are all effective only upon receipt. CPA exam questions frequently include offers that contain language modifying the mailbox rule, meaning that acceptances of that particular offer are effective only when received.

5. Consideration is a difficult topic. Courts, like the text, often talk about evaluating consideration in terms of benefits conferred. For purposes of the CPA exam, when analyzing whether consideration is present, one should focus always on the detriment, and see if each side has suffered a detriment in the situation, or if it fits into one of the other special circumstances discussed. Do not forget, though, that consideration can be defined in terms of a detriment suffered or a benefit received.

6. Candidates frequently mix up past consideration and preexisting duty. Analyze such situations carefully. If one party's act has already been completed when the other party makes its promise, it is past consideration. If the act has not been completed, but the party making the promise was already obligated to perform that act before making the new promise, it is a case of preexisting duty.

KEY CONCEPTS LIKELY TO BE TESTED ON THE CPA EXAM

1. Issues of contract formation where there might be offers, counteroffers, rejections, revocations, and acceptances crossing in the mail. Examine if the mailbox rule has been modified, then step by step determine whether offers are outstanding or terminated, a contract has been formed, etc. Remember that once a contract is formed, it is too late to reject or revoke.

2. The basic requirements of consideration.

3. The situations where consideration is lacking, including being able to identify the situation, such as preexisting duty.

4. Outputs and requirements contracts, how to identify each, and the fact that they do meet consideration requirements.

5. Promissory estoppel, likely in a question where they will make it clear that the promise was a gratuitous promise, and the candidate must determine if the elements of promissory estoppel are present.

KEY TERMS

Offer	Supervening Illegality	Illusory Promise
Offeree	Acceptance	Moral Obligation
Offeror	Unequivocal	Past Consideration
Objective Intent	Mirror Image Rule	Preexisting Duty
Definiteness of Terms	Mailbox Rule	Illegal Consideration
Communication	Consideration	Output and Requirements
Auction With Reserve	Legal Detriment	Accord and Satisfaction
Auction Without Reserve	Bargained-For Exchange	Unliquidated Debt
Revocation	Gratuitous Promise	Liquidated Debt
Option Contract	Option-to-Cancel Clause	Promissory Estoppel
Rejection	Best Efforts Contract	Detrimental Reliance
Counteroffer		

MULTIPLE CHOICE QUESTIONS

1.   Law May 88 #16

For an offer to confer the power to form a contract by acceptance, it must have all of the following elements except

A. Be communicated to the offeree in a communication made or authorized by the offeror.
B. Be sufficiently definite and certain.
C. Be communicated by words to the offeree by the offeror.
D. Manifest an intent to enter into a contract.

2.   Law May 89 #24

Dye sent Hill a written offer to sell a tract of land located in Newtown for $60,000. The parties were engaged in a separate dispute. The offer stated that it would be irrevocable for 60 days if Hill would promise to refrain from suing Dye during this time. Hill promptly delivered a promise not to sue during the term of the offer and to forego suit if Hill accepted the offer. Dye subsequently decided that the possible suit by Hill was groundless and therefore phoned Hill and revoked the offer 15 days after making it. Hill mailed an acceptance on the 20th day. Dye did not reply. Under the circumstances,

A. Dye's offer was supported by consideration and was **not** revocable when accepted.
B. Dye's written offer would be irrevocable even without consideration.
C. Dye's silence was an acceptance of Hill's promise.
D. Dye's revocation, **not** being in writing, was invalid.

3.   Law May 89 # 25

To announce the grand opening of a new retail business, Hudson placed an advertisement in a local newspaper quoting sales prices on certain items in stock. The grand opening was so successful that Hudson was unable to totally satisfy customer demands. Which of the following statements is correct?

A. Hudson made an invitation seeking offers.
B. Hudson made an offer to the people who read the advertisement.
C. Anyone who tendered money for the items advertised was entitled to buy them.
D. The offer by Hudson was partially revocable as to an item once it was sold out.

4.   Law Nov 84 #11

The following conversation took place between Mary and Ed: "Ed, if you wanted to sell your table, what would you ask for it?" Ed: "I suppose $400 would be a fair price." Mary: "I'll take it, if you will have it refinished." Ed: "Sold." Thus,

A. Ed's statement: "I suppose $400 would be a fair price" constituted an offer.
B. Mary's Reply: "I'll take it, if you will have it refinished" was a conditional acceptance, terminating Ed's offer.
C. No contract resulted because Ed never stated he would actually sell the table for $400.
D. A contract was formed when Ed said: "Sold."

5.   Law Nov 74 #17

An offer to sell a tract of real property is terminated at the time the

A. Buyer learns of the seller's death.
B. Seller mails his/her revocation if the original offer was made by mail.
C. Buyer mails a revocation of the offer if the original offer was received by mail.
D. Buyer learns of the sale of the property to a third party.

6.   CPA Law May 88 #18

In deciding whether consideration necessary to form a contract exists, a court must determine whether

A. The consideration given by each party is of roughly equal value.
B. There is mutuality of consideration.
C. The consideration has sufficient monetary value.
D. The consideration conforms to the subjective intent of the parties.

ESSAY QUESTION (Estimated time -- 15 to 25 minutes)

Law May 94 #5

Suburban Properties, Inc. owns and manages several shopping centers.

On May 4, 1993, Suburban received from Bridge Hardware, Inc., one of its tenants, a signed letter proposing that the existing lease between Suburban and Bridge be modified to provide that certain utility costs be equally shared by Bridge and Suburban, effective June 1, 1993. Under the terms of the original lease, Bridge was obligated to pay all utility costs. On May 5, 1993, Suburban sent Bridge a signed letter agreeing to share the utility costs as proposed. Suburban later changed its opinion and refused to share in the utility costs.

On June 4, 1993, Suburban received from Dart Associates, Inc. a signed offer to purchase one of the shopping centers owned by Suburban. The offer provided as follows: a price of $9,250,000; it would not be withdrawn before July 1, 1993; and an acceptance must be received by Dart to be effective. On June, 9, 1993, Suburban mailed Dart a signed acceptance. On June 10, before Dart had received Suburban's acceptance, Dart telephoned Suburban and

withdrew its offer. Suburban's acceptance was received by Dart on June 12, 1993.

On June 22, 1993, one of Suburban's shopping centers was damaged by a fire, which started when the center was struck by lightning. As a result of the fire, one of the tenants in the shopping center, World Popcorn Corp., was forced to close its business and will be unable to reopen until the damage is repaired. World sued Suburban claiming that Suburban is liable for World's losses resulting from the fire. The lease between Suburban and World is silent in this regard.

Suburban has taken the following positions:

- Suburban's May 5, 1993, agreement to share equally the utility costs with Bridge is not binding on Suburban.
- Dart could not properly revoke its June 4 offer and must purchase the shopping center.
- Suburban is not liable to World for World's losses resulting from the fire.

Required:

In separate paragraphs, determine whether Suburban's positions are correct and state the reasons for your conclusions.

EXPLANATIONS TO MULTIPLE CHOICE QUESTIONS

1. C is the correct answer. The three requirements for an offer are objective intent, definiteness of terms, and communication to the offeree. This question seeks the item **not** required. The question then becomes one of determining which of the two statements of the communication requirement is correct. The answer choices are similar, thus the candidate must focus on their differences. Choice A says that an offeror can authorize someone else to make the offer, which is true (see Chapter 18 on agency in this guide), and choice C says that the offer must be made by words, which is not true. An offer can be communicated by any means, including sign language, gestures, etc. Thus C, the choice not required, is the correct answer.

2. A is the correct answer. Under common law, which governs land contracts, a promise to hold an offer open is binding if the offeree has given consideration to the offeror to hold the offer open. Usually, that consideration is paid in money, but here the offeree's agreeing not to sue (even though only for a limited period) is the giving up of a legal right, which is a legal detriment. Thus there is a binding option contract, making the offer irrevocable for the option period. Choice D is incorrect because the revocation was ineffective whether or not in writing. This question has an unusual fact situation, illustrating the importance of candidates being able to apply legal rules in both common, less common, and sometimes truly strange situations.

3. A is the correct answer. Public advertisements are generally not considered offers, unless they are very specific. Beware of answer choices like D which lead to a correct result (Hudson is not obligated to sell to everyone who wants to buy) but for a wrong reason. Here the incorrect statement is that there was an offer in the first place. Note that Federal Trade Commission regulations on advertising (not tested on the CPA exam) could apply here, but under contract law a shopper usually cannot create a contract by responding to an advertisement.

4. D is the correct answer. A bilateral contract is formed when the offeree accepts an offer. Approach this question by analyzing each statement in chronological order as to whether it is an offer, acceptance, etc. Ed's statement, "I suppose $400 would be a fair price," does not show the necessary objective intent to be offering to sell the table. Mary's statement does meet all the requirements of an offer, but note that her offering price is implied from Ed's immediately preceding statement. Ed's statement, "Sold," is a valid acceptance and thereby forms the contract. Note that Ed's final statement did not explicitly make a promise but one is implied. Likewise, choice C is incorrect because the other terms, such as the price here, can be implied from all circumstances, including the parties' words, in the course of the negotiations.

5. D is the correct answer. Learning of the sale to another operates as a revocation of the offer because it notifies the offeree that the land is no longer available from the offeror. Note that the offer does not automatically terminate upon the sale to another, but only upon the offeree learning of it, because revocations, in any form, are effective only when notice is received. Contrast this with the death of the offeror, which terminates the offer by operation of law whether or not the offeree learns of the death, making choice A incorrect. Choices B and C are incorrect because rejections and revocations terminate offers only when received, not when sent.

6. B is the correct answer. Mutuality of consideration is another way of saying that each party must give consideration, and that each party's consideration must be given in exchange for the other's consideration, also referred to as the "bargained-for" requirement. Choices A and C both address the value of the consideration, and courts generally do not care about the value of the consideration, so long as there is at least some consideration.

UNOFFICIAL AICPA ANSWER TO ESSAY QUESTION

Law May 94 #5

Suburban is correct concerning the agreement to share utility costs with Bridge. A modification of a contract requires consideration to be binding on the parties. Suburban is not bound by the lease modification because Suburban did not receive any consideration in exchange for its agreement to share the cost of utilities with Bridge.

Suburban is not correct with regard to the Dart offer. An offer can be revoked at any time prior to acceptance. This is true despite the fact that the offer provides that it will not be withdrawn prior to a stated time. If no consideration is given in exchange for this promise not to withdraw the offer, the promise is not binding on the offeror. The offer provided that Suburban's acceptance would not be effective until received. Dart's June 10 revocation terminated Dart's offer. Thus, Suburban's June 9 acceptance was not effective.

Suburban is correct with regard to World's claim. The general rule is that destruction of, or damage to, the subject matter of a contract without the fault of either party terminates the contract. In this case, Suburban is not liable to World because Suburban is discharged from its contractual duties as a result of the fire, which made performance by it under the lease objectively impossible.

Author's note:

The third paragraph covers concepts that are discussed in Chapter 9 of this outline.

In this question, the requirements specifically stated that each point be addressed in a separate paragraph. It is vitally important to pay attention to such instructions and follow them.

Note, also, the structure of each paragraph. The first sentence states clearly and concisely the outcome. The second sentence states the general rule applicable to the situation. From there, if necessary, the rule is further explained, as in the second paragraph. The rule is then applied to the facts of the question, and the outcome is restated as a direct consequence of the rule's application. This approach allows concise essay answers, and demonstrates to the examiners both mastery of the subject matter and an ability to clearly communicate such mastery, both of which factor into the grading.

CHAPTER 7
CAPACITY AND LEGALITY

OVERVIEW

This chapter covers the final two requirements for a valid contract, capacity and legality. **Capacity** focuses on whether the parties to a contract had the mental ability to know what they were committing to when the contract was formed. The three most common reasons that capacity is lacking are minority, intoxication, and insanity. The law's purpose is to protect these persons from their own mistakes or from being taken advantage of by others. The concept of legality holds that courts will not enforce contracts which have illegal subject matter. There are many reasons that a contract is illegal, including some contracts, the "public policy illegality," where the contract does not actually violate any laws, but will be treated by the court as if it did. Illegal contracts are considered void, or nonexistent. Capacity differs from the other three basic contract requirements in that contracts where a party lacks capacity are voidable, rather than void. The party lacking capacity has the option to enforce or avoid the contract. Parties who have capacity are often referred to as **competent** parties.

OUTLINE

I. **Minors**
   A. <u>Definition</u>. A minor is someone who has not yet reached the age of majority, which today is 18 in most states. CPA exam questions will not require you to know the age of majority.
   B. <u>Right to Disaffirm</u>. The basic protection for minors is the right to disaffirm a contract.
      1. *Purpose.* The law protects minors from their "youthful folly" or being taken advantage of by adults.
      2. *Contract Is Voidable.* The right to disaffirm makes the contract voidable by the minor. The minor has the option to enforce the contract or cancel and avoid it. The competent party is bound to the contract if the minor chooses to enforce it.
      3. *Disaffirmance.* The minor can disaffirm a contract orally, in writing, or by contract. The minor can disaffirm at any time while still a minor, and for a reasonable (based on all the facts and circumstances) time after reaching majority. If neither party has begun performance under the contract, then disaffirmance simply relieves each party of its obligation to perform.
      4. *Restoration and Restitution.* Once performance has begun, including cases where both parties have fully performed, the minor's disaffirmance will trigger duties to bring closure to the contract.
         a. **Restitution** is the duty, held by the competent party to return the minor to the **status quo,** or position that the minor was in prior to entering the contract. Where the minor was the buyer, this means that the minor is entitled to a full refund of amounts paid.
         b. **Restoration** is the duty of the minor to return, to the competent party, whatever property the minor has received. The minor is required to return only that portion of such property, if any, still held by the minor, and only required to return it in its present condition. **Exam tip # 1.**

       c. Some states have imposed a duty of restitution on minors when the minor has caused loss in value to the property intentionally or through gross negligence. Many states now also impose a duty of restitution where the minor misrepresents her age, and in some other situations where a duty of restoration only would be unfair. **Exam tip #2.**

   5. *Ratification.* This means that the minor, now an adult, will be bound by the contract. The right to disaffirm ends when ratification occurs. Ratification can take place only after reaching majority, and any attempt to ratify while still a minor can, itself, be disaffirmed. Ratification can occur by:

       a. Express words.

       b. Conduct, usually by continuing to use the property, or otherwise retaining benefits of the contract.

       c. Failure to disaffirm within a reasonable time after reaching majority. **Exam tip #3.**

   6. *Necessaries of Life.* Minors are obligated to pay for necessaries of life. However, the minor is obligated to pay only the <u>fair</u> value, if that is more than the contract price. What qualifies as a necessary is up to the court and can differ greatly based on circumstances such as the minor's age, station in life, lifestyle, etc. **Exam tip #4.**

   7. *Emancipated Minors.* Emancipated minors are those who have voluntarily left home to live apart from their parents. Being emancipated releases the parents from responsibility for furnishing necessaries to the minor.

II. Mental Incompetency.

  A. <u>Definition</u>. Mental incompetency is any mental condition, however caused, which renders the party incapable of understanding the nature of the transaction <u>at the time it was entered into</u>. Mental incompetency is also called **legal insanity**.

  B. <u>Adjudged, or Adjudicated, Insanity</u>. This is where a court has declared someone mentally incompetent. The legal effect of such a declaration is that such persons, for their own protection, have had the legal ability to enter into contracts taken away. Any attempted contract involving an adjudged insane person is void; the person's actual mental state at the time of entering into the contract is irrelevant. **Exam tip #5.**

  C. <u>Insane, but Not Adjudged Insane</u>. These are persons who are insane, but have not been declared so by a court. Contracts with such persons are voidable by the insane person. The key analysis is the person's mental state at the time the contract was entered into. Thus an insane person who contracts during a **lucid interval**, or period when he did understand the nature of the transaction, is a valid contract.

  D. <u>Restitution Owed to Insane Person</u>. The competent party owes a duty of restitution to the insane person if the contract is void or if the insane person avoids a voidable contract.

  E. <u>Ratification</u>. Ratification can occur if the insane person becomes sane, and then expressly ratifies the contract, or ratifies by conduct, such as by using property which was purchased while insane.

III.   Intoxicated Persons.

  A. <u>Definition</u>. Under contract law, a person is intoxicated if, due to alcohol or other drugs, he could not comprehend the nature of the transaction when he entered into the contract. Contracts are voidable by intoxicated persons.

B. <u>Purpose</u>. It is important to remember that contract law protects, not punishes, intoxicated persons. Other parties cannot take advantage of someone's intoxication.

C. <u>Degree of Intoxication</u>. For the contract to be voidable, the level of intoxication must be so great that the person could not comprehend the nature of the transaction. For example, assume that a bar patron, after a few too many drinks and thinking that the band sounded great, bought one of the band's cassettes. If he listened to it later when sober and thought it sounded terrible, he would not be able to avoid the contract assuming that he had known he was buying a cassette. On the other hand, if he had tried to take a bite of the cassette thinking it was a sandwich, he was probably sufficiently intoxicated that he could avoid the contract once sober.

D. <u>Restitution Owed to Intoxicated Person</u>. The competent party owes a duty of restitution to the intoxicated person if the intoxicated person avoids a contract.

E. <u>Ratification</u>. Ratification can occur if the intoxicated person becomes sober, and then expressly ratifies the contract, or ratifies by conduct, such as by using property which was purchased while intoxicated.

IV. **Illegal Contracts-Statutory Violations.**

A. <u>General Concepts</u>. Most contracts made in violation of a statute are void. Examples include a contract for someone to kill your wealthy uncle, or a price fixing arrangement violating antitrust laws. Most statutory violations are of state statutes, and because these differ from state to state, the CPA exam tests on general principles in this area.

B. <u>Effect of Illegality</u>.

1. *Contract Is Void*. Illegal contracts are void, which means that the court ignores the contract, and leaves the parties where they are. This is usually true even if it seems unfair, such as when the more culpable party has come out ahead.

2. *All or Part May Be Treated as Void*. Where the main purpose of the contract is void, the entire contract will be considered void and ignored. Where only a specific provision is void, the court might ignore only the illegal portion, or if reasonable, might modify the illegal provision to make it legal. For example, a rental lease allowing four occupants might be modified to one allowing three, if local zoning regulations allow only three.

3. *Contract Law Is Not Punishment*. Contract disputes are civil actions, and are totally separate from the punishment which occurs in criminal court. The only response of the court to a contract dispute over an illegal contract is to ignore the contract and do nothing. Totally separate, and not a CPA exam concern, is whether the appropriate criminal prosecuting authority decides to file a criminal action.

C. <u>Usury Statutes</u>. Usury statutes set maximum interest rates that can be charged on particular lending arrangements. State laws differ; if a usurious rate is charged, some states reduce the contract rate to the maximum legal rate; some enforce repayment of principal, but no interest; and some do not enforce any provisions, including principal repayment, of the contract.

D. <u>Gambling</u>. These include traditional gambling or wagering, but include other situations such as purchasing insurance where one does not have an insurable interest, such as insurance on someone else's property.

E. <u>Licensing Statutes</u>. These affect contracts entered into by persons who are required to have a license to practice their trade or profession. There are two types of these:

1. *Regulatory Statutes.* Where the purpose of a licensing statute is to protect the public by ensuring that persons in the profession are competent, trustworthy, etc., contracts entered into by unlicensed practitioners are void. For example, if someone not licensed as a doctor has a contract to perform medical services, that contract is void because the purpose of the medical licensing statute is to protect the public. **Exam tip #6.**

2. *Revenue Raising Statute.* Where the purpose of a licensing statute is merely to raise revenue, contracts entered into by the unlicensed person are enforceable. If all pharmacists are required to pay an annual license fee which does not require additional training or education, contracts by a pharmacist who has not paid the fee are enforceable.

V. Illegal Contracts-Contracts Contrary to Public Policy.

A. <u>General Concepts</u>. Public policy is a vague concept which courts have wide discretion in defining. These are contracts which do not violate any specific statute, but which the court believes should not be enforced nonetheless. It might be surprising, but these are indeed treated as illegal contracts even though no specific statute is violated by the contract.

B. <u>Definition</u>. There is no single definition, but generally contracts which have a negative impact on society, public welfare, or public safety are considered against public policy. Critics say that such a subjective definition means that a court can determine that any contract it does not like is against public policy and therefore illegal. **Exam tip #7.**

C. <u>Immoral Contracts</u>. Any contract that is considered to violate society's moral values can be considered against public policy. A contract in which one party agrees to divorce his current spouse has been found to be immoral because it encourages divorce.

D. <u>Covenants Not to Compete</u>. These are agreements (also known as **noncompete agreements**) where a party agrees for a specified period of time to not engage in specified business activities in a designated geographic area. Such restrictions are acceptable if reasonable, but against public policy if too broad in three aspects. Whether too broad depends on all the circumstances, including the line of business, the purpose of the agreement, etc. An employee's agreement not to compete is scrutinized more strictly (i.e. more likely to be found against public policy) than that of a business owner where the agreement is connected with the sale of a business. The three aspects analyzed are:

1. *Line of Business.* An agreement to not open another pizzeria might be acceptable, but not one that covers any type of restaurant.

2. *Geographic Area.* A limitation applying to a city might be acceptable, whereas one covering an entire state might be too broad.

3. *Time.* Shorter restrictions are more likely to be found acceptable than longer ones.

E. <u>Exculpatory Clauses</u>. These clauses release a party from blame for torts committed. They are generally acceptable for negligent acts, but not for gross negligence or intentional acts. Where the parties did not have equal bargaining power, courts sometimes invalidate them even for negligent acts.

F. <u>Innocent Parties</u>. In some cases courts will act in connection with an illegal contract (including contracts in violation of a statute) to protect a party who is innocent, or at least less culpable in the situation. The remedy can be in the form of restitution or enforcement, and can be awarded to parties such as;

1. *Persons Justifiably Ignorant of the Law or Facts.*
2. *Persons Induced by Fraud, Duress, or Undue Influence to Enter into the Illegal Contract.*
3. *Persons Who Withdraw from the Illegal Contract Prior to the Illegal Act's Performance.*
4. *Persons Less at Fault.* Historically, other than the first three situations, the degree of fault did not matter, and parties were always considered **in pari delicto** or equally at fault. Though still true in most states, courts of some states occasionally order more-at-fault parties to pay restitution to less-at-fault parties.

VI.   **Unconscionable Contracts**

A. <u>General Concepts</u>. Parties generally are bound by the terms of the contracts they negotiate, regardless of how one-sided or unfair. The exception is **unconscionable contracts**, which are contracts so one-sided that the court will protect the disadvantaged party.

B. <u>Requirements</u>. A party can get relief from an unconscionable contract only if the following requirements are met:

1. *Vastly Different Bargaining Power.*
2. *Abuse of That Power by the Powerful Party.*
3. *No Reasonable Alternative for the Weaker Party.*

C. <u>Remedies</u>. If a contract is found to be unconscionable, the court, depending on the circumstances, can refuse to enforce the contract, can refuse to enforce the unconscionable portion, or can modify the unconscionable part as it deems appropriate. **Exam Tip #8.**

EXAM TIPS

1. Restitution and restoration are heavily tested and frequently confused. Be sure to know the definition of each and to whom each applies. Restitution is a general contract remedy that often appears in other contract situations as discussed in other chapters of this guide.

2. Remember that although the law is designed to protect minors, minors can take advantage of the law in many circumstances, and, in response, several states have imposed a duty of restitution on minors in such cases. For purposes of the CPA exam, assume the minor has only a duty of restoration, unless stated otherwise.

3. In every contract with a minor, ratification becomes an issue, because every minor eventually reaches the age of majority, unless death intervenes. Ratification can also occur by insane or intoxicated persons, but only if the insanity or intoxication ends, which will not always occur.

4. Because what constitutes a necessary differs so much, CPA exam questions on this issue will state whether or not the item is a necessary.

5. In questions involving insane persons, always look to see if the person has been adjudged insane, and be sure to know in which case contracts are void and in which they are voidable.

6. Candidates must know the differences in licensing and revenue raising statutes. Note that the contract itself in these cases is not illegal, but it is illegal for a party to enter into that type of transaction. The liability for the statutory violation is a separate issue, and a party in violation of a revenue raising statute might be liable for the violation even though his contract is enforceable.

7. CPA exam candidates often struggle with the concept of contracts contrary to public policy. Be sure to understand that when a court says a contract is contrary to public policy, it means that the contract is illegal for contract law purposes only, meaning that the contract will not be enforced. Such a determination does not impose any criminal penalty on the parties.

8. Unfair terms, by themselves, do not make a contract unconscionable. Do not let a very lopsided contract in an exam question lead you to conclude unconscionability unless all required elements are present.

KEY CONCEPTS LIKELY TO BE TESTED ON THE CPA EXAM

1. Disaffirmance: when and how it can occur.
2. Restoration and restitution in the event a minor disaffirms.
3. Liability of a minor for necessaries.
4. Effect on contracts of insane parties; adjudged insane and insane but not adjudged.
5. Effect of illegality generally.
6. Effect of regulatory and revenue raising statute violations on a contract.
7. Requirement for an acceptable covenant not to compete.
8. Unconscionable Contracts.

KEY TERMS

Capacity	Emancipated Minor	Revenue Raising Statute
Competent Party	Legal Insanity	Public Policy
Minor	Adjudged Insane	Immoral Contract
Disaffirm	Lucid Interval	Covenants Not to Compete
Restoration	Intoxication	Exculpatory Clause
Restitution	Statutory Violation	*In Pari Delicto*
Ratification	Usury	Unconscionable Contract
Necessaries of Life	Regulatory Statute	

MULTIPLE CHOICE QUESTIONS

1.   Law Nov 90 #22
Which of the following would be unenforceable because the subject matter is illegal?
A. A contingent fee charged by an attorney to represent a plaintiff in a negligence action.
B. An arbitration clause in a supply contract.
C. A restrictive covenant in an employment contract prohibiting a former employee from using the employer's trade secrets
D. An employer's promise **not** to press embezzlement charges against an employee who agrees to make restitution.

2.   Law Nov 92 #15
Rail, who was 16 years old, purchased an $800 computer from Elco Electronics. Rail and Elco are located in a state where the age of majority is 18. Rail was unhappy with the computer. Two days after reaching the age of 18, Rail was still frustrated with the computer's reliability. He returned it to Elco, demanding an $800 refund. Elco refused, claiming that Rail no longer had a right to disaffirm the contract. Elco's refusal is
A. Correct, because Rail's multiple requests for service acted as a ratification of the contract.
B. Correct, because Rail could have transferred good title to a good faith purchaser for value.
C. Incorrect, because Rail disaffirmed the contract within a reasonable time after reaching the age of 18.
D. Incorrect, because Rail could disaffirm the contract at any time.

3.   Law Nov 89 #11
Kent, a 16-year-old, purchased a used car from Mint Motors, Inc. Ten months later, the car was stolen and never recovered. Which of the following statements is correct?
A. The car's theft is a de facto ratification of the purchase because it is impossible to return the car.
B. Kent may disaffirm the purchase because Kent is a minor.
C. Kent effectively ratified the purchase because Kent used the car for an unreasonable period of time.
D. Kent may disaffirm the purchase because Mint, a merchant, is subject to the UCC.

4.   Law May 91 #13
On reaching majority, a minor may ratify a contract in any of the following ways **except** by
A. Failing to disaffirm within a reasonable time after reaching majority.
B. Orally ratifying the entire contract.
C. Acting in a manner that amounts to ratification.
D. Affirming, in writing, some of the terms of the contract.

5.   Law May 90 #17
Payne entered into a written contract to sell a parcel of land to Stevens. At the time the agreement was executed, Payne had consumed alcoholic beverages. Payne's ability to understand the nature and terms of the contract was not impaired. Stevens did not believe that Payne was intoxicated. The contract is
A. Void as a matter of law.
B. Legally binding on both parties.
C. Voidable at Payne's option.
D. Voidable at Stevens' option.

ESSAY QUESTION (Estimated time -- 10 to 15 minutes)

Author

Sam went to work as a computer programmer for a California software firm in 1989. This firm specialized in software for dental offices. As a condition of beginning employment he was requried to sign an agreement which provided that if he left the employment of the software firm, whether initiatied by Sam or the firm, he would not work for "another software firm, or as a consultant doing programming, for ten years, anywhere in the state of California."

Sam had been heavily recruited for this position, and the signing of this agreement, and other documents, had occured after a reception where Sam had consumed a number of alcoholic beverages. Sam was definitely feeling the effects of the drinks when he signed the agreement, but understood its terms and general nature.

In 1998 Sam began to have difficulties with his boss, and in June quit his job.

Three months later, Sam accepted a position as a software engineer with a firm in Los Angeles. This firm specialized in software for small and medium-sized hospitals.

In late 1998 Sam's former employer notified Sam that he was in breach of the agreement he had signed in 1989 before starting work.

Sam then offered to provide trade secrets of his new employer to the former employer in exchange for the former employer not enforcing the agreement and in exchange for cash payments of $1,000 per month, with the first five months paid in advance. This would help the former employer expand its software offerings.

Sam received $5,000 from the former employer and provided trade secrets for three months. Sam then stopped providing any trade secrets, fearing that he might get caught.

The former employer has sued Sam seeking:

- A return of the $5,000 paid to Sam, alleging that the limited trade secrets provided have no value.
- An injunction prohibiting Sam from working in violation of the noncompete agreement signed in 1989.

Sam has responded claiming:

- The contract to provide the trade secret was an illegal contract, thus he can keep the $5,000.
- He (Sam) was intoxicated when he signed the noncompete agreeement, making it unenforceable.
- The noncompete agreement is illegal and therefore not a valid contract.

Required:

Discuss each of the claims along with Sam's responses and indicate the probable outcome of the former employer's lawsuit.

EXPLANATIONS TO MULTIPLE CHOICE QUESTIONS

1. D is the correct answer. There is a legal obligation to report illegal activity, therefore an agreement to not do so is illegal. Furthermore, the decision to press charges or prosecute is made by the prosecutor or the district attorney, not by the employer.

2. C is the correct answer. A minor's time for ratification extends for a reasonable time after reaching majority. The time of ratification in CPA exam questions will clearly be within or clearly be beyond a reasonable time. No action prior to reaching majority can ever amount to ratification.

3. B is the correct answer. Even though the car was stolen, the minor can disaffirm. The seller might have a claim to any insurance proceeds, but that does not affect the minor's right to disaffirm.

4. D is the correct answer. Affirmation of a contract requires affirmation of all terms, but that affirmation can be accomplished orally, in writing, by conduct or by failure to disaffirm.

5. B is the correct answer. Intoxication makes a contract voidable only if the intoxicated person could not understand the nature or terms of the contract.

EXPLANATION TO ESSAY QUESTION

Author

The contract to steal the trade secrets is an illegal contract and would be a void contract which the courts would not enforce. A contract is illegal if it requires the violation of a statute or it is against public policy. The stealing of trades secrets likely violates a statute, but if not, the contract would certainly be considered against public policy. As an illegal contract, the court would leave the parties where they are. Thus Sam would not be ordered to pay back any of the $5,000 to the former employer. He would not even be required to pay the $2,000 for which he has not delivered any trade secrets.

Sam's claim that he was intoxicated would not affect his liability under the noncompete agreement. Intoxication allows the intoxicated party to void a contract only if the intoxication was so great that the intoxicated party could not comprehend the nature or the terms of the contract that was entered into. In this case, Sam was able to comprehend the contract when he signed it.

Sam's claim that the noncompete agreement is illegal is probably correct. Not all noncompete agreements are illegal. They are considered against public policy, and therefore illegal only if the limits are excessive with respect to the breadth of type of work prohibited, the geographic area, or the length of time that the restriction applies. The noncompete agreement in this case probably is excessive in all three areas. In evaluating whether the restrictions are excessive, a court will consider the legitimate business interests of the former employer in enforcing the restricitions and the effect on Sam's ability to earn a living if the restriction is enforced.

Where the restricitons are excessive, a court can modify the restriction so that it is reasonable. For example, a ten-year restriction might be reduced to two years. Sam will probably be able to keep his new job unless it poses a legitimate business threat to the former employer.

Author's note:

Sam might also be liable to his current employer for the theft of the trade secrets, but this was not asked for in the question. It will generally not hurt your score to briefly mention such related points but doing more than that will usually be more harmful than helpful.

CHAPTER 8
DEFENSES TO THE ENFORCEMENT OF CONTRACTS

OVERVIEW

Even though the basic elements required to form a contract are present, there are many reasons that a party might not be required to perform a contract. A **defense** allows a party to avoid its obligations under the contract, and in most situations, allows a party to recover any property already transferred away under the contract. There are two general categories of defenses. The first group covers situations where the assent, or agreement, of the parties is somehow flawed by a mistake, fraud, or by somehow being forced into the agreement. The second general type arises where an oral contract is used for one of the types of contracts which is required to be in writing.

OUTLINE

I. **Mistakes**
   A. General Concepts. A contract is based on a meeting of the minds about the contract. Mistakes as to the contract prevent this meeting of the minds. Mistakes are placed in two general categories based on whether one party is mistaken, or both are. When a party is allowed to get out of a contract based on a mistake, the general remedy is **rescission**, or an "undoing" of the contract, returning the parties to where they were before the contract.
   B. Unilateral Mistake. A **unilateral mistake** occurs where only one party is mistaken about the contract. The general rule is that such contracts are enforceable despite the mistake of one party. For example, Doug purchased a used car in the mistaken belief that it had air conditioning. Doug is bound by the contract because he is the only party who had that mistaken impression. Generally there is no rescission, but there are three circumstances where a party is allowed to rescind a contract based on a unilateral mistake.
      1. *Nonmistaken Party Knew of Other Party's Mistake.* If the nonmistaken party knew of the other party's mistake and made no attempt to correct the mistaken party's impression, the mistaken party can rescind. In the example of Doug, above, if the salesperson knew Doug erroneously thought the car had air conditioning and said nothing, Doug could rescind.
      2. *Clerical or Mathematical Error.* Mathematical and clerical errors, such as errors in preparing a bid for a construction contract, will allow rescission so long as the error was not caused by gross negligence.
      3. *Unconscionable if Enforced.* If the enforcement of the contract with the error would make the contract unconscionable, it can be rescinded. **Exam tip #1.**
   C. Mutual Mistake. A **mutual mistake** results when both parties have made a mistake about a past or existing material fact.
      1. *Past or Present Fact.* The subject of the mistake cannot be an opinion, nor can it relate to the future such as how an investment might perform. From the example above, if both Doug and the salesperson erroneously thought that the car had air conditioning, either could rescind the contract.
      2. *Mistake of Value.* A **mistake of value** is never grounds for rescission; the mistake must relate to fact.

3. *Application.* Mistake can be an issue with counterfeit items (artwork, coins, etc.) when neither party is aware the item is counterfeit or where an item, such as a painting, is sold with neither party realizing that it is a valuable masterpiece. Applying the above:

   a. Counterfeit Item. If two parties contract for the sale of a "Rembrandt painting" which both parties honestly believed to be a Rembrandt, but turns out to be counterfeit, there is a mutual mistake. They mistakenly believed that the contract was for a "Rembrandt painting" but the item was not a "Rembrandt painting."

   b. Unknown Masterpiece. A buyer and seller negotiated the sale of a "painting" at a yard sale. Unknown to either, the painting was a valuable Picasso masterpiece. There was no mistake of fact here. The parties negotiated a contract for the sale of a "painting" and the item actually was a "painting." There was no mistake of fact; the only mistake, if any, was of the painting's value. Neither party can rescind the contract.

   c. Summary. A contract for a particular item (painting by a master, a coin of a certain date, a pink Cadillac owned by Elvis Presley) which is not the particular item that the parties thought it was, is a mutual mistake of fact. A contract for an ordinary item which, unknown to the parties is a particularly valuable example of that item, is not a mutual mistake of fact. A mistake as to perceived value is not a mistake of fact.

II. Fraud.

A. <u>Fraud in the Inducement</u>. **Fraud in the inducement** occurs when one parties lies, or makes a misrepresentation in order to induce the other party to enter a contract. In order to recover for fraud, the victim must prove more than the fact of a misstatement. The plaintiff must prove all six of the following. If they are proven, the victim can recover damages. **Exam tip #2.**

1. *False Representation.* This **false representation** can take many forms, such as a picture on the box of a product which shows a different item than the product enclosed.

2. *Material Fact.* The statement must relate to a existing **material fact**. Items which do not meet this requirement include:

   a. Opinions. "This car has the most attractive styling out this year," is a mere **opinion**.

   b. Puffing. "This is the greatest car available this year," is **puffing** or sales talk.

   c. Immaterial Fact. "This car was driven by a woman in her golden years who drove it only to church," when in fact she drove it to the bingo parlor. Where she drove the car is not material in this case.

   d. Future events. "Because this car is a limited edition, it will increase in value as the years go by." Because this is a prediction of a future event, the failure of the event to occur cannot meet this requirement. Note that if the car was not, in fact, a limited edition, such a misstatement might relate to a material fact.

3. *Intent to Deceive.* Generally this means that the wrongdoer must have known that the statement was false. This knowledge of the falsity is sometimes known as **scienter**, which means knowledge, and comes from the same Latin word as science.

4. *Reliance on the False Statement.* The victim must have **relied on** the false statement and it must have been a factor in entering into the contract. Where the seller of a car falsely claims that a car has only 10,000 miles on it, the buyer has not relied if, prior to purchasing the car, she learns that the mileage is incorrect, or she purchases the car with its mileage otherwise not being a factor. The false statement need not be the only factor.

5. *Reliance Is Justified.* If a reasonable person should have known that the false statement was not true, then any reliance would not be justified. If a car which is claimed to have only 10,000 miles on it is so beat up and in such terrible condition that it is unreasonable to believe the statement, then **justifiable reliance** is missing.

6. *Injury.* There must be some loss to the plaintiff. Two common measures are the difference in value of the actual item and the item as represented, and costs incurred to correct or repair a misrepresented item.

B. <u>Fraud in the Inception</u>. **Justifiable reliance** occurs when someone is deceived about the document he is signing. If an attorney told a client he was signing an agreement about his legal representation when in fact the document that the client had signed was a will leaving all his property to the attorney, the attorney has committed fraud in the inception. These contracts are void.

C. <u>Fraud by Concealment</u>. **Fraud by concealment** is similar to fraud in the inducement, but rather than making an affirmative representation, the wrongdoer takes specific action, to hide a material fact or facts in some way from the other party.

D. <u>Silence as Misrepresentation</u>. Normally there is no duty to disclose facts, but **silence is misrepresentation** when:
   1. *Nondisclosure Would Cause Bodily Injury or Death.* The seller of a used car has no duty to disclose defects in the radio, but does have a duty to disclose brake defects.
   2. *There Is an Existing Fiduciary Relationship.* A fiduciary relationship is an existing relationship of trust and confidence.
   3. *A Statute Requires Disclosure.* In many states, home sellers are required to disclose certain known defects, as one example.

E. <u>Innocent Misrepresentation</u>. This occurs where there was no scienter, or intent to deceive the victim. The only remedy here is rescission; damages are not recoverable. In many aspects, innocent misrepresentation cases are similar to mutual mistake cases. **Exam tip #3.**

III. **Undue Influence.**
   A. <u>Definition</u>. **Undue influence** occurs when an individual takes advantage of a preexisting fiduciary relationship with a party by inducing the other party to enter into a contract.
   B. <u>Fiduciary Relationship</u>. A **fiduciary relationship** is one based on trust where one person generally should look out for the interests of another. They can arise from either family relationships or from contractual arrangements such as an attorney representing a client, or an agency arrangement.
   C. <u>Rationale</u>. Normally each party is expected to look after her own interests in a contract, but with a fiduciary relationship, one party has a duty to act in the other's best interest, so it is reasonable for the protected person to not look out for his own interests.
   D. <u>Example</u>. A son, who is an estate planning attorney, induced his mother to transfer her home to a trust, explaining that the trust would reduce estate taxes, but actually would result in the son getting the house upon the mother's death, denying the mother's desire that the house go equally to all her children. The law allows the mother to rely on her son, and if he takes advantage of the situation, the other party (possibly the surviving children here if the problem is not discovered until after the mother's death) can undo the contract.
   E. <u>Remedy</u>. The remedy for undue influence is rescission of the contract.

IV. Duress.
  A. Definition. Duress is any wrongful threat that induces a party to enter into a contract.
  B. Wrongful Threats. There are several types of wrongful threats under duress:
    1. *Physical Harm.* "I will break your arm if you do not sign this agreement."
    2. *Threat of Frivolous Civil Lawsuit.* "I will sue you for patent infringement." This is duress if there is no legitimate lawsuit against the victim, but it is not duress if there is a legitimate claim.
    3. *Threat of Criminal Lawsuit, Frivolous or Not.* "I will press charges against you for stealing my bike." This is duress even if the suit is valid because the person actually did steal the bike.
  C. Rationale. These contracts were not a meeting of minds. The victim did not agree to anything, but merely acted out of the fear of the threatened consequences.
  D. Economic Duress. Traditionally, desperate economic circumstances which led one party to agree to a one-sided contract did not amount to duress. In some cases where the powerful party was a cause of the situation, and the victim had no other alternative, **economic duress** has been recognized by the courts.
  E. Remedy. Contracts are not enforceable against victims of duress. **Exam tip #4.**

V. Statute of Frauds.
  A. Definition. The **Statute of Frauds** is a requirement that certain types of contracts be in writing in order to be enforceable. The original purpose was to prevent persons from committing fraud on the court by lying about oral contracts, thus the name. Contracts where reliable oral evidence is likely to be difficult to obtain must be in writing. **Exam tip #5.**
  B. Remedy. A contract which the statute requires to be in writing, but is not in writing, is unenforceable, meaning that the court will take no action with respect to it. There are some circumstances where courts will enforce oral contracts covered by the statute. In many cases, parties will voluntarily perform an oral contract that the statute requires to be in writing.
  C. Contracts Covered. The following are the most common contracts required to be in writing:
    1. *Interest in Land.*
      a. Interests Covered. Covered contracts include not only sales of land and improvements, but also grants of limited interests such as life estates (a right to use land for one's lifetime), easements, and in most states, leases of more than one year.
      b. Part Performance Exception. If neither party has performed, the court will not enforce the contract. But if one party has performed (i.e. the buyer has paid for the land or the seller has transferred the land to the buyer) the court will enforce the contract against the other party.
    2. *Cannot Possibly Be Performed Within One Year.*
      a. Measurement of the Year. The key is whether the end of the contract can be reached within one year of the date it is entered into, rather than the length of the contract performance. If a consulting agreement is entered into on March 1, 2000, which covers the period from January 1, 2001 to June 30, 2001, this contract must be in writing. The completion date of June 30, 2001, is more than one year from March 1, 2000, the date the contract is entered into. The six-month duration of the contract is not relevant.

       b. **Cannot Possibly Be Performed.** A contract to perform services for one's lifetime, or "the remainder of one's life," does not need to be in writing because it is <u>possible</u> that the service provider would die within a year, completing the contract in less than a year. Only contracts that <u>cannot</u> be performed in a year need to be in writing.

    3. *A Promise to Answer for the Debt of Another.* These are promises, such as surety arrangements, where a party promises to pay another's debt if the other person fails to do so. An unconditional promise to pay another's debt ("I will pay John's car loan.") is not required to be in writing.

    4. *A Promise Made in Consideration of Marriage.* A promise to marry need not be in writing. But any promise where marriage is the consideration does need to be in writing. Basically, this means that prenuptial agreements must be in writing. The promises in such agreements are of the general form, "If you marry me, I promise, that in the event of divorce...." Such promises, made in exchange for marriage, must be in writing.

    5. *A Contract for the Sale of Goods of $500 or More.* This is a requirement of the Uniform Commercial Code, and is based on the total contract price, not the price of individual items.

    6. *Certain Agency Contracts.* Where the underlying transaction must be in writing, an agency arrangement related to that transaction must also be in writing.

D. <u>Promissory Estoppel</u>. Just as promissory estoppel can be used to enforce a promise lacking consideration, promissory estoppel can be used to enforce an oral promise otherwise required to be in writing. See Chapter 6 of this guide for the requirements of promissory estoppel.

E. <u>The Required Writing</u>. A formal writing is not required. Any writing sufficient to determine the terms of the contract is adequate.

F. <u>Integration of Several Writings</u>. The requirement can be met with several **integrated writings** which together are sufficient. One writing can refer to another writing as part of the agreement through **incorporation by reference**. Airline tickets, for example, have a page entitled "Notice of Incorporated Terms" which means that the referred-to document is part of the agreement even though it is not physically present with the ticket.

G. <u>Signature Required</u>. The signature of the party against whom enforcement is sought is required. This is often stated as the signature of the "party to be charged." The plaintiff's signature is not needed because, by filing the lawsuit, the plaintiff is admitting the existence of the contract. **Exam tip #6.**

VI.   **Contract Interpretation.**

A. <u>General Concept</u>. A contract is based on a meeting of the minds, or the intent of the parties, but the words used and the way the contract is written is often, vague, contradictory, or incomplete. In these cases, the court must try to determine the party's intent by interpreting the contract. Courts have developed a number of general rules of **contract interpretation**. These include:

    1. *Ordinary Words.* These are given their ordinary dictionary meaning.

    2. *Technical Words.* These are given their technical meaning unless another meaning is clearly intended.

3. *Specific Terms.* Specific terms control or qualify general terms. If a residential lease prohibits pets in one provision, but allows cats in a different one, the specific allowance of cats would control over the inconsistent general prohibition against all pets.
4. *Changed Terms.* Terms typed onto a preprinted form contract control over the preprinted form. Handwritten terms control over either preprinted or typed terms.
5. *Ambiguities.* Ambiguous terms will be interpreted against the party who drafted the contract.
6. *Principal Object.* All interpretation of specific terms will be accomplished keeping in mind the overall object or purpose of the agreement.
7. *Words and Numerals.* Where a monetary amount is represented by both words, "One Thousand Dollars" and numerals, "$10,000.00" the words control over the numerals.

VII.   Parol Evidence Rule.
   A. General Rule. Where a contract is evidenced by a final written agreement that is intended to be the complete agreement, the court will not consider any earlier evidence, oral or written, from outside that final written agreement. This outside evidence is parol (rhymes with parole, but has no final "e") evidence and is not admissible. The **parol evidence rule** is sometimes called the **four corners rule** because only the words between the four corners of the written agreement are admissible. **Exam tip #7.**
   B. Rationale. Parties should not be able to claim that despite the terms of the written agreement, they really intended something different. Furthermore, many of these oral statements were made in the negotiation process, and get changed by the time of the final agreement.
   C. Example. A written contract for a used car provides that there is no warranty, but during negotiations the seller said that he would repair any problems that arose in the first month. The oral statement about the repairs cannot be heard by the court, because the written contract is assumed to be the final agreement between the parties, and if the earlier-discussed commitment to repair the car is not in the final agreement, the law assumes the parties changed their minds and ultimately did not want a repair obligation.
   D. Integration. Only if the agreement is intended to be the final agreement between the parties, does the parol evidence rule apply. This is often assumed, but the parties often use a **merger** or **integration clause** which specifically states that all earlier promises, provisions, or agreements have been incorporated into the written agreement. Such a clause prevents a party from claiming that the written agreement is not a complete integration, although the parol evidence rule would frequently apply even without the merger clause.
   E. Exceptions. If one of the following exceptions applies, it means that the court will allow the outside evidence to be admitted. The court is not obligated to decide in favor of that evidence, but the party at least has a chance to state its case.
      1. *Proof of Voidability.* If the evidence would make the contract voidable, it can be admitted. If the plaintiff is using the outside evidence to try to prove fraud in the inducement, it would be admissible despite the parol evidence rule. Proof of lack of contractual capacity or the failure of a condition precedent could also be admitted under this exception.
      2. *Interpretation of Ambiguous Language.* If a contract provides for the sale of the seller's "Honda Accord" but the seller owns two Honda Accords, outside evidence can be admitted to resolve a dispute over which Accord was intended.

3. *Fill in Gaps.* If a contract for a European tour omitted which hotel was to be provided on two nights in Paris, outside evidence could be admitted to resolve any disputes on that issue.

4. *Correct an Obvious Clerical Error.* For example, where the contract price is obviously in error, outside evidence can be introduced as to the correct price.

5. *Uniform Commercial Code.* For sales of goods under the UCC, parol evidence can be admitted to prove course of dealing, course of performance, or usage of trade. See Chapter 11 of this guide.

F. <u>Rule of Evidence</u>. The parol evidence rule does not directly determine the outcome in a contract dispute. It is a rule of evidence which determines if a court will allow or not allow a party to introduce evidence. If the rule applies, the party does not get to state its case in court. If the rule does not apply, the party gets to state its case, but that does not guarantee a decision in its favor. Of course, whether or not a party can present evidence on an issue will affect the outcome of a dispute.

G. <u>Does Not Apply to Later Agreements</u>. The parol evidence does not apply to agreements, oral or written, made <u>after</u> the main contract was formed. Thus, evidence of such agreements can always be admitted. The rationale is that if both parties agree, they should always be able to change the terms of a contract. There might be other problems with these later agreements, but they can be admitted into evidence. Where a party sold a car without warranties, but later promised to fix it at no charge, evidence of that later promise could be admitted, but the promise might lack consideration if the car owner gave up nothing, and the promise might be viewed as an unenforceable gift promise.

EXAM TIPS

1. These exceptions to the general unilateral mistake rule are frequently tested. Candidates must know them.

2. If even one of the elements of fraud in the inducement is missing, there is no fraud case, even if the elements which are present seem to scream for a remedy. There are six elements here, rather than the four in the text, because two of the textbook elements are shown here broken down into component parts. Various texts and courts break the fraud requirements down into four, five, or six elements; regardless of the number of elements, together the requirements are always the same.

3. A victim generally tries to prove a fraud case, if the elements are present, because of the recoverability of damages. If the victim cannot prove the intent element, then she might be able to prove an innocent misrepresentation case, but could only rescind the contract, and could not recover damages.

4. Candidates frequently confuse duress and undue influence. The key to duress is an improper threat, and the key to undue influence is the violation of a trust relationship.

5. The Statute of Frauds is an entirely separate concept from Fraud in the Inducement. Candidates absolutely must understand each thoroughly, and must not mix them up, despite the term "Fraud" appearing in the names of both. The Statute of Frauds has to do with writing, not with fraud.

6. In Statute of Frauds questions, be sure to see if the defendant's signature is present; the signature of the plaintiff (the party seeking enforcement of the contract) is not needed.

7. The parol evidence rule is very tricky. First, it is complex. Another common source of confusion is that it is a "negative" rule. If the rule applies, evidence is <u>not</u> allowed in, and when the rule does <u>not</u> apply, evidence <u>is</u> allowed in. Multiple choice questions should be analyzed very carefully. Be sure to know the exceptions because questions often require the candidate to determine applicability of the rule based on whether an exception is present.

KEY CONCEPTS LIKELY TO BE TESTED ON THE CPA EXAM

1. Whether a mistake is unilateral or bilateral, and whether a party can rescind a particular contract.
2. The required elements for fraud in the inducement and whether all are present in a fact situation to support a fraud claim.
3. Whether duress or undue influence are present, and the ability to distinguish them.
4. The general definition and types of contracts covered by the statute of frauds, and based on the rules and exceptions, whether a particular oral contract can be enforced.
5. The general rules of contract interpretation and their application.
6. The basic parol evidence rule, and how it works, and its exceptions.

KEY TERMS

Defense	Puffing	Economic Duress
Rescission	Scienter	Statute of Frauds
Unilateral Mistake	Reliance	Integrated Writings
Mutual Mistake	Justifiable Reliance	Incorporation by Reference
Mistake of Value	Fraud in the Inception	Contract Interpretation
Fraud in the Inducement	Fraud by Concealment	Parol Evidence Rule
False Representation	Silence as Misrepresentation	Four Corners Rule
Material Fact	Undue Influence	Merger Clause
Opinion	Fiduciary Relationship	Integration Clause

MULTIPLE CHOICE QUESTIONS

1.   Law May 92 #30
Under the parol evidence rule, oral evidence will be excluded if it relates to
A. A contemporaneous oral agreement relating to a term in the contract.
B. Failure of a condition precedent.
C. Lack of contractual capacity.
D. A modification made several days after the contract was executed.

2.   Law Nov 89 #12
The Statute of Frauds
A. Prevents the use of oral evidence to contradict the terms of a written contract.
B. Applies to all contracts having consideration valued at $500 or more.
C. Requires the independent promise to pay the debt of another to be in writing.
D. Applies to all real estate leases.

3.   Law May 90 #20

With regard to an agreement for the sale of real estate, the Statute of Frauds

A. Does **not** require that the agreement be signed by all parties.

B. Does **not** apply if the value of the real estate is less than $500.

C. Requires that the entire agreement be in a single writing.

D. Requires that the purchase price be fair and adequate in relation to the value of the real estate.

4.   Law May 90 #15

King sent Foster, a real estate developer, a signed offer to sell a specified parcel of land to Foster for $200,000. King, an engineer, had inherited the land. On the same day that King's letter was received, Foster telephoned King and accepted the offer. Which of the following statements is correct under the Statute of Frauds?

A. No contract was formed because Foster did **not** sign the offer.

B. No contract was formed because King is **not** a merchant and, therefore, King's letter is **not** binding on Foster.

C. A contract was formed, although it would be enforceable only against King.

D. A contract was formed and would be enforceable against both King and Foster because Foster is a merchant.

5.   Law Nov 90 #23

For a purchaser of land to avoid a contract with the seller based on duress, it must be shown that the seller's improper threats

A. Constituted a crime or tort.

B. Would have induced a reasonably prudent person to assent to the contract.

C. Actually induced the purchaser to assent to the contract.

D. Were made with the intent to influence the purchaser.

6.   Law May 92 #28

Which of the following, if intentionally misstated by a seller to a buyer, would be considered a fraudulent inducement to make a contract?

A. Nonexpert opinion.

B. Appraised value.

C. Prediction.

D. Immaterial fact.

7.   Law May 91 #17

Bond and Spear orally agreed that Bond would buy a car from Spear for $475. Bond paid Spear a $100 deposit. The next day, Spear received an offer of $575, the car's fair market value. Spear immediately notified Bond that Spear would not sell the car to Bond and returned Bond's $100. If Bond sues Spear and Spear defends on the basis of the Statute of Frauds, Bond will probably

A. Lose because the agreement was for less than the fair market value of the car.

B. Win, because the agreement was for less than $500.

C. Lose because the agreement was **not** in writing and signed by Spear.

D. Win, because Bond paid a deposit.

8.   Law May 86 #8

Sardy, a famous football player, was asked to autograph a pad of paper held by Maple. Unknown to Sardy, Maple had carefully concealed a contract for the sale of Sardy's home to Maple in the pad that Sardy signed. If Maple seeks to enforce the contract, Sardy's best defense to have the contract declared void would be

A. Fraud in the inducement.

B. Fraud in the execution.

C. Mistake.

D. Duress.

9.   Law May 91 #21

To prevail in a common law action for innocent misrepresentation, the plaintiff must prove

A. The defendant made the false statements with a reckless disregard for the truth.
B. The misrepresentations were in writing.
C. The misrepresentations concerned material facts.
D. Reliance on the misrepresentations was the only factor inducing the plaintiff to enter into the contract.

10.   Law Nov 88 #16

On April 6, Apple entered into a signed contract with Bean, by which Apple was to sell Bean an antique automobile having a fair market value of $150,000, for $75,000. Unknown to either party, the auto had been destroyed by fire on April 4. If Bean sues Apple for breach of contract, Apple's best defense is

A. Unconscionability.
B. Risk of loss had passed to Bean.
C. Lack of adequate consideration.
D. Mutual mistake.

11.   Law May 89 #27

Able hired Carr to restore Able's antique car for $800. The terms of their oral agreement provided that Carr was to complete the work within 18 months. Actually, the work could be completed within one year. The agreement is

A. Unenforceable because it covers services with a value in excess of $500.
B. Unenforceable because it covers a time period in excess of one year.
C. Enforceable because personal service contracts are exempt from the Statute of Frauds.
D. Enforceable because the work could be completed within one year.

12.   Law Nov 92 #23

Rogers and Lennon entered into a written computer consulting agreement that required Lennon to provide certain weekly reports to Rogers. The agreement also stated that Lennon would provide the computer equipment necessary to perform the services, and that Rogers' computer would not be used. As the parties were executing the agreement, Rogers and Lennon orally agreed that Lennon could use Rogers' computer. After executing the agreement, Rogers and Lennon orally agreed that Lennon would report on a monthly, rather than a weekly, basis. The parties now disagree on Lennon's right to use Rogers' computer and how often Lennon must report to Rogers. In the event of a lawsuit between the parties, the parol evidence rule will

A. Not apply to any of the parties' agreements because the consulting agreement did not have to be in writing.
B. Not prevent Lennon from proving the parties' oral agreement that Lennon could use Rogers' computer.
C. Not prevent the admission into evidence of testimony regarding Lennon's right to report on a monthly basis.
D. Not apply to the parties' agreement to allow Lennon to use Rogers' computer because it was contemporaneous with the written agreement.

ESSAY QUESTIONS

(Estimated time -- 15 to 25 minutes)

Essay #1.   Law May 93 #4
West Corp. is involved in the following disputes:

On September 16, West's president orally offered to hire Dodd Consultants, Inc. to do computer consulting for West. The offer provided for a 3-year contract at $5,000 per month. West agreed that Dodd could have until September 30 to decide whether to accept the offer. If Dodd chose to accept the offer, its acceptance would have to be received by September 30.

On September 27, Dodd sent West a letter accepting the offer. West received the letter on October 2. On September 28, West's president decided that West's accounting staff could handle West's computer problems and notified Dodd by telephone that the offer was withdrawn. Dodd argued that West had no right to revoke its offer, and that Dodd had already accepted the offer by mail.

Dodd claims that it has a binding contract with West because:

- West's offer could not be revoked before September 30
- Dodd's acceptance was effective on September 27, when the letter accepting the offer was mailed.

West's president claims that if an agreement exists, that agreement should not be enforceable against West because of the Statute of Frauds requirement that the contract be in writing.

On March 1, West signed a lease with Abco Real Estate, Inc. for warehouse space. The lease required that West repair and maintain the warehouse. On April 14, West orally asked Abco to paint the warehouse. Despite the lease provision requiring West to repair and maintain the warehouse, Abco agreed to do so by April 30. On April 29 Abco advised West that Abco had decided not to paint the warehouse. West demanded that Abco paint the warehouse under the April 14 agreement. Abco refused and has taken the following positions:

- Abco's April 14 agreement to paint the warehouse is not binding on Abco because it was a modification of an existing contract.
- Because the April 14 agreement was oral and the March 1 lease was in writing, West would not be allowed to introduce evidence in any litigation relating to the April 14 oral agreement.

Required:

a. State whether Dodd's claims are correct and give the reasons for your conclusions.

b. State whether West's president's claim is correct and give the reasons for your conclusion.

c. State whether Abco's positions are correct and give the reasons for your conclusions.

(Estimated time -- 15 to 20 minutes)

Essay #2.   Law Nov 91 #3

In a signed letter dated March 2, 1991, Stake offered to sell Packer a specific vacant parcel of land for $100,000. Stake had inherited the land, along with several apartment buildings in the immediate vicinity. Packer received the offer on March 4. The offer required acceptance by March 10 and required Packer to have the property surveyed by a licensed surveyor so the exact legal description of the property could be determined.

On March 6, Packer sent Stake a counteroffer of $75,000. All other terms and conditions of the offer were unchanged. Stake received Packer's counteroffer on March 8, and, on that day, telephoned Packer and accepted it. On learning that a survey of the vacant parcel would cost about $1,000, Packer telephoned Stake on March 11 requesting that they share the survey cost equally. During this conversation, Stake agreed to Packer's proposal.

During the course of the negotiations leading up to the March communications between Stake and Packer, Stake expressed concern to Packer that a buyer of the land might build apartment unites that would compete with those owned by Stake in the immediate vicinity. Packer assured Stake that Packer intended to use the land for a small shopping center. Because of these assurances, Stake was willing to sell the land to Packer. Contrary to what Packer told Stake, Packer had already contracted conditionally with Rolf for Rolf to build a 48-unit apartment development on the vacant land to be purchased from Stake.

During the last week of March, Stake learned that the land to be sold to Packer had a fair market value of $200,000. Also, Stake learned that Packer intended to build apartments on the land. Because of this information, Stake sued Packer to rescind the real estate contract, alleging that:

- Packer committed fraud in the formation of the contract thereby entitling Stake to rescind the contract.
- Stake's innocent mistake as to the fair market value of the land entitles Stake to rescind the contract.
- The contract was not enforceable against Stake because Stake did not sign Packer's March 6 counteroffer.

Required:

State whether Stake's allegations are correct and give the reasons for your conclusions.

EXPLANATIONS TO MULTIPLE CHOICE QUESTIONS

1. A is the correct answer. Evidence of any contemporaneous (made at the same time as the primary written contract) agreement, oral or written, is not allowed into evidence under the parol evidence rule. Choice D is incorrect because agreements made after the primary agreement are allowed into evidence on the theory that parties, by agreement, should always be able to change their minds.

2. C is the correct answer. Independent promises to pay the debt of another is one of types of contracts required to be in writing under the Statute of Frauds. Choice A describes the parol evidence rule, not the Statute of Frauds. Choice B is incorrect because the $500 rule applies only to sales of goods. These rules must be thoroughly understood; a general idea is insufficient.

3. A is the correct answer. Only the party being sued needs to have signed the contract. The plaintiff in a lawsuit need not have signed the contract because by bringing the lawsuit, the plaintiff admits to the contract. Choice B is incorrect because the $500 limit applies only to sales of goods. Choice C is incorrect because the writing requirement can be met with multiple writings.

4. C is the correct answer. For a real estate contract, to which common law rules apply, enforcement can occur only against parties whose signature appears on the contract. Choice D is incorrect. It refers to the written confirmation rule under the UCC (discussed in Chapter 11 of this guide) but would not apply to a sale of real estate.

5. C is the correct answer. For duress, the test is generally based on whether the victim was actually forced by the improper threat to enter into the contract. Thus, choice B is incorrect because it states an objective standard test. Note, however, that where the threat was weak or was not genuine, it will be difficult for an alleged victim to prove that the threat actually induced assent to the contract. Thus, if a professional wrestler was threatened with physical harm by the proverbial 90-pound weakling, the wrestler could avoid the contract if he could prove that he really was in fear of his safety, but that would be a hard case for him to prove.

6. B is the correct answer. The misstatement in a fraud case must be of a material fact. An appraisal is a type of expert opinion, and any misstatement about the appraised amount is a misstatement of a material fact.

7. B is the correct answer. Contracts for the sale of goods need to be in writing only if the contract amount is $500 or more. D is incorrect because the existence and enforceability of the contract does not depend on a deposit being paid. It is usually for a seller to demand a deposit in this situation, but the purpose of the deposit is to help ensure that the buyer will live up to the obligation created by the contract. The deposit does not make the obligation any more binding where the contract does not need to be in writing. Note that in some questions, such as this one, the names of the parties relate to their roles. **B**ond is the **b**uyer and **S**pear is the **s**eller.

8. B is the correct answer. Fraud in the execution occurs when a party is misled about the document being signed. Although fraud in the inducement occurs far more often in practice, CPA exam candidates must know both types thoroughly.

9. C is the correct answer. An innocent misrepresentation case requires existence of the same elements as a fraud in the inducement case except that intent need not be proven.

10. D is the correct answer. Mutual mistake occurs when both parties share the same mistaken impression about the contract subject matter. The mutual mistake allows either party to rescind the contract, thus either party could avoid liability for any claimed breach. It is important to realize that the mistake here is about the existence of the automobile. Any mistake in value is not considered a mutual mistake. This is one of very few CPA exam questions where incorrect reasoning (thinking that there was a mistake in value which was a mutual mistake allowing rescission) would nonetheless lead to the correct answer.

11. D is the correct answer. This question addresses the special circumstance of the one year rule under the Statute of Frauds. Because it is possible for the contract to be performed within one year, the contract does not need to be in writing to be enforceable.

12. C is the correct answer. The parol evidence rule prevents admission of evidence of prior or contemporaneous agreements related to a written agreement, but does not prevent the admission of evidence related later agreements. Note that the agreement regarding the reporting on a monthly basis was reached after the main agreement, thus the parol evidence rule does not apply. Because the parol evidence rule does not apply, Lennon will be able to present evidence of the later agreement. He will not necessarily win his case, but he does get a chance to try to convince the judge or jury that the parties did, in fact, agree to change the reporting from weekly to monthly. Lennon cannot even present evidence about the oral agreement to use Rogers' computer.

UNOFFICIAL AICPA ANSWERS TO ESSAY QUESTIONS

Essay #1.   Law May 93 #4
a. Dodd's claim, that West's offer could not be revoked before September 30, is incorrect. Offers can be revoked at any time before acceptance unless the offeror receives consideration to keep the offer open. West did not receive any consideration from Dodd in exchange for its promise to keep the offer open until September 30. Therefore, West effectively revoked its offer during the September 28 telephone conversation.

Dodd's claim, that the September 27 letter accepting West's offer was effective when mailed to West, is incorrect. The general rule is that an acceptance is effective when dispatched if the acceptance is made using a reasonable mode of communication. In this case, the offer required that the acceptance be received by West to be effective. Therefore, Dodd's acceptance could not have been effective until after the offer expired, because it was received after September 30.

b. West's claim, that any agreement that existed between West and Dodd would not be enforceable against West because of the Statute of Frauds, is correct. The term of the agreement was for three years. The Statute of Frauds requires that contracts that cannot be performed within one year from the date made must be in writing. Because this was an oral contract for a period of three years, it would not be enforceable under the Statute of Frauds. Dodd's attempted acceptance of the offer would not be such a writing because it was not signed by West and could not be enforceable against West.

c. Abco's first position, that the oral April 14 agreement regarding the painting of the warehouse is not binding, is correct. This agreement was intended to modify the existing lease between the parties. Under common law, agreements modifying existing contracts require consideration to be binding. Abco did not receive any consideration in exchange for its promise to paint the warehouse; therefore, the agreement is not enforceable against Abco.

Abco's second position, that evidence of the April 14 oral agreement could not be admitted into evidence, is incorrect. The parol evidence rule allows the admission of proof of a later oral agreement that modifies an existing written contract.

Essay #2.   Law Nov 91 #3

Stake's first allegation, that Packer committed fraud in the formation of the contract, is correct and Stake may rescind the contract. Packer had assured Stake that the vacant parcel would be used for a shopping center when, in fact, Packer intended to use the land to construct apartment units that would be in direct competition with those owned by Stake. Stake would not have sold the land to Packer had Packer's real intentions been known. Therefore, the elements of fraud are present:

- A false representation;

- Of a fact;

- That is material;

- Made with knowledge of its falsity and intention to deceive;

- That is justifiably relied on.

Stake's second allegation, that the mistake as to the fair market value of the land entitles Stake to rescind the contract, is incorrect. Generally, mistakes as to adequacy of consideration or fairness of a bargain are insufficient grounds to entitle the aggrieved party to rescind a contract.

Stake's third allegation, that the contract was not enforceable against Stake because Stake did not sign the counteroffer, is correct. The contract between Stake and Packer involves real estate and, therefore, the Statute of Frauds requirements must be satisfied. The Statute of Frauds requires that a writing be signed by the party against whom enforcement is sought. The counteroffer is unenforceable against Stake, because Stake did not sign it. As a result, Stake is not obligated to sell the land to Packer under the terms of the counteroffer.

Author's Note:

Note that the AICPA unofficial answer did not list injury or damages as a required element of fraud. You should list all the elements in your answers. Most likely, it was not listed because it was not an issue in this particular question and was perhaps assumed.

Note also that what is listed in the outline as one requirement, "material fact" was shown here as two separate elements. Conversely, the justifiable reliance is shown as a single element by the AICPA but consists of the two separate elements of reliance and whether that reliance is justified. How you break down the elements in your answer is not important so long as you list all of them in some manner.

Note how in the second sentence of the last paragraph of the unofficial answer that the reason (that the contract involves real estate) is clearly stated as the reason for the result (that the Statute of Frauds applies). It is all too common for candidates to make a statement that the Statute of Frauds applies without explaining the reason why. Be sure to always give the legal reasons for outcomes.

Lastly, although a purchaser of land generally can use that land for any lawful purpose, the right to do so can be lost if the purchaser, as here, voluntarily promises to limit her use of the land.

CHAPTER 9
THIRD-PARTY RIGHTS AND DISCHARGE OF CONTRACTS

OVERVIEW

This chapter covers the rights of third parties in connection with a contract. A **third party** is anyone other than the original parties to a contract. The term is actually a misnomer because a third party is actually a non-party to the contract. These third parties can gain rights based on the initial terms of the contract, or based on later actions of a contract party. In some circumstances a third party can acquire enforceable rights under a contract, in others the third party might receive some benefits, but has no enforceable rights. The second main topic in this chapter is the discharge of duties under a contract. The simplest way that duties are discharged is by the completion of performance. However, discharge can occur in a number of ways other than by performance.

OUTLINE

I. **Assignment of Contract Rights.**
   A. <u>Assignment</u>. Contract rights are a form of property, and can be transferred to others, by sale or gift, as most other property can be transferred. Any transfer of contract rights is an **assignment**.
   B. <u>Definitions</u>. The **assignor** is the party who assigns a right to the **assignee**. With respect to a duty, the one who owes the duty is the **obligor**, and the duty is owed to the **obligee**.
   C. <u>Terminology</u>. Technically speaking, contract rights are assigned, and contract duties are delegated. Frequently, an assignment of rights and delegation of duties occur simultaneously. For example, if Fran has a contract to clean an office building for $1,000, she might simultaneously delegate to a friend the duty to clean the building and the right to receive the $1,000. She could also have done either separately. When doing both, there is both a delegation and assignment, but such a situation is often imprecisely referred to as merely an "assignment of the contract" even though it includes the delegation aspect. **Exam tip #1.**
   D. <u>Nonassignable Rights</u>. Most rights can be assigned, but in some cases they cannot be. Rights that cannot be assigned include:
      1. *Future Rights.* **Future rights**, such as an expected bequest to be received under a will, cannot be assigned.
      2. *Assignment Would Alter the Risk or Increase the Duty.* An insurance contract generally cannot be assigned by the insured to cover someone else. Likewise, a homeowner who has a contract for her home to be re-roofed cannot assign that right to another homeowner if that would increase or materially alter the work of the roofer.
      3. *Personal Injury Claims.* A legal right to recover for personal injury claims cannot be assigned. Legal rights arising out of a contract dispute can, however, be assigned, such as the right to collect an unpaid account receivable.

4. *Rights of the Assignee.* An assignee gets all the rights of the assignor, but no greater rights than the assignor. If the assignor could have sued under the contract, so too can the assignee. Any defense the other party could have raised against the assignor can be raised against the assignee. For example, if the other party could avoid a payment to the assignor, that party could also avoid paying the assignee. When the assignee gives consideration to the assignor for the assignment, the assignor is liable to the assignee for the rights assigned.

E. Notice of Assignment. The assignee is not entitled to receive the obligor's performance until the assignee gives notice of the assignment to the obligor. Once this notice is given, the obligor must render performance to the assignee, even if, after the notice was given, performance was rendered to the assignor. When a mortgage loan is sold by one lender to another, the purchaser of the loan receives an assignment of the right to collect the payments, and then gives notice to the homeowner. The homeowner is the obligor of the duty to make the payments, and once given notice, must make payments to the new holder of the loan.

F. Anti-Assignment Clauses. Some contracts prohibit assignment of rights, although these are sometimes not enforced. A similar type of clause allows assignment, but only with the obligor's approval. Most states prevent the obligor from unreasonably withholding the approval.

G. Successive Assignments. Problems occur if the holder of a contract right assigns that right to more than one assignee. The states follow one of two rules:

1. *American Rule.* The **American Rule** provides that the first assignment in time prevails. This rule is followed in most states.

2. *English Rule.* The **English Rule** provides that the first assignee to give notice of her assignment to the obligor prevails.

II. Delegation of Duties.

A. Delegation. A **delegation** of duty occurs when a party transfers her obligation to perform a duty to someone else.

B. Definitions. The party who owes the duty is an obligor. When that party delegates that duty, it becomes a **delegator** and the one who agrees to take on the duty becomes a **delegatee**.

C. Duties Which Can Be Delegated. Most duties can be delegated. A major exception is personal service contracts where the personal skills and abilities of the obligor were a factor in the choice of the obligor. For example, a professor hired to teach college courses could not delegate that duty to another, nor could an athlete delegate her duty to play her particular sport.

D. Delegator Remains Liable. Although duties can be delegated, the delegation does not change the liability of the delegator for the proper performance of the duty. If Bob has a duty to repair a car and delegates that duty to Mary, Bob remains responsible for Mary's proper repair of the car, and is liable if Mary does not properly complete the repair. In a novation, explained under discharge in this chapter, the delegator is discharged.

E. Assumption. **Assumption** occurs when the delegatee agrees to be responsible for the performance of the duty. In such cases, the obligee can sue either the delegatee or the delegator, or both, for failure to perform. In the example above, if Mary had assumed the duty to repair the car, the car's owner could sue either Bob or Mary if the car was not properly repaired. Without an assumption, the delegatee is not legally responsible for performance of the duty even though the delegatee performs the duty. **Exam tip #2.**

F. <u>Anti-Delegation Clauses</u>. Clauses prohibiting delegation are usually enforced, although sometimes the delegate of a duty to merely pay money has been held by the courts to be delegable despite the anti-delegation clause.

III.   Third-Party Beneficiaries.
   A. <u>Definition</u>. **Third-party beneficiaries** are persons who claim rights under a contract in which they are not a party. Any rights of third-party beneficiaries usually exist from the inception of the contract, rather than arising later as in an assignment.
      1. *Intended Beneficiaries.*
         a. Donee Beneficiary. A **donee beneficiary** is a third party who receives a benefit under a contract without any payment required from the third party. In most life insurance contracts a named beneficiary other than the insured is a donee beneficiary.
         b. Creditor Beneficiary. This arrangement usually arises where one party has purchased an item on credit in the past, and later sells the item with the second purchaser simultaneously agreeing to continue paying the debt. In the secondhand sale contract, which is between the original buyer and the new buyer, the creditor from the original transaction is a **creditor beneficiary**.
         c. Rights to Enforce. Intended beneficiaries have enforceable contract rights and can sue to compel performance.
      2. *Incidental Beneficiaries.* **Incidental beneficiaries** are persons who might derive a benefit from a contract even though the parties to the contract did not intend for the third party to receive a benefit. For example, if Jan owns a small store, and a shopping center developer and construction firm enter into a contract to construct a nearby shopping center which will increase Jan's business, Jan is an incidental beneficiary and has no rights against the contracting parties should a breach by either lead to a loss for Jan.

III.   Promises of Performance.
   A. <u>Covenant</u>. A **covenant** is an unconditional promise to perform, and failure to perform is a breach of the contract.
   B. <u>Condition</u>. A **condition** is a qualification of a promise that will convert a conditional promise into a covenant if the condition is met. There are three kinds of conditions:
      1. *Condition Precedent.* A **condition precedent** is a condition which must be satisfied before the party becomes obligated to perform. Its occurrence triggers the obligation to perform. A common type of condition precedent is a requirement that one party's performance meet the satisfaction of the other party before the other party is obligated to pay. There are two kinds.
         a. Personal Satisfaction Test. The **personal satisfaction test** is used where the satisfaction depends on personal taste, such as decorating, and requires only that the party act in good faith if choosing to reject the contract.
         b. Reasonable Person Test. The **reasonable person test** is an objective test used in most commercial contracts where the test is whether a reasonable person would be satisfied with the performance.

    c. Time of Performance. If a contract contains a **time is of the essence** clause, performance by the stated time in an express condition. There is a breach if the performance is not completed on time. Without such a clause, courts often allow additional time to perform if the other party is not hurt by the delay.

  2. *Condition Subsequent.* A **condition subsequent** is a condition which must occur after the other party's obligation arises. For example, car insurance contracts provide that the company incurs an obligation to the insured when the loss occurs, but after that, the insured must cooperate in any investigation of the loss and in getting estimates for repairs. Failure of the insured to do so releases the company from its obligation.

  3. *Concurrent Conditions.* **Concurrent conditions** arise where parties must perform simultaneously, such as in a contract for the sale of goods where payment is due upon delivery.

  4. *Express and Implied Conditions.* The above conditions are **express conditions** if they were expressly stated in the contract, or **implied-in-fact conditions** if they are implied from the surrounding circumstances.

IV.   **Discharge of Performance.**

  A. <u>Definition.</u> **Discharge** of performance is the release of a party from any further obligation of performance. There are many circumstances that will release a party from further performance. **Exam tip #3.**

  B. <u>Discharge by Completion of Performance.</u> The most basic way to discharge performance is to complete the performance. Once completed, the party is discharged.

  C. <u>Discharge by Agreement of the Parties.</u> The parties to a contract are free to agree, prior to the completion of performance, that one or both parties have no further duty to perform, or are discharged from further performance. This can occur in several ways.

    1. *Mutual Rescission.* **Mutual rescission** is a new agreement by both parties that the original contract is canceled (rescinded). Duties under the original contract are discharged.

    2. *Substituted Contract.* A **substituted contract** is a new contract in which the parties agree that the new contract will replace the old. At the time the new contract is formed, duties under the original contract are discharged. Note that implicit with a substituted contract is rescission of the original contract. A substituted contract usually does not involve a dispute over the original contract, but rather is a case where the parties change their mind.

    3. *Novation.* A **novation** is a three-party agreement where all three parties agree that one of the original two parties will be replaced with a new party. There is a simultaneous assignment of rights and delegation of duties from the replaced party to the new party. Unlike a in a simple delegation of duties, in a novation the delegator is discharged and thus not responsible for the performance of the new party (the delegator). **Exam tip #4.**

    4. *Accord and Satisfaction.* An **accord** is a new agreement to settle a legitimate dispute concerning an existing contract or to settle a claim. It replaces the original contract. A **satisfaction** is the act of completing performance of the accord. Duties under the original contract are discharged, but <u>only</u> upon the satisfaction of the accord. Failure to satisfy the accord when due allows the nonbreaching party the choice to enforce either the original contract or the accord. **Exam tip #5.**

D. Discharge by Impossibility. The doctrine of **impossibility** will discharge the parties under certain conditions. This doctrine applies to some circumstances where the performance is actually possible, but the law considers it "impossible."

   1. *Impossibility of Performance.* **Impossibility of performance** occurs when it is not possible for a contract to be performed. Such situations include the following:

      a. Death or Incapacity of Promisor. If a promisor of a personal service dies or becomes incapacitated prior to performance of the service, the promisor is discharged.

      b. Destruction of Subject Matter. If the subject matter of a contract is destroyed, then performance is discharged, so long as the destruction was not the fault of the party owing the performance. If a car, which has been contracted to be sold, is destroyed by hail prior to being transferred to the buyer, the parties' duties are discharged.

      c. Supervening Illegality. If a contract calls for an act that was legal when the contract was entered into, but has become illegal prior to being completed, the parties are discharged. **Exam tip #6.**

   2. *Commercial Impracticability.* **Commercial impracticability** is a situation where unforeseeable circumstances have caused a contract to become impractical, extremely difficult, or too expensive to perform. This is a subjective doctrine, and a mere change in costs is generally not sufficient. If a gasoline wholesaler has agreed to supply gasoline to a large corporation for its fleet of vehicles at a price of $1.15 per gallon, an increase in the wholesaler's cost to $1.25 would not be commercial impracticability because gasoline price fluctuations are foreseeable. But if all three of the wholesaler's normal suppliers incurred refinery problems that would triple the wholesaler's cost of acquiring the gasoline, that would probably qualify as commercial impracticability.

   3. *Frustration of Purpose.* **Frustration of purpose** occurs when unforeseeable circumstances cause the contract to no longer be of value to the promisor. The performance is no more difficult, it simply no longer makes sense in light of the original purpose. If a traveler enters into a contract for a 10-day travel package to Salt Lake City during the 2002 Olympics, but the Olympics are unexpectedly canceled or moved to another location, discharge occurs. In order for discharge to occur, both parties must have been aware of the purpose (as they would have in this example). **Exam tip #7.**

   4. *Force Majeure Clauses.* A **force majeure clause** is a provision which specifies in advance events which will excuse performance. Such clauses eliminate the need to apply the above doctrines, and typically might include natural disasters, materials shortages, etc.

E. Discharge by Operation of Law. Certain events automatically discharge contractual obligations, including:

   1. *Statutes of Limitation.* A **statute of limitation** sets a time limit for bringing a lawsuit based on breach of contract. They differ by state, but most are from one to five years. For a breach of contract suit, the time period is measured from the time the breach occurs. Once the period has expired, the parties are discharged.

   2. *Bankruptcy.* Bankruptcy law generally provides a discharge of the bankrupt party's unpaid debts. See Chapter 17 of this outline for further explanation.

   3. *Alteration of the Contract.* If one party alters a contract, such as by unilaterally changing the price, the other party can either enforce the contract with the altered terms or treat the contract as discharged.

EXAM TIPS

1. For the CPA Exam you must know that you ass<u>i</u>gn <u>ri</u>ghts and <u>d</u>elegate <u>d</u>uties. A party may assign some or all rights, and a party may delegate some or all duties. Assignment and delegation may occur together, or each may occur separately.

2. Duties cannot be delegated without the consent of the delegatee. If the delegatee performs the duty, it is assumed that the delegatee has consented to do so. In performing the duty, the delegatee does not automatically assume legal responsibility for its proper performance. That happens only in an assumption of the duty.

3. Discharge addresses only whether the party in question is released from performing its own duty. A closely related, but separate issue is the remedy available when the other party fails to perform its duty. This is covered in the next chapter.

4. In a substituted contract, the same two parties survive, but they have replaced the first contract with a different one, discharging both parties from the first contract. In a novation, one of the parties is new, but the terms of the contract are usually, but not necessarily, the same. Only one party, the party who has been replaced, is discharged of any duties.

5. A substituted contract discharges the original contract upon its formation, but with accord and satisfaction, the original contract is discharged only upon performance (the satisfaction) of the new contract (the accord).

6. Do not confuse supervening illegality here with the attempted formation of a contract which is illegal at the time of attempted formation.

7. Commercial impracticability and frustration of purpose are often confused. Commercial impracticability is based on difficulty of performance and frustration of purpose is based on whether the original purpose would still be served by performance. Both apply only if the causal event is unforeseeable.

KEY CONCEPTS LIKELY TO BE TESTED ON THE CPA EXAM

1. Assignment and delegation terminology.
2. The ability to assign rights and delegate duties, as well as the liabilities of the parties where there has been an assignment or delegation.
3. The types of duties which can and cannot be delegated.
4. Identification of the type of third-party beneficiary based on a fact situation, and the rights of each type.
5. Types of conditions and how they affect a party's obligation to perform.
6. The requirements and consequences of the ways to discharge a contract by agreement, and the differences between them.
7. Definitions and ability to identify the different ways a contract can be discharged based on impossibility.

KEY TERMS

Third Party	Assumption	Implied-in-fact Condition
Assignment	Donee Beneficiary	Discharge
Assignor	Creditor beneficiary	Mutual Rescission
Assignee	Incidental Beneficiary	Substituted Contract
Obligor	Covenant	Novation
Obligee	Condition Precedent	Accord
Future Rights	Personal Satisfaction Test	Satisfaction
American Rule	Reasonable Person Test	Impossibility of Performance
English Rule	Time is of the Essence	Commercial Impracticability
Delegation	Condition Subsequent	Frustration of Purpose
Delegator	Concurrent Conditions	Force Majeure Clause
Delegatee	Express Condition	Statute of Limitation

MULTIPLE CHOICE QUESTIONS

1.   Law May 92 #31
Baxter Inc. and Globe entered into a contract. After receiving valuable consideration from Clay, Baxter assigned its rights under the contract to Clay. In which of the following circumstances would Baxter **not** be liable to Clay?
A. Clay released Globe.
B. Globe paid Baxter.
C. Baxter released Globe.
D. Baxter breached the contract.

2.   Law May 89 #33
Generally, which one of the following transfers will be valid without the consent of the other parties?
A. The assignment by the lessee of a lease contract where rent is a percentage of sales.
B. The assignment by a purchaser of goods of the right to buy on credit without giving security.
C. The assignment by an architect of a contract to design a building.
D. The assignment by a patent holder of the right to receive royalties.

3.   Law May 91 #23
Maco Corp. contracted to sell 1,500 bushels of potatoes to LBC Chips. The contract did not refer to any specific supply source for the potatoes. Maco intended to deliver potatoes grown on its farms. An insect infestation ruined Maco's crop but not the crops of other growers in the area. Maco failed to deliver the potatoes to LBC. LBC sued Maco for breach of contract. Under the circumstances, Maco will
A. Lose, because it could have purchased potatoes from other growers to deliver to LBC.
B. Lose, unless it can show that the purchase of substitute potatoes for delivery to LBC would make the contract unprofitable.
C. Win, because the infestation was an act of nature that could **not** have been anticipated by Maco.
D. Win, because both Maco and LBC are assumed to accept the risk of a crop failure.

4.   Law Nov 92 #24

Wilcox Co. contracted with Ace Painters, Inc. for Ace to paint Wilcox's warehouse. Ace, without advising Wilcox, assigned the contract to Pure Painting Corp. Pure failed to paint Wilcox's warehouse in accordance with the contract specifications. The contract between Ace and Wilcox was silent with regard to a party's right to assign it. Which of the following statements is correct?

A. Ace remained liable to Wilcox despite the fact that Ace assigned the contract to Pure.

B. Ace would **not** be liable to Wilcox if Ace had notified Wilcox of the assignment.

C. Ace's duty to paint Wilcox's warehouse was nondelegable.

D. Ace's delegation of the duty to paint Wilcox's warehouse was a breach of the contract.

5.   Law May 89 #34

In September 1988, Cobb Company contracted with Thrifty Oil Company for the delivery of 100,000 gallons of heating oil at the price of $.75 per gallon at regular specified intervals during the forthcoming winter. Due to an unseasonably warm winter, Cobb took delivery on only 70,000 gallons. In a suit against Cobb for breach of contract, Thrifty will

A. Lose, because Cobb acted in good faith.

B. Lose, because both parties are merchants and the UCC recognizes commercial impracticability.

C. Win, because this is a requirements contract.

D. Win, because the change of circumstances could have been contemplated by the parties.

6.   Author

Smith and Jones had a dispute over a contract for some landscaping. To settle the dispute, they reached a new agreement which resulted in a reduced amount of landscaping work to be done, along with a reduction in the contract price. The revised work is not yet complete. The completed actions of Smith and Jones can best be described as

A. An accord.

B. A novation.

C. An accord and satisfaction.

D. A substituted contract.

7.   Law May 95 #24

Under a personal services contract, which of the following circumstances will cause the discharge of a party's duties.

A. Death of the party who is to receive the services.

B. Cost of performing the services has doubled.

C. Bankruptcy of the party who is to receive the services.

D. Illegality of the services to be performed.

8.   Law May 90 #24

Rice contracted with Locke to build an oil refinery for Locke. The contract provided that Rice was to use United pipe fittings. Rice did not do so. United learned of the contract and, anticipating the order, manufactured additional fittings. United sued Locke and Rice. United is

A. Entitled to recover from Rice only, because Rice breached the contract.

B. Entitled to recover from either Locke or Rice because it detrimentally relied on the contract.

C. Not entitled to recover because it is a donee beneficiary.

D. Not entitled to recover because it is an incidental beneficiary.

9.   Law Nov 92 #19

The statute of limitations for an alleged breach of contract

A. Does **not** apply if the contract was oral.
B. Requires that a lawsuit be commenced and a judgment rendered within a prescribed period of time.
C. Is determined on a case by case basis.
D. Generally commences on the date of the breach.

10.   Law Nov 91 #24

Yost contracted with Egan for Yost to buy certain real property. If the contract is otherwise silent, Yost's rights under the contract are

A. Assignable only with Eagan's consent.
B. Nonassignable because they are personal to Yost.
C. Nonassignable as a matter of law.
D. Generally assignable.

ESSAY QUESTION (Estimated time -- 15 to 20 minutes)

Law Nov 90 #2

The following letters were mailed among Jacobs, a real estate developer, Snow, the owner of an undeveloped parcel of land, and Eljay Distributors, Inc., a clothing wholesaler interested in acquiring Snow's parcel to build a warehouse.

- *January 21, 1990* -- Snow to Jacobs: "My vacant parcel (Lot 2, Birds Addition to Cedar Grove) is available for $125,000 cash; closing within 60 days. You must accept by January 31 if you are interested."

This was received by Jacobs on January 31.

- *January 29, 1990* -- Snow to Jacobs: "Ignore my January 21 letter to you; I have decided not to sell my lot at this time."

This was received by Jacobs on February 3.

- *January 31, 1990* -- Jacobs to Snow: "Per your January 21 letter, you have got a deal."

Jacobs inadvertently forgot to sign the January 31 letter which was received by Snow on February 4.

- *February 2, 1990* -- Jacobs to Eljay: "In consideration of your promise to pay me $10,000, I hereby assign to you my right to purchase Snow's vacant lot (Lot 2, Birds Addition to Cedar Grove)."

This was received by Eljay on February 5.

All of the letters were signed, except as noted above, and properly stamped and addressed.

Snow has refused to sell the land to Jacobs or Eljay, asserting that no contract exists because:

- Jacobs' acceptance was not received on a timely basis.
- Snow had revoked the January 21 offer.
- Jacobs' acceptance was not signed.
- Jacobs had no right to assign the contract to Eljay.

Required:

For each of Snow's assertions, indicate whether the assertion is correct, setting forth the reasons for your conclusions.

EXPLANATIONS TO MULTIPLE CHOICE QUESTIONS

1. A is the correct answer. Where an assignee gives consideration to receive rights in an assignment, the assignor is liable to the assignee if the party owing the duty of performance does not perform. Thus, in this question, Baxter is responsible to Clay if Globe does not perform, but if Clay releases Globe, Baxter is simultaneously released. Choice B is incorrect because if Globe pays Baxter, Baxter then has a duty to pay that amount to Clay because he is entitled to it under terms of the assignment. Choice C is incorrect because Baxter's action cannot operate to cut off Clay's rights against Baxter if Globe does not perform. D is incorrect because, again, action by Baxter cannot operate to cut off Clay's rights against Baxter. In all assignment and delegation questions, it is usually helpful to draw a diagram.

2. D is the correct answer. Assignment of the right to receive royalties does not affect the rights or duties of the party paying the royalties. Choice A is incorrect because delegating the duty to pay rent will alter the amount of rent received by the lessor. Thus this duty cannot be delegated. Choice B is incorrect because the assignment of the right will alter the risk of the lender based on the creditworthiness of the assignor. Choice C is incorrect because the duty to perform personal services usually cannot be delegated. Answer choices A, C, and D are actually simultaneous delegations of duties and assignments of rights, although simply called assignments.

3. A is the correct answer. One aspect of a contract is allocation of risks. In this contract, the seller of the potatoes bears the risk of increased cost of acquiring the potatoes unless the contract states otherwise. Only if some unforeseeable event causes it to become unreasonably expensive does the doctrine of commercial impracticability apply. A crop failure is foreseeable and does not excuse the seller's performance, nor does the mere fact that a contract becomes unprofitable.

4. A is the correct answer. When Ace "assigned the contract" to Pure, Ace assigned the right to payment and delegated the duty to paint the warehouse. Because Ace originally had the duty to paint the warehouse, Ace remains liable for the proper completion of the painting. Ace would be released if all three parties executed a novation in which Wilcox released Ace and Pure agreed to take on all the duties of Ace.

5. D is the correct answer. Cobb had an absolute obligation to purchase 100,000 gallons under the contract. The mild winter was foreseeable and would not excuse performance. Choice C is incorrect because this was not a requirements contract. In fact, Cobb would have been better off with a requirements contract because it would have been obligated to purchase only what was needed.

6. A is the correct answer. An accord is a new agreement arising out of a dispute over an existing contract or to settle a claim. The satisfaction is the performance of the accord, which has not yet occurred in the facts of the question. Choice D is incorrect because a substituted contract generally arises where there was no dispute around the first contract.

7. D is the correct answer. Note that this refers to services that become illegal after the formation of the contract. Choice A is incorrect because some services, such as the preparation of a tax return, are not discharged upon the recipient's death. Other services are discharged, such as a massage.

8. D is the correct answer. Incidental beneficiary status confers no rights on the beneficiary.

9. D is the correct answer. Choice B is incorrect because the lawsuit must only be commenced, but not completed, by the end of the limitations period.

10. D is the correct answer. With a few exceptions, contract rights are generally assignable.

UNOFFICIAL AICPA ANSWER TO ESSAY QUESTION

Law Nov 90 #2

Snow's assertion that Jacobs' acceptance was not received on a timely basis is incorrect. Jacobs' January 31 acceptance was effective when dispatched (mailed) under the complete-when-posted doctrine because:

- The letter was an authorized means of communication (because Snow's offer was by mail); and
- The letter was properly stamped and addressed.

Therefore, Jacobs' acceptance was effective on January 31, the last possible day under Snow's January 21 offer.

Snow's assertion that the January 21 offer was effectively revoked is incorrect because a revocation is not effective until received. In this case, the revocation was effective on February 3, and Jacobs' acceptance was effective on January 31.

Snow's assertion that Jacobs' failure to sign the January 31 acceptance prevents the formation of a contract is incorrect. The Statute of Frauds, which applies to contracts involving interests in real estate, requires only the signature of the party to be charged with enforcement of the contract. Therefore, because Snow had signed the January 21 offer, which was accepted by Jacobs, the contract is enforceable against Snow.

Snow's assertion that Jacobs had no right to assign the contract is incorrect. Contract rights, including the right to purchase real estate, are generally assignable unless the assignment:

- Would materially increase the risk or burden of the obligor;
- Purports to transfer highly personal contract rights;
- Is validly prohibitied by the contract; or
- Is prohibited by law.

None of these limitations applies to the assignment by Jacobs to Eljay.

CHAPTER 10
CONTRACT REMEDIES AND TORTS ASSOCIATED WITH CONTRACTS

OVERVIEW

Contracts are entered into with the expectation that each party's duties will be carried out as agreed. Failure to perform an absolute duty owed under a contract results in a breach of the contract. Where there is a breach, the nonbreaching party is usually entitled to a remedy of some sort from the breaching party. Because of the infinite variety of contracts and contract duties, and the nearly unlimited number of ways that a contract can be breached, there is no single formula for determining remedies. Instead, there are a few general guiding principles, several types of remedies, and within this framework each breach of contract situation must be evaluated individually.

OUTLINE

I. **Performance and Breach.**
   A. <u>Complete performance</u>.
      1. *Definition.* **Complete** or **strict performance** occurs when a party has carried out all of its duties exactly as required by the contract. Once a party has done this, that party's obligations are discharged. Once all parties have done this, the contract becomes an **executed** contract.
      2. *Tender of Performance.* **Tender of performance** is an unconditional offer or attempt by a party to perform his obligations under the contract. If the other party interferes with or refuses the tender of performance, the party who tendered performance is discharged. For example, Mariam contracted to do landscaping work for Doug, but was confronted by a vicious dog in Doug's yard when she arrived at the agreed time to do the work. If Doug refused to constrain the dog, or Doug could not be contacted to constrain the dog, Mariam's tender of performance would discharge her duty to perform. Because she was ready, willing, and able to perform, Mariam owes no further duty.
   B. <u>Substantial Performance</u>. **Substantial performance** occurs when there is some minor deficiency in the performance, but otherwise it is complete. Such a breach is a **minor breach**, sometimes called an immaterial breach. A minor breach does not result in a general discharge of the nonbreaching party's duties. When one party has substantially performed, the nonbreaching party has the choice to:
      1. *Convince the Breaching Party to Complete Performance.*
      2. *Deduct the Cost to Correct the Defect from the Amount Paid to the Breaching Party.*
      3. *Recover the Cost to Correct the Defect from the Breaching Party if Payment Has Already Been Made.*
      4. *Exception: Cost to Correct Not Allowed.* Where the cost to correct is large compared to the difference in value of the actual and contracted performance, the nonbreaching party might be allowed to recover only that difference. The use of the wrong building materials can have this result due to the high cost to replace items which are only slightly inferior.

C. <u>Inferior Performance</u>. **Inferior Performance** occurs when there is a breach so significant that the essence of the contract is impaired. Such a breach is a **material breach**. The dividing line between minor and material breaches is subjective and based on all the surrounding circumstances in each individual case. When there has been a material breach, the nonbreaching party has two general options. **Exam tips #1 and #2.**

   1. *Rescind and Seek Restitution.* The nonbreaching party can rescind, or cancel the contract and can recover any consideration which has already been transferred to the breaching party. In some circumstances, the nonbreaching party might be entitled to receive some cash as part of its restitution.

   2. *Recover Damages.* The nonbreaching party can recover damages, or compensation for the loss caused by the breach, from the breaching party. Damages are explained in detail below.

D. <u>Anticipatory Breach</u>. An **anticipatory breach** (or repudiation) occurs when there is advance notification that a party will not perform her contractual duty when due. The notification can be express or implied from the party's conduct. Anticipatory breach discharges the nonbreaching party from his duties and allows the nonbreaching party to sue as soon as the anticipatory breach occurs without having to wait until the actual performance deadline occurs.

II. Monetary Damages.

A. <u>General Concepts</u>. **Monetary damages** compensate the nonbreaching party for its losses resulting from the breach. "Damages" in the contract remedy context really means "compensation for damages" but over the years has become known simply as "damages." The general goal is to place the nonbreaching party in the same position she would have been in if the contract had been fully performed. Note that this is not the same as placing the parties in the position where they were prior to the contract. Placing the nonbreaching party in the same position as she would have been in if the contract had been performed is also called giving her the **benefit of the bargain** or giving her **expectation damages** because the attempt is to give her what she expected out of the contract. There are many special applications of these general concepts, and sometimes it is simply not possible to put the nonbreaching party in the position she would have been in without the breach. In such cases, the courts will often try to return the nonbreaching party to her position prior to the contract or use another type of remedy.

B. <u>Compensatory Damages</u>. **Compensatory damages** are amounts awarded to the nonbreaching party to compensate that party for any loss caused by the breach. This loss is based on benefit of the bargain and is the basic measure of damages. A few examples follow.

   1. *Breach by Seller.* Barb contracted to purchase a house for $180,000, at a time when the house was worth $195,000. The seller breached by selling the house to someone else. Because Barb had contracted to pay only $180,000 for a house worth $195,000, Barb expected, in one sense, to come out $15,000 "ahead." As a consequence of the seller's breach, Barb would be entitled to a refund of any amounts already paid to the seller <u>and</u> would be entitled to receive an additional $15,000 from the seller. In this way, Barb would come out $15,000 "ahead" as she would have if the contract had been performed.

2. *Breach by Buyer.* Sandy contracted to sell her house for $170,000 even though the house was worth $150,000. The buyer breached by not purchasing the house. Sandy then was able to find another buyer at a price of $166,000. Sandy originally contracted to receive $170,000 for the house and the court will attempt to give her this benefit of her bargain. Sandy would be awarded damages of $4,000 from the original buyer because this $4,000 plus the $166,000 she received from the second buyer, would give her the benefit of her original bargain, or $170,000. Note that the original contract price was relevant, not the market value. Remedy law attempts to give the seller here the originally contracted price, not a "fair market" price.

3. *Breach by Service Provider.* A client contracted with a computer consulting firm for the installation (labor only) of a new computer system for a fee of $8,000. The consulting firm did half the work and quit. A second consulting firm had to be hired at a cost of $5,500 to complete the job. The original firm would be entitled to only $2,500 for its work. The client had a contract to receive a computer installation at a cost of $8,000. After paying the second firm $5,500, the client need only pay an additional $2,500 to end up with a computer installation at a total cost of $8,000. Notice that the original breaching party received far less than half of its fee even though it did half the work. The breaching party only gets the "leftovers" after giving the nonbreaching party the benefit of the bargain. Remember, also, that who actually pays whom after a lawsuit depends on how much, if any, has already been paid.

4. *Breach by Service Recipient.* Joe contracted with a homeowner to build a wooden deck for a price of $600. The homeowner told Joe a couple of days before he was to build the deck that she did not want a deck built and would not pay for it. If the materials would have cost Joe $200, he expected to make a $400 net profit on the deck. If he could find no other work for the time he planned to build the deck, he could recover $400 from the homeowner. If he could find another job which would net him $225, then he could recover $175 from the breaching homeowner. There are many possible circumstances, but they would be aimed at preserving Joe's $400 expected net profit for the time he was to spend on the deck. These same principles would be used in the tender of performance example on the first page of this chapter to calculate Mariam's damages, if any, when the vicious dog prevented her from performing. **Exam tip #3.**

C. Consequential Damages. **Consequential damages,** or **special damages,** are damages from outside the contract that are foreseeable. They can sometimes be thought of as damages that are "one step removed" from the contract itself, but occur as a consequence of the breach. They can also be thought of as additional damages needed to preserve the benefit of the bargain.

1. *Foreseeable Because of General Circumstances.* Consequential damages can be recovered where the nature of the contract makes the consequential damages foreseeable. For example, if a nightclub entered into a contract with a performer, but the performer breached by not appearing on the designated nights, the nightclub could not only recover any amounts already paid to the performer, but could recover the consequential damages of lost profits. It is foreseeable that a nightclub would lose revenues if an advertised performer fails to appear.

2. *Foreseeable Because Notice Was Given*. If one party, at the time of contracting, notified the other party of special circumstances, consequential damages related to that special circumstance can be recovered. For example, Jan took her car in for major repair work on a Friday morning and explained that she needed the car back by the close of business that day because she was leaving Friday evening on a one week trip in the car. If the car was not ready, Jan could recover her cost to rent a car for the week. Because Jan had notified the repair shop of her special circumstances, any related consequential damages would be foreseeable and thus recoverable.

3. *Lost Profits*. **Lost profits** are a common consequential damage. Lost profits are recoverable, but only if they can be proven with a reasonable degree of certainty. Proving this degree of certainty is often difficult, because the party is trying to prove how much would have been earned in hypothetical (if the breach had not occurred) circumstances. In many cases courts deny lost profits as being too speculative.

D. Incidental Damages. **Incidental damages** are minor costs incurred as the result of a breach. Incidental damages often consist of transaction costs. For example, where a seller must advertise an item for sale again because the original buyer breached, the additional advertising costs would be incidental damages. **Exam tip #4.**

E. Nominal Damages. **Nominal damages** are awarded as a formality where the nonbreaching party cannot prove an actual financial loss. They are generally small, often $1.

F. Liquidated Damages. **Liquidated damages** occur when parties, at the time they enter into a contract, agree in advance on the amount of damages if a breach should occur. Liquidated damages are valid only if the actual damages would be difficult to determine and if the amount specified is not unreasonably high. Amounts unreasonably high are considered a **penalty** and are disallowed by the courts. For example, an apartment lease might provide that the landlord retain the $500 security deposit if the tenant moves out prior to the end of the lease term. This fixes the damages at $500 whether the landlord's actual loss from the early termination is more or less than the $500. **Exam tip #5.**

E. Mitigation of Damages. **Mitigation of damages** is the requirement of a nonbreaching party to take reasonable steps to minimize his damages. If a car repair shop has improperly repaired a car in such a way that continuing to drive the car will damage it, the owner has a duty to not drive it until the problem can be corrected. If a tenant has terminated a lease five months early, the landlord has a duty to seek a replacement tenant.

F. Rescission and Restitution. **Rescission** is the undoing of the contract, and **restitution** is returning items to the other party to place that party to the position he was in prior to the contract. Sometimes money will have to be paid in place of goods in order to get a party back to where they were before the contract. **Exam tip #6.**

III. **Equitable Remedies.**

A. General Concepts. **Equitable remedies** are those remedies originally developed in the courts of equity. Courts of equity came about because the rules in the regular courts of law gradually became so rigid that unfair results sometimes occurred. In such circumstances, the person treated unfairly could seek a remedy in the equity courts. Specific to contracts, the awarding of damages sometimes did not give a fair result, leading the equity courts to act. Generally, these equitable remedies are available only if the award for damages would not be adequate.

B. Specific Performance. **Specific performance** is an order by the court compelling a party to do what was called for under the contract. Courts disfavor specific performance because it can place the court in a supervisory role to ensure that the ordered performance is properly carried out. It can be awarded in connection with: **Exam tip #7.**

1. *Purchase of Real Property.* The purchaser of real property can obtain a court order of specific performance. All real property is unique. This is true even of a three bedroom house in a subdivision of 100 identical homes because there is only one home at a specific location, thereby making it unique. Because each parcel of real property is unique, monetary damages might not adequately compensate for not acquiring that particular property. Note that the circumstances of a particular case might make specific performance impossible. If an unscrupulous seller contracted to sell his house to four different individuals, only one of them, at most, could obtain specific performance because there is only one house that can be sold. The others could only be awarded monetary damages.

2. *Purchase of Unique Artwork, Antiques, etc.* Purchasers of these items can obtain specific performance in the same way and with the same limitations as with real property. Unlike real property, which is all considered unique, a court will have to determine if the particular item is rare enough for an award of specific performance.

3. *No Specific Performance to Sellers of These Items.* Sellers are not entitled to specific performance because a seller can usually find another buyer, and if the second buyer's price is lower, the seller can recover the difference as damages from the original breaching buyer, and by doing so receive the full benefit of the bargain.

4. *No Specific Performance for Personal Service Contracts.* Parties will not be ordered to perform personal service contracts. For example, if a patient entered into a contract for heart bypass surgery with a heart surgeon, but the heart surgeon then refused to do the operation thereby breaching the contract, the court will not order specific performance. In addition to the practical problem of being operated on by a surgeon being forced to do the surgery against her will, the court does not want the supervisory role over the surgeon.

C. Reformation. **Reformation** is a rewriting of a contract to express the true intentions of the parties, often done to correct clerical errors, but used in other circumstances as well where it is determined that the stated terms of the contract are not a expression of the party's intent.

D. Quasi-contract. **Quasi-contract** (also known as **quantum meruit** or an **implied-in-law contract**) allows the court to order compensation in order to prevent **unjust enrichment**. Unjust enrichment occurs when there is no contract, but someone receives a benefit without paying for it in circumstances where it would be unfair for him to not pay for it.

E. Injunction. An **injunction** is a court order preventing an action or compelling a party to some action. Most contract law injunctions prohibit a party from undertaking a certain act. Often the injunction prohibits conduct which is in breach of the contract. For example, where there is a valid covenant not to compete, a court can issue an injunction preventing a party from working for competitors in violation of the agreement.

IV. **Torts Associated With Contracts.**

A. General Concepts. Most contract disputes are adjudicated using only contract remedies. In other cases, there are torts associated with the conduct of the breaching party, or the tort of a third party might affect a contract.

B. Intentional Interference with Contractual Relations.   **Intentional interference with contractual relations** occurs when a third party, who has knowledge of a contract, induces one of the contractual parties to break the contract. This is the tort most directly connected with contracts. Dealing with someone who has already breached a contract does not result in liability for this tort.

EXAM TIPS

1. When a party has breached, remember that there are two general issues for the nonbreaching party. The first is what the nonbreaching party must or can do, and the second is what remedy, if any, is available to the nonbreaching party.
2. Remember that: "minor breach = substantial performance" and
                     "material breach = inferior performance."
3. There are endless breach of contract situations, and not all can be learned in advance. Consider the question, "How many ways can people break agreements?" The answer is "an infinite number of ways," or something to that effect. Candidates should be familiar with the more common situations such as the examples given. However, candidates must also be able to take a big picture approach to an unfamiliar situation to determine, in a situation they have not memorized, what must be done to give the nonbreaching party the benefit of the bargain. Remedies questions can require the candidate to integrate the application of legal rules with mathematical problem solving.
4. Do not confuse incidental and consequential damages. The terms themselves are helpful in distinguishing between the two terms.
5. Excessively high liquidated damages provisions are considered penalties and not allowed. Contract law does not allow punishment. Very small liquidated damages are acceptable. An example is a photo developing contract providing only for the replacement of the film if the developer damages or loses it regardless of the value of the lost photographs.
6. Rescission and restitution can be ordered by a court as a remedy, but can also occur voluntarily as explained in the previous chapter.
7. Many persons unfamiliar with the law are surprised that courts seldom "make people do what they are supposed to do" and are surprised that specific performance is seldom awarded. It is simply easier for a court to order a cash payment of damages by a breaching party.

KEY CONCEPTS LIKELY TO BE TESTED ON THE CPA EXAM

1. The concept of substantial performance and the nonbreaching party's options and remedies.
2. General damages concepts related to benefit of the bargain.
3. The specific types of damages available in a particular situation.
4. Compensatory damages, including the ability to calculate the outcome in a given fact situation.
5. Consequential damage requirements.
6. The definition of liquidated damages and requirements for them to be allowable.
7. Specific performance and when it is available.

KEY TERMS

Complete Performance	Expectation Damages	Rescission
Strict Performance	Compensatory Damages	Restitution
Executed Contract	Consequential Damages	Equitable Remedies
Tender of Performance	Special Damages	Specific Performance
Substantial Performance	Lost Profits	Reformation
Minor Breach	Incidental Damages	Quasi Contract
Inferior Performance	Nominal Damages	Quantum Meruit
Material Breach	Liquidated Damages	Implied-in-law Contract
Anticipatory Breach	Penalty	Unjust Enrichment
Monetary Damages	Mitigation of Damages	Injunction
Benefit of the Bargain	Intentional Interference with Contractual Relations	

MULTIPLE CHOICE QUESTIONS

1.   Law Nov 93 #26
Ames Construction Co. contracted to build a warehouse for White Corp. The construction specifications required Ames to use Ace lighting fixtures. Inadvertently, Ames installed Perfection lighting fixtures which are of slightly lesser quality than Ace fixtures, but in all other respects meet White's needs. Which of the following statements is correct?
A. White's recovery will be limited to monetary damages because Ames' breach of the construction contract was **not** material.
B. White will **not** be able to recover any damages from Ames because the breach was inadvertent.
C. Ames did **not** breach the construction contract because the Perfection fixtures were substantially as good as the Ace fixtures.
D. Ames must install Ace fixtures or White will **not** be obligated to accept the warehouse.

2.   Law May 92 #32
To cancel a contract and return the parties to their original positions before the contract, the parties should execute a
A. Novation.
B. Release.
C. Rescission.
D. Revocation.

3.   Law May 89 #35
Jones, CPA, entered into a signed contract with Foster Corp. to perform accounting and review services. If Jones repudiates the contract prior to the date performance is due to begin, which of the following is **not** correct?
A. Foster could successfully maintain an action for breach of contract after the date performance was due to begin.
B. Foster can obtain a judgment ordering Jones to perform.
C. Foster could successfully maintain an action for breach of contract prior to the date performance is due to begin.
D. Foster can obtain a judgment for the monetary damages it incurred as a result of the repudiation.

4.   Law Nov 89 #18

Moss entered into a contract to purchase certain real property from Shinn. Which of the following statements is **not** correct?

A. If Shinn fails to perform the contract, Moss can obtain specific performance.

B. The contract is nonassignable as a matter of law.

C. The Statute of Frauds applies to the contract.

D. Any amendment to the contract must be agreed to by both Moss and Shinn.

5.   Law Nov 87 #1

On June 1, 1986, Nord Corp. engaged Milo & Co., CPAs, to perform certain management advisory services for nine months for a $45,000 fee. The terms of their oral agreement required Milo to commence performance any time before October 1, 1986. On June 30, 1987, after Milo completed the work to Nord's satisfaction, Nord paid Milo $30,000 by check. Nord conspicuously marked on the check that it constituted payment in full for all services rendered. Nord has refused to pay the remaining $15,000 arguing that although it believes the $45,000 fee is reasonable, it had received bids of $20,000 and $38,000 from other firms to perform the same services as Milo. Milo endorsed and deposited the check. If Milo commences an action against Nord for the remaining $15,000, Milo will be entitled to recover

A. $0 because there has been an accord and satisfaction.

B. $0 because the Statute of Frauds has **not** been satisfied.

C. $8,000 because the $38,000 was the highest other bid.

D. $15,000 because it is the balance due under the agreement.

6.   Law Nov 92 #14

Castle borrowed $5,000 from Nelson and executed and delivered to Nelson a promissory note for $5,000 due on April 30. On April 1 Castle offered, and Nelson accepted, $4,000 in full satisfaction of the note. On May 15, Nelson demanded that Castle pay the $1,000 balance on the note. Castle refused. If Nelson sued for the $1,000 balance Castle would

A. Win because the acceptance by Nelson of the $4,000 constituted an accord and satisfaction.

B. Win, because the debt was unliquidated.

C. Lose, because the amount of the note was not in dispute.

D. Lose, because no consideration was given to Nelson in exchange for accepting only $4,000.

7.   Law May 78 #22

The Johnson Corporation sent its only pump to the manufacturer to be repaired. It engaged Travis, a local trucking company to deliver the pump, and to redeliver it to Johnson promptly upon completion of the repair. Travis did not know that Johnson's entire plant was inoperative without the pump. Travis delayed several days in returning the repaired pump. During the time it expected to be without the pump, Johnson incurred $5,000 in lost profits. At that end of that time, Johnson rented a replacement pump at $200 per day. What is Johnson entitled to recover from Travis?

A. The $200 a day cost incurred in renting the pump.

B. The $200 a day cost incurred in renting the pump plus the lost profits.

C. Actual damages plus punitive damages.

D. Nothing because Travis is not liable for damages.

8.   Law May 91 #24

In general, a clause in a real estate contract entitling the seller to retain the purchaser's down payment as liquidated damages if the purchaser fails to close the transaction, is enforceable

A. In all cases, when the parties have a signed contract.
B. If the amount of the down payment bears a reasonable relationship to the probable loss.
C. As a penalty, if the purchaser intentionally defaults.
D. Only when the seller cannot compel specific performance.

9.   Law May 92 #35

Kaye contracted to sell Hodges a building for $310,000. The contract required Hodges to pay the entire amount at closing. Kaye refused to close the sale of the building. Hodges sued Kaye. To what relief is Hodges entitled?

A. Punitive damages and compensatory damages.
B. Specific performance and compensatory damages.
C. Consequential damages or punitive damages
D. Compensatory damages or specific performance.

ESSAY QUESTION (Estimated time -- 15 to 20 minutes)

Law Nov 83 #4

Bar manufacturing and Cole enterprises were arch rivals in the high technology industry and both were feverishly working on a new product which would give the first to develop it a significant competitive advantage. Bar engaged Abel Consultants on April 1, 1983, for one year, commencing immediately, at $7,500 a month to aid the company in the development of the new product. The contract was oral and was consummated by a handshake. Cole approached Abel and offered them a $10,000 bonus for signing, $10,000 a month for nine months, and a $40,000 bonus if Cole was the first to successfully market the new product. In this connection, Cole stated that the oral contract Abel made with Bar was unenforceable and that Abel could walk away from it without liability. In addition, Cole made certain misrepresentations regarding the dollar amount of its

commitment to the project, the stage of its development, and the expertise of its research staff. Abel accepted the offer.

Four months later, Bar successfully introduced the new product. Cole immediately dismissed Abel and has paid nothing beyond the first four $10,000 payments plus the initial bonus. Three lawsuits ensued: Bar sued Cole, Bar sued Abel, and Abel sued Cole.

Required:

Answer the following, setting forth reasons for any conclusions stated.

Discuss the various theories on which each of the three lawsuits is based, the defenses which will be asserted, the measure of possible recovery, and the probable outcome of the litigation.

EXPLANATIONS TO PRACTICE MULTIPLE CHOICE QUESTIONS

1. A is the correct answer. This breach is a minor breach. As a consequence, White Corp. must accept the building with the defective performance, and must pay for the building, but will be allowed to deduct compensatory damages from its payment to the construction company. The measure of damages will be the cost to correct (by replacing the light fixtures with the ones specified) the breach or the difference in the market value of the building with the incorrect fixtures and the market value if the correct fixtures had been used. This latter measure would be used if the cost to correct is large compared to the difference in value.

2. C is the correct answer. The rescission is the agreement to cancel the contract. It will usually be accompanied by each party paying restitution to the other party to put them in same position as before the contract. Rescission can occur by agreement of the parties or it can be ordered by the courts as a remedy.

3. B is the correct answer. This question seeks the incorrect statement, and specific performance is not available as a remedy to force someone to perform a personal service. Choice C is a correct statement because when there is an anticipatory breach (also called repudiation) the nonbreaching party can sue immediately without having to wait until the actual performance deadline.

4. B is the correct answer. This question seeks the incorrect statement, and contracts are generally assignable unless stated otherwise. Rights to payment are usually assignable even when there is a provision prohibiting assignment.

5. D is the correct answer. The obligation to pay the $45,000 was liquidated (fixed in dollar amount) and was not in dispute. Choice A is incorrect because a "payment in full" provision on a payment for a liquidated debt is ineffective even if the check is cashed or deposited. Thus there was no accord and satisfaction. Choice B is incorrect because the contract could possibly have been performed within a year, thus it did not need to be in writing. The actual time of performance is not relevant for the Statute of Frauds. Choice C is incorrect because the other bids are irrelevant to the obligations of the parties under this contract.

6. A is the correct answer. The April 1 agreement is an accord and satisfaction because it settled an existing claim. Note that unlike in the previous question, here the new agreement resulted in paying the note earlier than required by the original contract. Thus, choices B and C are incorrect because by agreeing to pay the note earlier, the satisfaction of the accord discharged all duties under the original agreement, including the duty to pay the last $1,000.

7. A is the correct answer. This question requires a careful reading of the facts. The ordinary measure of compensatory damages attempts to put the nonbreaching party in the same position as if the contract had been performed. The rental of the pump gave Johnson Corporation the same use of the pump it would have had with proper delivery. Note that the lost profits relate to the time that Johnson expected to be without the pump, thus the breach did not cause the lost profits. Therefore lost profits are not recoverable here.

8. B is the correct answer. Liquidated damages clauses are disfavored by the courts. They are allowed if they are not excessive, which requires that they bear some relation to the expected actual damages. Excessive liquidated damages are considered a penalty, and punitive damages are generally not allowed in contracts. Another factor making liquidated damages more likely to be acceptable is if the computation of actual damages, in the event of a breach, would be difficult. This question has a terminology problem with respect to the term "down payment." The question would be more realistic if the term "earnest money" or "deposit" had been used instead because the seller does not have the full down payment prior to closing, and thus could not "retain" it. Furthermore, it is forfeiture of the earnest money that real estate contracts often set as liquidated damages.

9. D is the correct answer. The buyer of real estate is entitled to specific performance or compensatory damages, but not both. The compensatory damages compensate the buyer for not getting the building. If the buyer gets specific performance, then there would be no need for compensatory damages. Punitive damages are generally not available in breach of contract cases. Also, remember that a real estate seller cannot get specific performance forcing the buyer to buy.

UNOFFICIAL AICPA ANSWER TO ESSAY QUESTION

Law Nov 83 #4

Bar's lawsuit against Cole will be based upon the intentional tort of wrongful interference with a contractual relationship. The primary requirement for this cause of action is a valid contractual relationship with which the defendant knowingly interferes. This requirement is met in the case of Cole. The contract is not required to be in writing since it is for exactly one year from the time of its making. It is, therefore, valid even though oral. Cole's knowledge of the contract is obvious. The principal problem, however, is damages.

Since Bar was the first to successfully market the product, it would appear that damages are not present. It is possible there were actual damages incurred by Bar (for example, it hired another consulting firm at an increased price). It also might be possible that some courts would permit the recovery of punitive damages because this is an intentional tort.

Bar's cause of action against Abel would be for breach of contract. Once again, damages would appear to be a serious problem. Furthermore, punitive damages would rarely be available in a contract action. Finally, Bar cannot recover the same damages twice. Hence, if it proceeds against Cole and recovers damages caused by Abel's breach of contract, it will not be able to recover a second time.

Abel's lawsuit against Cole will be based upon fraud and breach of contract. There were fraudulent statements made by Cole with the requisite intent and that were possibly to Abel's detriment. The breach of contract by Cole is obvious. However, the contract that Cole induced Abel to enter into and which it subsequently breached was an illegal contract, that is, one calling for the commission of a tort. Therefore, both parties are likely to be treated as wrongdoers, and Abel will be denied recovery.

CHAPTER 11
FORMATION OF SALES AND LEASE CONTRACTS

OVERVIEW

Contracts for the sale or lease of goods are governed by the **Uniform Commercial Code**, a model law which has been adopted by all 50 states. Some states made minor changes when adopting it, and Louisiana has only adopted portions. Unlike the common law of contracts, the UCC is statutory law. The UCC adds to and sometimes changes contract law when applied to the sale of goods compared to other contracts. The UCC was developed because of the need for uniformity in contract law affecting goods. **Goods** are any items of movable, tangible personal property, thus contracts involving goods frequently cross state lines making uniformity desirable. Note that real property is unmoveable by its nature, and, historically, services have not often crossed state lines, so uniformity is much less important for laws covering such contracts.

OUTLINE

I. **Uniform Commercial Code.**
   A. <u>Definition</u>. The Uniform Commercial Code is a model statute which was promulgated in the early 1950s and recommended to all jurisdictions for adoption. Its various articles cover several areas of commercial law. It is state law, even though it is nearly the same in all states.
   B. <u>Sales and Lease Articles</u>. Article 2 of the UCC applies to contracts for the sale of goods. As leasing became more widespread as an alternative means to finance the acquisition of goods, Article 2A covering leasing transactions was drafted and has since been adopted by many jurisdictions, with more expected to in the future. Article 2A closely parallels Article 2 in many respects, though deviating where the nature of leasing calls for different provisions.
   C. <u>Applicability</u>. The appropriate Article applies to any covered contract. The UCC operates as a "default" statute in that the parties are free, by agreement, to modify almost any of its provisions. Thus specific contract terms control where they differ from the standard UCC rule.
   D. <u>General Philosophy</u>. In addition to the goal of uniformity, the UCC is designed to encourage and facilitate business transactions. This means that some of the common law contract formalities and requirements are either relaxed or eliminated under the UCC.
   E. <u>Statutory Detail</u>. The UCC contains many detailed provisions, some of which are quite technical. Unlike common law, which can change over time as circumstances change, UCC provisions seldom change.
   F. <u>General Issues</u>.
      1. *Sale*. A **sale** is any transaction, however paid for, where title transfers from seller to buyer for a price. **Title** is legal ownership; it is not, as many believe, a document, such as the owner of a car might possess. That document, a <u>certificate</u> of title, is proof of ownership while title itself is the legal concept of ownership.
      2. *Goods*. All sales of goods are covered by Article 2. Money and intangible items such as stocks are not goods and not covered under Article 2.

3. *Mixed Sale.* A **mixed sale** is a transaction that involves both a sale of goods and the providing of services. The law applicable to a mixed sale contract depends on which component is predominant. If the transaction is predominantly a sale of goods, then the UCC applies to all portions of the contract, even the service component. If predominantly a service contract, common law applies, even to the sale of goods component. The question of which predominates depends on various factors, including the overall purpose of the contract and the values of the goods portion and services portion relative to each other. **Exam tip #1.**

4. *Merchants.* The UCC applies to all parties in contracts for the sale of goods, whether merchant or nonmerchant. Some specific provisions apply only to merchants, and some provisions apply differently to each, but most UCC provisions apply equally to both. A **merchant** is (1) a person who deals in the goods of the kind involved in transaction or (2) a person who by his or her occupation holds himself out as an expert in the goods involved in the transaction. A tire store is a merchant in any transaction involving tires, but not in purchasing a computer. Note that in part (2) of the definition above that it is the holding out, or <u>claiming</u> to be an expert that classifies one as a merchant; whether or not the person really is an expert is irrelevant. **Exam tip #2.**

G. <u>Leases</u>. A **lease** is the transfer of the right of possession and use (but not title) of the named goods for a set term in return for certain consideration. The **lessor** is party who transfers the right of possession and use to the **lessee**.

H. <u>Good Faith</u>. All contracts for goods have an implied covenant of **good faith**, with merchants being held to a higher standard.
1. *Nonmerchants.* Good faith means honesty in fact.
2. *Merchants.* Good faith means honesty in fact and fair dealing in the trade.

II. Formation of Sales and Lease Contracts.
A. <u>Offer</u>. Offer requirements under the UCC are more lenient than under common law. Offers can have **open terms** which are not stated, but will be implied using **gap-filling rules**. Under common law, omitting any item usually results in the offer not meeting the definiteness of terms requirement. Common open terms include:
1. *Open Price.* A reasonable price will be implied. If a contract allows one party to later set the price, that must be done in good faith.
2. *Open Payment.* If not specified, payment is due at the time and place where the buyer is to receive the goods. If a document of title is involved, payment is when and where the document of title is delivered regardless of where the goods are to be received.
3. *Open Delivery.* If not specified, the goods are to be delivered at the seller's place of business, or if none, at the seller's residence.
4. *Open Time.* If not specified, the contract must be performed within a reasonable time.
5. *Open Assortment.* If not specified, such as the colors and sizes for a shipment or lot of clothing, the buyer can choose from the seller's stock, subject to good faith and commercial reasonableness.
6. *Open Quantity.* An open quantity term usually results in the offer being too vague because it is seldom possible to determine a reasonable quantity term. **Exam tip #3.**

B. <u>Firm Offer Rule</u>. The **firm offer rule** makes certain offers by merchants irrevocable even if there is no consideration to hold the offer open. Essentially, it eliminates the consideration requirement for an option contract. It applies only if the offeror:
   1. *Is a Merchant,*
   2. *Offers to Buy, Sell, or Lease Goods,*
   3. *Promises to Hold the Offer Open,* and
   4. *Gives a Written and Signed Assurance.*

   The offer cannot be revoked if the above requirements are met. The irrevocability period is the period stated in the offer, or if none is stated, a reasonable period, but can never be longer than three months.

C. <u>Acceptance of an Offer</u>. An offer to buy goods can be accepted either by a promise to ship the goods, or by promptly shipping goods. Note that the mere act of shipping the goods operates as an acceptance. The offer can be accepted by any reasonable method.

D. <u>Accommodation Shipment</u>. Nonconforming goods shipped along with notice to the buyer that they are sent as an **accommodation** is neither an acceptance nor a breach, but a counteroffer.

D. <u>Additional Terms in Acceptance</u>. The mirror image rule under common law makes an acceptance ineffective if it contains any terms different from the offer, thus no contract would be formed. Under the UCC, a contract might still be formed. There are two sets of rules based on the merchant status of the parties.
   1. *One or Both Parties Are Nonmerchants.* The additional terms are considered **proposed additions** to the contract. If the original offeror accepts the additional terms in the acceptance, the contract will include the additional terms. If the additional terms are not accepted, a contract is formed on the basis of the original offer without the additional terms.
   2. *Both Parties Are Merchants.* The additional terms automatically become part of the contract unless any one of the following applies:
      a. The offer expressly limits acceptance to the terms of the offer.
      b. The additional terms materially alter the express terms of the contract.
      c. The offeror notifies the offeree that he objects to the additional terms within a reasonable time after receiving the acceptance with the additional terms.

      This situation is commonly called the **battle of the forms** because it often arises where a standard form document, such as a purchase order, of one party operates as the offer, and a different standard form document, such as a sales confirmation or invoice, of the other party operates as the acceptance. These often contain different terms. **Exam tip #4.**

E. <u>Consideration in a Contract Modification</u>. Under the UCC, a contract modification does not need consideration, a change from common law where both parties must give consideration in a modification.

F. <u>Statute of Frauds</u>. Contracts with a contract price of $500 or more must be in writing in order to be enforceable. There once was a CPA exam question that required the candidate to know that a contract of exactly $500 needed to be in writing. Lease contracts involving payments of $1,000 or more must be in writing.

G. <u>Statute of Frauds in a Contract Modification</u>. Whether a contract modification is required to be in writing or not depends on whether the contract price, as modified, is $500 or more. If a contract requires that all modifications be in writing, any oral modification is unenforceable.

H. <u>Statute of Frauds Exceptions</u>. There are three exceptions to the writing requirement. With each of these exceptions, there are usually other sources of evidence such that the writing is not so crucial.

1. *Specially Manufactured Goods.* An oral contract can be enforced against the buyer or lessee if (1) the goods are not suitable for sale or lease to others in the seller's ordinary course of business and (2) the seller or lessor has made a substantial beginning of their manufacture or procurement.

2. *Admissions in Pleadings or Court.* An oral contract can be enforced against a party who has admitted the existence of the contract, but only up to the quantity admitted.

3. *Part Acceptance.* Oral contracts can be enforced to the extent that the related goods have been accepted by the buyer.

I. <u>Written Confirmation Rule</u>. Under common law, a contract required to be in writing can be enforced against a party only if that party's signature is a part of the writing. Under the UCC, the signature of the party against whom enforcement is sought is not always needed. The signature is not needed if there is a **written confirmation** meeting the following requirements.

1. *Both Parties Are Merchants,*

2. *There Is an Oral Agreement,*

3. *One Party Sends a Written Confirmation of the Agreement to the Other Within a Reasonable Time of the Oral Agreement,* and

4. *The Party Receiving the Confirmation Did Not Object in Writing Within Ten Days.*

For example, a retailer ordered $2,000 of merchandise from a wholesaler over the phone. A few days later the wholesaler sends a written confirmation to the retailer, who does not object within 10 days. The written confirmation meets the writing requirement and the contract can be enforced against the retailer even without the retailer's signature. **Exam tip #5.**

J. <u>Parol Evidence</u>. Under common law, one of the exceptions (meaning that the oral evidence can be admitted) to the parol evidence rule is evidence used to clear up ambiguities in the contract. This is true also under the UCC, but the UCC prioritizes three specific types of evidence to be used in clearing up ambiguities. Evidence of the following is used, in order of priority.

1. *Course of Performance.* **Course of performance** is the previous conduct of the parties in performing earlier portions of the contract in dispute.

2. *Course of Dealing.* **Course of dealing** is the conduct of the parties in prior transactions and contracts between them.

3. *Usage of Trade.* **Usage of trade** is any practice or method of dealing that is regularly observed or adhered to in a place, a vocation, a trade, or an industry.

Where there is a dispute over an ambiguous term, the court will first look to see if course of performance can give guidance about the ambiguous term, and if not, will then try course of dealing, and lastly usage of trade. For example, if a contract called for delivery of 10 "large widgets" per month, "large" could be ambiguous. In deciding what constituted a "large" widget, the court would look to see if any widgets were accepted as "large" (or refused because they were not large enough) in earlier shipments, of the current contract. Such evidence would be used by the court in interpreting "large." If that provided no guidance, the court would next look to prior contracts, if any, between the same parties, and lastly to what the industry norm was for "large" widgets.

III.   Identification, Passage of Title, and Risk of Loss.

A. Identification of Goods. **Identification of goods** occurs when the goods are distinguished from other goods of the seller. It can occur at the time of contracting for specifically identified goods, such as a car purchased from a dealer, or later when the contracted quantity of similar goods are separated for the particular buyer out of the seller's general stock. Identification must occur before title can pass.

B. Passage of Title. Remember that title is the legal concept of ownership, not a document. Thus this is the passage of legal ownership, not necessarily the transfer of a document. The parties' contract can determine when title passes, otherwise the UCC rules will control.

1. *General Rule.* Passage of title usually occurs when the seller's obligations with respect to delivery are completed. Sometimes this occurs at the moment the contract is formed, on other occasions it does not occur until the goods reach the buyer's place of business. The UCC has separate rules for risk of loss, making passage of title less important than it was previously.

C. Risk of Loss. **Risk of loss** determines who bears the loss if the goods are damaged through no fault of the parties. Risk of loss rules take into account whether a common carrier is used for the transport of the goods and whether there has been a breach of the contract. Risk of loss is always initially on the seller, and usually will pass to the buyer at some point. In some cases it may never leave the seller, or may shift back to the seller after it is on the buyer.

1. *Carrier Cases.* When a common carrier, such as a railroad or trucking company is used to transport the goods, there is a period of time when the goods are in the possession of neither the buyer nor the seller. There are two general rules, based on who is responsible for the shipping of the goods. If goods are lost or destroyed while in the hands of a common carrier, the common carrier is liable. The risk of loss rules apply if, for any reason, the common carrier is unable to cover the loss. **Exam tip #6.**

   a. Shipment Contract. A **shipment contract** requires that the seller place the goods in the hands of a common carrier, at which point the seller's responsibilities end. Risk of loss passes from seller to buyer when the goods are placed in the hands of the common carrier. The buyer bears the risk of loss while the goods are in transit.

   b. Destination Contract. A **destination contract** places the responsibility and cost of delivery on the seller until the goods reach the destination called for in the contract. Risk of loss does not pass from seller to buyer until the goods reach their destination. The seller bears the risk of loss while they are in transit.

2. *Shipping Terms.* There are several common shipping terms which are used to indicate whether a contract is a shipment or destination contract.

   a. F.O.B. This stands for **free on board**. The letters are usually followed by the name of the city (such as F.O.B. Detroit) which is the free on board point, or the point at which the seller's responsibility ends. If the named location is that of the seller, it is a shipment contract, and if the named location is that of the buyer, it is a destination contract. In other cases the terms can simple read "F.O.B. shipping point" or "F.O.B. destination."

b. F.A.S. This stands for **free alongside**. This is a type of shipping point contract where a ship or railroad is named (such as F.A.S. *The Peerless)*, indicating that the seller's duty and risk of loss end when the goods are placed alongside the named vessel. This indicates a shipment contract.

3. *Noncarrier Cases.* In a noncarrier case, the goods are transferred directly from the seller to the buyer without going through a common carrier. Any transporting of goods from the seller to the buyer will be done by either the seller or the buyer. There are two rules, depending on if the seller is a merchant.

a. Merchant Seller. With a merchant seller, the risk of loss passes when actual delivery is made to the buyer.

b. Nonmerchant Seller. With a nonmerchant seller, risk of loss passes when the seller tenders delivery to the buyer. **Tender of delivery** occurs when the seller makes the goods available to the buyer and notifies the buyer of this fact. For example, Hank went to Jean's home to look at a carpet which Jean was selling. They agreed on a price and Jean told Hank he could take the carpet. Hank then asked Jean if she could hold the carpet until the following week. Tender of delivery occurred when Jean told Hank that he could take the carpet, thus passing risk of loss. If anything happened to the carpet through no fault of Jean before Hank picked it up, Hank would bear the loss.

c. Rationale. Merchant sellers are in the business of holding goods until sold, and likely have insurance covering such losses, making it reasonable to bear the risk of loss until actual delivery. Nonmerchant sellers are not in the storage business, so a seller like Jean in the example above should not bear the risk of loss when doing a favor of holding the goods for the buyer.

4. *Conditional Sales.*

a. Sale on Approval. With a **sale on approval**, a potential buyer takes physical possession of goods and has a certain period of time to decide if she wants to buy them. Title and risk of loss do not pass until she accepts the goods, which might never occur.

b. Sale or Return. With a **sale or return**, the goods are delivered with the understanding that they can be returned if not used or resold within a certain period of time. Title and risk of loss pass to the buyer as soon as the goods are in the buyer's possession. Of course title and risk of loss would pass back to the seller for any goods returned.

c. Consignment Sale. In a **consignment sale**, the seller of goods delivers them to a buyer who then tries to sell them, charging a fee if successful. The UCC treats a consignment sale as a sale or return.

5. *Risk of Loss in Breach of Contract Situation.*

a. In General. The risk of loss rules change when a party breaches the contract. Generally, the breaching party is more likely to bear the risk of loss than would be the case without a breach.

b. Seller in Breach. When the seller breaches (usually for delivering nonconforming goods), the risk remains on the seller until either the nonconformity is cured or the buyer accepts the goods with the nonconformity. Thus, the breaching seller can continue to bear the risk of loss after the goods are in the hands of the buyer.

      c. Buyer in Breach. When the buyer breaches (usually for nonpayment, repudiation of the contract, or refusal to take delivery of conforming goods), the risk of loss shifts immediately to the buyer if it has not already done so. This applies only to goods that have been identified to the contract, and lasts only for a commercially reasonable time. For example, if a buyer wrongfully refused to take delivery of goods, the buyer would bear the risk of loss while in transit back to the seller, and for a reasonable time after they were back in the seller's hands.

IV.   Sales by Nonowners.

A. <u>Stolen Goods</u>. A thief acquires no title, or **void title**, to any goods stolen. If stolen goods are then sold, and resold any number of times, even in good faith, no one in the line of possession ever acquires title. The true owner, the victim of the theft, can always reclaim the goods, even if many years later. In some cases, such as with artwork, the heirs of the victim might be the ones to recover the goods. Void title is no title and can never become good title.

B. <u>Voidable Title Situation</u>. Persons holding **voidable title** have the ability to transfer the goods and good title to a **good faith purchaser for value** (also known as a **bona fide purchaser for value**, and sometimes abbreviated BFP). This is one of the few cases in the law where a buyer can receive more (good title) than the seller had (voidable title).

    1. *Voidable Title*. Voidable title usually arises when a buyer acquires goods in a contract but does not pay for them or otherwise breaches the contract. The seller in such a situation can void the title of the buyer by reclaiming the goods.

    2. *Resale by Buyer*. If the buyer holding voidable title resells the goods to a good faith purchaser for value, that good faith purchaser acquires good title. Thus if the first buyer never paid, the original seller could reclaim them while they were still in the hands of the original buyer, but not after the original buyer sold them to a good faith purchaser.

    3. *Good Faith Purchaser for Value*. In order to be a good faith purchaser for value, the purchase must be made at such a price and under such circumstances that the buyer honestly believed that the seller held good title.

    4. *Example*. Lynn sold a bicycle to Bob's Secondhand Shop, whose check to Lynn was dishonored for lack of funds. Lynn could reclaim the bicycle from Bob if he still had it, but could not claim the bicycle from a good faith purchaser to whom Bob resold it.

    5. *Policy and Consequences*. The rule, which seems harsh to many candidates, encourages commerce by reducing the title worries of potential buyers. Lynn, in the example above, does have a remedy. She could sue Bob. Furthermore, Lynn could have prevented the situation from occurring by accepting only cash from Bob.

C. <u>Entrustment Rule</u>. The **entrustment** rule applies when someone entrusts the possession of a good to a merchant who deals in the goods of that kind. The owner gives <u>no</u> title to the merchant, yet the merchant can pass good title to a **buyer in the ordinary course of business**. For example, Paula took a diamond ring to a jewelry dealer for cleaning and to reset the stone. If the dealer were to sell the ring to a buyer in the ordinary course of business, Paula could not force the buyer of the ring to return it, and could only sue the jewelry dealer. The buyer has acquired good title even though the jewelry dealer had no title at all. The rule applies only if a merchant deals in the type of item. Taking a computer in for repair puts the owner of the computer at risk of losing title only if the repair shop also sells computers. **Exam tip #7.**

EXAM TIPS

1. In any contract question, it is crucial that the candidate first determine the kind of contract because this determines which rules, those of the UCC or common law, apply. It is all too easy to blindly proceed applying the wrong set of rules to the situation. Always check first what kind of contract is present. An essay question might involve more than one contract, including some covered by the UCC, and some not.

2. CPA exam questions will describe the merchant status either by telling you that the party is or is not a merchant, or by describing the party so that merchant status can be determined based on the definition. Candidates should be alert for descriptions stating that a party "is in the business of selling widgets," etc. A manufacturer is a merchant in the goods manufactured because the manufacturer is in the business of selling its output. Remember that merchant status depends on whether the merchant regularly sells the goods of the kind in the particular transaction.

3. Be sure to know which of these have specific gap-filling terms (e.g., place of delivery) and which merely imply a reasonable term (e.g., price), and remember that an open quantity term usually results in no contract.

4. In a fact situation where an acceptance differs from the offer, the first issue is whether common law or the UCC applies. If common law applies, the acceptance with the altered terms violates the mirror image rule and will operate as a counteroffer. If the UCC applies, then the merchant status of the parties must be determined, and based on this, the relevant rule applied.

5. Candidates need to know all of these specific UCC rules precisely, especially as to the merchant requirements. Some rules apply only if both parties are merchants, some if either is a merchant, some only if a specific party is a merchant. These rules are easily confused if not thoroughly known. Multiple choice questions can be very tricky in this area.

6. In a risk of loss case, always determine first whether there is a common carrier involved and whether either party is in breach of contract. Then apply the appropriate rule.

7. One can buy from either a merchant or a nonmerchant and be a good faith purchaser for value. But in order to be a buyer in the ordinary course of business, one must have bought from a merchant. Be sure to keep straight the distinctions in the various nonowner sale situations, and remember that no one other than the original owner ever acquires title to stolen goods.

KEY CONCEPTS LIKELY TO BE TESTED ON THE CPA EXAM

1. General definitions under the UCC, such as goods, merchant, etc.
2. Contracts covered by Article 2, and those not covered.
3. The UCC contract formation rules which differ from common law.
4. Parol evidence rules for contract interpretation.
5. Who bears a loss when goods are destroyed or lost.
6. Rules and application in void and voidable title situations.

KEY TERMS

Uniform Commercial Code	Gap-Filling Rules	Risk of Loss
Goods	Firm Offer Rule	Shipment Contract
Sale	Accommodation Shipment	Destination Contract
Title	Proposed Additions	Free On Board
Mixed Sale	Battle of the Forms	Free Alongside
Merchant	Written Confirmation Rule	Tender of Delivery
Lease	Course of Performance	Sale on Approval
Lessor	Course of Dealing	Sale or Return
Lessee	Usage of Trade	Consignment Sale
Good Faith	Identification of Goods	Void Title
Voidable Title	Good Faith (or Bona Fide) Purchaser for Value	
Entrustment Rule	Buyer in the Ordinary Course of Business	
Open Terms		

MULTIPLE CHOICE QUESTIONS

1.   Law May 94 #42

Under the UCC Sales Article, which of the following statements is correct concerning a contract involving a merchant seller and a non-merchant buyer?

A. Whether the UCC Sales Article is applicable does **not** depend on the price of the goods involved.

B. Only the seller is obligated to perform the contract in good faith.

C. The contract will be either a sale or return or sale on approval contract.

D. The contract may **not** involve the sale of personal property with a price of more than $500.

2.   Law May 90 #40

To satisfy the UCC Statute of Frauds regarding the sale of goods, which of the following must generally be in writing?

A. Designation of the parties as buyer and seller.

B. Delivery terms.

C. Quantity of the goods.

D. Warranties to be made.

3.   Law Nov 89 #46

Cookie Co. offered to sell Distrib Markets 20,000 pounds of cookies at $1.00 per pound, subject to certain specified terms for delivery. Distrib replied in writing as follows:

"We accept your offer for 20,000 pounds of cookies at $1.00 per pound, weighing scale to have valid city certificate."

Under the UCC

A. A contract was formed between the parties.

B. A contract will be formed only if Cookie agrees to the weighing scale requirement.

C. No contract was formed because Distrib included the weighing scale requirement in its reply.

D. No contract was formed because Distrib's reply was a counteroffer.

4.   Law Nov 94 #50

Under the Sales Article of the UCC, which of the following statements is correct?

A. The obligations of the parties to the contract must be performed in good faith.
B. Merchants and nonmerchants are treated alike.
C. The contract must involve the sale of goods for a price of more than $500.
D. None of the provisions of the UCC may be disclaimed by agreement.

5.   Law May 92 #54

On May 2, Mason orally contracted with Acme Appliances to buy for $480 a washer and dryer for household use. Mason and the Acme salesperson agreed that delivery would be made on July 2. On May 5, Mason telephoned Acme and requested that the delivery date be moved to June 2. The Acme salesperson agreed with this request. On June 2, Acme failed to deliver the washer and dryer to Mason because of an inventory shortage. Acme advised Mason that it would deliver the appliances on July 2 as originally agreed. Mason believes that Acme has breached its agreement with Mason. Acme contends that its agreement to deliver on June 2 was not binding. Acme's contention is

A. Correct, because Mason is **not a** merchant and was buying the appliances for household use.
B. Correct, because the agreement to change the delivery date was **not** in writing.
C. Incorrect, because the agreement to change the delivery date was binding.
D. Incorrect, because Acme's agreement to change the delivery date is a firm offer that **cannot** be withdrawn by Acme.

6.   Law May 90 #44

Cey Corp. entered into a contract to sell parts to Deck, Ltd. The contract provided that the goods would be shipped "F.O.B. Cey's warehouse." Cey shipped parts different from those specified in the contract. Deck rejected the parts. A few hours after Deck informed Cey that the parts were rejected, they were destroyed by fire in Deck's warehouse. Cey believed that the parts were conforming to the contract. Which of the following statements is correct?

A. Regardless of whether the parts were conforming, Deck will bear the loss because the contract was a shipment contract.
B. If the parts were nonconforming, Deck had the right to reject them, but the risk of loss remains with Deck until Cey takes possession of the parts.
C. If the parts were conforming, risk of loss does **not** pass to Deck until a reasonable period of time after they are delivered to Deck.
D. If the parts were nonconforming, Cey will bear the risk of loss, even though the contract was a shipment contract.

7.   Law May 85 #41

Taylor signed and mailed a letter to Peel that stated: "Ship promptly 600 dozen grade A eggs." Taylor's offer

A. May be accepted only by a prompt shipment.
B. May be accepted by either a prompt promise to ship or prompt shipment.
C. Is invalid because the price term was omitted.
D. Is invalid because the shipping term was omitted.

8.   Law Nov 95 #41

Under the Sales Article of the UCC, a firm offer will be created only if the

A. Offer states the time period during which it will remain open.
B. Offer is made by a merchant in a signed writing.
C. Offeree gives some form of consideration.
D. Offeree is a merchant.

9.   Law Nov 89 #48

Which of the following factors is most important in deciding who bears the risk of loss between merchants when goods are destroyed during shipment?

A. The agreement of the parties.
B. Whether the goods are perishable.
C. Who has title at the time of the loss.
D. The terms of applicable insurance policies.

ESSAY QUESTIONS

(Estimated time -- 15 to 20 minutes)

Essay #1.   Law Nov 89 #4

Anker Corp., a furniture retailer, engaged Best & Co., CPAs, to audit Anker's financial statements for the year ended December 31, 1988. While reviewing certain transactions entered into by Anker during 1988, Best became concerned with the proper reporting of the following transactions:

- On September 8, 1988, Crisp Corp., a furniture manufacturer, signed and mailed a letter offering to sell Anker 50 pieces of furniture for $9,500. The offer stated it would remain open until December 20, 1988. On December 5, 1988, Crisp mailed a letter revoking this offer. Anker received Crisp's revocation the following day. On December 12, 1988, Anker mailed its acceptance to Crisp, and Crisp received it on December 13, 1988.
- On December 6, 1988, Dix Corp. signed and mailed a letter offering to sell Anker a building for $75,000. The offer stated that acceptance could only be made by certified mail, return receipt requested. On December 10, 1988, Anker telephoned Dix requesting that Dix keep the offer open until December 20, 1988 because it was reviewing Dix's offer. On December 12, 1988, Dix signed and mailed a letter to Anker indicating that it would hold the offer open until December 20, 1988. On December 19, 1988, Anker sent its acceptance to Dix by a private express mail courier. Anker's acceptance was received by Dix on December 20, 1988.

After reviewing the documents concerning the foregoing transactions, Best spoke with Anker's president who made the following assertions:

- The September 8, 1988 offer by Crisp was irrevocable until December 20, 1988, and therefore a contract was formed by Anker's acceptance on December 12, 1988.
- Dix's letter dated December 12, 1988 formed an option contract with Anker.
- Anker's acceptance on December 19, 1988 formed a contract with Dix.

Required: In separate paragraphs, discuss the assertions made by Anker's president. Indicate whether the assertions are correct and the reasons therefor.

(Estimated time -- 15 to 25 minutes)

Essay #2.   Law Nov 92 #5

Debco Electronics, Inc. sells various brands of computer equipment to retail and business customers. An audit of Debco's 1991 financial statements has revealed the following transactions:

- On September 1, 1991, a Debco salesperson orally agreed to sell Rapid Computers, Inc. eight TMI computers for $11,000, to be delivered on October 15, 1991. Rapid sells computers to the general public. The Debco salesperson sent Rapid a signed confirmation of the sales agreement. Rapid received the confirmation on September 3, but did not respond to it. On October 15, 1991, Debco tendered delivery of the computers to Rapid. Rapid refused to accept delivery, claiming it had no obligation to buy the computers because it had not signed a contract with Debco.

- On October 12, 1991, Debco mailed TMI Computers, Inc. a signed purchase order for certain specified computers for delivery by November 30, 1991. The purchase order also stated the following:
    > This purchase order will not be withdrawn on or before October 31, 1991. You must accept by that date or we will assume you cannot meet our terms. Ship F.O.B. -- our loading dock.

TMI received the purchase order on October 15, 1991.

- On October 25, Debco mailed the following signed correspondence to TMI, which TMI received on October 29:
    > Cancel our October 12, 1991, purchase order. We have found a better price on the computers.

- On October 31, 1991, TMI mailed the following signed correspondence to Debco received on November 3:
    > We have set aside the computers you ordered and turned down other offers for them. Therefore, we will ship the computers to you for delivery by November 30, 1991, F.O.B. -- your loading dock with payment terms 2/10; net 30.

There were no further communications between TMI and Debco.

TMI shipped the computers on November 15, and Debco received them on November 29. Debco refused to accept delivery. In justifying its refusal to accept delivery, Debco claimed the following:

- Its October 25 correspondence prevented the formation of a contract between Debco and TMI;
- TMI's October 31 correspondence was not an effective acceptance because it was not received by Debco until November 3;
- TMI's October 31 correspondence was not an effective acceptance because it added payment terms to Debco's purchase order.

Debco, Rapid, and TMI are located in a jurisdiction that has adopted the UCC.

Required:
   a. State whether Rapid's claim is correct and give the reasons for your conclusions.
   b. State whether Debco's claims are correct with regard to the transaction involving TMI and give the reason for your conclusions.

EXPLANATIONS TO MULTIPLE CHOICE QUESTIONS

1. A is the correct answer. The UCC applies to all contracts for the sale of goods regardless of the price of the goods, although contracts for an amount of $500 or more must be in writing under the Statute of Frauds. Choice B is incorrect because all parties must perform in good faith under the UCC, although the good faith standard for nonmerchants is more lenient than that for merchants.

2. C is the correct answer. The UCC has gap-filling rules for situations where certain terms, such as the price or delivery terms, are missing. Because it is usually not possible to determine what a "reasonable" quantity would be, lack of a quantity term generally results in no contract.

3. A is the correct answer. This question addresses the effect, under the UCC, of different or additional terms in the acceptance to an offer. Choice D is incorrect because unlike at common law, a contract is formed under the UCC. Whether the additional terms become part of the contract depends on the merchant status of the parties. This question requires only that the candidate know that under the UCC a contract will be formed in all cases. Choices B and C are essentially the same, and thus both incorrect.

4. A is the correct answer. Choice B is incorrect because although the UCC applies to both merchants and nonmerchants, they are treated differently in some provisions. Choice D is incorrect because most provisions of the UCC can be disclaimed or modified by the terms of the contract, although the good faith requirement is one provision that cannot be disclaimed.

5. C is the correct answer. The oral modification is binding because the contract, as modified, was for less than $500 and therefore was not required to be in writing. Furthermore, no new consideration is necessary for modifications under the UCC. Choice D is incorrect because this situation is nowhere close to a firm offer. Beware of incorrect answer choices like this where a totally inapplicable rule or doctrine given as an answer choice can trip up unprepared candidates.

6. D is the correct answer. The risk of loss rules are changed when a party breaches the contract, generally to the detriment of the breaching party. If a seller breaches by delivering nonconforming goods, the risk of loss stays on the seller until the nonconformity is cured or the buyer accepts the goods with the nonconformity, neither of which happened here. The seller's belief that the goods were conforming is not relevant; whether they actually conform is. Choice A is incorrect because with a breach the risk of loss would remain on the breaching seller even in a shipment contract. Note the structure of answer choices B, C, and D, where a further assumption is made about facts (whether the goods did conform) of the question.

7. B is the correct answer. Either shipment or a promise to ship will operate as an acceptance. Choices C and D are incorrect because the UCC has gap filling provisions for contracts where certain terms are omitted.

8. B is the correct answer. The correct choice concisely states the three requirements of a firm offer, and is an easy question for candidates who know the rule.

9. A is the correct answer. The most important factor under the UCC for risk of loss is the contract's shipping terms. That does not appear as an answer choice, but because the contract's shipping terms are part of the agreement of the parties, choice A is the correct choice. Many candidates mistakenly believe that title is the most important factor. Choice D might be important in determining who actually bears a loss, but the rules for risk of loss are determined independently of insurance coverage of the parties. In reality, the risk of loss rules determine who will bear a loss if no one else (e.g., insurance, or the party causing the loss, such as the common carrier) covers the loss.

UNOFFICIAL AICPA ANSWERS TO ESSAY QUESTIONS

Essay #1.   Law Nov 89 #4

The president's assertion that the September 8, 1988 offer by Crisp was irrevocable until December 20, 1988, and that, therefore, a contract was formed by Anker's acceptance on December 12, 1988, is incorrect. Because the offer made by Crisp involves a transaction in goods, i.e. furniture, the UCC Sales Article applies. The UCC Sales Article provides that an offer by a merchant to buy or sell goods in a signed writing which by its terms gives assurance that it will be held open is not revocable, for lack of consideration, during the time stated or, if no time is stated, for a reasonable time, but in no event may such period of irrevocability exceed three months. Under the facts of this case, Crisp's offer was a firm offer that could not be revoked because the offer was made by Crisp, a merchant, concerning the kind of goods being sold (furniture); was in writing and signed by Crisp; and stated that it would remain open until December 20, 1988. Despite the provision that the offer will remain open until December 20, 1988, a firm offer remains irrevocable for a three-month period. Therefore, Crisp's letter of revocation on December 5, 1988 did not terminate the firm offer because the three-month period had not yet expired. The revocation was effective on December 8, 1988, when the three-month period expired. Therefore, Anker's attempted acceptance on December 12, 1988 did not form a contract with Crisp. Instead, Anker's attempted acceptance is likely to be treated as an offer.

The president's assertion that Dix's December 12, 1988 letter formed an option contract is incorrect. To form an option contract, where the subject matter is real estate, all of the elements necessary to form a contract must be met. In this case, Anker did not furnish any consideration in return for Dix's promise to keep the offer open until December 20, 1988; therefore, an option contract was not formed.

The president's assertion that Anker's acceptance on December 19, 1988 formed a contract with Dix is incorrect. In general, acceptance of an offer is effective when it is dispatched. If, however, an offer specifically stipulates the method of communication to be utilized by the offeree, the acceptance to be effective must conform to that method. Thus, an acceptance by another method of communication is ineffective and no contract is formed. Under the facts of this case, Anker's acceptance on December 19, 1988 by a private express mail courier is ineffective, despite Dix's receipt of the acceptance on December 20, 1988, because Dix's offer specifically stipulated that acceptance could only be made by certified mail, return receipt requested. Instead, Anker's attempted acceptance is likely to be treated as a counteroffer.

a. Rapid's claim is incorrect. Both Debco and Rapid are merchants under the UCC because they both deal in the type of goods involved in the transaction (computers).

The UCC provides that a confirmation satisfies the Statute of Frauds, if an oral contract between merchants is:

- Confirmed in writing within a reasonable period of time, and
- The confirmation is signed by the party sending it and received by the other party.

Both parties are bound even though the party receiving the confirmation fails to sign it. This is correct unless the party receiving the confirmation submits a written objection within 10 days of receipt. Rapid will be bound even though it did not sign the confirmation because no written objection was made.

b. Debco's first claim, that its October 25 correspondence prevented the formation of a contract, is incorrect. Debco's October 12 purchase order will be regarded as a firm offer under the UCC because:

- Debco is a merchant.
- The purchase order is in writing and signed.
- The purchase order states that it will not be withdrawn for the time specified.

Because Debco's October 12 purchase order is considered a firm offer, Debco cannot revoke it, and its October 25 attempt to do so is ineffective.

Debco's second claim, that TMI's October 31 correspondence is not an effective acceptance because it was not received until November 3, is incorrect. An acceptance of an offer is effective when dispatched (in this case, when mailed), provided that an appropriate mode of communication is used. The UCC provides that an offer shall be construed as inviting acceptance in any manner and by any medium reasonable in the circumstances. In this case, Debco made its offer by mail, which, if adequately addressed with proper postage affixed, would be considered a reasonable manner and medium for acceptance. As a result, TMI's acceptance was effective when mailed on October 31.

Debco's third claim, that TMI's acceptance is not effective because it added payment terms to Debco's offer, is also incorrect. The UCC provides that a definite and timely expression of acceptance of an offer will form a contract, even if the terms of the acceptance are different from those in the offer, unless acceptance is expressly made conditional on accepting the different terms. Therefore, TMI's October 31 correspondence, which expressly stated that TMI would ship the computers ordered by Debco, was an effective acceptance, and a contract was formed despite the fact that TMI added payment terms.

Author's Note:
The last paragraph of this answer would have been more complete if the rules for an acceptance containing terms different from the offer were more thoroughly explained. Specifically, the answer could have stated the relevant rule and then applied it to the facts of this question.

CHAPTER 12
PERFORMANCE OF SALES AND LEASE CONTRACTS

OVERVIEW

This chapter covers the law affecting the parties after the contract has been formed. The obligations in most goods contracts are fairly similar, and the vast majority of these are performed without a problem. And when problems do arise, the parties often work out a settlement. The rules in this chapter apply when the contract does not provide for other remedies and the parties have been unable to work out a solution. In general, this chapter first addresses the obligations of buyer and seller, and then discusses the actions and remedies available to each party in the event of a breach by the other. Most of the provisions discussed are also applicable to lessors and lessees even though not specifically stated in the outline. For example, a nonbreaching lessee can lease similar goods from another lessee just as a nonbreaching buyer can buy similar goods from another seller.

OUTLINE

I. **Acceptance and Rejection of Goods.**
   One of the issues that arises in the performance of a sales contract is the buyer's **acceptance of goods** or **rejection of goods** delivered by the seller. It is crucial to not confuse these with the acceptance or rejection of an offer. Unfortunately, identical terms are used in these two different situations, often without specifying which. In other words the term "acceptance" might be used without specifying whether it refers to acceptance of an offer or acceptance of the delivered goods. Often only the surrounding circumstances will indicate the specific situation. To summarize:
   A. <u>Offers.</u> If an offer is rejected, there is no contract, and the parties have no obligations to each other. One party or the other must make a new offer to revive negotiations. If an offer is accepted, a contract is formed, both parties are bound, and after that point neither party can unilaterally cancel the contract. The offeree can never revoke acceptance of an offer.
   B. <u>Goods.</u> If acceptance or rejection of goods is an issue, the contract should have already been formed, including the acceptance of the offer. If delivered goods are rejected, the contract is not terminated. Issues might arise as to breach of contract or whether the rejection of goods was proper. Unlike with an offer, an acceptance of goods can later be revoked under certain circumstances. These rules are explained further in this chapter.
   In this chapter and in any contract for the sale of goods, it is important to be aware that the terms acceptance and rejection are used in these two different contexts. References to acceptance and rejection in this chapter refer to acceptance or rejection of delivered goods.

II. **Seller and Lessor Obligations.**
   A. <u>Tender of Delivery.</u> The seller's basic obligation is tender of delivery of conforming goods. **Tender of delivery** consists of an unconditional readiness and willingness to deliver and present ability to do so. Generally this means that the seller must:
      1. *Put and Hold Conforming Goods at the Buyer's Disposition* and

2. *Give the Buyer Any Notification Reasonably Necessary to Enable Delivery.*
The time, place and manner of delivery can be agreed to by the parties, or without an agreement the delivery must be at a reasonable time, and the goods must be kept available for a reasonable period of time. The goods must be delivered in a single delivery unless the contract calls for delivery in lots (separate shipments).

B. Place of Delivery. If not specified in the contract, the place of delivery is as follows:

   1. *Noncarrier Cases.* Normally the place of delivery is the seller's place of business, or if none, the seller's home. This means that if nothing else is specified regarding delivery, then the buyer must go to the seller's place of business (or home) to take delivery of the goods. If, at the time of contracting, the contracted goods are known to be located elsewhere, that location is the place of delivery.

   2. *Goods in Possession of Bailee.* A **bailee** is any holder of goods, such as a public warehouse, who is neither the buyer nor seller. Such goods are frequently "delivered" by transferring documents without moving the goods themselves. Delivery in such circumstances can occur by the seller:
      a. Tendering to the buyer a negotiable document of title covering the goods,
      b. Procuring acknowledgment from the bailee of the buyer's right to possession, or
      c. Tendering to the bailee a nonnegotiable document of title or written direction to deliver the goods to the buyer.

   3. *Carrier Cases.* The seller's duties depend on the contract's shipping terms.
      a. Shipment Contracts. The seller must place the goods in the carrier's possession and contract for their proper transportation; obtain and deliver any documents necessary to enable the buyer to take delivery, or required by the contract or usage of trade; and promptly notify the buyer of the shipment. The buyer may reject the goods if a material delay or loss is caused by the seller's failure to comply.
      b. Destination Contracts. The seller is responsible to deliver the goods to the buyer's place of business, or other specified location. The delivery must be at a reasonable time, in a reasonable manner, with proper notice, and with any appropriate documents provided by the seller.

C. Perfect Tender Rule. The **perfect tender rule** requires that the seller delivers **conforming goods** at the time and place agreed. Conforming goods are the goods specified in the contract, and conformity generally requires that the goods be the correct goods and that they not be defective. The perfect tender rule requires that the tendered goods be exactly what is specified in the contract. If the tendered shipment of goods is nonconforming in any way, the buyer can:

   1. *Reject the Entire Shipment.*
   2. *Accept the Entire Shipment.*
   3. *Reject Part and Accept Part of the Shipment.*

Note that the UCC allows a buyer to reject an entire shipment of 1,000 units if even one item is defective. Note that the third option above does not limit which items are accepted or rejected. Thus if 20 items out of 1,000 are nonconforming, the buyer can accept 15 of the nonconforming items and 346 of the conforming, and reject the remainder. Stated differently, the buyer can could accept all 1,000 items, could reject all 1,000 items, or could accept any combination of conforming and nonconforming items and reject the remainder.

D. <u>Perfect Tender Rule Is Often Modified</u>. Because the perfect tender can be harsh, the parties often agree to limit the buyer's options in the event that the tendered delivery is less than perfectly conforming. The parties are free to make any modification they want, but common provisions include:

1. *Only Nonconforming Items Can Be Rejected*. If 27 out of 100 items were nonconforming, the buyer would only have the option to reject some or all of the 27 defective ones.
2. *The Seller May Replace or Repair Nonconforming Items*. Such a provision would give the seller a right to repair or replace any nonconforming items.
3. *Buyer Will Accept Nonconforming Goods With Appropriate Compensation*. The buyer would be obligated to accept even nonconforming goods, but would be compensated through a reduced price or otherwise. **Exam tip #1.**

E. <u>Substitution of Carrier</u>. If the agreed upon manner of delivery or type of carrier cannot be used, the seller is required to use a commercially reasonable substitute, and the buyer cannot reject the goods because of the substitute carrier.

F. <u>Cure</u>. The right to **cure** gives the seller an opportunity to repair or replace nonconforming goods.

1. *The Right to Cure Lasts Only Until Performance Deadline*. The seller has a right to cure only until the original deadline for performance. If a contract called for delivery of 100 green shirts by May 30, but the seller delivered 100 blue shirts on May 28, the seller would have only two days to cure. If the seller delivered the 100 blue shirts on May 30, the seller could cure only until the end of that day.
2. *Extension of Time to Cure*. The right to cure can be extended beyond the contract performance deadline if the seller delivered nonconforming goods in the reasonable belief that the nonconforming goods would be accepted by the buyer. This commonly happens in a couple of circumstances.
   a. Past Conduct. If, from the example above, in past shipments the buyer had accepted shirts of a different color from those ordered, the right to cure would last a reasonable time from when the seller received notice of the nonconformity. Notice that the past conduct does not relieve the seller of the duty to make a perfect tender, but simply gives an extended period of time to correct a nonconforming shipment.
   b. Delivery of Higher Quality Good. For example, Lisa ordered a new car specifying various optional equipment, but a sunroof was not among those items ordered. The dealer delivered a car to Lisa which is exactly as ordered except that it has a sunroof. The dealer did not change the price to Lisa and assumed Lisa would accept the car with the sunroof. Lisa, however, is a basketball player over six feet tall and did not want a sunroof because of the limited head room. The seller of the car has a reasonable time beyond the performance deadline to cure. **Exam tip #2.**

G. <u>Installment Contracts</u>. An **installment contract** is a contract where delivery in separate lots is either allowed or required. If such a contract states that it is an installment contract, a nonconformity in a particular installment allows rejection of that installment only, and not the entire contract, unless the nonconformity in the one installment impairs the value of other installments.

H. <u>Destruction of Goods</u>. If the goods are totally destroyed through the fault of neither party before risk of loss passes to the buyer, the contract is terminated and both parties are then excused from performing. If they are partially destroyed, the buyer may inspect them and treat the contract as void or accept them, and if accepted, the price will be lowered accordingly.

III.   Buyer and Lessee Obligations.

A. <u>Inspection Right</u>. The buyer has the right to inspection of the goods prior to accepting or paying for the goods. This may be after arrival for goods that are shipped. When the contract provides for goods to be shipped **C.O.D.**, or **cash on delivery**, the buyer does not have a right of inspection prior to payment, although may, of course, reject if they turn out to be nonconforming.

B. <u>Payment</u>. Unless otherwise agreed, payment is due when and where the goods are delivered.

C. <u>Acceptance of Goods</u>. **Acceptance** of goods occurs when, after a reasonable opportunity to inspect, the buyer does any one of the following:
   1. *Signifies to the Seller That the Goods Are Acceptable*. This can be by words or conduct, and can apply to conforming goods or goods where the buyer accepts them with the nonconformity.
   2. *Fails to Reject Within a Reasonable Time After Delivery*.
   3. *Acts Inconsistently With the Seller's Ownership Interest*. Using the goods as one's own or putting the goods up for sale are two examples.

D. <u>Revocation of Acceptance</u>. Under certain conditions a buyer can revoke acceptance of goods already accepted. In order to revoke acceptance, there are three requirements, the third of which can be met in one of three different ways. Revocation can occur if:
   1. *The Goods are Nonconforming,*
   2. *The Nonconformity Substantially Impairs the Value to The Buyer*, and
   3. *One of the Following Is Present*:
      a. A promise by the seller to cure is not met,
      b. The goods were accepted before discovery of the nonconformity and the particular nonconformity was difficult to detect, or
      c. The goods were accepted before discovery of the nonconformity and the seller had assured the buyer that the goods were conforming. **Exam tip #3.**

IV.   Doubts of Performance.

A. <u>Assurance of Performance</u>. If a party has reasonable doubts that the other party will perform, the party with the doubts may demand an **adequate assurance** in writing. If reasonable, the requesting party may suspend performance until the adequate assurance is received or until the performance occurs. For example, Barb has a contract calling for delivery of office furniture on June 15, but learns on June 10 that the seller's warehouse was totally destroyed by fire. Barb can demand adequate assurance and can suspend her performance until the seller either gives assurance or actually delivers conforming furniture on time. **Exam tip #4.**

B. <u>Anticipatory Repudiation</u>. **Anticipatory repudiation** is a clear indication in advance that one party will breach. The other party can await the performance deadline to see if the party will actually perform, or can treat the contract as breached at the point of the anticipatory repudiation. The latter would give the nonbreaching party an immediate right to sue without waiting until the performance deadline. The nonbreaching party could also safely enter into an alternate contract with another party. For example, if a buyer filed bankruptcy and would not be able to pay for goods purchased, the seller could treat that as anticipatory repudiation.

V. Seller's Remedies for Breach by Buyer.

A. <u>In General</u>. Remedies under the UCC have the same general goal as common law remedies, namely to provide the nonbreaching party with the benefit of the bargain, or stated differently, to put the nonbreaching party in the position she would have been in had the contract been fully performed. The UCC identifies a number of specific remedies available in reaching that goal. Some of the UCC remedies are aimed at reducing the nonbreaching party's loss. The nonbreaching party can usually choose from a number of remedies, and might be entitled to a combination of remedies if necessary to get the benefit of the bargain. The seller's remedies generally focus on getting the goods back from the breaching buyer, allowing the seller to find another buyer, and awarding damages to make the total recovery equal to the benefit of the bargain.

B. <u>Right to Withhold Delivery</u>. The seller may **withhold delivery** if the goods are in the possession of the seller at the time the buyer breaches. This includes any goods remaining in the seller's possession if partial delivery has already been made. If the buyer becomes insolvent prior to delivery, the seller can withhold delivery unless the buyer pays cash.

C. <u>Right to Stop Delivery of Goods in Transit</u>. Goods which are in the possession of common carriers and other bailees such as warehouses are said to be **in transit**. If the seller learns of the buyer's insolvency, the seller can stop delivery of goods in transit regardless of the shipment's size. If the buyer repudiates the contract, fails to make payment when due, or otherwise gives the seller the right to withhold goods, delivery can be stopped in transit, but only if the shipment constitutes a carload, truckload, planeload, etc. or larger shipment.

D. <u>Right to Reclaim Goods</u>. A seller can **reclaim** goods within 10 days of delivery if the seller discovers that the buyer was insolvent when the goods were received. If the buyer misrepresented his insolvency in writing within three months before delivery, the 10 day limit does not apply. Nor does the 10 day limit apply if the buyer paid with a check that was later dishonored. A lessor may recover leased goods any time the lessee is in default on the lease contract.

E. <u>Right to Dispose of Goods</u>. If the buyer repudiates before delivery, or if the seller has reacquired the goods, the seller can sell the goods to another buyer in any commercially reasonable manner in a public or private sale. The seller must notify the buyer in advance unless the goods threaten to decline quickly in value or are perishable.

F. <u>Unfinished Goods</u>. If the contract is breached while goods are in the process of being made, the seller has the choice to either:
   1. *Cease Production and Resell for Scrap or Salvage* or
   2. *Complete Production and Sell to Another Buyer.*

G. <u>Right to Recover the Purchase Price</u>. In some circumstances the seller can sue the buyer for the entire contract price, sometimes known as an **action for the price**. Any of the following allows an action for the price:
   1. *The Buyer Has Accepted the Goods, but Failed to Pay for Them When Due.*
   2. *The Buyer Breached After the Goods Were Identified, and the Seller Cannot Sell Them to Another Buyer or Otherwise Dispose of Them.*
   3. *The Goods Are Damaged or Lost After Risk of Loss Has Passed to the Buyer.*

   In each of these situations, the goods are either not in the possession of the seller, or they are unable to be sold to anyone other than the original buyer. Because the seller can receive no money elsewhere for the goods, the seller can recover the entire contract price from the buyer.

H. <u>Damages</u>. In addition to or in place of the above, the seller can recover damages for the breach. The seller is entitled to recover damages sufficient to put the nonbreaching seller in the place she would have been in if the contract had not been breached. This includes the right to recover incidental damages, such as transaction costs in selling to another buyer, and consequential damages, which can include lost profits in some circumstances.

I. <u>Lost Profits of Lost Volume Seller</u>. The damages recoverable by a retail seller can be computed one of two ways, depending on if the seller is a lost volume seller. A **lost volume seller** is a seller who has an unlimited supply of the item which was the subject of the breached contract. For example, a car dealer contracted to sell a car to Larry for $20,000 which had cost the dealer $17,000. Larry breached, and the dealer then sold the car to a different buyer for $19,000. The amount of damages recoverable depends on if the dealer is a lost volume seller with respect to the model car sold to Larry.
   1. *Dealer Is Not a Lost Volume Seller.* If this was a limited supply car, meaning that the dealer can buy only a fixed amount from the manufacturer, the dealer is entitled to the difference in the original contract price and the amount paid by the second buyer. A new popular car such as the new Volkswagen Beetle when first introduced, is an example. In this case, Larry's breach did not affect the number of cars sold, but only affected the amount of money received by the dealer for that particular car. If the dealer could only get five of these cars, for example, all that changed by Larry's breach is that one of the cars was sold for $19,000 which should have been sold to Larry for $20,000. The dealer can recover the $1,000 difference from Larry to preserve the benefit of its bargain.
   2. *Dealer Is a Lost Volume Seller.* If the dealer could get as many of this model car as it desired, it would be considered a lost volume seller with respect to this car. In this case, the dealer is entitled to the entire profit of $3,000 which it would have made from the sale to Larry. This is because Larry's breach caused the dealer to sell one less car, thereby losing the entire profit on that car. The dealer could have acquired another car from the manufacturer and sold it to the second buyer even if Larry had performed the contract.

J. <u>Multiple Remedies Available</u>. In many circumstances it will take several of these remedies to give the seller the benefit of the bargain. For example, a seller might reclaim goods from the seller, then resell them to a new buyer, and be entitled to damages if the price to the second buyer was lower than the contract price. The nonbreaching party is not entitled to collect from the breaching party such that he comes out better off than if the contract had been performed.

VI.   Buyer's Remedies.

A. <u>In General</u>. The buyer's remedies are also focused on getting the benefit of the bargain. Most often, the seller breaches by not delivering conforming goods. The buyer's remedies are generally focused on getting the contracted goods, or a substitute, to the buyer, and allowing the buyer to recover any additional costs from the seller.

B. <u>Right to Reject</u>. The buyer can reject nonconforming goods or goods that have been improperly tendered. Remember that the perfect tender rule, if not modified in the particular contract, allows the buyer to reject none, some, or all of a nonconforming shipment. The buyer must notify the seller of the rejection within a reasonable time and must hold the rejected goods with reasonable care for a reasonable time after rejection. The buyer must notify the seller of the specific defects on which the rejection is based. If the buyer fails to do so, the buyer cannot use those defects to justify the rejection if the seller could have cured with the proper notification.

C. <u>Revocation of Acceptance</u>. The buyer has the right to revoke an earlier acceptance if the conditions to do so have been met.

D. <u>Recover Goods from an Insolvent Seller</u>. If the buyer has made partial or full payment prior to receiving them and the seller becomes insolvent within 10 days after receiving the first payment, the buyer can recover, or **capture** the goods, so long as the buyer pays any remaining amount due under the contract.

E. <u>Specific Performance</u>. The buyer can obtain an order of specific performance ordering the seller to deliver unique goods, such as works of art, antiques, and coins, if other remedies such as damages would not be adequate for the buyer.

F. <u>Cover</u>. A buyer may **cover** its need for the contracted goods by purchasing substitute goods from another seller if the original seller has failed to deliver conforming goods to the buyer. Cover must be made in a commercially reasonable manner, and entitles the buyer to recover damages for any amount by which the cover price exceeds the contract price. For example, if a buyer contracted to purchase 100,000 pounds of bananas for $20,000, and after failure of the seller to deliver purchases the same quantity of bananas from another source for $24,000, the buyer could recover the $4,000 difference from the breaching seller. **Exam tip #5.**

D. <u>Replevy</u>. The term **replevy** describes a legal action to recover goods which are wrongfully in the possession of another, and applies in many areas of law other than contracts for the sale of goods. But where the goods are scarce and attempts at cover are unsuccessful (for replevy, it need not be shown that the goods are unique), the buyer can institute a replevy action to recover any goods that have been identified to the contract. **Exam tip #6.**

E. <u>Right to Cancel</u>. The seller's repudiation of the contract or failure to deliver goods gives the buyer the right to cancel the contract, at which point all obligations of the buyer are canceled. The buyer retains other applicable remedies against the seller, such as the right to collect damages.

F. <u>Damages</u>. In addition to these other remedies, the buyer has the right to recover damages from the breaching seller. This includes damages for failure to deliver conforming goods as well as damages resulting from the buyer accepting nonconforming goods.

G. <u>Multiple Remedies Available</u>. As with the seller, the buyer can use any consistent combination of the remedies necessary in order to receive the benefit of the bargain, or to be placed where the buyer would have been if the seller had breached.

VI.   Other Remedies Provisions.

A. <u>Statute of Limitations</u>. The **statute of limitations** for remedies under the UCC is four years, measured from the time of breach, whether or not the nonbreaching party was aware of the breach at the time it occurred. The parties may agree in their contract to shorten the period to as little as one year, but may not extend it beyond four years.

B. <u>Agreements Affecting Remedies</u>. The parties may agree to remedies in addition to or in place of those provided by the UCC. For example, the contract may provide a repair obligation on the seller in place of the buyer's right to reject for nonconformity.

1. *Consequential Damages*. A limitation or exclusion of consequential damages will be enforced unless it is unconscionable.

2. *Liquidated Damages*. A **liquidated damages** provision which fixes in advance the amount of damages in the event of a breach will be enforceable if it is reasonable in light of the anticipated actual harm and difficulties of determining actual damages. As under common law, an unreasonably large liquidated damages provision is void as against public policy, but very small liquidated damages provisions are acceptable.

EXAM TIPS

1. The perfect tender rule, if not modified, is absolute. A buyer is entitled to receive the exact goods agreed to in the contract, and any nonconformity allows the buyer to reject. This is why the parties frequently include contract provisions modifying the perfect tender rule.

2. Cure is a crucial concept. It is important to know both the basic rule and the circumstances under which the time is extended. It is also important to understand the interplay between cure and the perfect tender rule, and any modification to the perfect tender rule that the contract provides. For example, a provision allowing the seller to replace defective items might both limit the ability to reject goods <u>and</u> extend the cure period.

3. Revocation of acceptance can be confusing. First, remember that under the perfect tender rule, a nonconforming good can be rejected for any nonconformity. Once accepted, however, that acceptance can be revoked only under certain circumstances. Lastly, keep in mind the structure of the requirements where the third requirement can be met in three different ways.

4. Adequate assurance and anticipatory repudiation are often confused. Adequate assurance usually involves a substantial doubt, whereas with anticipatory repudiation it is more definite that there will be a breach. In the adequate assurance situation, the doubting party can merely suspend its own performance, whereas anticipatory repudiation allows the party to not only suspend its own performance, but to immediately treat the contract as breached. With adequate assurance, no breach can occur until the actual performance deadline passes without performance.

5. Cover is a remedy of the <u>buyer</u> only, even though the buyer has a parallel remedy, namely selling to another and collecting an additional amount as damages if appropriate. The term **cover**, though, is a remedy of the buyer only.

6. For replevy, uniqueness need not be shown, only scarcity. Replevy can be used where there might be thousands of an item, such as a popular new toy, but the item is in short supply because of great demand.

KEY CONCEPTS LIKELY TO BE TESTED ON THE CPA EXAM

1. The duties and obligations of the buyer and seller in a contract for the sale of goods.
2. The perfect tender rule, including the common modifications.
3. The right to cure, especially the general rule that it lasts only until the performance deadline.
4. Acceptance of goods and the different ways that acceptance can occur.
5. Revocation of acceptance.
6. Adequate assurance and anticipatory repudiation.
7. Remedies. The candidate should know all the remedies available to the buyer and all available to the seller. The candidate should know which are buyer's remedies and which are seller's remedies. The candidate should also be able to determine the dollar amount of damages which would be awarded in a particular fact situation.

KEY TERMS

Acceptance of Goods	Installment Contract	Action for the Price
Rejection of Goods	C.O.D. or Cash on Delivery	Lost Volume Seller
Tender of Delivery	Adequate Assurance	Capture of Goods
Bailee	Anticipatory Repudiation	Cover
Perfect Tender Rule	Withhold Delivery	Replevy
Conforming Goods	Goods in Transit	Statute of Limitations
Cure	Reclaim Goods	Liquidated Damages

MULTIPLE CHOICE QUESTIONS

1.   Law Nov 95 #48
Under the Sales Article of the UCC, and unless otherwise agreed to, the seller's obligation to the buyer is to
A. Deliver the goods to the buyer's place of business.
B. Hold conforming goods and give the buyer whatever notification is reasonably necessary to enable the buyer to take delivery.
C. Deliver all goods called for in the contract to a common carrier.
D. Set aside conforming goods for inspection by the buyer before delivery.

2.   Law Nov 93 #57
Cara Fabricating Co. and Taso Corp. agreed orally that Taso would custom manufacture a compressor for Cara at a price of $120,000. After Taso completed the work at a cost of $90,000, Cara notified Taso that the compressor was no longer needed. Taso is holding the compressor and has requested payment form Cara. Taso has been unable to resell the compressor for any price. Taso incurred storage fees of $2,000. If Cara refuses to pay Taso and Taso sues Cara, the most Taso will be entitled to recover is
A. $ 92,000.
B. $105,000.
C. $120,000.
D. $122,000.

3.   Law May 90 #46

Jefferson Hardware ordered three hundred Ram hammers from Ajax Hardware. Ajax accepted the order in writing. On the final date allowed for delivery, Ajax discovered it did not have enough Ram hammers to fill the order. Instead, Ajax sent three hundred Strong hammers. Ajax stated on the invoice that the shipment was sent only as an accommodation. Which of the following statements is correct?

A. Ajax's note of accommodation cancels the contract between Jefferson and Ajax.
B. Jefferson's order can only be accepted by Ajax's shipment of the good ordered.
C. Ajax's shipment of Strong hammers is a breach of contract.
D. Ajax's shipment of Strong hammers is a counteroffer and **no** contract exists between Jefferson and Ajax.

4.   Law May 92 #56

On February 15, Mazur Corp. contracted to sell 1,000 bushels of wheat to Good Bread, Inc. at $6.00 per bushel with delivery to be made on June 23. On June 1, Good advised Mazur that it would not accept or pay for the wheat. On June 2, Mazur sold the wheat to another customer at the market price of $5.00 per bushel. Mazur had advised Good that it intended to resell the wheat. Which of the following statements is correct?

A. Mazur can successfully sue Good for the difference between the resale price and the contract price.
B. Mazur can resell the wheat only after June 23.
C. Good can retract its anticipatory breach at any time before June 23.
D. Good can successfully sue Mazur for specific performance.

5.   Law Nov 94 #56

Rowe Corp. purchased goods from Stair Co. that were shipped C.O.D. Under the Sales Article of the UCC, which of the following rights does Rowe have?

A. The right to inspect the goods before paying.
B. The right to possession of the goods before paying.
C. The right to reject nonconforming goods.
D. The right to delay payment for a reasonable period of time.

6.   Law Nov 94 #55

Under the Sales Article of the UCC, which of the following events will release the buyer from all its obligations under a sales contract?

A. Destruction of the goods after risk of loss passed to the buyer.
B. Impracticability of delivery under the terms of the contract.
C. Anticipatory repudiation by the buyer that is retracted before the seller cancels the contract.
D. Refusal of the seller to give written assurance of performance when reasonably demanded by the buyer.

7.   Law May 92 #59

Under the UCC Sales Article, a seller will be entitled to recover the full contract price from the buyer when the

A. Goods are destroyed after title passed to the buyer.
B. Goods are destroyed while risk of loss is with the buyer.
C. Buyer revokes its acceptance of the goods.
D. Buyer rejects some of the goods.

OTHER OBJECTIVE FORMAT QUESTION (Estimated time -- 10 to 15 minutes)

Law May 95 #3(a)

Question Number 3 consists of two parts. Each part consists of 6 items. Select the **best** answer for each item. Use a No. 2 pencil to blacken the appropriate ovals on the *Objective Answer Sheet* to indicate your answers. **Answer all items**. Your grade will be based on the total number of correct answers.

a. On February 1, 1995, Grand Corp., a manufacturer of custom cabinets, contracted in writing with Axle Co., a kitchen contractor, to sell Axle 100 unique, custom-designed, kitchen cabinets for $250,000. Axle had contracted to install the cabinets in a luxury condominium complex. The contract provided that the cabinets were to be ready for delivery by April 15 and were to be shipped F.O.B. sellers loading dock. On April 15, Grand had 85 cabinets complete and delivered them, together with 15 standard cabinets, to the trucking company for delivery to Axle. Grand faxed Axle a copy of the shipping invoice, listing the 15 standard cabinets. On May 1, before reaching Axle, the truck was involved in a collision and all the cabinets were damaged beyond repair.

Required:

Items 1 through 6 refer to the above fact pattern. For each item, determine whether A, B, or C is correct. On the *Objective Answer Sheet*, blacken the oval that corresponds to the correct statement.

1. A. The contract between Grand and Axle was a shipment contract.
   B. The contract between Grand and Axle was a destination contract.
   C. The contract between Grand and Axle was a consignment contract.

2. A. The risk of loss for the 15 custom cabinets passed to Axle on April 15.
   B. The risk of loss for the 100 cabinets passed to Axle on April 15.
   C. The risk of loss for the 100 cabinets remained with Grand.

3. A. The contract between Grand and Axle was invalid because **no** delivery date was stated.
   B. The contract between Grand and Axle was voidable because Grand shipped only 85 custom cabinets.
   C. The contract between Grand and Axle was void because the goods were destroyed.

4. A. Grand's shipment of the standard cabinets was a breach of the contract with Axle.
   B. Grand would **not** be considered to have breached the contract until Axle rejected the standard cabinets.
   C. Grand made a counteroffer by shipping the standard cabinets.

5. A. Had the cabinets been delivered, title would **not** transfer to Axle until Axle inspected them.
   B. Had the cabinets been delivered, title would have transferred on delivery to the carrier.
   C. Had the cabinets been delivered, title would **not** have transferred because the cabinets were nonconforming.

6. A. Axle is entitled to specific performance from Grand because of the unique nature of the goods.
   B. Axle is required to purchase substitute goods (cover) and is entitled to the difference in cost from Grand.
   C. Axle is entitle to punitive damages because of Grand's intentional shipment of nonconforming goods.

ESSAY QUESTIONS

Essay #1.   Law R98 #1

On June 1, Classic Corp., a manufacturer of desk chairs, orally agreed to sell 100 leather desk chairs to Rand Stores, a chain of retail furniture stores, for $50,000. The parties agreed that delivery would be completed by September 1, and the shipping terms were "F.O.B. seller's loading dock." On June 5, Classic sent Rand a signed memorandum of agreement containing the terms orally agreed to. Rand received the memorandum on June 7 and made no response.

On July 31, Classic identified the chairs to be shipped to Rand and placed them on its loading dock to be picked up by the common carrier the next day. That night, a fire on the loading dock destroyed 50 of the chairs. On August 1, the remaining 50 chairs were delivered to the common carrier together with 50 vinyl chairs. The truck carrying the chairs was involved in an accident, resulting in extensive damage to 10 of the leather chairs and 25 of the vinyl chairs.

On August 10, the chairs were delivered to Rand. On August 12, Rand notified Classic that Rand was accepting 40 of the leather chairs and 10 of the vinyl chairs, but the rest of the shipment was being rejected. Rand also informed Classic that, due to Classic's failure to perform under the terms of the contract, Rand would seek all remedies available under the Sales Article of the UCC. Classic contended that it has no liability to Rand and

that the shipment was strictly an accommodation to Rand because Rand failed to sign the memorandum of agreement, thus preventing a contract from being formed.

The above parties and transactions are governed by the provisions of the Sales Article of the UCC.

Required:

a. Determine whether Classic's contention is correct and give the reason for your conclusion.

b. Assuming that a valid contract exists between Classic and Rand, answer the following questions and give the reasons for your conclusions. Do not consider any possible liability owed by the common carrier.

1. Who bears the risk of loss for the 50 destroyed leather chairs?

2. Who bears the risk of loss for the 25 damaged vinyl chairs?

3. What is the earliest date that title to any of the chairs would pass to Rand?

c. With what UCC requirements must Rand comply to be entitled to recover damages from Classic?

d. Assuming that a valid contract exists between Classic and Rand, state the applicable remedies to which Rand would be entitled. Do not consider any possible liability owed by the common carrier.

(Estimated time -- 15 to 20 minutes)
Essay #2.   Law Nov 91 #4

On October 10, Vesta Electronics contracted with Zap Audio to sell Zap 200 18" stereo speakers. The contract provided that the speakers would be shipped F.O.B. seller's loading dock. The contract was silent as to when risk of loss for the speakers would pass to Zap. Delivery was to be completed by November 10.

On October 18, Vesta identified the speakers to be shipped to Zap and moved them to the loading dock. Before the carrier picked up the goods, a fire on Vesta's loading dock destroyed 50 of the speakers. On October 20, Vesta shipped, by common carrier, the remaining 150 18" speakers and 50 16" speakers. The truck carrying the speakers was involved in an accident resulting in damage to 25 of the 16" speakers. Zap received the 200 speakers on October 25, and on October 27 notified Vesta that 100 of the 18" speakers were being accepted, but the rest of the shipment was being rejected. Zap also

informed Vesta that, due to Vesta's failure to comply with the terms of the contract, Zap would contest paying contract price and would sue for damages. The above parties and transactions are subject to the Uniform Commercial Code (UCC).

Required:

Answer the following questions, and give the reasons for your conclusions.

a. 1. Who bears the risk of loss for the 50 destroyed 18" speakers?

2. Who bears the risk of loss for the 25 damaged 16" speakers?

b. 1. Was Zap's rejection of the 16" speakers valid?

2. Was Zap's rejection of some of the 18" speakers valid?

c. Under the UCC, what duties are required of Zap after rejecting all or part of the shipment?

EXPLANATIONS TO MULTIPLE CHOICE QUESTIONS

1. B is the correct answer. The gap filling rule where a contract does not specify anything with respect to delivery is for the buyer to pick up the goods at the seller's place of business. In addition, the seller must give reasonable notification to the buyer. Choices A and D are incorrect because there is no obligation to deliver the goods to the buyer unless the contract specifically provides for it.

2. D is the correct answer. Where a seller cannot resell the goods to another buyer, the seller is entitled to recover the full purchase price from the breaching buyer. Such a lawsuit is known as an action for the price. In addition, the seller is entitled to recover any other reasonable costs related to the breach. Choice A is incorrect because the seller is entitled to recover the benefit of the bargain by recovering the entire contract price, not merely the cost of the goods.

3. C is the correct answer. This is a difficult question. An accommodation shipment operates as a counteroffer only where the seller has not already accepted the offer by promising to ship conforming goods. Here, because the seller has already accepted the offer (the order from Jefferson), shipment of goods other than those called for in the contract is a breach. Choice D would be correct if only Ajax had not already accepted the order by promising to ship conforming goods.

4. A is the correct answer. Good Bread committed an anticipatory breach of the contract when it notified Mazur that it would not accept or pay for the wheat. Upon anticipatory breach, the nonbreaching party can immediately treat the contract as breached without waiting until the actual performance deadline. By treating the contract as breached, the seller can seek to resell the goods to a different buyer, and usually must seek to do so because of the duty to mitigate damages. The seller must notify the buyer of the intent to resell the goods unless they must be sold quickly due to spoilage or other deterioration in value. If successful in finding another buyer, the seller is entitled to recover the difference in the original contract price and the price received from the alternate buyer. This enables the seller to preserve the benefit of the bargain.

5. C is the correct answer. Under a C.O.D. the buyer is not entitled to possess or inspect the goods until they have been paid for. The buyer is still able to reject nonconforming goods, but under a C.O.D. contract such a rejection normally would occur only after payment has been made.

6. D is the correct answer. Choice A is incorrect because the seller's duty to pay for the goods would not be discharged. Choice B is incorrect because it is possible that the impracticality of delivery was caused by the buyer, and it is possible that alternate delivery arrangements can be made. Choice C is incorrect because the retraction of the anticipatory repudiation would reinstate the seller's obligations so long as the seller has not yet canceled the contract.

7. B is the correct answer. If the risk of loss is on the buyer when the goods are destroyed, the goods cannot be resold, and the seller is entitled to receive the full contract price. Choice A is incorrect because risk of loss is not always on the party who has title to the goods. Under the UCC, risk of loss is primarily determined by the contract's shipping terms, not by title.

EXPLANATION TO OTHER OBJECTIVE FORMAT QUESTION

Law May 95 #3(a)

This question can be viewed as a set of multiple choice questions or, more accurately, a series of true/false questions. Each set of three statements requires that the candidate choose the one true statement from among the three. Note that there is no separate question related to each of the three statements, thus the candidate must merely determine whether each statement is true or false and select the true one. The structure of this question is different from the situation where there are several different specific multiple choice questions based on a single set of facts.

1. A is the correct answer. The term "F.O.B. shipping point" means that this is a shipment contract because the F.O.B. point is the point of shipment rather than destination.

2. C is the correct answer. The perfect tender rule allows rejection of all items shipped if the tender is less than exactly as called for in the contract. Here, the shipping of the 15 nonconforming cabinets allows the buyer to reject any or all of the goods. Choice A is incorrect because with such a breach, the risk of loss remains on the seller, even for the 85 conforming cabinets.

3. B is the correct answer. Because Axle Corp. could reject all 100 cabinets, the contract was voidable. Choice C is incorrect because Grand Corp. bore the risk of loss at the time the goods were destroyed, and their destruction does not discharge the obligation to deliver the goods under the terms of the contract.

4. A is the correct answer. Grand had already agreed to ship the conforming cabinets prior to the shipping of the nonconforming cabinets. Choice C is incorrect because the nonconforming shipment would be considered a counteroffer only if it was an accommodation shipment. It would qualify as such only if Grand was responding to an offer to buy made by Axle, if Grand had not yet promised to send conforming goods, and if Grand notified Axle that the nonconforming goods were being shipped as an accommodation. These requirements were not met here.

5. C is the correct answer. Title would transfer only if Axle accepted the nonconforming goods, which did not happen here.

6. A is the correct answer. Choice B is incorrect because Axle is not required to take any particular action. If Axle were able to purchase substitute goods, then Axle would be entitled to the difference in price, but Axle would not be required to purchase the substitute goods. Choice C is incorrect because punitive damages are generally not available in breach of contract actions.

UNOFFICIAL AICPA ANSWERS TO ESSAY QUESTIONS

Essay #1.   Law R98 #1

a. Classic's contention is incorrect. Under the provisions of the Sales Article of the UCC, a written memorandum stating an agreement between merchants does not have to be signed by both parties. The contract is enforceable against Classic because Classic signed the memorandum and against Rand because Rand did not object to the memorandum within 10 days after receiving it.

b. 1. Classic bears the risk of loss for the 50 leather chairs destroyed in the fire. Even though the goods were identified to the contract and placed on the loading dock, the risk of loss remains with Classic. The shipping terms "F.O.B. seller's loading dock" provide that risk of loss remains with the seller until the goods are delivered to the common carrier. The 50 leather chairs destroyed in the fire had not yet been delivered to the carrier.

2. Classic bears the risk of loss for the damaged vinyl chairs. Even though these goods were delivered to the common carrier, the risk of loss did not pass to Rand because the vinyl chairs were nonconforming goods.

3. August 1 was the earliest date that title to any of the chairs passed to Rand. Title passed when goods identified to the contract were delivered to the carrier.   [continued]

c. Under the Sales Article of the UCC, for Rand to be entitled to damages from Classic, Rand must comply with the following requirements:

- Rand has to notify Classic of the rejection of the goods within a reasonable time.
- Rand must act in good faith with respect to the rejected goods by following any reasonable instructions from Classic.

d. Rand would be entitled to the following remedies:

- The right to cancel the contract.
- The right of cover.
- The right to recover monetary damages for nondelivery.

Essay #2.   Law Nov 91 #4

a. 1. Vesta Electronics would bear the risk of loss for the 18" speakers destroyed by the fire on its loading dock. Even though Vesta identified and segregated the goods on its loading dock, the risk of loss remained with the seller because the contract's shipping terms "F.O.B. sellers's loading dock" made it a shipment contract. Thus, risk of loss does not pass to Zap until the goods are delivered to the carrier.

2. The risk of loss for the 16" speakers also remained with Vesta. Even though the goods were delivered to the common carrier, risk of loss did not pass because Vesta shipped nonconforming goods.

b. 1. Zap may validly reject the 16" speakers because any buyer may reject nonconforming goods. To avoid potential liability, the rejection must be made within a commercially reasonable time of receipt and must be communicated to the seller.

2. Zap may also validly accept some of the 18" speakers. A buyer may accept none, all, or any commercial unit of a shipment when nonconforming goods are shipped.

c. To be entitled to damages, Zap must comply with the UCC by notifying Vesta of the rejection of the goods within a reasonable time; acting in good faith with respect to the rejected goods by following any reasonable instructions of the seller; and giving Vesta the opportunity to cure until the contract time of performance expires.

Author's Note:

These two essay questions are very similar, but do contain important fact differences. More important, note that the structure of the answers differs more than that of the questions. In the first essay, the answer for part **(c.)** does not mention the right to cure which would be just as applicable as in the second essay question. Also notice that the answer to the first question, which is more recent, made use of bullet points in the answer. It also probably would be worth mentioning in either answer that the risk of loss for the conforming items also remained on the seller until acceptance due to the fact that some of the items were nonconforming.

CHAPTER 13
WARRANTIES AND PRODUCT LIABILITY

OVERVIEW

This is the last chapter covering contracts for the sale of goods. The first part of the chapter addresses the warranties made in a sale of goods contract. It is important to understand that the familiar warranty obligating a seller to repair or replace an item for a fixed period of time is only one of the many possible kinds of warranties. Some warranties arise automatically and others exist only if the parties specifically agree to them. The rules can be confusing but it is vital for CPA exam candidates to keep them straight. The second part of this chapter covers products liability. Products liability law is not actually part of Article 2 of the UCC, but is based primarily on common law. Products liability law relates to goods which have been sold as part of an Article 2 contract and has begun to be tested in recent years.

OUTLINE

I. **Warranties.**
   A. <u>In General</u>. In a sales contract, there are several warranties which can apply. Some are **implied warranties** meaning that they automatically apply, while others are **express warranties** which apply only if there has been some expression of the warranted characteristic or obligation. Some warranties relate to the seller's ownership of the goods and right to sell them and others relate to the quality or other characteristics of the goods themselves. A last issue that frequently arises is the effect of an attempted disclaimer of a warranty. The various warranties are discussed first, followed by a discussion of the disclaimer rules. The warranties also generally apply to lease transactions even though this outline focuses on warranties in the sale context.
   B. <u>Warranties of Title</u>. There is a general **implied warranty of good title** that applies to all sales unless it is properly disclaimed. This is a warranty to the buyer that the seller's transfer of title (ownership) to the buyer is rightful. There are other implied warranties that relate to specific aspects of title:
      1. *Warranty of No Security Interests*. The **warranty of no security interests** warrants that there are no undisclosed liens, security interests, etc. applicable to the goods.
      2. *Warranty of No Infringements*. The **warranty of no infringements** applies to merchants and warrants that the goods sold are free of any third-party patent, copyright, or trademark infringement claim.
      3. *Warranty Against Interference*. The **warranty against interference,** or **warranty of quiet possession**, applies to leased goods because the lessor does not purport to transfer title to the lessee. The lessor does warrant to the lessee that the lessee's use of the goods as provided for in the contract will not be interfered with as a consequence of any action or failure to act by the lessor.

C. <u>Warranties of Quality</u>. Warranties of quality can be grouped into express and implied categories.
   1. *Express Warranties.* Express warranties arise from any express factual affirmation, by words or conduct, of the seller. Express warranties can be written or oral. The factual affirmation does not need to state that it is a warranty or otherwise use the word warranty for it to be one. Express warranties can arise in many ways, including:
      a. Affirmation of Fact. For example, "This desk is made of solid oak." The warranty is breached if the desk is not solid oak.
      b. Promise About the Product. For example, "This carpet will not show any wear for at least 5 years."
      c. Description of the Product. For example, "This shoe is made of Italian leather." The warranty is breached if the shoe is not made of Italian leather.
      d. Model or Sample. For example, the fabric in draperies ordered based on a sample must be the same as the sample.
      e. Picture of Product in an Advertisement or on a Package.
      In order for a buyer to recover for the breach of an express warranty, it must have been a factor, though not necessarily the only factor, in inducing the buyer to purchase the item. In much the same way that **statements of opinion** or **puffing** cannot form the basis of a fraud claim, such statements do not amount to an express warranty. **Exam tip #1.**
   2. *Implied Warranty of Merchantability.* The **implied warranty of merchantability** warrants that goods are fit for their ordinary use and would pass in the trade as being acceptable. The warranty applies only if the seller is a merchant in the goods of the transaction. The UCC specifies a number of standards which must be met:
      a. The goods must be fit for the ordinary purposes for which they are used.
      b. The goods must be adequately contained, packaged, and labeled.
      c. The goods must be of an even kind, quality, and quantity within each unit.
      d. The goods must conform to any promise or affirmation of fact made on the container or label.
      e. The quality of the goods must pass without objection in the trade.
      f. Fungible goods must meet a fair average or middle range of quality. A **fungible good** is an item which does not differ significantly among different producers where a unit from one producer can be substituted for that of another, such as wheat or gasoline.
   3. *Implied Warranty of Fitness for a Particular Purpose.* The **implied warranty of fitness for a particular purpose** warrants that a product will be satisfactory for a particular use. It applies only if certain conditions exist, but it can apply to either a merchant or nonmerchant seller. This warranty applies if all of the following exist:
      a. The seller has reason to know the particular purpose for which the buyer is purchasing the goods.
      c. The the seller knows that the buyer is relying on the seller's skill or judgment.
      b. The seller makes a statement that the goods will serve this purpose.
      For example, Sam told a salesperson at a hardware store that he needed a power drill that he would be using to drill through half-inch thick steel. The salesperson recommended a particular model in stock. There would be a breach of warranty if the drill was not powerful enough for half-inch thick steel. **Exam tip #2.**

D. <u>Overlapping and Inconsistent Warranties</u>. Multiple warranties can exist in a transaction and will be cumulative unless they are inconsistent. The UCC provides rules to determine which applies if they are inconsistent:
   1. Express warranties displace inconsistent implied warranties other than implied warranties of fitness for a particular purpose.
   2. Exact or technical specifications displace inconsistent models or general language of description.
   3. A sample from an existing bulk displaces inconsistent general language of description.
E. <u>Warranty Disclaimers</u>. A **warranty disclaimer** is a provision stating that a warranty does not apply. Some of the warranties can be disclaimed only with specific language. Problems arise when warranties and disclaimers are both present and are inconsistent with one another. Written disclaimers must be conspicuous. The disclaimer rules are:
   1. If an express warranty is made, it can be limited if the disclaimer and warranty can be reasonably construed with each other, but to the extent that is unreasonable, the disclaimer is inoperative.
   2. All implied warranties of quality can be disclaimed by language such as "with all faults" or "as is" or other language that clearly indicates that there are no implied warranties.
   3. If the above language is not used to disclaim all implied warranties, the implied warranty of merchantability can be disclaimed only by using the word "merchantability."
   4. The implied warranty of fitness for a particular purpose can be disclaimed without using the word "fitness." "There are no warranties which extend beyond the description on the face hereof," is sufficient.
   5. If the seller demands that the buyer examine goods, and the buyer examines them as fully as she desires or refuses to examine them, there are no implied warranties with respect to any defects that the examination should have discovered. The examination would not eliminate implied warranties related to latent defects that the examination would not be expected to uncover.
   6. The warranty of title can be disclaimed <u>only</u> by using the word "title" or by the seller clearly indicating that the seller was only conveying whatever title the seller had, if any. Thus a statement saying that "there are absolutely no warranties, express or implied," would <u>not</u> disclaim the warranty of title. **Exam tip #3.**
F. <u>Damages for Breach of Warranty</u>. Breach of warranty is a type of breach of contract. If the buyer seeks damages for breach of warranty, the measure of damages is generally the difference in value of the good as warranted and the actual good, both measured as of the time the goods were accepted. Consequential and incidental damages are allowable as they are for other breaches of contract.
G. <u>Statute of Limitations</u>. The four year statute of limitations applies to breach of warranty claims, and like other breach of warranty claims can be limited by terms of the contract to a period as short as one year. The period begins to run when the goods are tendered to the buyer. The statute of limitations cannot be extended except if the warranty applies to future performance of the good, such as a five-year warranty to repair any problems that arise.

II. Strict Liability for Injuries Caused by Goods.

A. <u>Negligence</u>. Although it is possible to bring a case based on **negligence** for an injury caused by a product, it is seldom done anymore. This is because there is so much less to prove in a products liability case based on strict liability. In general, a negligence case involves fault on the part of the defendant, and for the plaintiff to win requires the plaintiff to prove:

1. *A Duty Owed by the Defendant to the Plaintiff.*
2. *A Breach of That Duty.*
3. *An Injury to the Plaintiff.*
4. *Actual Causation.*
5. *Proximate Causation, or Foreseeability.*

The CPA exam has not tested much on this recently, but it is presented here to distinguish negligence from strict liability products liability which has been recently tested.

B. <u>Products Liability Cases Based on Strict Liability</u>. Most cases today for injuries caused by products are brought on the basis of **strict liability**, which means that defendant can be liable even though there is no fault on the part of the defendant.

1. *Required Elements.* In order to prove a products liability case, the plaintiff must prove:
   a. That the plaintiff was injured.
   b. The injury was caused by the product.
   c. The injury was due to a defect in the product.
   d. The product was sold by the defendant with that defect present.
   e. The defendant was in the business of selling goods.

2. *Not Required to Be Proven.* For the CPA exam, it is just as important to know what does <u>not</u> need to be proven by the plaintiff:
   a. Negligence. Proof of negligence is not required in a products liability suit, nor are some of its components which are separately listed below. Even if the defendant did nothing wrong, the defendant can be held liable if the required elements are proven.
   b. Duty and Breach of Duty. These components of negligence need not be proven.
   c. Foreseeability of the Injury. This component of negligence need not be proven.
   d. Privity of Contract. To be in **privity of contract** simply means that two parties are in a contractual relationship. To recover in products liability, the plaintiff need not be in privity of contract with the defendant.
   e. That the plaintiff was the purchaser, owner, or user of the product that caused the injury. Any user of a product can recover in products liability, and in most states bystanders can recover as well. **Exam tip #4.**

3. *Who Can Be Liable.* Any party who sold the good after the defect occurred can be held liable. Thus, anyone who sold the good prior to the occurrence of the defect is not liable. For example, a tire manufacturer sold a defective tire to a car manufacturer who installed the tire on a car. If the retail purchaser was injured by the tire, the tire manufacturer, car manufacturer, and car dealer could all be liable because each of them sold the tire with the defect present. If, on the other hand, the car dealer damaged the tire, then only the car dealer could be held liable because the defect was not present in the tire when sold by the tire manufacturer and was not present when sold by the car manufacturer. Sales by persons not in the business of selling goods do not result in liability.

4. *Defects.* Only safety-related defects which make a product unreasonably dangerous can result in liability. There are four main types of defects. **Exam tip #5.**
   a. Manufacturing Defect. A **manufacturing defect** is a defect affecting only the particular sample (or all items for a relatively short period of time) resulting from a problem in the manufacture of that particular item.
   b. Design Defect. A **design defect** is a defect where the design itself is unreasonably dangerous so that all manufactured items have the same defect.
   c. Failure to Warn or Provide Adequate Instructions. A **failure to warn** will result in the product being considered defective even though the only problem is the lack of a warning of instructions.
   d. Defect in Packaging. A **packaging defect** generally applies to medicines and poisons where the packaging itself does not cause the injury, but allows access to the product which then causes an injury. The contained product is not defective. A soft drink bottle which explodes causing injury to the user is not a defect in packaging because the product itself, the bottle, was defective and caused the injury. It would be either a design or manufacturing defect in the bottle depending on the circumstances.
5. *Defenses.* Because there is so little that the plaintiff must prove, the defenses are crucial in many products liability cases. If the plaintiff can prove the elements of the case, the defendant gets a chance to try to prove the existence of a defense. If successful in proving the presence of any one defense, the defendant will not be liable and thus will win the case.
   a. Supervening Event. A **supervening event** is an event that occurred after the product was sold by the defendant. This could be a later event causing the defect (thus the defect was not present with the defendant sold it), or some other event which led to the injury.
   b. Assumption of the Risk. **Assumption of the risk** occurs if the plaintiff knew and appreciated the risk and voluntarily assumed the risk.
   c. Generally Known Danger. A **generally known danger** is one which the general population is aware of, such as the dangers of a cigarette lighter, or, at least today, of cigarettes themselves.
   d. Correction of a Defect. **Correction of a defect** applies if the defendant has tried to correct the problem in the particular item that caused the injury. This is usually done through a recall. The focus here is the manufacturer's efforts, and if adequate, the defense will be effective even if the owner ignored the recall notice. Merely redesigning the product to eliminate the defect in future production does not qualify as correction of a defect.
   e. Unforeseeable Misuse of a Product. The **unforeseeable misuse** defense is effective only if the misuse was unforeseeable. For example, a car designed to hold five passengers must be designed so that the axles will support the car with six or seven passengers because this is foreseeable misuse, but it need not be designed to support the car while carrying 20 passengers. If the plaintiff's misuse was unforeseeable, the defendant is not liable.
   f. Unavoidable Danger. Some products have **unavoidable dangers** which cannot be designed away, and because of the product's usefulness, the risk is considered acceptable. Generally known danger often will also apply in the situation.

6. *Not a Defense.* **Contributory** and **comparative negligence** are negligence on the part of the plaintiff which was a contributing cause of the injury. They are usually not allowed as a defense in products liability, but some courts have recently allowed the defense, especially if the plaintiff's conduct amounts to gross negligence. Also not recognized as a defense is any claim that the design is the industry norm. The mere fact that everyone in an industry is posing the same danger does not protect a defendant.

EXAM TIPS

1. Because there is no limit to the statements or affirmations a seller might make, there is no limit to the situations where an express warranty might exist. It is important to remember that the statement does not have to be labeled as a warranty in order to be a warranty.
2. The implied warranties of merchantability and fitness for a particular purpose are easily confused. The candidate must know the conditions under which each can apply, what each warrants, and to whom each can apply.
3. Exam candidates should be sure to know exactly what is required to disclaim each of the implied warranties.
4. It is important to know what is required and what is not required to be proven in a products liability case.
5. The defects that apply in products liability are only those defects that make a product unreasonably dangerous. The examiners seem to have focused on the basic elements needed to prove a products liability case, but there is nothing to prevent them from asking more detailed questions on defects and defenses.

KEY CONCEPTS LIKELY TO BE TESTED ON THE CPA EXAM

1. General characteristics of warranties, especially the implied warranties.
2. Classification of a particular warranty as express or implied.
3. Whether a particular warranty applies in a specific situation.
4. Ability to recognize representations leading to the presence of an express warranty.
5. Disclaimers of implied warranties.
6. The elements required to prove a products liability case, and who can be held liable.
7. The concept of defect as an unreasonably dangerous condition.

KEY TERMS

Express Warranty
Implied Warranty
Statement of Opinion
Puffing
Merchantability
Fitness for a Particular Purpose
Warranty Disclaimer
Negligence
Strict Liability

Privity of Contract
Manufacturing Defect
Design Defect
Failure to Warn
Packaging Defect
Supervening Event
Assumption of the Risk
Generally Known Danger
Correction of a Defect

Implied Warranty of Good Title
Warranty of No Security Interests
Warranty of No Infringements
Warranty Against Interference
Warranty of Quiet Possession
Unforeseeable Misuse
Unavoidable Danger
Contributory Negligence
Comparative Negligence

MULTIPLE CHOICE QUESTIONS

1.   Law May 92 #57
Under the UCC Sales Article, an action for breach of the implied warranty of merchantability by a party who sustains personal injuries may be successful against the seller of the product only when
A. The seller is a merchant of the product involved.
B. An action based on negligence can also be successfully maintained.
C. The injured party is in privity of contract with the seller.
D. An action based on strict liability in tort can also be successfully maintained.

2.   Law May 92 #60
Which of the following factors result(s) in an express warranty with respect to a sale of goods?

I. The seller's description of the goods as part of the basis of the bargain.
II. The seller selects goods knowing the buyer's intended use.

A. I only.
B. II only.
C. Both I and II.
D. Neither I nor II.

3.   Law Nov 95 #43
Under the Sales Article of the UCC, the warranty of title
A. Provides that the seller cannot disclaim the warranty if the sale is made to a bona fide purchaser for value.
B. Provides that the seller deliver the goods free from any lien of which the buyer lacked knowledge when the contract was made.
C. Applies only if it is in writing and signed by the seller.
D. Applies only if the seller is a merchant.

4.   Law May 92 #55
Which of the following conditions must be met for an implied warranty of fitness for a particular purpose to arise in connection with a sale of goods?

I. The warranty must be in writing.
II. The seller must know that the buyer was relying on the seller in selecting the goods.

A. I only.
B. II only.
C. Both I and II.
D. Neither I nor II.

5.   Law Nov 95 #44

To establish a cause of action based on strict liability in tort for personal injuries that result from the use of a defective product, one of the elements the injured party must prove is that the seller

A. Was aware of the defect in the product.
B. Sold the product to the injured party.
C. Failed to exercise due care.
D. Sold the product in a defective condition.

6.   Law Nov 94 #51

Under the Sales Article of the UCC, which of the following statements is correct regarding the warranty of merchantability arising when there has been a sale of goods by a merchant seller?

A. The warranty must be in writing.
B. The warranty arises when the buyer relies on the seller's skill in selecting the goods purchased.
C. The warranty cannot be disclaimed.
D. The warranty arises as a matter of law when the seller ordinarily sells the goods purchased.

7.   Law Nov 94 #53

High sues the manufacturer, wholesaler, and retailer for bodily injuries caused by a power saw High purchased. Which of the following statements is correct under strict liability theory?

A. Contributory negligence on High's part will always be a bar to recovery.
B. The manufacturer will avoid liability if it can show it followed the custom of the industry.
C. Privity will be a bar to recovery insofar as the wholesaler is concerned if the wholesaler did **not** have a reasonable opportunity to inspect.
D. High may recover even if he **cannot** show any negligence was involved.

8.   Law May 94 #43

Vick bought a used boat from Ocean Marina that disclaimed "any and all warranties" in connection with the sale. Ocean was unaware the boat had been stolen from Kidd. Vick surrendered it to Kidd when confronted with proof of the theft. Vick sued Ocean. Who is likely to prevail and why?

A. Vick, because the implied warranty of title has been breached.
B. Vick, because a merchant **cannot** disclaim implied warranties.
C. Ocean, because of the disclaimer of warranties.
D. Ocean, because Vick surrendered the boat to Kidd.

9.   Law May 94 #44

Larch Corp. manufactured and sold Oak a stove. The sale documents included a disclaimer of warranty for personal injury. The stove was defective. It exploded causing serious injuries to Oak's spouse. Larch was notified one week after the explosion. Under the UCC Sales Article, which of the following statements concerning Larch's liability for personal injury to Oak's spouse would be correct?

A. Larch **cannot** be liable because of a lack of privity with Oak's spouse.
B. Larch will **not** be liable because of a failure to give proper notice.
C. Larch will be liable because the disclaimer was **not** a disclaimer of all liability.
D. Larch will be liable because liability for personal injury **cannot** be disclaimed.

ESSAY QUESTION (Estimated time -- 15 to 20 minutes)

Law Nov 90 #4

Pharo Aviation, Inc. sells and services used airplanes. Sanders, Pharo's service department manager, negotiated with Secure Equipment Co. for the purchase of a used tug for moving airplanes in and out of Pharo's hangar. Secure sells and services tugs and related equipment. Sanders was unfamiliar with the various models, specifications, and capacities of the tugs sold by Secure; however, Sanders knew that the tug purchased needed to have the capacity to move airplanes weighing up to 10,000 pounds. Sanders and the sales representative discussed this specific need because Sanders was uncertain as to which tug would meet Pharo's requirements. The sales representative then recommended a particular make and model of tug. Sanders agreed to rely on the sales representative's advice and signed a purchase contract with Secure.

About a week after Sanders took delivery, the following occurred:

- Sanders determined that the tug did not have the capacity to move airplanes weighing over 5,000 pounds.
- Sanders was advised correctly by Maco Equipment Distributors, Inc. that Maco was the rightful owner of the tug, which it had left with Secure for repairs.

Pharo has commenced a lawsuit against Secure claiming that implied warranties were created by the contract with Secure and that these have been breached. Maco has claimed that it is entitled to the tug and has demanded its return from Pharo.

Required:

Answer each of the following questions, and set forth the reasons for your conclusions.

a. Were any implied warranties created by the contract between Pharo and Secure and, if so, were any of those warranties breached?

b. Is Maco entitled to the return of the tug?

EXPLANATIONS TO MULTIPLE CHOICE QUESTIONS

1. A is the correct answer. The implied warranty of merchantability applies only if the seller is a merchant in the type of good which was sold. This could be a difficult question because it relates to a personal injury claim under the warranty of merchantability. Most personal injury claims are brought under strict liability, which has different requirements. However, the requirement that the seller be a merchant of the type of good sold also applies to strict liability cases. Choice C is incorrect because the implied warranty of merchantability extends to parties other than the purchaser. Choices B and D are incorrect because an action based on breach of warranty is separate from other causes of action and does not require that the other causes of action also be successful.

2. A is the correct answer. Any description of the goods, including pictures and models, result in an express warranty. The seller's knowledge of the buyer's intended use relates to the implied warranty of fitness for a particular purpose and not to express warranties.

3. B is the correct answer. The warranty of title is an implied warranty which warrants that good title is being conveyed to the buyer. The warranty of good title includes a requirement that the goods be free from any security interest. If the existence of a security interest is disclosed to the buyer, the warranty is not breached. Choice A is incorrect because it is possible to disclaim the warranty of title. Choice D is incorrect because the warranty of title applies to all sellers.

4. B is the correct answer. The seller must have known that the buyer was relying on the seller in selecting the appropriate goods for the warranty of fitness for a particular purpose to apply. Because it is an implied warranty, there is no requirement that it be in writing. Implied warranties arise automatically without any statement, oral or written, by the seller.

5. D is the correct answer. Any party who sold a product when it was in a defective condition can be held liable for any injuries arising from the defect. A defendant can use the intervening event defense if she can show that the defect first occurred in the product after it left her hands. Choice A is incorrect because a defendant's knowledge of a defect need not be proven. Choice B is incorrect because privity of contract need not be proven. Choice C is incorrect because lack of due care need not be proven.

6. D is the correct answer. The warranty of merchantability is an implied warranty, and thus arises automatically in a sale by a merchant. Choice A is incorrect because no writing is needed for implied warranties. Choice B is incorrect because the reliance on the seller's skill in selecting a product relates to the implied warranty of fitness for a particular purpose. Choice C is incorrect because it is possible to disclaim the warranty of merchantability.

7. D is the correct answer. Negligence need not be proven in a strict liability products liability case. Choice A is incorrect because contributory negligence by the plaintiff usually does not prevent recovery for the injuries suffered. Choice B is incorrect because a defendant cannot escape liability because the defect (here, usually a design defect) was also present in all or most of the similar products of competitors. If industry custom were a defense, then competitors would have an incentive to design equally dangerous products. Choice C is incorrect because the existence of the defect when the product is sold is all that the plaintiff must prove. Note that answer choice C says "Privity" will be a bar to recovery. The CPA exam, and others, sometimes use the word "privity" when they mean "lack of privity." Remember that privity simply means being in a contractual relationship. Choice C is actually referring to lack of privity. Beware of this poor use of terminology.

8. A is the correct answer. The implied warranty of title can be disclaimed, but only by specifically mentioning the word "title" in the disclaimer or by a statement that the seller is selling "only that right, title, ownership, etc. that the owner has" in the goods sold. A statement disclaiming "all warranties" will not accomplish that.

9. D is the correct answer. Liability for personal injuries cannot be disclaimed. One reason for this is that many of the persons injured by a product, as in this question, were not a party to the contract of sale and could not know of any disclaimer.

OFFICIAL AICPA ANSWER TO ESSAY QUESTION

Law Nov 90 #4

a. Under the UCC Sales Article, the contract between Pharo and Secure creates the following implied warranties:

- Implied warranty of merchantability;
- Implied warranty of fitness for a particular purpose;
- Implied warranty of title.

The implied warranty of merchantability requires the tug to be merchantable; that is, fit for the ordinary purposes intended. It is probable that the tug was fit for such ordinary purposes and, therefore, the implied warranty of merchantability was not breached.

The implied warranty of fitness for a particular purpose requires that the tug be fit for the particular purpose for which it was purchased. To show that the implied warranty of fitness for a particular purpose is present as a result of the contract, Pharo must show that:

- Secure knew of the particular needs of Pharo;
- Pharo relied on Secure to select a suitable tug;
- Secure knew that Pharo was relying on Secure to select a tug suitable for Pharo's needs.

The implied warranty of fitness for a particular purpose has been breached because the tug was not suitable for Pharo's particular needs (i.e., to move airplanes weighing up to 10,000 pounds).

The implied warranty of title requires that:

- Secure have good title;
- The transfer to Pharo would be rightful;
- The tug would be delivered free from any security interest or other lien.

The implied warranty of title has been breached because Maco was the rightful owner.

b. Maco will be entitled to recover the tug from Pharo because:

- Maco had entrusted the tug to Secure, which deals in similar goods;
- That, as a result of such entrustment, Secure had the power to transfer Maco's rights to the tug to a buyer in the ordinary course of business;
- Pharo was a buyer in the ordinary course of business because Pharo purchased the tug in good faith and without knowledge of Maco's ownership interest.

CHAPTER 14
CREATION AND TRANSFER OF NEGOTIABLE INSTRUMENTS

OVERVIEW

Negotiable instruments are formal contracts, meaning that they must be in a particular form in order to be valid as a negotiable instrument. If the formal requirements are not met, it is still possible for the contract to be valid, but it will not be a negotiable instrument and will not have the special characteristics that negotiable instruments have. The primary feature of a negotiable instrument is that one can become a **holder in due course** of such an instrument. A holder in due course can obtain better right to payment of the instrument than the party from whom it was received. In this sense, a holder in due course is somewhat like a good faith purchaser for value. The rules and requirements for negotiable instruments are complicated and detailed, but once they are learned, the rules' applications are generally straightforward.

OUTLINE

I. **Introduction to Negotiable Instruments.**
    A. <u>Source of Law</u>. Negotiable instruments are covered in Revised Article 3 of the UCC which was released in 1990 and is in the process of being adopted by the states to replace the prior Article 3. The earlier Article 3 referred to "Commercial Paper" instead of the current use of "Negotiable Instruments."
    B. <u>General Concept</u>. Negotiable instruments serve as substitute for money in commerce. They do not have all the characteristics of money, but can substitute for money in many circumstances. Although still very important, both in commerce and on the CPA exam, they are not used as much as in the past because of the increasing use of various forms of electronic banking and wire transfers, often used in place of paper checks.
    C. <u>Negotiability</u> The key feature of these instruments is their **negotiability**, or transferability, to other parties. The negotiability feature makes these instruments more like money than other contract rights. When a payee endorses a check over to someone else, that payee has negotiated the check. Negotiability is further discussed below.

II. **Types of Negotiable Instruments.**
    A. <u>Draft</u>. A **draft** is a three-party instrument in which there is an unconditional written **order** by one party (the **drawer**) that orders a second party (the **drawee**) to pay money to a third party (the **payee**). In order be obligated to pay, the drawee must accept the draft and in so doing becomes the **acceptor** of the draft. Often the drawee owes money to the drawer, while the drawer owes money to a third party. The draft orders the drawee to pay this third party, making the third party the payee. Drafts have other characteristics that can differ.
        1. *Sight Draft*. A **sight draft**, or **demand draft**, is payable on sight. It will use language such as "pay on demand" or "pay on sight." These mean to "pay upon the demand of the payee," and "pay upon sight of this draft." The drawee is ordered to pay immediately upon the draft being presented to the drawee.

2. *Time Draft.* A **time draft** is payable at some specified time, such as "pay on May 28, 1999," or "pay 90 days after date." The latter means to pay 90 days after the date of the draft, which is presumably the date the draft was written.

3. *Trade Acceptance.* A **trade acceptance** is a sight draft used when a seller extends credit to a buyer, and in which the seller is both drawer and payee.

B. <u>Check</u>. A **check** is a particular type of draft which has two special characteristics:

1. *Payable on Demand.* Drafts can be payable either on demand or at a particular time. Checks can be payable only on demand.

2. *Drawee Is a Financial Institution.* Drafts can be drawn on any kind of party, but checks can be drawn only on financial institutions.

Because they are a particular type of draft, a check is a three-party instrument that contains an order to pay. When a student writes a check to pay tuition, the student is the drawer, the bank is the drawee, and the college is the payee. By writing the check, the student is essentially saying to the bank, "I order you to pay money, in the amount of this check, to the college when the college presents this check to you."

C. <u>Promissory Note</u>. A **promissory note** is a two-party instrument in which one party, the **maker**, makes an unconditional promise to pay money to another party, the **payee**. A note can be either a **demand note** (payable at any time upon the demand of the payee to be paid) or a **time note**, (payable only at the time specified). They can be payable in one lump sum, or an **installment note** would be payable in multiple payments. Most notes provide for the payment of interest, but payment of interest is not necessary.

D. <u>Certificate of Deposit</u>. A **certificate of deposit (CD)** is a particular type of note with one special characteristic, which is a requirement that the maker is a financial institution. With a CD, after the bank receives the depositor's money the bank makes an unconditional promise to pay the depositor at some time in the future, the maturity date of the CD. **Exam tip #1.**

III. **Requirements for an Instrument to be Negotiable.**

A. <u>A Writing</u>. The writing is often on a preprinted form, such as a check which is filled in by the drawer. The writing must be permanent and portable, so the writing cannot be done on a fixed object. Even though most instruments are written on paper they can be written on any portable object, such as the oversized poster board checks sometimes used in large charitable contributions or for large lottery winners.

B. <u>Signed by the Drawer or Maker</u>. The drawer must sign a draft or check, and the maker must sign a note or CD. Any signature or other identifying mark will meet this requirement. The signature can be made by an authorized representative, as is done when a corporate officer signs a check for the corporation. The representative should clearly indicate the representative capacity in the signature.

C. <u>Unconditional Promise or Order to Pay</u>. The promise (for a note or CD) or order (for a draft or check) must be **unconditional**. A statement such as "I owe you $1,000," merely acknowledges a debt but is not a promise to pay it off. A promise or order is conditional, and therefore nonnegotiable if it states any one of the following:

1. *An Express Condition to Payment.*

2. *That It Is Subject to or Governed by Another Writing.*

3. *That the Rights or Obligations With Respect to the Promise or Order Are Stated in Another Writing.*

Thus the promise or order cannot contain conditions which promise payment "when the job is finished," or "if the product is satisfactory." Also conditional would be payment "as provided in the services agreement dated September 1, 1999." Note however that a negotiable instrument can simply refer to another agreement, such as a note which refers to a security agreement affecting collateral in the event of a default by the maker of the note.

D. Fixed Amount of Money.
   1. *Fixed Amount.* The amount due must be fixed in the instrument. A variable interest rate is acceptable, even if it requires reference to information not contained in the instrument. If the instrument provides for interest without stating the rate, the rate is the judgment rate in effect at the place of payment of the instrument.
   2. *Payable in Money.* To be negotiable, the instrument must be payable in **money**, which is a medium of exchange adopted by a government as part of its currency. Instruments payable in a recognized foreign currency are negotiable. Instruments payable in gold, stocks, bonds, goods, or services are not negotiable.

E. Not Require Any Undertaking in Addition to the Payment of Money. If an instrument requires payment in goods or services in addition to the payment of money, it is not negotiable. There are three undertakings that are acceptable and will not destroy negotiability:
   1. *An Authorization to Protect Collateral.*
   2. *An Authorization to Dispose of Collateral.*
   3. *A Provision to Waive Any Law to Protect the Obligor.* An example would be a waiver of the right to a jury trial.

F. Payable on Demand or at a Definite Time.
   1. *Payable on Demand.* These are payable at any time after creation upon demand of the payee. Silence regarding payment creates a demand instrument. All checks are payable on demand. Instruments payable "at sight" or "on presentment" are demand instruments.
   2. *Payable at a Definite Time.* Examples include:
      a. At a Fixed Date.
      b. On or Before a Stated Date. The instrument must be paid by the stated date, but the maker or drawee has the option to pay it prior to the stated date.
      c. At a Fixed Period After Sight. Common with drafts (e.g., "Payable 60 days after sight"), this requires formal presentment, which establishes the date of sight.
      d. At a Date Ascertainable When the Instrument Is Issued. A common example is an instrument payable a fixed number of days after a stated date, such as "60 days after July 1, 2000.
   3. *Allowable Clauses.* The following clauses do not violate the definite time requirement even though they might alter that actual time of payment.
      a. Prepayment Clause. A **prepayment clause** allows the maker to pay the amount due prior to the due date.
      b. Acceleration Clause. An **acceleration clause** allows the payee or holder to require immediate payment upon the happening of certain events, usually default.
      c. Extension Clause. An **extension clause** allows the maturity date to be extended into the future.

G. Payable to Order or Bearer.
   1. *Order Instruments.* **Order instruments** can be either payable to the order of an identified person, or payable to an identified person or order. Thus it could be payable "to the order of Bob" or "to Bob or order." The word "order" must appear. Order instruments can be payable to multiple payees together or alternatively. Order instruments can be payable to artificial entities such as corporations or trusts.
   2. *Bearer Instruments.* A **bearer instrument** is payable to whomever is in possession of it. The person in possession "bears" it and is the **bearer**. The following language creates a bearer instrument:
      a. "Payable to bearer."
      b. "Payable to the order of bearer."
      c. "Payable to Jane Doe or bearer."
      d. "Payable to cash."
      e. "Payable to the order of cash." **Exam tip #2.**

IV. **Negotiability and Nonnegotiability.**
   A. Nonnegotiable Instrument Is a Contract. If less than all of the above requirements of negotiability are met, this does not mean the contract is invalid. It means that it will be treated as any other contract, but will not have the special characteristics of a negotiable instrument.
   B. Assignment of a Nonnegotiable Contract. When ordinary contract rights are assigned, as discussed in Chapter 9 of this guide, the assignee receives the rights of the assignor, but no more. Thus, where an assignor assigns a right to payment, if the other party to the contract had a defense to payment and could avoid paying the assignor, that party could also avoid paying the assignee.
   C. Assignment of a Negotiable Instrument. Assignment of negotiable instruments is done through the process of negotiation. **Negotiation** is the transfer of a negotiable instrument by someone other than the issuer. The person receiving the instrument becomes a **holder**. All holders get all the rights of the transferor. But a holder who qualifies as a holder in due course, could receive even greater rights that those of the transferor. The result is that the holder in due course can collect on the instrument in some circumstances when the transferor could not have.

V. **Negotiation.**
   A. Order Paper. **Order paper** is an instrument payable to a specific payee or endorsed to a specific endorsee. There are two requirements for negotiating order paper.
      1. *Endorsement.* An **endorsement** (also spelled **endorsement**) is a signature of someone other than as a maker, drawer, or acceptor that is placed on a negotiable instrument in order to negotiate it. Most often this is the signature of the payee, but it could also be the signature of an endorsee. Endorsements are discussed in detail below.
      2. *Delivery.* The instrument must be delivered to complete the negotiation.
   B. Bearer Paper. **Bearer paper** is an instrument which is not payable to a specific payee or endorsee. Bearer paper is negotiated by delivery alone. **Exam tip #3.**

VI.   Endorsements.

    A. <u>Generally</u>. Endorsements are required to negotiate order paper, and, although not required, may be used in negotiating bearer paper. The transferee of bearer paper sometimes requires the transferor's endorsement before accepting the instrument. The person making the endorsement is the **endorser** and if the endorser names a specific payee, that person is the **endorsee**. Endorsements can convert bearer paper to order paper and can convert order paper to bearer paper. There are three variable characteristics which all endorsements possess. For each of these, the endorsement can be classified as one or the other.

    B. <u>Blank or Special</u>. Every endorsement is either blank or special.

        1. *Blank Endorsement*. A **blank endorsement** does not name a specific payee. If Jim Johnson simply signs the back of a check payable to him, this is a blank endorsement.

            a. Converts to Bearer Paper. A blank endorsement converts order paper to bearer paper. This is why checks should not be endorsed until at the bank ready to be deposited.

            b. Bearer Paper Can Be Endorsed. Although bearer paper does not require an endorsement to be negotiated, it often is. The transferee may demand endorsement for identification purposes or to create additional liability for the transferor. This liability is explained in the next chapter of this guide.

        2. *Special Endorsement*. A **special endorsement** names a specific endorsee. A special endorsement results in the instrument being order paper, with the signature of the special endorsee needed to further negotiate the instrument. For example, a check payable to John Doe could be endorsed by John "Pay to Sue Doe" followed by John's signature. Sue's signature would be needed for further negotiation. **Exam tip #4.**

    C. <u>Qualified or Unqualified</u>. Every endorsement is either qualified or unqualified. An endorsement operates as a promise by the endorser to pay the holder or any subsequent endorsee the amount of the instrument if the maker, drawer, or acceptor defaults.

        1. *Unqualified Endorsement*. With an **unqualified endorsement** the endorser is subject to this liability in the event of default on the instrument.

        2. *Qualified Endorsement*. A **qualified endorsement** disclaims this liability to later endorsees. A qualified endorsement is made by including the words "without recourse" or similar language in the endorsement. The restrictive endorsement gives notice that the restrictive endorser will not be held liable if the instrument is not paid.

    D. <u>Restrictive or Nonrestrictive</u>. Every endorsement is either restrictive or nonrestrictive. Restrictive endorsements put requirements or conditions on the payment of the funds.

        1. *Nonrestrictive Endorsement*. A **nonrestrictive endorsement** contains no conditions or restrictions on the payment of funds. Endorsements are nonrestrictive unless there is language indicating a restriction.

        2. *Effective Restrictive Endorsement*. A **restrictive endorsement** contains a condition or instructions related to the payment of funds. The most common are:

            a. Endorsement For Deposit or Collection. For example, "for deposit only" conditions payment of the instrument on depositing the funds.

            b. Trust Endorsement. When an instrument is endorsed to an attorney, executor, or trustee for the benefit of the client, estate, or trust, the funds must be applied to the named beneficiary.

3. *Endorsements Where the Restriction Is Ignored.* Some restrictive endorsements contain restrictions which are not effective. This means that the endorsement is effective and is construed as if the restriction were absent.

   a. Prohibition of Further Restriction. If a restrictive endorsement read, "pay to George Doe only," the restrictive word "only" would be ignored, and George Doe could transfer the instrument to anyone else.

   b. Conditional Endorsement. If an endorsement contains a condition, the **conditional endorsement** is construed as if the condition were not there. For example, if an endorsement read, "Pay to Pam Doe if she completes her consulting engagement," the condition would be ignored and the endorsement would be construed as "Pay to Pam Doe." Thus, the instrument could be paid regardless of whether or not the condition had been met.

E. <u>Endorsement Characteristic Summary</u>. One of each of the three above pairs of terms applies to every endorsement. Some examples:

"John Doe" is a blank, unqualified, unrestricted endorsement.

"John Doe, without recourse, for deposit only" is blank, qualified, restricted.

"John Doe, without recourse" is blank, qualified, unrestricted.

"Pay to Sally Doe, John Doe without recourse" is special, qualified, unrestricted.

To fully describe an endorsement, each of the three relevant terms is needed. However, be aware that often the terms "blank," "unqualified," and "unrestricted" are assumed and omitted. Thus the third example might simply be called "qualified" and the fourth simply called "special, qualified." **Exam tip #5.**

F. <u>Misspelled Name</u>. Where the payee or endorsee's name is misspelled, that person can endorse with either the correct or incorrect spelling, although someone taking the instrument for value or collection may require both signatures.

VII. **Forged Endorsements.**

A. <u>Generally</u>. The general rule for forged endorsements is that the person who first takes the instrument after the forgery bears the loss if the forger cannot be found and made to pay. The first transferee is assumed to be the person who was in the best position to prevent the problem by being more careful in taking the instrument. There are two exceptions to this general rule:

   1. *Imposter Rule.* The **imposter rule** applies when someone impersonates another, and induces a maker or drawer to issue an instrument payable to the person being impersonated. If the imposter then forges the endorsement of the person who was impersonated, the maker or drawer is liable. In this circumstance, the drawer or maker could have best prevented the situation by knowing who the check was being written to.

   2. *Fictitious Payee.* A **fictitious payee** is either a fictitious person or someone the maker or drawer never intended to have an interest in the instrument. For example, the treasurer of a corporation issued a check of the corporation in the name of his brother-in-law and then forged the endorsement of the brother-in-law and cashed the check. The corporation, and not the party cashing the check, would bear the loss. Again, the corporation was in the best position to prevent the situation. **Exam tip #6.**

EXAM TIPS

1. Exam questions have required candidates to identify a pictured instrument, thus it is important to know the definitions and requirements of each type of negotiable instrument.
2. Questions asking for the identification of an instrument often also require knowledge of the requirements of negotiability. The pictured instrument might fail to meet one of the negotiability requirements, making the correct answer choice the one that indicates nonnegotiability. Candidates must know these requirements thoroughly, as well as any relevant exceptions to each.
3. Bearer paper is not the same as a bearer instrument. Whether an item is a bearer instrument or an order instrument is determined at the time the instrument is written and is based on the face of the instrument. Whether it is bearer paper or order paper depends also on any endorsements. Certain endorsements can convert an order instrument to bearer paper, or a bearer instrument to order paper. Thus a check payable to a named person is an order instrument and is order paper prior to endorsement. If the payee endorses in blank, it is converted to bearer paper.
4. Although "to the order of" is needed on the face of a negotiable instrument, those "magic words" of negotiability are not needed in endorsements. "Once negotiable, always negotiable," illustrates the fact that no endorsement can make a negotiable instrument nonnegotiable.
5. Exam questions often illustrate a series of endorsements on the back of an instrument. Candidates should be able to determine the type and effect of each endorsement as well as who made the endorsement. You should know for each endorsement what must be done for further negotiation. Remember that parties sometimes endorse items when it is not necessary, as with a holder of a bearer instrument making a special endorsement, converting the instrument to order paper. To help remember which endorsement is which:
   A **special** endorsement names a **specific** person.
   A **qualified** endorsement might reflect poor **quality** (whether it will be paid) of the instrument.
   A **restrictive** endorsement **restricts** what can be done with the proceeds.
   When an exam question shows endorsements on the back of a check, signatures are usually shown in italics. The last endorsement determines if the instrument is order or bearer paper.
6. Candidates should be able to recognize situations where the imposter rule or fictitious payee rule apply, and the outcome when it does. It is important to understand the factual situation where each applies and to not confuse them.

KEY CONCEPTS LIKELY TO BE TESTED ON THE CPA EXAM

1. Identification of a pictured instrument and determination whether it is negotiable.
2. The requirements of negotiability.
3. Knowledge of what items and conditions will destroy negotiability, including being able to recognize their presence in a pictured instrument.
4. Identification of the types of endorsements.
5. Effect of endorsements, or a series of endorsements shown on the back of an instrument, including whether the instrument, as endorsed, is order or bearer paper.
6. Knowledge and effect of the imposter and fictitious payee rules.

KEY TERMS

Holder in Due Course
Negotiability
Draft
Order to Pay
Drawer
Drawee
Payee
Acceptor
Sight Draft
Demand Draft
Time Draft
Trade Acceptance
Check
Promissory Note
Maker

Demand Note
Time Note
Installment Note
Certificate of Deposit
Unconditional Promise or Order
Money
Prepayment Clause
Acceleration Clause
Extension Clause
Order Instrument
Bearer Instrument
Bearer
Negotiation
Holder

Order Paper
Endorsement
Bearer Paper
Endorser
Endorsee
Blank Endorsement
Special Endorsement
Unqualified Endorsement
Qualified Endorsement
Nonrestrictive Endorsement
Restrictive Endorsement
Conditional Endorsement
Imposter Rule
Fictitious Payee Rule

MULTIPLE CHOICE QUESTIONS

1.   Law May 95 #42

```
To: Middlesex National Bank
    Nassau, N.Y.
                        September 15, 1994

Pay to the order of  Robert Silver   $4,000

 Four Thousand and xx/100   Dollars

 On October 1, 1994

                        Lynn Dexter
                        Lynn Dexter
```

The above instrument is a
A. Draft.
B. Postdated check.
C. Trade acceptance.
D. Promissory note.

2.   Law May 92 #46
The following endorsements appear on the back of a negotiable promissory note made payable "to bearer." Clark has possession of the note.

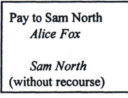

```
Pay to Sam North
    Alice Fox

    Sam North
(without recourse)
```

Which of the following statements is correct?
A. Clark's unqualified endorsement is required to further negotiate the note.
B. To negotiate the note, Clark must have given value for it.
C. Clark is **not** a holder because North's qualified endorsement makes the note nonnegotiable.
D. Clark can negotiate the note by delivery alone.

3.   Law May 93 #41

The following endorsements appear on the back of a negotiable promissory note payable to Lake Corp.

Pay to John Smith only
Frank Parker, President of Lake Corp.

John Smith

Pay to the order of Sharp, Inc., without recourse, but only if Sharp delivers computers purchased by Mary Harris by March 15, 1993
Mary Harris

Sarah Sharp, President of Sharp, Inc.

Which of the following statements is correct?

A. The note became nonnegotiable as a result of Parker's endorsement.

B. Harris' endorsement was a conditional promise to pay and caused the note to be nonnegotiable.

C. Smith's endorsement effectively prevented further negotiation of the note.

D. Harris' signature was **not** required to effectively negotiate the note to Sharp.

4.   Law Nov 92 #34

Which of the following conditions, if present on an otherwise negotiable instrument, would affect the instrument's negotiability?

A. The instrument is payable six months after the death of the maker.

B. The instrument is payable at a definite time subject to an accelerated clause in the event of a default.

C. The instrument is postdated.

D. The instrument contains a promise to provide additional collateral if there is a decrease in value of the existing collateral.

5.   Law May 89 #48

The following instrument is in the possession of Bill North:

On May 30, 1989, I promise to pay Bill North, the bearer of this document, $1,800.

            Joseph Peppers
            Joseph Peppers

Re: Auto Purchase Contract

This instrument is

A. Non-negotiable because it is undated.

B. Non-negotiable because it is **not** payable to order or bearer.

C. Negotiable even though it makes reference to the contract out of which it arose.

D. Negotiable because it is payable at a definite time.

6.   Law Nov 89 #42

Which of the following is required to make an instrument negotiable?

A. Stated date of issue.

B. An endorsement by the payee.

C. Stated location for payment.

D. Payment only in legal tender.

7.   Law Nov 92 #33

Which of the following negotiable instruments is subject to the UCC Negotiable Instruments Article?

A. Corporate bearer bond with a maturity date of January 1, 2001.

B. Installment note payable on the first day of each month.

C. Warehouse receipt.

D. Bill of lading, payable to order.

OTHER OBJECTIVE FORMAT QUESTION (Estimated time -- 10 to 15 minutes)

Law May 94 #3(A)

Question Number 3 consists of 2 parts. Part A consists of 6 items. Select the **best** answer for each item. Use a No. 2 pencil to blacken the appropriate oval on the Objective Answer Sheet to indicate your answers. **Answer all items.** Your grade will be based on the total number of correct answers.

A. Items 1 through 6 are based on the following documents:

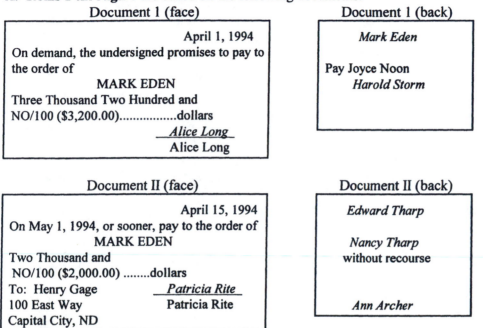

Document 1 (face)

> April 1, 1994
> On demand, the undersigned promises to pay to the order of
> MARK EDEN
> Three Thousand Two Hundred and
> NO/100 ($3,200.00)................dollars
> *Alice Long*
> Alice Long

Document 1 (back)

> *Mark Eden*
>
> Pay Joyce Noon
> *Harold Storm*

Document II (face)

> April 15, 1994
> On May 1, 1994, or sooner, pay to the order of
> MARK EDEN
> Two Thousand and
> NO/100 ($2,000.00) ....dollars
> To: Henry Gage   *Patricia Rite*
> 100 East Way   Patricia Rite
> Capital City, ND

Document II (back)

> *Edward Tharp*
>
> *Nancy Tharp*
> without recourse
>
> *Ann Archer*

Required:

Items 1 through 6 relate to the nature and negotiability of the above documents and the nature of several of the endorsements. For each item select from list A the response that best completes that statement and blacken the corresponding oval on the Objective Answer Sheet. A response may be selected more than once.

		List A
1. Document I is a (type of instrument)	A.	Blank
2. Document II is a (type of instrument)	B.	Check
3. Document I is (negotiability)	C.	Draft
4. Document II is (negotiability)	D.	Negotiable
5. The endorsement by Mark Eden is (type of endorsement)	E.	Nonnegotiable
6. The endorsement by Nancy Ferry is (type of endorsement)	F.	Promissory Note
	G.	Qualified
	H.	Special

EXPLANATIONS TO MULTIPLE CHOICE QUESTIONS

1. A is the correct answer. This is a draft because it is payable at a definite time rather than on demand. Without the terms "On October 1, 1994," it would be a check. Choice B is wrong for two reasons. It is a draft, and one cannot determine if it is postdated. One must know whether it is before or after September 15, 1994, to know if it is postdated.

2. D is the correct answer. This instrument is payable to bearer, so initially it could be negotiated without endorsing a signature. But when Alice Fox gave the special endorsement to Sam North, it became order paper requiring North's signature. Once North endorsed it, it again became bearer paper, negotiable by delivery alone. The last endorsement determines whether it is bearer or order paper.

3. D is the correct answer. After Frank Parker's endorsement, the note was order paper requiring Smith's signature to negotiate it. Smith's signature converted it to bearer paper, thus not requiring a signature to further negotiate it. Choices A and B are incorrect because endorsements can never destroy negotiability. The condition in Mary Harris' endorsement would be ignored.

4. A is the correct answer. A date six months after the maker's death is neither a definite time nor on demand, making the note nonnegotiable. The other conditions are acceptable.

5. B is the correct answer. The words "pay Bill North" do not include the required language of "to order" or "to bearer."

6. D is the correct answer. The legal tender can be any recognized currency. This is an easy question if the requirements for negotiability have been memorized, and one common sense might not lead to the correct answer.

7. B is the correct answer. In this question, the installment note described in the correct answer choice is negotiable, and subject to Article 2, only if all negotiability requirements have been met, but the other three answer choices are never covered under Article 2. B is the best choice.

EXPLANATION TO OTHER OBJECTIVE FORMAT QUESTION

1. F is the correct answer. A two-party instrument with a promise to pay is a promissory note.
2. C is the correct answer. This is a draft, rather than a check, because the drawee, Henry Gage, is not a bank.
3. D is the correct answer. This note meets all negotiability requirements.
4. D is the correct answer. This draft meets all negotiability requirements.
5. A is the correct answer. A signature, with nothing more, is a blank endorsement.
6. G is the correct answer. The words "without recourse" create a qualified endorsement, meaning that Tharp will not be liable if the instrument is not paid.

CHAPTER 15
HOLDER IN DUE COURSE, LIABILITY, AND DEFENSES

OVERVIEW

This chapter completes the material on negotiable instruments. The requirements of becoming a holder in due course are discussed. The holder in due course is a holder who meets certain requirements and enjoys special rights with respect to the negotiable instrument that he holds. This is followed by discussion of the various liabilities that can be incurred by a party associated with a negotiable instrument. Lastly, the defenses to payment are discussed. **Defenses** are the reasons, or excuses, that the law recognizes as allowing an instrument to not be paid. This is where the holder in due course has special rights. There are certain defenses which, although good against other holders, are ineffective against a holder in due course. Thus, the maker of a note might have a defense and be able to avoid paying the payee of a note, but if that same note is transferred so that it is held by a holder in due course, the maker might, depending on the particular defense, be required to pay the note despite the defense. The holder in due course, by being able to collect on the note, has greater rights than other holders. Although many defenses are not good against a holder in due course, others are effective. Thus a holder in due course gets greater, but not absolute, rights to collection. For example, if the seller of a car committed fraud on the buyer, who paid with a check, the buyer could avoid paying the check to the seller, but if the seller transferred the check to someone qualifying as a holder in due course, the buyer would be required to pay the check to that holder in due course.

OUTLINE

I. **Holder in Due Course.**
   A. Holder. To become a holder in due course, one must first become a holder. A **holder** of bearer paper is anyone in possession of the instrument. The holder of an instrument payable to an identified person is that specific person with possession. A holder has rights similar to an assignee of a nonnegotiable contract, meaning that the holder has no greater rights than the transferor and is subject to the same defenses as the transferor.
   B. Holder in Due Course. A **holder in due course** (an HDC) can have greater rights than the transferor. The holder takes the instrument free of certain claims and defenses. A **claim** is an assertion by a third party that he, rather than the holder, is entitled to ownership of the instrument and thus entitled to payment. A defense would allow the instrument to not be paid. Either, if successful, would prevent the holder from being paid on the instrument. To qualify as an HDC, the holder must take the instrument:
   1. *For Value,*
   2. *In Good Faith,* and
   3. *Without Notice That It Is Defective or Overdue.*
   Any holder who meets these requirements is a holder in due course. Each requirement will be discussed further.

C. <u>Taking for Value</u>. The holder must have given value to qualify as an HDC. A promise which has not yet been performed does not qualify as value given. Where a the holder has promised to pay the transferor for the instrument, the new holder has given value only to the extent that the agreed amount has actually been paid. The instrument has been **taken for value** if the holder has done any of the following:

   1. *Performed the Agreed-upon Promise.*
   2. *Acquired a Security Interest or Lien on the Instrument.*
   3. *Taken the Instrument in Payment or as Security for an Antecedent Claim.*
   4. *Given a Negotiable Instrument as Payment.*
   5. *Given an Irrevocable Obligation as Payment.* **Exam tip #1.**

D. <u>Taking in Good Faith</u>. The instrument must have been **taken in good faith** in order to qualify as an HDC. Good faith is based on the UCC definition of honesty in fact in the conduct or transaction concerned; all surrounding circumstances are considered in whether good faith is present. Paying a stranger in a bar $200 for a $1,000 instrument would probably not meet the good faith test.

E. <u>Taking Without Notice</u>. The holder in due course rule is designed to protect innocent holders who had no notice of a problem with the particular instrument. The law will not protect a holder who should have been aware that there could be a problem, but nevertheless chose to take the instrument. A holder cannot qualify as an HDC if the holder had notice of any of the following at the time of taking the instrument:

   1. *It Is Overdue.* Time instruments become overdue on the day after their due date. An installment note is considered overdue if a single payment is late. If an instrument has been accelerated, it becomes overdue when the accelerated due date passes. If an instrument has not been accelerated and the only default is in the payment of interest, the instrument is not considered overdue. Checks are considered overdue after 90 days, and for other demand instruments the overdue point depends on the surrounding circumstances.
   2. *It Has Been Dishonored.* An instrument is **dishonored** if it is presented for payment and payment is refused.
   3. *It Contains an Unauthorized Signature or Has Been Altered.*
   4. *There Is a Claim to it by Another Person.*
   5. *There Is a Defense Against it.*

F. <u>No Evidence of Forgery, Alteration, or Irregularity</u>. If the instrument contained apparent evidence of forgery, alteration, or should have appeared suspicious due to incompleteness or irregularity, the holder cannot qualify as an HDC. If a reasonable person would not have recognized the problem, the holder could still qualify as an HDC. Postdating or antedating is not, by itself, an irregularity.

G. <u>Payee as Holder in Due Course</u>. A payee generally cannot become an HDC because the payee would be aware of any defenses. In a goods transaction, the payee would be the seller, and the seller/payee would be aware if the goods were defective, which would give the buyer a defense to the payment of a check issued to purchase the goods. There is one situation where a payee could become an HDC. If the buyer's check was made payable to a third party, most likely due to a prior debt of the seller to the third party, that third party, as payee, could likely qualify as an HDC if the third party were unaware of any defects in the seller's performance.

H. <u>Shelter Principle</u>. A person who does not qualify as an HDC can obtain the rights of an HDC if she acquires the instrument from someone who does qualify as an HDC. Thus an HDC can transfer an instrument to someone saying, "I got this instrument before I knew that there was a defense to its payment based on fraud, thus I am an HDC." The person taking from the HDC could not be an HDC himself because he received notice (from the statement of the HDC) prior to taking it that there was a defense to its payment. However, the **shelter principle** protects him by giving him the same rights that were held by his HDC transferor. An important exception to the shelter principle prevents the shelter principle from applying to any person who previously was a non-HDC holder, but who later reacquires the instrument from an HDC. Such a person would **not** receive the rights of an HDC, nor can any person involved in any fraud surrounding the transaction.

I. <u>Holder in Due Course Rule Not Applicable in Certain Consumer Credit Transactions</u>. Where a negotiable instrument is given by a consumer as part of a consumer goods purchase, later holders of that instrument will not receive most HDC protections. For example, Jack bought a home theater system from an electronics dealer, giving a negotiable promissory note as payment. If the home theater system was defective, Jack would have a defense to paying the note to the electronics dealer. Normally, if the dealer sold the promissory note to someone qualifying as an HDC, Jack would have to pay the note despite the fact that the home theater system was defective. But the Federal Trade Commission requires such notes to contain a notice that any later holder of the note is subject to all claims and defenses that could be used against the seller, meaning Jack would not have to pay any later holder of the note if he could have avoided paying the electronics dealer.

II. Signature Liability.

A. <u>Generally</u>. By placing a signature on an instrument, a party becomes liable on the instrument. The type of liability depends on the type of instrument and the capacity in which the instrument is signed. Liability can be primary or secondary. Qualified endorsers (those signing "without recourse") and agents who properly sign as an agent incur no liability. A signature can be a written signature or any mark used in place of a regular signature.

B. <u>Agent Signatures</u>. The liability of an agent who has signed an instrument on behalf of a principal depends on the precise details of the signature.

1. *Agent Unambiguously Indicates Agent Status*. A signature, "Polson, by Andersen, agent," would clearly indicate the agent role of Andersen, and would give Andersen no liability to any party. It indicates that there is an agency relationship, identifies the principal by name, and results in a fully disclosed agency as explained in Chapter 18 of this guide.

2. *Status of Agent Unclear*. Signatures such as "Polson, Andersen" or "Andersen" do not indicate the status of Andersen as agent. Depending on the circumstance and other notice to holders and HDCs, Andersen could be held liable even if he is, in fact, an agent of Polson.

3. *Liability of Principal*. The principal is liable on the instrument regardless of the form of the signature so long as the agent was in fact the authorized agent of the principal. If the agent was not authorized, the principal is not liable unless the principal later ratifies the unauthorized signature. An agent who signs an instrument falsely claiming agent authority can be liable for damages to any party who relies on the agent's claim of authority.

C. Primary Liability. A party has **primary liability** on an instrument if the terms on the face of the instrument indicate that the party will pay it. The maker of a note has primary liability. No one is primarily liable on a draft or check when it is written because it is an order to pay which contains no promises. But if the drawee becomes an acceptor, the acceptor has primary liability. When a bank certifies a check, this makes the bank primarily liable. Otherwise, a bank has no obligation to pay a payee or holder of the check, although if wrongfully dishonored, the bank could be liable to the drawer for certain damages suffered by the drawer.

D. Secondary Liability. **Secondary liability** arises upon the failure of the primarily liable party to pay the instrument when due. Drawers of checks and drafts and unqualified endorsers of negotiable instruments have secondary liability.

1. *Drawer of Check or Draft.* If the drawee (the bank) of a check does not pay it, the drawer becomes liable for payment to the payee or other holder who presented it for payment.

2. *Unqualified Endorser.* By indorsing a check, the endorsee incurs secondary liability. Thus if John makes a special, unqualified, unrestricted endorsement of a check naming Betty as endorsee, John becomes liable to Betty if the check is not paid. By making a qualified endorsement "without recourse," this liability is avoided.

3. *Requirements to Impose Secondary Liability.* Secondary liability is imposed only once the following three events have occurred:

   a. Presentment. **Presentment** is the proper demand for payment or acceptance upon the party obligated to pay or accept. Presentment can occur in any commercially reasonable manner and is effective when received by the person to whom presentment is made.

   b. Dishonor. Dishonor occurs if payment or acceptance is refused or cannot be obtained within any prescribed period (e.g., "60 days after sight") in the instrument.

   c. Notice of Dishonor. **Notice of dishonor** must be given to the secondarily liable party before that party can be held liable. That notice must be given in a timely manner. Banks must give notice by midnight of the following banking day, and other parties must give notice within 30 days of presentment.

E. Accommodation Party. An **accommodation party** is a party who lends his name and credit to another party, and signs along with that other party in whatever capacity the other party signs. If the accommodation party must pay, he has a right to recover from the party accommodated. Accommodation parties undertake one of two different obligations in signing.

1. *Guarantee of Payment.* By **guaranteeing payment**, the accommodation party becomes primarily liable, enabling the holder to seek payment directly from the accommodation party without first attempting to collect from the accommodated party.

2. *Guarantee of Collection.* By **guaranteeing collection**, the accommodation party is liable only after all legal steps have been taken against the accommodated party. This generally requires that the execution of a judgment against the accommodated party be returned unsatisfied, or that the party is insolvent, cannot be served with process, or it is otherwise apparent that the primarily liable party will not be able to pay. Only then does the accommodation party become liable.

III.   Warranty Liability.

A. <u>Generally</u>. **Warranty liability** is imposed on the transferor of an instrument solely due to the act of transfer. The liability does not depend on a signature. The rules generally impose liability on the party who was in the best position to prevent the loss, usually the party who dealt directly with the wrongdoer. There are two types of warranty liability. **Exam tip #2.**

B. <u>Transfer Warranties</u>. A **transfer** of an instrument is any passage other than its issuance or presentment. The act of transferring imposes five warranties on the transferor in favor of the immediate transferee. If the transfer is by endorsement, the warranties of the transferor also apply to all subsequent transferees. The five transfer warranties are:

1. *The transferor has good title to the instrument, or is authorized to obtain payment by one who does have good title.*
2. *All signatures are genuine or authorized.*
3. *The instrument has not been materially altered.*
4. *No defenses of any party are good against the transferor.*
5. *The transferor has no knowledge of any insolvency proceeding against the maker, the acceptor, or the drawer of an unaccepted instrument.*

Transfer warranties cannot be disclaimed with respect to checks, but can be disclaimed with respect to other instrument using the words "without recourse." Thus the transferor of a check which contains a material alteration has breached this warranty even if it was endorsed "without recourse."

C. <u>Presentment Warranties</u>. Anyone who presents a draft or check for payment or acceptance makes three presentment warranties.

1. *The presenter has good title to the instrument or is authorized to obtain payment or acceptance of the person who has good title.*
2. *The instrument has not been materially altered.*
3. *The presenter has no knowledge that the signature of the drawer is unauthorized.*

IV.   Defenses.

A. <u>Definition</u>. A defense is a legally sufficient reason that the party obligated to pay an instrument can avoid paying it. For example, forgery is a defense. Thus the drawer of a check with a forged signature has a defense to payment and can avoid liability for its payment.

B. <u>Real v. Personal Defenses</u>. There are two types of defenses to the payment of negotiable instruments. A **real defense** is one which can be used to avoid payment to any holder, including holders in due course (HDCs). A **personal defense** is one which is not effective to avoid payment to an HDC. This is the value or benefit of qualifying as an HDC. Breach of contract is a personal defense. If a buyer paid with a check to buy goods which turned out to be defective, the buyer would have a defense (breach of contract) against paying the check to the seller. But if the seller had transferred the check to someone qualifying as an HDC, the buyer's defense of breach of contract would be ineffective against the HDC. The buyer would be obligated to pay the HDC despite the fact that the goods were defective and would have to recover damages from the seller. **Exam tip #3.**

C. Real Defenses. The following real defenses will allow nonpayment to any party, whether or not an HDC. **Exam tip #4.**

1. *Minority*. A minor can avoid payment of negotiable instruments to the extent that she could avoid other contracts, subject to a minor's obligation to pay the fair value for necessaries of life.

2. *Extreme Duress*. **Extreme duress**, usually some form of force or violence, is a real defense. This is distinguished from ordinary duress which is a personal defense.

3. *Adjudicated Mental Incapacity*. This is a real defense because any contract entered into by someone who has been adjudicated insane is void.

4. *Illegality*. Instruments arising out of illegal transactions result in a real defense if the law declares the instrument void. This would be the case with most illegal contracts.

5. *Discharge in Bankruptcy*. Debts are discharged, or forgiven, in bankruptcy, thus a discharge in bankruptcy is a real defense.

6. *Fraud in the Inception*. Fraud in the inception occurs when a party is deceived as to the nature of the document being signed, as in the case of signing a negotiable instrument after being told it was something else. Assuming that the person took reasonable efforts, considering all the surrounding circumstances, to determine what he was signing, the defense would allow the maker or drawer to avoid paying an HDC.

7. *Forgery*. **Forgery** is the unauthorized signature of a maker, drawer, or endorser.

8. *Material Alteration*. A **material alteration** is any significant fraudulent change to an instrument. Removing part of an instrument, or adding to one, or changing the numbers are examples. Material alteration is a real defense, but only to the amount of the alteration. For example, if a note was altered from $1,000 to $10,000, the maker would be obligated to pay the $1,000 as it was originally written, but would have a real defense with respect to the additional $9,000 resulting from the material alteration.

D. Personal Defenses. Personal defenses are not valid against an HDC, thus an HDC must be paid despite the presence of the personal defense. A personal defense will allow payment to be avoided to a party who is not an HDC. Most of the personal defenses are situations where the maker (in the case of a note) or drawer (in the case of a check) set up the situation that allowed the problem to occur. Note that this is not the same as finding them at fault, but rather that different conduct (such as not writing a check before the related work was completed) would have prevented the situation.

1. *Breach of Contract*. If the underlying contract is breached, the maker or drawer could avoid paying the instrument to the breaching party, but would be required to pay an HDC. Thus if a purchaser paid for a service in advance with a check, and the provider of that service breached by not delivering the service, the drawer of the check could avoid payment to the breaching service provider. But if the breaching service provider transferred the check to an HDC, the breach of contract defense is ineffective and the check must be paid. Recovery must be obtained from the service provider. Note that the purchaser of the service could have avoided the problem by not writing the check prior to the completion of the service.

2. *Fraud in the Inducement.* A victim of fraud in the inducement can avoid paying the perpetrator, but could not use the fraud in the inducement to avoid paying an HDC. The rule here assumes that the victim of the fraud was in the best position (by being more careful) to avoid being defrauded. Certainly there is absolutely nothing that the HDC could have done to prevent the fraud. **Exam tip #5.**

3. *Unauthorized Completion.* **Unauthorized completion** is the completion of an instrument in a manner contrary to the instructions of the maker or drawer. Unauthorized completion can occur where a person gives a signed check which does not have the amount filled in to another person who then completes it contrary to instructions. For example, David gave a signed blank check to his gardener with instructions to complete the check based on the hours worked by the gardener that day, up to eight hours. If the gardener completed the check based on the hours worked, the completion would be authorized. But if the gardener completed the check for $2,000, it would be an unauthorized completion. As a personal defense, David could avoid payment to the gardener, but would have to pay any HDC who acquires the check. David could have prevented this situation by not giving the gardener the blank check. Thus, Dave must pay the HDC, who could not have prevented the unauthorized completion. Dave's remedy would be against the gardener. **Exam tip #6.**

4. *Nonadjudicated Mental Illness Which Makes a Contract Voidable.*

5. *Any Illegality Which Makes a Contract Voidable Rather Than Void.*

6. *Undue Influence or Ordinary Duress.*

7. *Discharge of an Instrument by Payment of Cancellation.*

V. Discharge.

A. <u>Definition.</u> **Discharge** is the release from liability of a party on an instrument. Discharge can occur in many ways.

1. *Payment of the Instrument.*

2. *Tender of Payment.* The tendering party, assuming that the tender was refused, is discharged for any later interest, costs, or fees, but not as to principal or interest accrued up to that point.

3. *Cancellation.* This can occur by marking "canceled" on the instrument or mutilating the instrument with the intent of eliminating the obligation.

4. *Impairment of the Right of Recourse.* **Impairment of the right of recourse** occurs when a party takes any action which adversely affects the right of a party to seek recourse from other obligors or from collateral. This usually happens by an obligor being released or by collateral being surrendered without the authorization of the party whose rights have been impaired.

5. *Striking the Signature of an Endorser.* The striking of an endorser's signature discharges that endorser's secondary liability to all later endorsers. The signature is no longer valid once stricken. Later endorsers have their recourse rights impaired because they can no longer look to the endorser whose signature was stricken, thus all the endorsers whose signatures appear below the stricken signature are discharged as well.

5. *Certification of a Check.* Certification discharges the drawer.

EXAM TIPS

1. A promise which has not yet been performed does not meet the requirement for giving value. Do not confuse this with the consideration requirement in the formation of a contract where the mere making of the promise constitutes valid consideration. If the new holder has promised to pay $1,000 for an instrument, but has only paid $700, the new holder has only given value to the extent of $700 and would be protected as a holder in due course only to that extent.

2. Do not forget warranty liability and the fact that it is imposed without a signature. It is in addition to any signature liability. Always check a fact situation to see if either transfer or presentment is present. Either of these will trigger warranty liability.

3. The terminology of "real" and "personal" confuses many candidates. Think of a **real** defense as one that works against everyone. A real defense is one that is always good. A **personal** defense is good against those with whom the party asserting the defense (usually the maker of a note or drawer of a check) dealt with personally. Personal defenses are also good against others who are not HDCs, but think of it as applying to those dealt with personally.

4. Candidates often memorize which defenses are personal and which are real without really understanding the significance of the difference. In addition to knowing which defenses are real and which are personal, candidates must thoroughly understand the general concept of a defense as well as the significance of whether a defense is real or personal.

5. Breach of contract and fraud in the inducement are the most common personal defenses to appear on the exam. Be sure to know these, and to not confuse fraud in the inducement with the real defense of fraud in the inception.

6. Unauthorized completion is a type of material alteration, but it operates as a personal defense because the maker or drawer must pay the instrument, as completed, to an HDC. Do not confuse **forgery** (a real defense where the signature is not genuine) with **material alteration** (a real defense as to the altered amount, where a validly completed instrument is later fraudulently changed) or **unauthorized completion** (a personal defense where a signed blank instrument is given to someone who then completes it contrary to instructions). And remember that even an HDC must be paid the unaltered amount of an instrument with a material alteration.

KEY CONCEPTS LIKELY TO BE TESTED ON THE CPA EXAM

1. The requirements to qualify as a holder in due course (HDC), including being able to determine from a fact situation if a person qualifies.
2. Identification of a pictured instrument as negotiable or not, and if negotiable, identification of the type of negotiable instrument.
3. The shelter principle.
4. Signature liability, primary and secondary.
5. Warranty liability.
6. General concept of defenses and the effect of a defense, real or personal.
7. Which defenses are real and which are personal.
8. Recognition of a defense from a fact situation and knowledge of whether that defense is real or personal.

KEY TERMS

Defense	Primary Signature Liability	Transfer
Holder	Secondary Signature Liability	Real Defense
Holder in Due Course	Presentment	Personal Defense
Claim	Notice of Dishonor	Extreme Duress
Take for Value	Accommodation Party	Forgery
Take in Good Faith	Guarantee of Payment	Material Alteration
Dishonor	Guarantee of Collection	Unauthorized Completion
Shelter Principle	Warranty Liability	Discharge
Impairment of the Right of Recourse		

MULTIPLE CHOICE QUESTIONS

1.   Law May 93 #42

Robb, a minor, executed a promissory note payable to bearer and delivered it to Dodsen in payment for a stereo system. Dodsen negotiated the note for value to Mellon by delivery alone and without endorsement. Mellon endorsed the note in blank and negotiated it to Bloom for value. Bloom's demand for payment was refused by Robb because the note was executed when Robb was a minor. Bloom gave prompt notice of Robb's default to Dodsen and Mellon. None of the holders of the note were aware of Robb's minority. Which of the following parties will be liable to Bloom?

	Dodsen	*Mellon*
A.	Yes	Yes
B.	Yes	No
C.	No	No
D.	No	Yes

2.   Law Nov 92 #40

A maker of a note will have a real defense against a holder in due course as a result of any of the following conditions **except**

A. Discharge in bankruptcy.
B. Forgery.
C. Fraud in the execution.
D. Lack of consideration.

3.   Law May 92 #47

To the extent that a holder of a negotiable promissory note is a holder in due course, the holder takes the note free of which of the following defenses?

A. Minority of the maker where it is a defense to enforcement of a contract.
B. Forgery of the maker's signature.
C. Discharge of the maker in bankruptcy.
D. Nonperformance of a condition precedent.

4.   Law Nov 90 #47

A $5,000 promissory note payable to the order of Neptune is discounted to Bane by blank endorsement for $4,000. King steals the note from Bane and sells it to Ott who promises to pay King $4,500. After paying King $3,000, Ott learns that King stole the note. Ott makes no further payment to King. Ott is:

A. A holder in due course to the extent of $5,000.
B. An ordinary holder to the extent of $4,500.
C. A holder in due course to the extent of $3,000.
D. An ordinary holder to the extent of $0.

5.   Law May 95 #47

Under the Negotiable Instruments Article of the UCC, which of the following circumstances would prevent a person from becoming a holder in due course of an instrument?

A. The person was notified that payment was refused.
B. The person was notified that one of the prior endorsers was discharged.
C. The note was collateral for a loan.
D. The note was purchased at a discount.

6.   Law May 95 #48

Under the Negotiable Instruments Article of the UCC, which of the following statements best describes the effect of a person endorsing a check "without recourse"?

A. The person has **no** liability to prior endorsers.
B. The person makes **no** promise or guarantee of payment on dishonor.
C. The person gives **no** warranty protection to later transferees.
D. The person converts the check into order paper.

7.   Law Nov 91 #48

For a person to be a holder in due course of a promissory note

A. The note must be payable in U.S. currency to the holder.
B. The holder must be the payee of the note.
C. The note must be negotiable.
D. All prior holders must have been holders in due course.

8.   Law May 90 #38

Bond fraudulently induced Teal to make a note payable to Wilk, to whom Bond was indebted. Bond delivered the note to Wilk. Wilk negotiated the instrument to Monk, who purchased it with knowledge of the fraud and after it was overdue. If Wilk qualifies as a holder in due course, which of the following statements is correct?

A. Monk has the standing of holder in due course through Wilk.
B. Teal can successfully assert the defense of fraud in the inducement against Monk.
C. Monk personally qualifies as a holder in due course.
D. Teal can successfully assert the defense of fraud in the inducement against Wilk.

9.   Law May 93 #43

Vex Corp. executed a promissory note payable to Tamp, Inc. The note was collateralized by some of Vex's business assets. Tamp negotiated the note to Miller for value. Miller endorsed the note in blank and negotiated it to Bilco for value. Before the note became due, Bilco agreed to release Vex's collateral. Vex refused to pay Bilco when the note became due. Bilco promptly notified Miller and Tamp of Vex's default. Which of the following statements is correct?

A. Bilco will be unable to collect from Miller because Miller's endorsement was in blank.
B. Bilco will be able to collect from either Tamp or Miller because Bilco was a holder in due course.
C. Bilco will be unable to collect from either Tamp or Miller because of Bilco's release of the collateral.
D. Bilco will be able to collect from Tamp because Tamp was the original payee.

OTHER OBJECTIVE FORMAT QUESTION (Estimated time -- 10 to 15 minutes)

Law Nov 94 #3

Question Number 3 consists of 2 parts. Part A consists of 5 items and Part B consists of 8 items. Select the **best** answer for each item. Use a No. 2 pencil to blacken the appropriate ovals on the Objective Answer Sheet to indicate your answers. **Answer all items.** Your grade will be based on the total number of correct answers.

During an audit of Trent Realty Corp.'s financial statements, Clark, CPA, reviewed the following instruments:

A. Instrument 1.

$300,000	Belle, MD
	September 15, 1993

For value received, ten years after date, I promise to pay to the order of Dart Finance Co. Three Hundred Thousand and 00/100 dollars with interest at 9% per annum compounded annually until fully paid.

This instrument arises out of the sale of land located in MD.

It is further agreed that:

1. Maker will pay all costs of collection including reasonable attorney fees.
2. Maker may prepay the amount outstanding on any anniversary date of this instrument.

G. Evans
G. Evans

The following transactions relate to Instrument 1.

* On March 15, 1994, Dart endorsed the instrument in blank and sold it to Morton for $275,000.
* On July 10, 1994, Evans informed Morton that Dart had fraudulently induced Evans into signing the instrument.
* On August 15, 1994, Trent, which knew of Evans' claim against Dart, purchased the instrument from Morton for $50,000.

Required:

Items 1 through 5 relate to Instrument 1. For each item, select from list I the correct answer and blacken the corresponding oval on the Objective Answer Sheet. An answer may be selected once, more than once, or not at all.

1. Instrument 1 is a (type of instrument)
2. Instrument 1 is (negotiability)
3. Morton is considered a (type of ownership)
4. Trent is considered a (type of ownership)
5. Trent could recover on the instrument from (liable party(s))

List I

A. Draft
B. Promissory Note
C. Security Agreement
D. Holder
E. Holder in due course
F. Holder with rights of a holder in due course under the Shelter Provision
G. Negotiable
H. Nonnegotiable
I. Evans, Morton, and Dart
J. Morton and Dart
K. Only Dart

B. Instrument 2.

Front

```
To:  Pure Bank
     Upton, VT
                              April 5, 1994

Pay to the order of M. West $1,500.00
One Thousand Five Hundred and 00/100
Dollars on May 1, 1994

                    W. Fields
                    W. Fields
```

Back

```
M. West

Pay to C. Larr
T. Keetin

C. Larr
without recourse
```

Required:

   Items 1 through 8 relate to Instrument 2. For each item, select from List II the correct answer and blacken the corresponding oval on the Objective Answer Sheet. An answer may be selected once, more than once, or not at all.

1. Instrument 2 is a (type of instrument)

2. Instrument 2 is (negotiability)

3. West's endorsement makes the instrument (type of instrument)

4. Keetin's endorsement makes the instrument (type of instrument)

5. Larr's endorsement makes the instrument (type of instrument)

6. West's endorsement would be considered (type of endorsement)

7. Keetin's endorsement would be considered (type of endorsement)

8. Larr's endorsement would be considered (type of endorsement)

List II

A. Bearer paper
B. Blank
C. Check
D. Draft
E. Negotiable
F. Nonnegotiable
G. Note
H. Order Paper
I. Qualified
J. Special

ESSAY QUESTION (Estimated time -- 15 to 20 minutes)

Law May 91 #3

River Oaks is a wholesale distributor of automobile parts. River Oaks received the promissory note shown below from First Auto, Inc., as security for payment of a $4,400 auto parts shipment. When River Oaks accepted the note as collateral for the First Auto obligation, River Oaks was aware that the maker of the note, Hillcraft, Inc., was claiming that the note was unenforceable because Alexco Co. had breached the license agreement under which Hillcraft had given the note. First Auto had acquired the note from Smith in exchange for repairing several cars owned by Smith. At the time First Auto received the note, First Auto was unaware of the dispute between Hillcraft and Alexco. Also, Smith, who paid Alexco $3,500 for the note, was unaware of Hillcraft's allegations that Alexco had breached the license agreement.

PROMISSORY NOTE
Date: 1/14/90

Hillcraft, Inc. promises to pay to Alexco Co. or Bearer the sum of $4,400 Four Thousand and 00/100 Dollars on or before May 15, 1991 (Maker may elect to extend due date by 30 days) with interest thereon at the rate of 9 ½ % per annum.

Hillcraft, Inc.
By: *P.J. Hill*
P.J. Hill, President

Reference: Alexco Licensing Agreement

The reverse side of the note was endorsed as follows:

Pay to the order of First Auto without recourse

E. Smith
E. Smith

Pay to the order of River Oaks Co.

First Auto
By: *G First*
G. First, President

First Auto is now insolvent and unable to satisfy its obligation to River Oaks. Therefore, River Oaks has demanded that Hillcraft pay $4,400, but Hillcraft has refused, asserting:

- The note is nonnegotiable because it references the license agreement and is not payable at a definite time or on demand.
- River Oaks is not a holder in due course of the note because it received the note as security for amounts owed by First Auto.
- River Oaks is not a holder in due course because it was aware of the dispute between Hillcraft and Alexco.
- Hillcraft can raise the alleged breach by Alexco as a defense to payment.
- River Oaks has no right to the note because it was not endorsed by Alexco.
- The maximum amount that Hillcraft would owe under the note is $4,000 plus accrued interest.

Required:
State whether each of Hillcraft's assertions are correct and give the reasons for your conclusions.

EXPLANATIONS TO MULTIPLE CHOICE QUESTIONS

1. D is the correct answer. Mellon incurred secondary liability by endorsing the note in blank. He could have avoided this liability by giving a restrictive endorsement, "without recourse." Dodsen made transfer warranties when he transferred the note to Mellon, but because Dodsen's transfer was without his signature, those warranties applied only to the immediate transferee, Mellon.

2. D is the correct answer. Lack of consideration is a personal defense. The incorrect answer choices all identify real defenses.

3. D is the correct answer. This question also seeks a personal defense, but unlike the previous question, does not ask directly. An HDC takes an instrument free of personal, but not real, defenses. Nonperformance of a condition is the only personal defense among the answer choices.

4. C is the correct answer. To be an HDC, Ott must have taken the note without notice of claims or defenses. The true owner, Bane, has a claim against it, but Ott was unaware of the theft when he took the note. However, another requirement to be an HDC is that value be given, which means that any promised payment must actually have been made. Here, Ott had actually paid only $3,000 for the instrument before he learned that it had been stolen. Even if he had paid additional amounts after learning of the theft (a foolish thing to do), he would be an HDC only to the extent of $3,000, the value given before receiving notice of the theft.

5. A is the correct answer. None of the incorrect choices prevent a holder from becoming a holder in due course.

6. B is the correct answer. This question illustrates the importance of reading the question carefully and choosing the option that best answers the question. Choice A, read in isolation, is a correct statement. Endorsers generally do not have liability to prior endorsers. Choice A is incorrect here because that fact is not a consequence of using the words "without recourse." Choice C is incorrect because the words "without recourse" do not negate warranty liability, and the signature accompanying the words "without recourse" extends the warranty liability to all later transferees.

7. C is the correct answer. The holder in due course doctrine applies only if an instrument is negotiable. Choice A is incorrect because an instrument must be payable in money, but it need not be United States currency.

8. A is the correct answer. Because Wilk acquired the instrument from an HDC (the assumption in the last sentence of the question), the shelter doctrine gives her the rights of an HDC even though she does not qualify as an HDC herself.

9. C is the correct answer. When Bilco released the collateral, it impaired the right of recourse, specifically the right against the collateral, in the event that the instrument was not paid. Choice B is incorrect because the discharge of Tamp and Miller is unaffected by Bilco's HDC status.

EXPLANATION TO OTHER OBJECTIVE FORMAT QUESTION

Part A

1. B is the correct answer. The words "I promise" in the instrument indicate that this is a note. Furthermore, a note is a two-party instrument, and there are only two parties to this instrument, Evans, the maker, and Dart, the payee.

2. G is the correct answer. This note includes all the requirements of negotiability and contains no promise or condition destroying negotiability.

3. E is the correct answer. Morton gave value and had no notice of any claim or defense when taking the note.

4. F is the correct answer. Trent cannot qualify as a holder in due course, but by acquiring the note from a holder in due course acquires the rights of a holder in due course under the shelter principle.

5. I is the correct answer. Evans must pay because fraud in the inducement is a personal defense and Trent has the rights of an HDC. Dart's endorsement gives him secondary liability. Morton made transfer warranties to Trent.

Part B

1. D is the correct answer. Because this three-party instrument is payable at a specific time, and not on demand, it is a draft rather than a check.

2. E is the correct answer. This draft meets all requirements of negotiability.

3. A is the correct answer. A blank endorsement results in bearer paper.

4. H is the correct answer. Keetin's special endorsement to Larr results in order paper.

5. A is the correct answer. Larr's qualified endorsement does not name a specific payee, thus the instrument is converted back to bearer paper.

6. B is the correct answer. A signature, with nothing more, is a blank endorsement.

7. J is the correct answer. Naming a specific payee results in a special endorsement.

8. I is the correct answer. Without recourse eliminates the endorser's signature liability to later transferees and is a qualified endorsement.

UNOFFICIAL AICPA ANSWER TO ESSAY QUESTION

Law May 91 #3

Hillcraft's first assertion, that the note is nonnegotiable because it references the license agreement and is not payable at a definite time or on demand, is incorrect. The note is negotiable despite the reference to the license agreement because it does not make the note subject to the terms of the agreement; rather, the reference is regarded only as a recital of its existence.

Also, Hillcraft's right to extend the time for payment does not make the note nonnegotiable because the extension period is for a definite period of time.

Hillcraft's second assertion, that River Oaks is not a holder in due course (HDC) because it received the note as security for an existing debt and, therefore, did not give value for it, is incorrect. Under the UCC Commercial Paper Article, a holder does give value for an instrument when it is taken in payment of, or as security for, an antecedent claim.

Hillcraft's third assertion, that River Oaks is not an HDC because River Oaks was aware of Alexco's alleged breach of the license agreement, is correct. If a holder of a note is aware of a dispute when it acquires the note, that holder cannot be an HDC because it took with notice.

Hillcraft's fourth assertion, that it can raise the alleged breach by Alexco as a defense to payment of the note, is incorrect. Even though River Oaks is not an HDC, under the UCC "shelter provision" it is entitled to the protection of an HDC because it took the instrument form First Auto, which was an HDC. Therefore, River Oaks did not take the note subject to Hillcraft's defense based on the alleged breach by Alexco. Hillcraft's defense is considered a personal defense and can only be used by Hillcraft against Alexco.

Hillcraft's fifth assertion, that River Oaks has no right to the note because it was not endorsed by Alexco, is incorrect. River Oaks acquired rights to the Hillcraft note without Alexco's endorsement because the note was a bearer instrument as a result of it being payable to "Alexco Company or bearer." A bearer instrument can be negotiated by delivery alone.

Hillcraft's final assertion, that the maximum amount Hillcraft would owe under the note is $4,000, plus accrued interest, is correct. If there is a conflict between a number written in numerals and also described by words, the word take precedence. Therefore, Hillcraft's maximum potential principal liability is $4,000 under the note.

Author's Note:

The "UCC Commercial Paper Article" referred to in the third paragraph is the former name of the Negotiable Instruments Article.

Notice the structure of this answer. Each of the assertions is discussed in a separate paragraph, and each paragraph begins with a clear statement of the assertion and whether it is correct or not. The question specifically asked for a statement about the correctness of each assertion supported by the reasons. It is important to follow directions carefully. A candidate could have easily discussed the legal issues correctly, but failure to address the correctness of the assertions would result in lost points.

CHAPTER 16
CREDIT, SURETYSHIP, AND SECURED TRANSACTIONS

OVERVIEW

This chapter addresses the rights of parties in various types of lending transactions. Each of these transactions will involve the lending of money, or extension of credit, by a lender, or **creditor** to a borrower, or **debtor**. In the basic lending transaction, the creditor has the right to sue the debtor for nonpayment if the debtor fails to pay the debt when due. This straightforward situation can be greatly complicated where the debtor has given a security interest to the creditor, especially where there are multiple creditors and multiple security interests. Issues often arise over which creditor(s), if any, has the right to collateral. These issues are complicated and constitute most of this chapter. The last major issue covered is suretyship, the situation where one person promises to pay the debt of another if the other person fails to do so. Although there are many complex and detailed rules to learn in this area, once they are learned, most fact situation questions can be answered fairly easily.

OUTLINE

I. **Introduction to Credit.**
   A. <u>General Terminology</u>. In a credit transaction, a creditor lends money to a debtor. With **unsecured credit** there is no security, or collateral, to make it more likely that the debt will be paid. If the debtor does not pay, the creditor's only recourse is to sue the debtor, often a futile exercise because in many cases the debtor simply does not have the assets to pay the debt. The creditor can obtain a judgment against the debtor, and can execute on the judgment, which means the courts will attach any of the debtor's assets so that those assets can be used to satisfy the judgment. This is a lengthy and costly process with no assurance that the debtor will have the assets to satisfy the judgment. The attachment cannot occur until after a judgment has been entered by the court, which is usually after a trial.
   B. <u>Secured Credit</u>. With secured credit, the debtor puts up **collateral** as part of a **security agreement**. The security agreement allows the creditor, in the event the debtor **defaults**, to use the collateral to satisfy the unpaid debt. This is usually done by selling the collateral and applying the proceeds to pay off the debt. The collateral is property identified in the security agreement. A default is any violation of the loan agreement. Failure to pay when due is the most common type of default, but other violations, such as allowing the checking account cash balance to fall below a certain level, can also constitute default. With secured credit, the creditor can fairly quickly gain possession of the collateral, and there is much greater assurance that the amount of the debt will be recovered. If the proceeds from the collateral cover only a portion of the unpaid debt, the creditor can obtain a **deficiency judgment** for the difference and will be treated as an unsecured creditor for that difference.
   C. <u>Real Property Security Interests</u>. Where the collateral for a loan is real property, the security interest is called a **mortgage**. Mortgages are covered in Chapter 28 of this guide.

II. Introduction to Security Interests in Personal Property.

A. <u>Definitions</u>. A **secured transaction** is a lending transaction where the debtor, in addition to being extended credit and promising to repay the amount borrowed, has entered into a security agreement with the creditor. The security agreement allows the creditor, the **secured party**, access to the goods covered by the agreement, the collateral, in order to satisfy the debt in the event of default. The security interests covered in this chapter apply only to **personal property**. Personal property is any property other than real property. Real property is land and any property, such as buildings, permanently attached to the land.

B. <u>Source of Law</u>. Security interests are covered in Article 9 of the UCC. Article 9 has been adopted by all states except Louisiana, although many states made minor changes to 9 when adopting it.

C. <u>Parties in a Secured Transaction</u>. Secured transactions can be entered into as either two-party transactions or three-party transactions.

1. *Two-Party Secured Transaction*. In a **two-party secured transaction**, the credit is extended by the seller of goods at the same time the goods are purchased. The seller is also the creditor in a two-party transaction, and the buyer is also the debtor. Any sale where the seller allows payment after the sale is a two-party credit transaction; if the parties enter into a security agreement, it is a two-party secured transaction.

2. *Three-Party Secured Transaction*. In a **three-party secured transaction**, the party who extends credit is a different party from the seller. In a three-party transaction, the buyer is also the debtor, as is the case in the two party transaction. A common example is where a bank lends money to a buyer of goods who purchases them from the seller. The seller does not extend credit. Lastly, in the three-party situation, the extension of credit does not necessarily occur at the same time as the purchase of goods. For example, a business may borrow money in 2001 for needed operating funds and at the same time enter into a security agreement covering equipment which it purchased several years earlier.

D. <u>Timing Is Often Crucial</u>. With secured transactions, it is often important not only <u>if</u> particular requirements have been met, but exactly <u>when</u> those requirements were first met. One common situation where timing is crucial is when multiple creditors seek the same collateral.

III.   Creating a Security Interest in Personal Property.

A. <u>Basic Requirements to Create a Security Interest</u>. The **security interest** is the right of the creditor to use the collateral to satisfy a debt after default. The security interest is created by the security agreement. The security interest does not come into existence until all three of the following requirements are met:

1. *Written Security Agreement*. A written security agreement is required, with one exception. That exception permits an oral agreement if the creditor takes physical possession of the collateral, as in the case of a pawn shop. But in the vast majority of cases where the creditor does not take possession of the collateral, there must be a written security agreement which contains the following:
   a. A Clear Description of the Collateral So It Can Be Readily Identified.
   b. The Debtor's Promise to Repay the Debt, Including Repayment Terms.
   c. The Rights of the Creditor in the Event of Default by the Debtor.
   d. The Signature of the Debtor. The creditor's signature is not needed.

2. *Value Given to the Debtor.* **Value** is any consideration that would support a simple contract. In a three-party transaction, value takes the form of cash paid by the creditor to, or on behalf of, the debtor. In a two-party transaction, the value given is the transfer of goods from the seller/creditor to the buyer/debtor. The value requirement can also be met where a security interest is given to satisfy or secure a preexisting claim or debt.

3. *Debtor Has Rights in Collateral.* The debtor must have a current or future right to the collateral, or its possession. The debtor's rights often amount to ownership, but rights less than ownership will meet this requirement.

B. Attachment. **Attachment** occurs at the moment all three of the above requirements have been met. The security interest is said to attach to the collateral. The creditor can use the collateral to satisfy an unpaid debt only after attachment has taken place. The order in which these three requirements are met will differ in various situations.

C. Types of Property. The following types of property can be the subject of a security interest:

1. *Goods.* Goods, for purposes of Article 9, are divided into four categories. The classification depends on how that good is used by the particular debtor and is not based on any inherent characteristics of the good.

   a. Consumer Goods. **Consumer goods** are items bought or used primarily for personal, family or household purposes.

   b. Equipment. **Equipment** includes goods bought or used primarily by a business.

   c. Farm Products. **Farm products** includes crops, livestock, or farming supplies.

   d. Inventory. **Inventory** includes goods held for sale or lease, including work in progress or materials.

   e. Fixtures. **Fixtures** are items of personal property which are attached to real property in such a way that they become part of the real property.

   The equipment category serves as the default category such that any good that cannot be clearly classified in any other category will be categorized as equipment. **Exam tip #1.**

2. *Instruments.* Examples include checks, notes, stocks, and bonds.

3. *Chattel Paper.* **Chattel paper** is a writing that evidences both a monetary obligation and a security interest.

4. *Documents of Title.* The most common are bills of lading and warehouse receipts.

5. *Accounts.* These include any obligation not evidenced by an instrument or chattel paper such as accounts receivable.

6. *General Intangibles.* Examples include patents, copyrights, money, and royalties.

Article 9 does not apply to transactions involving real estate mortgages, landlord's liens, artisan's liens, mechanic's liens, or judicial liens.

D. Floating Liens. A **floating lien** is a lien where the items of collateral covered can change over time and can include items acquired by the debtor after the security agreement was executed.

1. *After-Acquired Property.* An **after-acquired property** clause subjects the described after-acquired property to a preexisting security interest. For example, the security interest might cover all inventory of the debtor, currently (as of the date the security agreement is entered into) owned and acquired in the future. This is a common clause and is needed to protect the creditor because the inventory of the business is constantly changing, and a buyer in the ordinary course of business will take the item free of the security interest. Thus, new inventory items are covered by the security interest when they are acquired.

2. *Proceeds*. **Proceeds** refers to whatever is received (e.g., an account receivable or cash in the case of inventory) when a good is sold or otherwise disposed of. The creditor automatically has a security interest in the proceeds of any property in which a security interest is held, unless the security agreement provides otherwise.

3. *Future Advances*. Debtors often arrange a variable open line of credit with a lender, and, with a **future advances** clause, amounts drawn in the future against the line of credit will also be secured by the collateral. A future advances clause makes it unnecessary to enter into a new security agreement each time an additional advance is taken against the line of credit.

IV.   Perfection of a Security Interest.

A. Generally. Attachment of a security interest determines when the security interest comes into existence. **Perfection**, on the other hand, establishes the priority of security interests when there is more than one security interest in the same collateral. This priority is usually established by filing, which puts future potential lenders on notice that the property of the debtor has already been pledged as collateral and that the earlier creditor has a superior claim against the collateral in the event of default. There are many special rules for specific types of collateral and particular situations. **Exam tip #2.**

B. Perfection by Filing a Financing Statement. The most common way to perfect a security interest is to file a **financing statement**. Financing statements, once filed, are available to the public and put the world on notice of the security agreement's existence.

1. *Financing Statement Requirements*. The financing statement puts the world on notice of the existence of the security agreement. The financing statement must include the following:
   a. Debtor's Name and Mailing Address.
   b. Name and Address of Secured Party From Whom Information Concerning the Security Interest Can Be Obtained.
   c. A Statement of the Types of Collateral or a Description of the Collateral.
   d. The Debtor's Signature.

The purpose of the filing is to give notice so that further information about the security interest can be obtained. It is not necessary to file the security agreement itself, although the security agreement can be filed as the financing statement. **Exam tip #3.**

C. Where to File. Each state determines the place of filing. The UCC allows a state to choose either the office of the secretary of state or the county clerk. If the county clerk is used, the county of the debtor's residence is used unless the debtor is a nonresident, in which case the county where the property is located is the appropriate filing location. The required location can be different for different types of property.

D. Effective Period and Continuation Statements. A financing statement is effective for five years from the date of filing. To extend the period, a **continuation statement** must be filed during the last six months of the five-year period. It will extend the original financing statement for an additional five-year period. Successive continuation statements can be filed. The debtor's signature is **not** needed on a continuation statement; the secured party's signature is sufficient.

E. Perfection by Possession of Collateral. Where the creditor (the secured party) has possession of the collateral, there is no need to file because the possession of the collateral serves as perfection. The fact that the owner's property is possessed by someone else is considered notice, thus making filing unnecessary. A pawn shop is a common example, but possession of negotiable instruments and documents is the only way to perfect a security interest in them.

F. Purchase Money Security Interest in Consumer Goods. A **purchase money security interest (PMSI)** is a security interest granted in connection with the credit that allows the debtor to purchase the goods. A PMSI can be held by a seller of goods who sells the goods on credit or by a third-party lender such as a bank which lends the money to enable the purchase of the goods. Where a consumer debtor pledges previously acquired property as collateral to get a new loan, it would not be a PMSI.

1. *Automatic Perfection for Consumer Goods.* If the goods are consumer goods, perfection occurs automatically without the need to file a financing statement.

2. *Security Agreement Required.* It is only the perfection which is automatic. Attachment must occur, and it is only if all three attachment requirements are met, including having a security agreement, that perfection occurs.

3. *Not Applicable to Motor Vehicles or Fixtures.* The automatic perfection rule does not apply to motor vehicles or to consumer goods which become fixtures.

4. *Exception for Second-Hand Consumer Purchaser.* The holder of a PMSI in consumer goods is automatically perfected so long as the consumer goods remain in the hands of the original purchaser. If they are sold by the original consumer to a second-hand consumer buyer, the automatic perfection is lost, and the creditor cannot recover the goods from the second-hand buyer based on automatic perfection. If the creditor had filed (even though not required to) the PMSI, it would be good against the second-hand buyer. The second-hand buyer would have constructive notice due to the filing. The PMSI is good against the second-hand buyer also if the second-hand buyer had actual notice of the PMSI.

G. Changes to an Existing Financing Statement. The following changes to an existing financing statement must be filed in the same location where the original is filed.

1. *Statement of Assignment.* A **statement of assignment** assigns the creditor's rights to another party.

2. *Amendment.* An **amendment** may be filed, but must have the debtor's signature.

3. *Release.* A **release** ends the secured party's interest in the collateral. A release can apply to some or all of the collateral covered by a security agreement.

H. Termination Statement. A **termination statement** gives notice to the world that a particular financing statement is no longer effective. The creditor is required to file within one month of the satisfaction of the underlying debt, or within 10 days of the debtor's demand. Note that even if no termination statement has been filed, a secured party has no claim to collateral if the underlying debt has been satisfied in accordance with the debt agreement.

V. Priority of Claims.

A. Generally. Where more than one party has a claim to a debtor's collateral, several factors determine who will have the first priority claim. The factors include whether or not the creditor is secured, if and when perfection occurred, and whether any special priority rules apply. Priority becomes an issue only where there are competing claims to the same collateral.

B. <u>Priority Rules</u>. The following priority rules will resolve many disputes over competing claims.
   1. *Secured Claims Take Priority Over Unsecured Claims.*
   2. *Competing Unperfected Claims Are Resolved Based on First to Attach.*
   3. *Perfected Claims Take Priority Over Unperfected Claims.*
   4. *Competing Perfected Claims Are Resolved Based on First to File or Perfect.* The **first to file or perfect rule** means that normally the perfection date determines priority. However, in some cases a creditor will not be perfected until sometime after filing, but in such a case the earlier filing date will determine the priority. This situation arises when the filing occurs before the requirements for attachment are met. Because perfection can never occur before attachment, the filing will not immediately cause perfection to occur. For example, a bank entered into an agreement on June 15 to lend a debtor $100,000 to buy a piece of equipment with the bank having a security interest in the equipment. The bank filed the financing statement on June 16, advanced the funds to the debtor on June 20, and the debtor purchased the equipment on June 24. Even though the financing statement was filed on June 16, perfection did not occur until June 24 because attachment did not occur until the debtor acquired the equipment on June 24. Remember that perfection cannot occur until there is attachment. Nonetheless, the priority date is June 16 because priority is determined by the date of filing <u>or</u> perfection, whichever occurs first. **Exam tip #4.**
   5. *Security Interest in Fungible Commingled Goods Is Determined on a Pro Rata Basis.* Where a creditor has a perfected security interest in fungible goods which have been commingled (such as 1,000 bushels of wheat commingled with other wheat in a storage silo), the security interests rank equally with all perfected security interests which have become part of the commingled whole. The amount of each interest is based on the portion that the cost of each holder's secured goods is of the whole. Note that for such commingled goods the creditors' order of perfection is not relevant.
C. <u>Priority Rule Exceptions</u>. There are many special cases which change these rules. Some involve a grace period in which the priority date will "relate back" to some other date, usually the date goods are acquired by the debtor, if the filing is done within the grace period.
   1. *Purchase Money Security Interest in Inventory.* A PMSI in inventory takes priority only if certain steps are taken. These requirements exist because after-acquired property clauses are common with security interests in inventory. With an after-acquired property clause, a prior lienholder would reasonably believe that any new inventory received by the debtor would be subject to the prior lien. The PMSI in the new inventory takes priority over the earlier-perfected security interest only if the new PMSI lienholder has:
      1. Filed its Financing Statement Prior to the Delivery of the Inventory to the Debtor, and
      2. Given Written Notice to Any Holders of Perfected Security Interests in the Same Inventory Prior to the Delivery of the Inventory to the Debtor.
      This second requirement exists because an after-acquired property clause of a prior lienholder would apply to any new inventory the moment it becomes property of the debtor. This gives the earlier lienholder advance notice that the particular delivery of inventory will <u>not</u> be covered under any after-acquired property clause.

2. *Purchase Money Security Interest in Equipment.* A PMSI in equipment will have priority over an earlier perfected security interest if the PMSI is filed within 10 days of the date that the debtor takes possession. This 10-day grace period means that a filing within that 10-day period will be treated as if it were filed when the debtor took possession, thus giving the PMSI priority over existing perfected security interests as well as priority over any new non-PMSI security interests filed after the equipment is acquired. Unlike with an inventory PMSI, no written notice to the earlier secured parties is needed. **Exam tip #5.**

3. *Buyers in the Ordinary Course of Business.* A buyer in the ordinary course of business takes goods free of any security interests in the inventory of the seller, even those of which a buyer has knowledge. **Exam tip #6.**

4. *Other Grace Periods.* There are other situations where the creditor is given a grace period to file. This generally means that a filing within the grace period will be treated as if it occurred at the beginning of the grace period and will give that filer priority. Failure to file within the grace period will cause the priority date to be determined as of the actual filing date.

    a. Proceeds: 10 days. Many times filing is not needed because the perfection requirement for proceeds can often be met without filing.

    b. Collateral Moved to Another State: Four Months. Because security interests are filed at the state level, the creditor must file in the new state when collateral is moved into another state. If the creditor files within four months of the collateral being moved into the new state, the priority date of the filing in the old state will apply in the new state.

    c. Documents and Instruments: 21 Days. A secured party who advances new value has 21 days to perfect, which must be by possession for documents and instruments.

    d. Collateral Released to Debtor for Disposition: 21 Days. Where the creditor has perfected by possessing the collateral, if the creditor releases the collateral to the debtor so that the debtor can sell it, the creditor remains perfected for 21 days. After 21 days, the creditor must either file or take possession of the collateral again to maintain priority.

5. *Artisan's and Mechanic's Liens.* Most states have statutes providing that persons who provide labor or materials with respect to goods will obtain an **artisan's lien** or **mechanic's lien** on the goods benefitted which will have priority over even preexisting perfected security interests in the same property.

VI.   Remedies of Secured Creditor.

A. <u>Default</u>. Article 9 does not define **default**, but leaves that up to the parties in their security agreement. Typically, default is defined to include items such as failure to make payments when due, bankruptcy of the debtor, breach of the warranty of ownership of the collateral or moving the collateral to another state. Default is the event that triggers the ability of the creditor to use the collateral to obtain payment of the debt. The rules provide a balancing of the rights of creditors and debtors.

B. <u>Repossession</u>. The first step most creditors take to satisfy a defaulted debt is to **repossess** the collateral. Upon repossession the creditor can either retain the collateral, sell or otherwise dispose of it, and apply the proceeds to the debt. The secured party must act in good faith, with commercial reasonableness, and with reasonable care to preserve the collateral. In repossessing the property, the creditor cannot **breach the peace**. This generally means that if the debtor objects or resists, the creditor cannot take the property by force.

1. *Retention of Collateral.* The debtor can **retain the collateral** in satisfaction of the debtor's obligation. The creditor must give notice to the debtor unless the debtor has waived this right. For all collateral except consumer goods the creditor must also give notice to any other creditor who has given written notice of a claim to the collateral. The creditor can then retain the collateral unless either of the following occurs, in which case the collateral must be sold:

    a. Written Objection. If any party entitled to the notice gives written objection to the creditor within 21 days, the collateral must be sold, or

    b. Consumer Goods 60 Percent Paid. If the debt involves consumer goods and the debtor has paid at least 60 Percent of the cash price or the loan, the goods must be sold unless the consumer has waived this right.

2. *Disposition of Collateral.* The secured party may sell, lease, or otherwise dispose of the collateral in any commercially reasonable manner including public or private sale. Notice must be given to the debtor, and except for consumer goods, others who have given written notice of a claim to the collateral. No notice is needed if the collateral is perishable, threatens to decline in value, or is customarily sold on a recognized market. The sale also discharges all subordinate security interests or liens. **Exam tip #7.**

3. *Disposition of Proceeds from a Sale of Collateral.* Proceeds from the sale are distributed in the following order:

    a. Expenses of the Sale. These include costs of taking, holding and preparing the collateral, and can include attorneys' fees if the security agreement provides for them and state law does not prohibit attorneys' fees to be paid from the sale proceeds.

    b. Satisfaction of the Indebtedness Owed to the Secured Party.

    c. Satisfaction of Subordinate Liens. The written notification of demand must be received before the distribution of proceeds is completed.

    d. Any Remaining Surplus Goes to the Debtor.

4. *Deficiency Judgment.* In the event of a sale that does not provide funds to fully satisfy the indebtedness, the creditor can bring an action to obtain a **deficiency judgment** for the unsatisfied amount of the debt.

5. *Redemption Rights.* Prior to the sale of the collateral, or the creditor exercising a right to retain the collateral, the debtor can **redeem** the collateral by payment of all obligations secured by the collateral as well as expenses in taking and holding the collateral, and attorneys' fees if provided in the security agreement and not prohibited by state law.

C. <u>Proceeding to Judgment on the Underlying Debt</u>. The secured party may relinquish the security interest and proceed to judgment on the underlying debt. This is seldom done unless the collateral has declined in value and the debtor has other assets.

VII.   Surety and Guaranty Arrangements.

A. <u>Generally</u>. A **surety** or **guaranty** arrangement involves three parties with the surety or guarantor promising to pay a debtor's debt in the event that the debtor does not. Sureties and guarantors can be either compensated, or uncompensated, with more favorable treatment for uncompensated sureties or guarantors in some instances.

B. <u>Surety</u>. A surety assumes liability for another person's debt. A surety has primary liability for the debt along with the principal debtor, thus the creditor can attempt to collect from the surety without first attempting to collect from the principal debtor and without the principal debtor being in default. A surety can also be known as an **accommodation party** or **cosigner**.

C. <u>Guaranty</u>. A guarantor also assumes liability for another person's debt, but that liability is secondary, and does not arise until the default of the principal debtor. Guaranty agreements can differ greatly, and with some the guarantor's liability does not arise until the creditor has sued the principal debtor and exhausted all legal remedies. Such a guarantor is a guarantor of collection.

D. <u>Defenses</u>. Most defenses of the principal debtor against the creditor can be used by a surety or guarantor to avoid payment to the creditor.

   1. *Defenses of Principal Debtor Available to Surety or Guarantor.*
      a. Forgery of Debtor's Signature.
      b. Debtor Has Performed the Contract.
      c. Debtor Was Fraudulently Induced to Enter the Contract.
      d. Debtor Tendered Performance Which Was Refused by the Creditor.
      e. Creditor Has Breached Contract So as to Excuse Debtor's Performance.

   2. *Defenses of Principal Debtor Not Available to Surety or Guarantor.* These defenses of the principal debtor do not excuse the surety or guarantor from payment.
      a. Bankruptcy of Principal Debtor.
      b. Lack of Capacity (infancy or insanity) of the Principal Debtor.

   3. *Surety's or Guarantor's Own Defenses.* These defenses arise from conduct of the creditor which result in the surety or guarantor being released.
      a. Creditor's Action Which Impairs the Value of Collateral.
      b. Release of the Principal Debtor Unless the Creditor Has Reserved Her Rights Against the Surety or Guarantor.
      c. Modification of the Principal Debtor's Obligation Without the Surety's or Guarantor's Consent. With uncompensated sureties and guarantors, any modification of the obligation will result in a total release of the surety. Compensated sureties and guarantors are released only for material changes in the obligation that actually injure the compensated surety.
      d. Fraud in the Inducement Committed by the <u>Creditor</u>. Note that fraud committed by the principal debtor on the surety or guarantor is <u>not</u> a defense unless the creditor was aware of it. For example, if a debtor misrepresented his financial condition in order to get a party to sign as a surety, this fraud, unless known to the creditor, would not be a defense of the surety. **Exam tip #8.**

E. Rights of Surety or Guarantor Against the Principal Debtor.
   1. *Subrogation.* If the surety or guarantor pays the debt, the right of **subrogation** allows the surety to take the place of the creditor and collect from the principal debtor, or to use any collateral that the creditor could have.
   2. *Reimbursement.* **Reimbursement** is the right to collect from the principle debtor for amounts that the surety or guarantor has paid on the principal debtor's behalf.
   3. *Exoneration.* An action for **exoneration** is a suit to compel the principal debtor to pay the debt. If the debtor is insolvent with other debts, bankruptcy or other laws might limit the amount that the debtor pays on any one debt.

F. Rights of Surety or Guarantor Against Cosurety
   1. *Cosureties and Coguarantors.* A **cosurety** or **coguarantor** arrangement arises when more than one party promises to be secondarily liable for the same debt. They are equally liable unless the agreement specifies a different sharing of the obligation. Cosureties and coguarantors are liable in proportion to their maximum liabilities under their agreements. Thus if one of two cosureties has a maximum liability twice that of the other cosurety, for any loss, the first will be liable for two thirds of the loss and the other cosurety for one third of the loss, up to their contractual limits.
   2. *Reimbursement and Exoneration.* These rights are similar to the same rights applicable against the principal debtor.
   3. *Contribution.* **Contribution** is a right that applies only against a cosurety or coguarantor. It is the right of one cosurety or coguarantor to recover amounts paid by one cosurety or coguarantor on behalf of other cosureties or coguarantors. Thus it is similar to reimbursement, but applies only to cosureties or coguarantors.

F. Rights of Surety or Guarantor Against Creditor. The surety or guarantor's rights against the creditor are limited.
   1. *Right to Compel Collection.* There is generally no right of a surety or guarantor to compel collection from the principal debtor, but a surety or guarantor can compel collection when the surety is likely to become insolvent or leave the state without paying once there is a cause of action on the payment obligation.
   2. *Use of Secured Property.* There is generally no right of a surety to compel the creditor to proceed against the collateral before proceeding against the surety. However, the surety can compel the creditor to proceed against the collateral if the surety's right of reimbursement against the principal debtor is worthless and proceeding against the collateral would not result in unreasonable expense or delay to the creditor. Guarantor agreements often require steps be taken against the collateral before seeking payment from the guarantor.
   3. *Use of Funds Received.* Where a surety or guaranty agreement covers only certain obligations of the principal debtor, the creditor is not obligated to apply the funds to any particular obligations unless the **principal** debtor objects.
   4. *Notice.* The surety or guarantor does not have a right to receive notice of the principal debtor's failure to pay.

VIII. Collection Remedies.

A. <u>Generally</u>. These remedies apply to the collection of any debt. A security interest is not necessary. Secured creditors usually first proceed against the collateral, and resort to the following remedies only if the collateral proceeds do not satisfy the debt. The creditor usually has the choice of which remedy to pursue, and can pursue more than one if the first does not result in full payment of the amount owed.

B. <u>Attachment</u>. **Attachment** is a prejudgment remedy where the court will seize property of the purported debtor prior to the conclusion of a lawsuit. Because the court has not yet determined if the debtor actually owes the debt, attachment is allowed only if the plaintiff shows:

1. *That There Is a Default*,
2. *The Statutory Grounds for the Attachment*, and
3. *That the Debtor Is Attempting to Transfer the Property Before the Trial.*

If the plaintiff loses the trial, the plaintiff must compensate the defendant for any monetary loss associated with the loss of use of the property, including court costs. **Exam tip #9.**

C. <u>Execution</u>. **Execution** is a postjudgment remedy where the court will seize property of a party who has not paid a valid court judgment. The existence of the judgment allows the property to be taken by the court and sold to satisfy the debt, with any excess being returned to the debtor. State laws exempt certain property, such as clothing or furniture to a set amount, or a homestead exemption, limiting the ability to take the judgment debtor's home.

D. <u>Garnishment</u>. **Garnishment** is similar to execution but applies when the property is held by someone other than its owner. Bank accounts are often garnished, as are wages (property of the employee held by the employer). Wage garnishments are limited to 75 percent of after tax income or 30 hours pay at the federal minimum wage, whichever is greater. Stricter state limits apply in many states.

E. <u>Composition Agreement</u>. A **composition agreement** is an agreement among several creditors of a debtor who is unable to pay all her debts. Typically, each creditor forgives a portion of the debt. If the debtor fails to perform the composition agreement, affected creditors can seek to enforce either the composition agreement or the original debt.

F. <u>Assignment for the Benefit of Creditors</u>. Debtors can voluntarily assign title to their property to a trustee to be sold to satisfy creditors' claims. If the assignment is made to more than one creditor, creditors are paid pro rata based on the amount of their claims.

EXAM TIPS

1. Exam questions often describe the debtor's use of secured property. Because the classification of the type of goods depends on their use, pay attention to this information.
2. Candidates must know the difference between **attachment** and **perfection**, as well as the relationship between them. Be sure to know the attachment requirements as well as the perfection requirements. To remember that Attachment must occur before Perfection, remember that "A" occurs before "P" in the alphabet. Remember also that <u>P</u>erfection and <u>P</u>riority both start with the letter "P."

3. Do not confuse the security agreement and the financing statement. The security agreement sets out the terms of the agreement between the debtor and creditor. The financing statement is the document filed to put the world on notice of the existence (though not necessarily all the terms) of the security agreement and tells how to find more information about the security agreement itself.

4. Be sure to understand the first to file or perfect rule. With priority questions, first determine the exact situation (whether secured, perfected, etc.) of the creditors before applying the priority rules. Also, remember that perfection can also occur by possession, so be alert for fact situations where the creditor has possession of collateral.

5. Questions involving purchase money security interests appear fairly often on the exam. Candidates should always be on the lookout for facts indicating that the debtor is using the borrowed funds to <u>buy</u> the secured property or that the seller is extending the credit. If a PMSI situation, then apply the appropriate rule for the particular type of goods. Be sure to know the PMSI rules for each type of goods as they differ greatly.

6. Remember that a buyer in ordinary course of business will obtain property free of any security interest in the seller's inventory, even if the buyer has knowledge of that security interest.

7. A private sale is acceptable, so long as commercially reasonable. Be sure to know that all subordinate security interests are discharged upon the sale. The proceeds distribution rules provide that these subordinate interests will be paid to the extent the sale provides funds; but whether or not those claims are satisfied, the sale eliminates them.

8. If a surety or guarantor is a victim of fraud, be sure to determine who committed the fraud since only fraud by the creditor operates as a defense.

9. Be aware that the term "attachment" applies to two unrelated situations. Attachment by a court of a purported debtor's property is unrelated to the attachment of a security interest pursuant to a security agreement.

KEY CONCEPTS LIKELY TO BE TESTED ON THE CPA EXAM

1. Attachment and perfection requirements and whether they exist in a fact situation.
2. Classification of types of goods.
3. The general priority requirements.
4. The rules for PMSIs and other special rules affecting priority.
5. Rights of a secured party upon the debtor's default.
6. The defenses to payment of a surety or guarantor.
7. The rights of a surety, including what a surety does not have a right to.

KEY TERMS

Creditor	Floating Lien	Retention of Collateral
Debtor	After-Acquired Property	Redemption Rights
Unsecured Credit	Proceeds	Surety
Collateral	Future Advances	Guaranty
Security Agreement	Perfection	Accommodation Party
Default	Financing Statement	Cosigner
Deficiency Judgment	Continuation Statement	Subrogation
Secured Transaction	Statement of Assignment	Reimbursement
Secured Party	Amendment	Exoneration
Personal Property	Release	Cosurety or Coguarantor
Security Interest	Termination Statement	Contribution
Value Given	First to File or Perfect	Attachment (by a Court)
Attachment (Security Interest)	Artisan's Lien	Execution
Consumer Goods	Mechanic's Lien	Garnishment
Equipment	Default	Composition Agreement
Farm Products	Repossession	Purchase Money Security Interest
Inventory	Buyer in the Ordinary Course of Business	(PMSI)
Fixtures	Two-Party Secured Transaction	
Chattel Paper	Three-Party Secured Transaction	

MULTIPLE CHOICE QUESTIONS

1.   Law May 94 #52

Under the UCC Secured Transactions Article, what is the order of priority for the following security interests in store equipment?

I.   Security interest perfected by filing on April 15, 1994.

II.   Security interest attached on April 1, 1994.

III.   Purchase money security interest attached April 11, 1994 and perfected by filing on April 20, 1994.

A. I, III, II.
B. II, I, III.
C. III, I, II.
D. III, II, I.

2.   Law Nov 93 #59

Grey Corp. sells computers to the public. Grey sold and delivered a computer to West on credit. West executed and delivered to Grey a promissory note for the purchase price and a security agreement covering the computer. West purchased the computer for personal use. Grey did not file a financing statement. Is Grey's security interest perfected?

A. Yes, because Grey retained ownership of the computer.

B. Yes, because it was perfected at the time of attachment.

C. No, because the computer was a consumer good.

D. No, because Grey failed to file a financing statement.

3.   Law Nov 94 #58

Under the Secured Transactions Article of the UCC, which of the following purchasers will own consumer goods free of a perfected security interest in the goods?

A. A merchant who purchases the goods for resale.
B. A merchant who purchases the goods for use in its business.
C. A consumer who purchases the goods from a consumer purchaser who gave the security interest.
D. A consumer who purchases the goods in the ordinary course of business.

4.   Law May 94 #48

Under the UCC Secured Transactions Article, which of the following events will always prevent a security interest from attaching?

A. Failure to have a written security agreement.
B. Failure of the creditor to have possession of the collateral.
C. Failure of the debtor to have rights in the collateral.
D. Failure of the creditor to give present consideration for the security interest.

5.   Law Nov 89 #53

Perfection of a security interest permits the secured party to protect itself by

A. Avoiding the need to file a financing statement.
B. Preventing another creditor from obtaining a security interest in the same collateral.
C. Establishing priority over the claims of most subsequent secured creditors.
D. Denying the debtor the right to possess the collateral.

6.   Law Nov 93 #58

Winslow Co., which is in the business of selling furniture, borrowed $60,000 from Pine Bank. Winslow executed a promissory note for that amount and used all of its accounts receivable as collateral for the loan. Winslow executed a security agreement that described the collateral. Winslow did not file a financing statement. Which of the following statements best describes this transaction.

A. Perfection of the security interest occurred even though Winslow did **not** file a financing statement.
B. Perfection of the security interest occurred by Pine having an interest in accounts receivable.
C. Attachment of the security interest did **not** occur because Winslow failed to file a financing statement.
D. Attachment of the security interest occurred when the loan was made and Winslow executed the security agreement.

7.   Law May 93 #49

A party who filed a security interest in inventory on April 1, 1993, would have a superior interest to which of the following parties?

A. A holder of a mechanic's lien whose lien was filed on March 15, 1993.
B. A holder of a purchase money security interest in after acquired property filed on March 20, 1993.
C. A purchaser in the ordinary course of business who purchased on April 10, 1993.
D. A judgment lien creditor who filed its judgment on April 15, 1993.

8.   Law R96 #13
Which of the following will enable a creditor
to collect money from a debtor's wages?
A. An order of receivership.
B. An order of garnishment.
C. A writ of execution.
D. A writ of attachment.

9.   Law Nov 92 #28
A distinction between a surety and a co-surety
is that only a co-surety is entitled to
A. Reimbursement (Indemnification).
B. Subrogation.
C. Contribution.
D. Exoneration.

OTHER OBJECTIVE FORMAT QUESTION (Estimated time -- 10 to 15 minutes)

Law R96 #2(b)

b. Under the Secured Transactions Article of the UCC, any transaction intended to establish a
security interest in personal property is governed by requirements for the creation and satisfaction of
that interest.

Required:

Items 1 through 5 relate to situations involved in the creation and/or satisfaction of a security
interest. For each item, select the effect that will result from each situation form List II and blacken
the corresponding oval on the *Objective Answer Sheet*. An answer may be selected once, more than
once, or not at all.

1. The security interest obtained by a creditor
   who lends money to a debtor to purchase
   goods used in the debtor's business will
   be

2. A seller of consumer goods who obtains
   an oral security agreement from a
   purchaser in the ordinary course of
   business will have

3. A creditor who is transferred collateral to
   hold as security by a debtor, pursuant to
   agreement, will have

4. A creditor who files a financing statement
   would, at the most, have

5. A creditor who files a financing statement
   on October 15 will have priority over
   another creditor who has a signed but
   unfiled security agreement dated October
   1 because of

List II--Effect
A. An attached security interest.
B. A priority due to attachment.
C. A priority due to perfection.
D. A priority due to chronological order.
E. A purchase money security interest.
F. A security interest in receivables.
G. A security interest perfected by filing.
H. A security interest perfected without filing.
I. No security interest.

ESSAY QUESTION (Estimated time -- 15 to 20 minutes)

Law Nov 91#5

Mead, a junior member of a CPA firms's audit staff, was assigned to assist in auditing Abco Electronics, Inc.'s financial statements. Abco sells various brands of computer equipment to the general public, and to distributors who sell the equipment to retail customers for personal and business use. One of Mead's assignments was to evaluate the following transactions:

- On September 1, Abco sold a CDM computer out of its inventory to Rice, who intended to use it for businsess purposes. Rice paid 25% of the purchase price and executed and delivered to Abco a promissory note for the balance. A security agreement was signed only by the Abco sales representative. Abco failed to file a financing statement. Rice is in default under the promissory note. Rice claimed that Abco does not have an effective security interest in the computer because Rice did not sign the security agreement, and because Abco did not file a financing statement.

- On August 18, Abco sold a computer to Baker, who intended to use it for business inventory and accounts payable control, and payroll processing. Baker paid 20% of the purchase price and executed and delivered to Abco a promissory note for the balance and a security agreement covering the computer. Abco filed a financing statement on August 27. On August 25, Baker borrowed $5,000 from Condor Finance Co., giving Condor a promissory note for the loan amount and a security agreement covering the computer. Condor filed a financing statement on August 26. Baker defaulted on the promissory note given to Abco and its obligation to Condor. Condor has asserted that its security interest in the computer is superior to Abco's.

Required:

State whether the claims of Rice and Condor are correct and give the reasons for your conclusions.

EXPLANATIONS TO MULTIPLE CHOICE QUESTIONS

1. C is the correct answer. A purchase money security interest in equipment has priority over earlier perfected security interests if it is filed within 10 days of the debtor taking possession of the equipment. A perfected security interest always has priority over an unperfected security interest, thus the security interest perfected on April 15 has second priority here.

2. B is the correct answer. This was a Purchase Money Security Interest in consumer goods, and thus perfection is automatic (no financing statement need be filed) once attachment occurs.

3. D is the correct answer. Goods purchased in the ordinary course of business will be free of any security interest in the inventory of the seller, even if known to the buyer. Choice C is incorrect because the second-hand buyer will be free from any automatically-perfected PMSI, but will be subject to any prior security interest (including a PMSI) which has been perfected by filing.

4. C is the correct answer. Choices A and B are incorrect because a written security agreement is usually required, but taking possession of the collateral eliminates the requirement for a written agreement. Choice D is incorrect because a security interest can validly be given in connection with a preexisting debt.

5. C is the correct answer. The correct answer is a statement of the general effect of perfection.

6. D is the correct answer. This question tests the difference in attachment and perfection. Choice C is incorrect because filing relates to perfection, not to attachment.

7. D is the correct answer. The priority date of a judgment lien is determined by its filing date. Choice A is incorrect because the mechanic's lien was filed prior to April 1. Note that the filing date is not important because a mechanics lien takes priority over earlier perfected security interests as well.

8. B is the correct answer. Garnishment applies where the debtor's property (here, the wages) is in the hands of another party (here, the employer). Choice C is incorrect because execution applies to property in the debtor's possession and is used to satisfy a judgment. Choice D is incorrect because attachment applies to property in the debtor's possession prior to a judgment.

9. C is the correct answer. Contribution is the right of one cosurety against to recover amounts paid on behalf of another cosurety. Choices A and D represent rights against a cosurety which are also rights of any surety against the principal debtor.

EXPLANATION TO OTHER OBJECTIVE FORMAT QUESTION

1. E is the correct answer. A creditor who lends money to acquire the goods covered by a security interest will obtain a purchase money security interest, or PMSI, in the goods. A PMSI can be held either by the seller of the goods in a two-party transaction or by a third party such as a bank.

2. I is the correct answer. An oral security agreement is valid only if the secured party retains or obtains possession of the goods.

3. H is the correct answer. Possession of the collateral results in perfection without filing. Thus, possession of collateral has two effects. It eliminates the requirement for a written security agreement and results in perfection without filing.

4. G is the correct answer. The words "at the most" appear because filing the financing statement is no assurance that there is perfection. Attachment must occur in order for there to be perfection. Thus, if the security interest has not attached, the filing does not result in perfection. Always remember that there can be no perfection without attachment.

5. C is the correct answer. A perfected security interest has priority over one that is unperfected.

UNOFFICIAL AICPA ANSWER TO ESSAY QUESTION

Law Nov 91 #5

Rice's assertion that Abco does not have an effective security in the CDM computer purchased by Rice is correct. For Abco to have an enforceable security interest in the collateral, the security interest claimed must have attached. Attachment requires that:

- The secured party (Abco) has given value;

- The debtor (Rice) has rights in the collateral; and

- The debtor (Rice) has executed and delivered to the creditor (Abco) a security agreement covering the collateral.

In this case, all but one of the requirements are met. The security agreement is ineffective because it was not signed by the debtor (Rice). Abco's failure to perfect its security interest by filing a financing statement would have no effect on the enforceability of the security interest against Rice.

Condor's assertion that its security interest in the computer is superior to Abco's incorrect. Both Condor's and Abco's security interests are perfected. Condor's security interest was perfected when it filed its financing statement on August 26. Because Abco's security interest was a purchase money security interest in collateral other than inventory, its security interest was perfected at the time of the sale to Baker (August 18), provided it filed a financing statement at the time Baker took possession of the computer or within the UCC time period for perfection. Abco's security interest was perfected on August 18 before Condor's was perfected (on August 26), because Abco filed a financing statement within the applicable UCC time period. Therefore, Abco's security interest is superior to Condor's.

Author's Note:

The reference to collateral other than inventory generally means equipment, as consumer goods have separate rules for a purchase money security interest.

Remember that attachment, but not perfection, is needed for the creditor to have rights in the collateral against the debtor.

The last paragraph of the answer refers to the "UCC time period for perfection." This is a reference to the 10-day grace period for filing a purchase money security interest in noninventory (equipment). This answer would be more complete if it explained that the period is 10 days and that the period is measured from when the debtor takes possession of the equipment.

CHAPTER 17
BANKRUPTCY AND REORGANIZATION

OVERVIEW

Bankruptcy law is based on federal statute, although the federal statute allows the states to make certain modifications. The four chapters of bankruptcy cover different types of debtors and achieve different results. The two possible results of bankruptcy are liquidation and reorganization. Bankruptcy cases are tried in special federal courts and proceed through a series of steps in a specified order. These steps differ depending on whether the debtor is an individual or a business, and whether the case is a liquidation or reorganization. The liquidation process aims to provide an equitable distribution of the assets of the debtor to the creditors in an orderly process. Certain debts have higher priority than others, and will be more likely to be paid. Liquidation of a business results in its termination, whereas an individual debtor receives a **fresh start**. The reorganization process for a business aims to save the business through concessions from creditors in which the creditors might forgive part of the debt or extend payment terms. CPA exam candidates must understand the steps in the different bankruptcy processes, and the many special rules. Candidates must also be able to determine the distribution of the bankruptcy estate proceeds to various creditors in a liquidation case.

OUTLINE

I. **General Concepts of Bankruptcy.**
   A. <u>Source of Law</u>. Bankruptcy law is based on the **Bankruptcy Reform Act of 1978** and the various amendments to it since 1978. Together, these are referred to as the **Bankruptcy Code.**
   B. <u>Bankruptcy Courts</u>. All bankruptcy cases are heard in special federal bankruptcy courts which handle bankruptcy cases only.
   C. <u>Goal of Law</u>. The past practice of putting bankrupt persons in prisons proved unsatisfactory. The current bankruptcy law has several goals in liquidation cases.
      1. *Single Proceeding*. The bankruptcy case replaces separate lawsuits by each creditor.
      2. *Orderly Liquidation*. The bankruptcy law determines the amounts (based on the assets available in each case) to be distributed to each creditor. This eliminates the "race to the courthouse" if the assets were distributed according to who sued first.
      3. *Equitable Distribution*. The distribution rules are designed so that creditors share the loss from the bankrupt in an equitable manner. This includes giving certain types of debts priority over others.
      4. *Fresh Start*. Individuals receive a fresh start, free of most or all of their past debts.
      5. *Reorganization Goals*. A reorganization is designed to allow the business to survive by not liquidating it, but rather adjusting the debts in an equitable manner.
   D. <u>The Bankruptcy Chapters</u>. The chapter numbers are based on the Bankruptcy Code.
      1. *Chapter 7--Liquidation*. A **liquidation** is also known as straight bankruptcy and can be filed by an individual or business.
      2. *Chapter 9--Municipal Debt Adjustment*. This has not been tested on the CPA exam.
      3. *Chapter 11--Reorganization*. A **reorganization** is generally available to businesses only.

4. *Chapter 13--Consumer Debt Adjustment.* A **consumer debt adjustment** is similar in some ways to a reorganization because the debtor will remain liable for a portion of the debts.

II. Chapter 7--Liquidation.

A. Overview. In a liquidation, the assets of the debtor are gathered, sold, and the proceeds are used to pay the debts of the debtor in priority order to the extent that there are funds to do so. Unpaid debts are discharged, meaning that they are no longer a legal obligation. Individuals then receive a fresh start. There are exceptions to many of the rules; for example, the debtor is allowed to keep some property, and certain debts cannot be discharged. The specific steps that follow will occur in most liquidations. **Exam tip #1.**

B. Petition. All bankruptcy cases are initiated by the filing of a petition.

1. *No Insolvency Requirement.* There is no requirement that a debtor be unable to pay debts, although the person must have at least one debt.

2. *Voluntary Petition.* Any debtor can file a **voluntary petition.** For example, a debtor with $400,000 in assets and $20,000 in debts can file a voluntary petition, but such action would be pointless. It would result in the debt being paid, the remaining assets returned to the debtor, and the debtor paying court costs and attorney fees. A married couple can file one joint petition.

3. *Involuntary Petition.* An **involuntary petition** is filed by creditors when the creditors are not getting paid by the debtor. The creditors must show that the debtor is not paying his debts as they come due. The requirements to file differ based on the number of creditors.

   a. Fewer Than 12 Creditors. Where the debtor has fewer than 12 creditors, any one creditor with an amount owed to her of at least $10,775 can file an involuntary petition. If the creditor is owed less than this amount, the creditor must find other creditors to join in the petition such that the total owed to the petitioning creditors is at least the minimum amount. For example, a creditor who is owed $7,000 must find at least one other creditor, and the amount owed to the other creditor(s) must be at least $3,775.

   b. Twelve or More Creditors. Where there are 12 or more creditors, an involuntary petition has the same minimum debt requirement, but at least three creditors must join in the petition regardless of the amount owed. The law reasons that if only one or two creditors are not getting paid, it is likely that the cause is something other than bankruptcy, such as a contract dispute. **Exam tip #2.**

C. Order for Relief. The **order for relief** is the court order proclaiming that the case is accepted for further proceedings. It is automatic in voluntary cases, but in involuntary cases the debtor can object to the petition, with the court then deciding whether to issue the order of dismiss the petition. For example, where an involuntary petition was filed by a creditor owed $20,000 by a debtor with 10 creditors, the debtor might object, explaining that the particular creditor is not being paid because purchased merchandise was defective. The bankruptcy court could dismiss the petition and the creditor could file a collection suit in a regular court.

D. Meeting of Creditors. At the **meeting of creditors**, the debtor must appear and answer the questions of creditors.

E. <u>Appointment of Trustee</u>.   A **trustee** is elected by the creditors and becomes the legal representative of the bankrupt's estate (the debtor's assets). The trustee is paid for serving as such, and has many duties, most involving the gathering , collection, and sale of assets and the distribution of the proceeds. The trustee also files claims on behalf of the estate, including claims to recover voidable transfers, discussed below. The trustee is accountable to the court. The trustee is often a CPA or attorney, but this is not required.

F. <u>Proof of Claims</u>. Unsecured creditors must file **proof of claims** for amounts owed to them.

G. <u>Automatic Stay</u>. The **automatic stay** stops most pending legal actions against the debtor, and prevents most new ones from being filed.

   1. *Most Actions Stayed.* Most actions by creditors such as collections suits or repossessions of collateral are suspended pending the outcome of the bankruptcy proceedings.

   2. *Bankruptcy Court Addresses All.* These other actions are stayed because the bankruptcy court will essentially handle most of them through the bankruptcy process, and the bankruptcy court's award, if any, will make a separate judgment of another court meaningless.

   3. *Protections of Collateral.* Relief from the stay will be granted if it is necessary to give the creditor quick access to the collateral to protect against spoilage or a rapid decline in market value. The creditor would then be able to repossess and dispose of the collateral.

   4. *Other Exceptions.* Certain other actions are not stayed, including criminal proceedings, alimony cases, child support cases, and tax proceedings.

H. <u>Property of the Bankruptcy Estate</u>. All property of the debtor is part of the bankruptcy estate, including gifts, inheritances, life insurance proceeds, and property from divorce settlements.

I. <u>Exempt Property</u>. An individual debtor can keep certain **exempt property** from being used to satisfy creditors. There is no exempt property for business debtors.

   1. *Federal Exempt Property Limits.* The federal limits are quite low, such as $7,500 for an interest in a residence, also known as the homestead exemption.

   2. *States Can Set Own Limits.* The Bankruptcy Code specifically allows states to set their own exempt property rules and limits. The states which have set their own limits generally allow debtor to keep more property. Some of these states mandate use of their limits while others give debtors the choice of using the state or federal limits. **Exam tip #3.**

J. <u>Voidable Transfers</u>. Certain transfers of property (cash or any other assets) by the debtor before the date of the petition are **voidable transfers** which the trustee can recover from the recipient. Any transfer or payment which meets the requirements of a voidable transfer will be brought back into the bankruptcy estate and thus become available for distribution to the creditors. There are two types of these transfers, preferential transfers and fraudulent transfers. **Exam tip #4.**

K. <u>Preferential Transfers</u>. A **preferential transfer** is a transfer (in many cases the "transfer" is a payment of cash; the two terms are often used interchangeably) made prior to the filing of the petition that allows one creditor to receive an amount which might be unfairly large compared to what the other creditors would get in the bankruptcy. Preferential payments are not illegal when made. It is not illegal for a debtor to pay one creditor in full, such as an electronics store, while not paying another, such as a furniture store. Although such a payment is legal, in a bankruptcy case the payment might be taken back from the electronics store to be distributed among all creditors (including the electronics store).

1. *Requirements for Preferential Transfers*. A payment is considered preferential, and thus recoverable by the trustee, if it is a transfer:
   a. Made by a debtor to a creditor,
   b. Is made within 90 days before the filing of the petition,
   c. Is made for antecedent debt, and
   d. Gives the creditor who received it a larger payment than that creditor would receive under a Chapter 7 liquidation if the transfer had not been made.

   Under these rules, if a petition is filed on August 1, any payment made by the creditor in the 90 days prior to August 1 will be examined by the trustee to see if it qualifies as preferential and does not meet any of the exceptions below. The determination that a payment is preferential has no effect on the debtor, but results in recovering an amount from one creditor which is then made available for the general distribution.

2. *One-Year Period for Insiders*. The 90-day period is changed to one year for payments made to **insiders** of the debtor, which includes relatives, partners, officers, directors, and corporations having a relationship with the debtor.

3. *Exceptions*. Many payments made by a debtor that meet the requirements above are not recoverable because they meet one of the following exceptions:
   a. Current Consideration. Any transfer made where consideration is received at the same time, or nearly the same time, as the payment was made is not recoverable by the trustee from the recipient.
   b. Ordinary Course of Business. Any payments made in the ordinary course of business are not recoverable. Regular payments on installment loans would qualify for this exceptions, as would payments consistent with a long-term pattern.
   c. Consumer Debtor--$600. Any payment of less than $600 made by a consumer debtor is not recoverable.
   d. Alimony and Child Support. These payments are also not recoverable.

4. *Preferential Liens*. The definition of transfer includes liens granted. A lien is considered a transfer because it transfers rights in the collateral, allowing the lienholder, rather than the general bankruptcy estate, to benefit from the collateral. A preferential lien is simply invalidated, making the collateral available to the bankruptcy estate. The same exceptions apply. If a bank advanced $20,000 to the debtor and the debtor gave the bank a lien as part of the transaction, the lien would not be preferential because the amount advanced, the $20,000, would qualify as current consideration.

L. Fraudulent Transfers. A **fraudulent transfer** is any transfer made with the intent to "hinder, delay, or defraud" creditors.

1. *Time Period*. The Bankruptcy Code provides a one-year period to examine whether transfers were fraudulent, but many states have a longer period which applies.

2. *To Any Transferee*. Fraudulent transfers can be made to anyone, whether or not a creditor, unlike preferential transfers which apply only to transfers made to creditors.

3. *Fraudulent Intent*. There must have been an improper, or fraudulent intent for the transfer to be fraudulent.

4. *Inadequate Consideration*. Where an asset was sold for less than its fair value, the fraudulent intent need not be shown, and the asset can be recovered. Any good faith purchasers are entitled to be refunded the amount they paid.

5. *Examples of Fraudulent Transfers.* If a debtor gave his mother a valuable antique before filing bankruptcy, that transfer could be avoided, meaning the antique would become part of the estate. If the debtor sold his $20,000 sports car to a good faith purchaser for $14,000, the trustee could recover the car from its purchaser, but would be required to refund the $14,000 paid. Of course, the lower the price paid relative to the asset's value, the harder it will be for the purchaser to show good faith. **Exam tip #5.**

M. Priority of Distribution. Once any voidable transfers have been recovered by the trustee and the other assets of the debtor sold, the estate will consist of cash for distribution. Assets are distributed in **distribution priority** order. Creditors at one level are fully satisfied before those at the next level receive anything. Where there is some money for creditors at a level, but not enough to satisfy all those claims, all creditors will receive the same percentage of their claim amount. Thus where $4,000 is available for claims of $10,000, it would often be stated as receiving 40 cents on the dollar. Once all assets are distributed, any unpaid claims will remain unpaid.

1. *Secured Creditors.* Secured creditors have first claim to the amount of their debt, or the value of the collateral, whichever is less. If the collateral, such as the such as the auto in an auto loan, does not fully satisfy the debt, the creditor becomes an unsecured creditor for the shortage.

2. *Priority Unsecured Creditors.* Unsecured creditors receive payment in the following priority order:

   a. Administrative Expenses. These include fees of the trustee and other experts, such as attorneys, CPAs, and appraisers.

   b. Gap Creditors. A party who extends credit to a debtor (in involuntary cases only) in the period between the filing of the petition and the granting of the order for relief is a **gap creditor.**

   c. Wage Claims. This priority is limited to the first $4,300 of unpaid wages per employee and applies only to amounts earned in the 90 days prior to the filing of the petition.

   d. Employee Benefit Plan Contributions. This limit is also $4,300, but applies to amounts applicable for 180 days prior to the filing of the petition.

   e. Grain Farmers and Fishermen. Grain farmers and fishermen have a priority for up to $4,3000 against grain or fish storage facilities.

   f. Consumer Deposits. The priority claim for deposits for goods or services not delivered is limited to $1,950.

   g. Alimony and Child Support.

   h. Most Tax Claims. **Exam tip #6.**

3. *General Unsecured Creditors.* General unsecured creditors have the last priority, with such claims sometimes called nonpriority claims. Amounts in excess of any priority claim limits are considered general unsecured claims. For example, an employee claimant with $5,000 in unpaid wages would have a third-priority claim for $4,300 and a nonpriority claim for $700.

N. Discharge of Remaining Unpaid Debts. Any debts remaining unpaid after all assets are distributed are discharged. There are a number of exceptions below.

O. <u>Nondischargeable Debts</u>. Nondischargeable debts include:
   1. *Tax Claims Within Three Years of Filing the Petition*. Older tax claims are discharged. Also nondischargeable are any debts incurred to pay taxes.
   2. *Certain Government Fines*.
   3. *Claims for Wilful or Malicious Injury to Persons of Property*.
   4. *Claims Arising From Fraud, Larceny, or Embezzlement by the Debtor Acting as a Fiduciary*.
   5. *Alimony, Maintenance, or Child Support*.
   6. *Unscheduled Claims*. These are debts that the debtor did not list on the petition.
   7. *Luxury Goods*. Amounts for luxury goods acquired within 60 days of filing the petition are not dischargeable to the extent the debts exceed $500 to any one creditor, and in their entirety if they exceed $1,075 to one creditor.
   8. *Credit Cards*. Charges and cash advances within 60 days of the petition on credit cards and other open-ended credit are not discharged if the total of such charges exceeds $1,075.
   9. *DUI Judgments*. Judgments against the debtor for operating a motor vehicle while intoxicated are not dischargeable. **Exam tips #7 & 8.**

P. <u>Student Loans</u>. Student loans are not dischargeable within the first seven years of when they became due, which usually means when repayment began. Thereafter, they are dischargeable as other debts. However, even within the first seven years they can be discharged if the debtor can show it would be an undue hardship if they were not discharged. With other nondishargeable debts, the debtor does not have the opportunity to show undue hardship and be discharged.

Q. <u>Reaffirmation Agreements</u>. A **reaffirmation agreement** is an agreement to pay a debt even though it could be discharged in the bankruptcy. In order to prevent coercion by creditors and to prevent debtors from reaffirming amounts that they will not be able to pay back, reaffirmation agreements:
   1. *Must Be Entered Into Prior to Discharge,*
   2. *Must Be Filed With the Court,*
   3. *Must Be Approved by the Court if the Debtor Does Not Have an Attorney*, and
   4. *Can Be Rescinded*. The debtor can rescind the reaffirmation agreement up until discharge, and until 60 days after the agreement is filed with the court, whichever is later.

R. <u>Actions of Debtor Which Prevent Discharge</u>. Certain debtor conduct will prevent a discharge of any debts, including:
   1. *Making False Representations About Financial Condition in Obtaining Credit.*
   2. *Concealing Property or Making Fraudulent Transfers.*
   3. *Falsifying, Concealing, or Destroying Records of the Debtor's Financial Condition.*
   4. *Failing to Account for Any Assets.*
   5. *Failing to Answer a Creditor's Questions.*
   6. *Refusing to Follow a Court Order.*

S. <u>No Discharge for Corporations and Partnerships</u>. Corporations and partnerships are not granted a discharge. Unpaid debt of a bankrupt corporation will probably never be paid because the corporation will cease to exist. Partnership debts might be paid because of the unlimited personal liability of the partners.

T. <u>Six-Year Limit</u>. Only one discharge is allowed every six years.

III.   Chapter 11--Reorganization.

    A. <u>Overview</u>. In a reorganization, the goal is for the business to survive. In a reorganization, the creditors and the court develop and adopt a plan by which the business hopes to survive its current difficulties. Often, the creditors will lose less than if the business were liquidated, although in some reorganizations the creditors would have been better off with a liquidation.

    B. <u>Petitions</u>. The requirements for petitions, orders for relief, and the automatic stay are similar to those under a Chapter 7 bankruptcy.

    C. <u>Debtor in Possession</u>. The debtor will usually continue to operate the business as a **debtor in possession** unless there is a showing of cause, such as fraud or gross mismanagement, to appoint a trustee.

    D. <u>Creditors' Committees</u>. After the order for relief, a creditors' committee is appointed, usually consisting of the holders of the seven largest unsecured claims. Committees of secured creditors and equity holders are also sometimes appointed.

    E. <u>Plans of Reorganization</u>. For the first 120 days after the order for relief, only the debtor can propose a **plan of reorganization**, and has the right to obtain creditor approval of any plan within 180 days. Thereafter, any party of interest can propose a plan.

    F. <u>Executory Contracts</u>. The debtor in possession can reject executory contracts with court approval.

    G. <u>Collective Bargaining Agreements</u>. Collective bargaining agreements require special steps in order to be rejected or modified:

        1. *The Modification Proposal Must Be Given by the Debtor to the Union,*

        2. *A Meeting Must Be Held With the Union to Discuss it,* and

        3. *A Court Hearing Will Be Held if the Union Does Not Accept the Proposal.*

    H. <u>Confirmation of the Plan</u>. Only the court can confirm the plan. This can be done by two methods:

        1. *Acceptance Method.* The **acceptance method** is used if the court determines that:

           a. The plan is in the best interest of each class of claims and interests,

           b. The plan is feasible,

           c. At least one class of claims has voted to accept the plan, and

           d. Each class of claims and interests is not impaired.

        2. *Cram Down Method.* The **cram down method** is used where an impaired class of claimants opposes the plan. The court can confirm the plan over the objections of the dissenting class (hence the term) if it determines that:

           a. At least on impaired class has accepted the plan, and

           b. The plan is fair and equitable to all dissenting impaired classes.

    I. <u>Discharge</u>. A discharge will be granted for debts not included to be paid back in the plan of reorganization.

IV.   Chapter 13--Consumer Debt Adjustment.

    A. <u>Overview</u>. In a consumer debt adjustment, the individual debtor agrees to remain liable for a portion of the debts. Chapter 13 appears to be lightly tested on the CPA exam. The following are the primary differences of a Chapter 13 case from a Chapter 7 individual case.

    B. <u>Voluntary Petitions Only</u>. Individuals cannot be forced into a Chapter 13. The petition must state that the debtor seeks a reduction in debts or an extension of time to pay them, or both.

C. Automatic Stay. In Chapter 13, the automatic stay stops most actions, but does not stop attempts to collect business debts.

D. Repayment Plan. A plan or repayment is developed under which the debtor makes payments to the court which then remits the payments to the creditors.

E. Plan of Repayment. The plan is determined by the debtor, and will be approved by the court so long as the plan is:
   1. *Made in Good Faith*,
   2. *Feasible for the Debtor*, and
   3. *In the Best Interest of the Creditors*.
   Any plan which gives the creditors more than they would receive in a liquidation is in their best interest.

F. Discharge. The portion of debts not agreed to be repaid will be discharged upon completion of the plan.

G. Hardship Discharge. Discharge will be granted if the plan is not completed and the following requirements are met:
   1. *The Failure to Complete Payment Is Due to Unforeseen Circumstances*,
   2. *The Unsecured Creditors Are at Least as Well Off as in a Chapter 7 Case*, and
   3. *It Is Not Practical to Modify the Plan*.

EXAM TIPS

1. Most aspects of a Chapter 7 case are the same whether the debtor is an individual or a business. Certain aspects apply only to one or the other. For example, exempt property applies only to individual debtors. Candidates must know the steps in a liquidation, and should pay attention in exam questions to whether the debtor is an individual or a business.

2. The requirements to file both voluntary and involuntary petitions are heavily tested. Remember that any debtor can file a voluntary petition, and be sure to know the requirements for involuntary petitions. Many dollar amounts in the Bankruptcy Code are now indexed for inflation, thus the former $10,000 minimum here is now $10,775. Before these amounts were indexed, they were tested. It is unclear how these amounts will be tested in the future, if at all. Questions might use numbers that are so high or so low that a minor inflation adjustment would not affect the answer.

3. Because the exemptions are different in different states, the exam has not recently tested on the specific exempt property limits. As of the middle of 1999, there are several proposals in Congress to limit the ability of states to set their own exemptions.

4. Voidable transfers, especially preferential transfers, are very difficult for many exam candidates to understand. It is just as important to understand the general concept and flow of assets as it is to know the specific requirements. Remember that voidable transfer is a general term for both preferential and fraudulent transfers.

5. Preferential and fraudulent transfers are often confused. A preferential transfer was proper when made and does not change the total amount received by the creditors because what is taken back from one creditor goes to other creditors. With fraudulent transfers, the transfer was wrongful when made and will usually result in recovering the asset from a noncreditor for the benefit of creditors, thus increasing the total amount available to the creditors.

6. Note that taxes are a low priority, contrary to the belief of many. This misconception can be traced to the fact that taxes **are** paid ahead of general unsecured creditors, and for many individual debtors, taxes are the only priority claim other than administrative expenses.

7. Be sure to understand the interplay between the priority distribution rules and nondischargeable debts. Some items appear on only one list and others appear on both. Remember that whether or not a debt is nondischargeable becomes an issue only if it was not satisfied in the distribution of assets. Thus, if an alimony debt is paid off in the distribution, it is then irrelevant that it is nondischargeable because the distribution from the estate discharged it when it was paid. To the extent not paid, whether it is dischargeable becomes an issue.

8. Candidates should be prepared to determine amounts received by various creditors when assets (usually cash) are distributed. Pay very close attention to any amounts (such as administrative expenses) that the question states have already been paid from the amount given as available for distribution.

KEY CONCEPTS LIKELY TO BE TESTED ON THE CPA EXAM

1. Requirements to file a petition, both voluntary and involuntary.
2. The effect of the automatic stay.
3. The general rules for preferential and fraudulent transfers, and whether a particular transfer in a fact situation can be recovered by the trustee.
4. Distribution of assets, including the priority of claims and dollar amounts received by specific creditors.
5. Nondischargeable debts.
6. The general process of Chapter 11, including the role of the trustee and the process of confirmation of the plan.

KEY TERMS

Fresh Start	Bankruptcy Trustee	Distribution Priority
Bankruptcy Reform Act	Proof of Claims	Gap Creditor
Bankruptcy Code	Automatic Stay	Discharge
Liquidation	Exempt Property	Nondischargeable Debt
Reorganization	Voidable Transfer	Reaffirmation Agreement
Consumer Debt Adjustment	Preferential Transfer	Debtor in Possession
Voluntary Petition	Insider	Plan of Reorganization
Involuntary Petition	Preferential Lien	Acceptance Method
Order for Relief	Fraudulent Transfer	Cram Down Method
Meeting of Creditors		

MULTIPLE CHOICE QUESTIONS

1.   Law Nov 93 #31
Which of the following acts by a debtor could result in a bankruptcy court revoking the debtor's discharge?

I. Failure to list one creditor.
II. Failure to answer correctly material questions on the bankruptcy petition.

A. I only.
B. II only.
C. Both I and II.
D. Neither I nor II.

2.   Law Nov 93 #32
Robin Corp. incurred substantial operating losses for the past three years. Unable to meet its current obligations, Robin filed a petition for reorganization under Chapter 11 of the Federal Bankruptcy Code. Which of the following statements is correct?
A. The creditors' committee must select a trustee to manage Robin's affairs.
B. The reorganization plan may only be filed by Robin.
C. A creditors' committee, if appointed, will consist of unsecured creditors.
D. Robin may continue in business only with the approval of a trustee.

3.   Law Nov 90 #32
Chapter 7 of the Federal Bankruptcy Code will deny a debtor a discharge when the debtor
A. Made a preferential transfer to a creditor.
B. Accidentally destroyed information relevant to the bankruptcy proceeding.
C. Obtained a Chapter 7 discharge 10 years previously.
D. Is a corporation or a partnership.

4.   Law Nov 91 #29
To file for bankruptcy under Chapter 7 of the Federal Bankruptcy Code, an individual must
A. Have debts of any amount.
B. Be insolvent.
C. Be indebted to more than three creditors.
D. Have debts in excess of $5,000.

5.   Law Nov 89 #22
Rolf, an individual, filed a voluntary petition in bankruptcy. A general discharge in bankruptcy will be denied if Rolf
A. Negligently made preferential transfers to certain creditors within 90 days of filing the petition.
B. Unjustifiably failed to preserve Rolf's books and records.
C. Filed a fraudulent federal income tax return two years prior to filing the petition.
D. Obtained a loan by using financial statements that Rolf knew to be false.

6.   Law Nov 89 #28
Which of the following unsecured debts of $500 each would have the highest priority in the distribution of a bankruptcy estate in a liquidation proceeding?
A. Tax claims of state and municipal governmental units.
B. Liabilities to employee benefit plans arising from services rendered during the month preceding the filing of the petition.
C. Claims owed to customers who gave deposits for the purchase of undelivered consumer goods.
D. Wages earned by employees during the month preceding the filing of the petition.

OTHER OBJECTIVE FORMAT QUESTION (Estimated time -- 10 to 15 minutes)

Law Nov 95 #3(a)

Question Number 3 consists of two parts. Each part consists of five items. Select the **best** answer for each item. Use a No. 2 pencil to blacken the appropriate ovals on the *Objective Answer Sheet* to indicate your answers. **Answer all items.** Your grade will be based on the total number of correct answers.

a. Items 1 through 5 are based on the following:

On June 1, 1995, Rusk Corp. was petitioned involuntarily into bankruptcy. At the time of the filing, Rusk had the following creditors:

- Safe Bank, for the balance due on the secured note and mortgage on Rusk's warehouse.
- Employee salary claims.
- 1994 federal income taxes.
- Accountant's fees outstanding.

Prior to the bankruptcy filing, but while insolvent, Rusk engaged in the following transactions:

- On February 1, 1995, Rusk repaid all corporate directors' loans made to the corporation.
- On May 1, 1995, Rusk purchased raw materials for use in its manufacturing business and paid cash to the supplier.

Required:

Items 1 through 5 relate to Rusk's creditors and the February 1 and May 1 transactions. For each item, select from List I whether only statement I is correct, whether only statement II is correct, whether both statements are correct, or whether neither statement I nor II is correct. Blacken the corresponding oval on the *Objective Answer Sheet.*

List I
A. I only.
B. II only.
C. Both I and II.
D. Neither I nor II.

1. I. Safe Bank's claim will be the first paid of the listed claims because Safe is a secured creditor.
    II. Safe Bank will receive the entire amount of the balance of the mortgage due as a secured creditor regardless of the amount received from the sale of the warehouse.

2. I. The employee salary claims will be paid in full after the payment of any secured party.
    II. The employee salary claims up to $4,300 per claimant will be paid before payment of any general creditors' claims.

3. I. The claim for 1994 federal income taxes due will be paid as a secured creditor claim.
    II. The claim for 1994 federal income taxes due will be paid prior to the general creditor claims.

4. I. The February 1 repayment of the directors' loans were preferential transfers even though the payments were made more than 90 days before the filing of the petition.
    II. The February 1 repayments of the directors' loans were preferential transfers because the payments were made to insiders.

5. I. The May purchase and payment was **not** a preferential transfer because it was in the ordinary course of business.
    II. The May 1 purchase and payment was a preferential transfer because it occurred within 90 days of the filing.

ESSAY QUESTION (Estimated time -- 15 to 25 minutes)

Law R96 #1

In 1995, Fender was petitioned involuntarily into bankruptcy under the liquidation provisions of Chapter 7 of the Federal Bankruptcy Code.

At the time of the filing, Fender listed the following unsecured claims:

Judgment Creditor	$4,000
Alimony and maintenance due under divorce decree	1,200
IRS assessment for 1993 taxes	500
1994 state income tax due	750
Unsecured personal loan from Ranch Bank	7,000
Rent on residence	2,000
Electricity charges on residence	200
Ace Finance Co.	1,000

The Ace Finance Company claim is listed because, in 1993, Fender agreed to guarantee payment of a $1,000 loan by Ace Finance Co. to Fender's cousin. The cousin defaulted on the loan and Ace is attempting to collect from Fender.

Fender had not been paying bills and obligations as they became due.

Required:

a. State and name the fewest number of creditors which would have had to join in filing the petition against Fender and give the reasons for your decision.

b. State which two creditor claims would be satisfied first from the bankruptcy estate and give the reasons for your decision.

c. State which claim(s) would not be discharged if unpaid and give the reasons for your decision.

EXPLANATIONS TO MULTIPLE CHOICE QUESTIONS

1. B is the correct answer. The failure to list one creditor would result in that particular debt not being discharged, but would not result in the discharge being revoked for other debts.

2. C is the correct answer. The creditors' committee is composed of unsecured creditors because secured creditors are protected by their collateral. Choices A and D are incorrect because the debtor usually continues to run the business as a debtor in possession. Choice B is incorrect because after 120 days any party in interest can file a plan.

3. D is the correct answer. Neither a partnership nor a corporation can receive a discharge under Chapter 7. In the case of a corporation the debt will likely never be paid because the corporation will cease to exist. A partnership debt might be paid due to the personal liability of a partner.

4. A is the correct answer. The only requirement for an individual to file a voluntary petition is that the individual have at least one debt. The amount in choice D is the amount which was required for an involuntary petition when the question was used in 1991. It has since been increased to $10,000 and then to $10,775 due to indexing for inflation.

5. B is the correct answer. The key to choice B is that the failure to preserve the books and records was unjustifiable. Choice A is incorrect because a preferential payment merely affects the distribution of amounts among creditors and does not affect whether or not the debtor is entitled to discharge. A fraudulent transfer can result in a denial of discharge, but not a preferential payment. Choice D is incorrect because fraud in connection with obtaining an extension of credit will result in that particular debt not being discharged but will not result in a general denial of discharge.

6. D is the correct answer. Wages have a third priority, with administrative expenses and gap creditors being the only higher priority unsecured claims. The incorrect answer choices are, from highest to lowest priority: choice B, choice C, and lastly choice A.

EXPLANATION TO OTHER OBJECTIVE FORMAT QUESTION

1. A is the correct answer. Statement II is incorrect because Safe Bank will receive the lesser of the balance due on the note or the amount received upon sale or the warehouse. If the proceeds from the sale of the warehouse are less than the amount due, Safe Bank will become an unsecured creditor for the difference.

2. B is the correct answer. The first statement is incorrect because the administrative expenses will be paid before the payment of the wage claims. Note that this question was originally written with the limit of $4,000 which applied before the inflationary adjustment changed the limit to $4,300.

3. B is the correct answer. The claim for income taxes is the last priority claim, but would be paid ahead of general unsecured creditors.

4. C is the correct answer. Because these payments were made to insiders, they would be considered preferential if made at any time within one year prior to the filing of the bankruptcy petition.

5. A is the correct answer. Because this purchase was for raw materials used in the manufacturing process of the debtor, it is a payment made in the ordinary course of business and would not be considered preferential. It would also qualify for the exception of being a payment made for current consideration, which was the raw materials received.

UNOFFICIAL AICPA ANSWER TO ESSAY QUESTION

Law R96 #1

a. Ranch Bank and the judgment creditor would have had to join in the involuntary bankruptcy petition. Fender had fewer than 12 unsecured creditors. Under the liquidation provisions of Chapter 7 of the Federal Bankruptcy Code, when there are fewer than 12 creditors, one or more creditors having unsecured claims in the aggregate of $10,000 must join in the petition.

b. The $1,200 claim for alimony and maintenance due under a divorce decree would be the first creditor claim paid. The $500 IRS assessment for 1993 taxes and the $750 due for 1994 income tax would be paid next.

Unsecured debts are paid according to the priority established by the Federal Bankruptcy Code. The claim with the highest applicable priority is the claim for alimony and maintenance. The next highest applicable priority is for taxes owed to governmental units for which a return is required withing three years of the date of the filing of the petition. The IRS claim and the state tax claim would share *pro rata* if the assets of the bankruptcy estate were insufficient to pay both claims in full.

c. The alimony and maintenance claim and the tax claims would not be discharged if unpaid because these are two of the 10 types of debts specifically excepted from discharge under the Federal Bankruptcy Code.

d. Fender's discharge in bankruptcy would discharge the guarantee of payment given to Ace. Bankruptcy of the guarantor is an absolute defense to payment, and any claim by Ace would be included in the bankruptcy proceeding and be discharged.

Author's Note:

Although this question did not require a computation of amounts distributed to the different claimants, candidates should be prepared to make such a calculation. The main point for making the calculation are that claimants on one level are paid in full before any amounts are paid to the next lower level, and that all claimants at the same level are paid the same percentage of their claims if they cannot all be fully paid. Note the debt arising out of the guarantee of payment is discharged as any other debt.

Remember that the $10,000 amount mentioned in the first part of the answer has now been adjusted to $10,750 for inflation.

CHAPTER 18
AGENCY

OVERVIEW

An **agency** arrangement arises in any situation where two parties agree that one of them will act on behalf of the other in some capacity. In an agency relationship, a **principal** appoints an **agent** to act on behalf of the principal. The agent is often authorized to enter into contracts with third parties for the principal. Thus, agency arrangements often involve three parties. In addition to examining the requirements to form an agency arrangement and a review of other arrangements which are similar to an agency, this chapter addresses the common legal problems that can arise in an agency relationship. First is the question of the agent's and principal's rights and duties with respect to each other. This is followed by a look at the contract liability and tort liability of the principal and agent to third parties. Agency law underlies much other business law, so an understanding of agency is important in grasping other areas of law such as partnership law. Most business contracts involve agents because a corporation cannot itself enter into a contract. The employee who negotiates the contract is acting as an agent of the corporation.

OUTLINE

I. **The Nature of Agency.**
   A. <u>Fiduciary Relationship</u>. An agency is a fiduciary relationship where a principal appoints an agent to act on behalf of the principal. The agent owes the principal a fiduciary duty to act in the principal's best interest in matters covered by the agency.
   B. <u>Must Be Consensual</u>. An agency must be **consensual**, meaning that both parties must agree to the arrangement. No one can unknowingly be an agent or principal, nor can anyone be an agent or principal against her will.
   C. <u>Must Have a Legal Purpose</u>. The purpose of an agency must be lawful. Many actions, such as murder or theft, are illegal whether done directly or through an agent. Other actions, such as voting, are legal if performed directly, but are illegal when accomplished through an agent. Certain professionals, such as attorneys and CPAs, must have a license to operate as an agent. Agency arrangements are void if illegal for any reason.
   D. <u>Writing</u>. An agency arrangement must be in writing under the Statute of Frauds if it will last for more than one year or if the underlying transaction must be in writing, such as in an agency to purchase real estate.
   E. <u>Other Contract Requirements Need Not Be Met</u>. An agency arrangement can be valid without fully meeting the consideration and capacity requirements to form a contract.
      1. *Consideration.* Consideration is not required to form an agency relationship. If Paul asked his friend Amy to buy a couple of concert tickets for him as a favor, Amy has become Paul's agent for purposes of purchasing the concert tickets. Even though there is no contract between Paul and Amy because Paul has given no consideration (payment), it is a valid agency arrangement. Note, though, that if Amy failed to get the tickets, Paul could not sue Amy for her failure to perform. If Paul had agreed to pay Amy to get the tickets, there would be a contract and he could recover any damages caused by her failure to perform.

2. *Capacity.* In an agency arrangement, the principal must have contractual capacity, but capacity is not necessary for the agent. Many candidates think that this rule should be the other way. But the reason for the rule is that a principal should not be able to do indirectly what he cannot do directly. Thus, because a minor cannot directly enter into an enforceable contract, then the minor cannot have an agent do so on the minor's behalf. Because the contract rules for minors are for the protection of the minor, an adult is able to appoint a minor as agent because it is the adult, not the minor, who will live with the consequences of the minor's actions. In fact, an adult might be prudent to appoint a minor as an agent to select and buy a computer on the adult's behalf. **Exam tip #1.**

E. <u>Summary</u>. Of the four basic requirements to form an enforceable contract, agreement and legality are required in an agency. Consideration is not needed, and capacity is necessary for the principal, but not for the agent.

II. Employment Relationships.

A. <u>Generally</u>. Many employee relationships involve agency, with some employees being agents and others not. An **independent contractor** arrangement often exists where the person is not an employee.

B. <u>Employee or Independent Contractor</u>. In many situations where one person works for another, there is a question whether the person doing the work is an independent contractor or an employee. This determination is important for many purposes, including tax treatment and workers' compensation coverage. Here it determines whether the person doing the hiring is responsible for the actions of the person doing the work and any injuries caused by that person.

1. *Responsible for the Acts of an Employee.* An employer is responsible for the torts committed by the employee within the scope of employment.

2. *Not Responsible for the Acts of an Independent Contractor.* The person hiring an independent contractor is not responsible for the acts of the independent contractor.

3. *Factors to Determine if an Employee.* There are a number of factors to determine whether the person doing the work is an employee or an independent contractor. All the factors are examined in a particular case with an overall judgment then being made. The factors include:
   a. Right of the Employer to Control How the Work Is Done. This is the most important. Note that it is the right of control, not whether it is exercised, that is crucial.
   b. Length of Time the Arrangement Has Been in Existence.
   c. Amount of Time Worked Each Week or Month.
   d. Whether Work Hours Are the Same Each Week or Vary.
   e. Whether the Worker Supplies Her Own Tools and Supplies.
   f. Whether the Worker Hires His Own Assistants.
   g. Whether Payment Is Based on Time Worked or Job Completion.
   Generally, the more right of control by the employer and the more regular the work hours, the more likely that the worker will be treated as an employee.

C. <u>Agency</u>. A separate question is whether the worker is also an agent.

1. *Independent Contractors.* Independent contractors are usually not agents, but they can be. A homeowner could hire a contractor to build a deck and tell the contractor to buy the material at a certain lumber store and charge them to the homeowner's account. On the CPA exam, assume that an independent contractor is not an agent unless otherwise stated.

2. *Employees.* Whether an employee is also an agent depends on the employee's job. Any employee whose job involves entering into contracts on behalf of the employer is an agent. Employees at all levels can be agents. The person taking orders at a fast food restaurant is an agent because his job involves entering into contracts on behalf of the restaurant. A highly paid engineer, on the other hand, might have no authority to enter into contracts. An employer will be responsible for the contracts entered into by an employee who is an agent acting within authority. **Exam tip #2.**

III.   **Creation of the Agency Relationship.**

   A. Generally. Because an agency must be consensual, there must be some words or conduct to create the arrangement. The creation of the agency gives the agent **authority** to act on behalf of the principal. Agencies are often classified based on how the authority arises. In describing an agency, either the word "agency" or "authority" might be used. Thus, "express authority" and "express agency" have the same general meaning. It is possible for more than one type of authority to exist in a single agency.

   B. Express Agency. An **express agency**, or agency with express authority (also called actual authority), is created with express words, oral or written, of the parties. The agent has only the authority agreed to. Thus, where a principal gave an agent express authority to buy a piece of land up to 20 acres in size on the principal's behalf, there is no authority to buy a 25-acre parcel.

   C. Power of Attorney. A **power of attorney** is a formal express agency granting the agent the power to act for the principal on specified matters, often legal in nature. It can be **general**, by granting broad powers, or **special**, which would limit the power, perhaps even to a single transaction. The agent is also called an **attorney-in-fact** and is not required to be an attorney.

   D. Implied Agency. An **implied agency** is based on the conduct of the parties. It can also be based on past dealings, industry custom, or the agent's position.

   E. Incidental Implied Authority. When an express agency does not provide all the details of the agent's authority, there might be **incidental authority**, a type of implied authority, for certain actions. For example, where an agent has express authority to locate and purchase a piece of equipment, there would be incidental authority to enter into a shipping contract for the equipment. In such an agency, both express authority and implied authority are present.

   F. Apparent Authority. When a principal creates the impression of authority that does not actually exist, an **apparent agency** is created. Thus, the principal falsely stating to a third party that a person is her agent will create apparent authority. Apparent authority can be created only by actions or statements of the principal, not by actions of a supposed agent. Apparent authority exists where an employer gives a job title, such as purchasing manager, to someone who has no express authority to make purchases for the corporation. The employer's action of giving the title would lead a third party to believe that the employee had authority to make purchases, and thereby creates apparent authority in the employee.

   G. Lingering Apparent Authority. When certain agencies end, such as for sales agents, notice may need to be given (usually actual notice to actual customers and possibly publication notice as well) to avoid the principal being liable on contracts entered into by the former agent.

   H. Agency by Ratification. Where there was no authority for an action, but later the principal decides to ratify the contract, there is **agency by ratification**. Once ratified, the principal is bound even though the agent was not authorized when the contract was entered into.

IV.   **Agent's Duties.**
   A. <u>Duty of Performance</u>. The agent has a **duty of performance** under which the agent must do that which the agent agreed to. This includes performing the duty with reasonable care.
   B. <u>Duty of Notification</u>. The agent has a **duty of notification** to notify the principal of any important information related to the agency. Thus, an agent who is hired to find a tenant for a landlord must notify the landlord of problems with the property which the agent notices while showing the property.
   C. <u>Duty of Loyalty</u>. The **duty of loyalty** is a general duty to act in all ways in the principal's best interest in matters of the agency. There are numerous ways that this duty can be breached. The following situations are not violations of the duty, however, if the principal has been notified and consents to the situation.
      1. *Dual Agency.* An agent cannot be an agent for more than one principal in the same transaction, also known as **dual agency**.
      2. *Usurping an Opportunity.* When an agent locates an opportunity (such as a parcel of land for purchase) for the principal, the agent cannot **usurp the opportunity** by taking it for himself.
      3. *Self-Dealing.* The agent cannot simultaneously be on both sides of a transaction, one on her own behalf and the other as agent for the principal. This is **self-dealing**. Thus, an agent hired to purchase a piece of land for the principal could not sell her own land to the principal, unless the agent's ownership interest is disclosed.
      4. *Misuse of Confidential Information.* The agent breaches the duty of loyalty by **misusing confidential information** (usually about the principal) obtained in the course of the agency.
      5. *Competing With the Principal.* An agent cannot **compete with the principal** by attempting to do on his own behalf that which he is doing for the principal. An agent hired to sell the principal's house cannot attempt to sell his own house in competition with that of the principal. This duty is breached even if the agent is not successful in his attempts to sell his own house. **Exam tip #4.**
   D. <u>Duty of Obedience</u>. The agent has a **duty of obedience** requiring that instructions of the principal be followed so long as they are legal.
   E. <u>Duty of Accountability</u>. The agent has a **duty of accountability** to account for all assets received from the principal or received from others on the principal's behalf. This duty also requires that the agent maintain a separate account for the principal and that the agent use the principal's property in a reasonable manner.

V. **Principal's Duties.**
   A. <u>Duty of Compensation</u>. The **duty of compensation** requires that the agreed-to compensation be paid, or that a reasonable compensation be paid if none is specified. No compensation need be paid to a gratuitous agent.
   B. <u>Duty of Reimbursement</u>. The **duty of reimbursement** requires that the principal reimburse the agent for expenses and costs incurred by the agent in carrying out the agency.
   C. <u>Duty of Indemnification</u>. The **duty of indemnification** is similar to the duty of reimbursement, but applies to losses, usually unplanned, incurred by the agent in properly carrying out the agency arrangement. This can occur where the agent incurs a loss due to the principal's misconduct, such as the breach of a properly authorized contract.

D. <u>Duty of Cooperation</u>. The principal owes the agent a **duty to cooperate** with the agent so that the agent can carry out her duties. A homeowner who has hired an agent to sell the home violates this duty by not cooperating with the agent in making the home available to be shown.

E. <u>Duty to Provide Safe Working Conditions</u>. The principal has a **duty to provide safe working conditions** for the agent. **Exam tip #5.**

VI. Contract Liability to Third Parties.

A. <u>General Situation</u>. The principal hires the agent to enter into contracts on the principal's behalf. The principal generally wants to be liable on these contracts. The most common legal issue is whether the agent can be held liable on a contract following a breach by the principal.

B. <u>Principal Liability</u>. The principal will be liable on any contract that the agent enters into on her behalf so long as one of the types of authority is present. The presence of the authority means that the principal is liable without any further action by the principal, except in the case of authority by ratification.

C. <u>Agent Liability</u>. If the principal performs the contract, then there is no problem or liability for the agent. The question of agent liability arises if the principal does not perform.

   1. *Agent's Contract Liability Depends on Disclosure.* The agent's liability on a contract properly entered into on the principal's behalf depends on the degree of disclosure of the agency (usually by the agent) to the third party. There are three degrees of disclosure.

      a. Fully Disclosed Principal--Agent Not Liable. With a **fully disclosed principal**, the third party is told of both the existence and the identity of the principal prior to entering into the contract. Because the third party knows the true identity of the other party, the agent cannot be held liable on the contract. This disclosure can also be made by the principal.

      b. Partially Disclosed Principal--Agent Liable. With a **partially disclosed principal**, the third party is told of the existence of the principal (often by the agent simply saying that she is acting as someone's agent) but not the principal's identity. Because the third party knows the identity of only the agent, the third party can hold the agent liable on the contract if the principal fails to perform it.

      c. Undisclosed Principal--Agent Liable. With an **undisclosed principal**, the agent knows of neither the existence nor the identity of the principal. The agent can be held liable if the principal does not perform. **Exam tip #6.**

   2. *Exceeding Scope of Authority.* Where an agent exceeds the scope of authority, or has no authority at all, the agent is liable on the contract. The principal will not be liable unless the principal ratifies the agent's actions.

VII. Tort Liability to Third Parties.

A. <u>General Situation</u>. Agents and employees often commit torts in the performance of their duties. Unlike contracts, which are usually a planned part of an agency arrangement, torts are usually unplanned. The tortfeasor (one who commits a tort) is always liable. The most common issue surrounding torts in an agency situation is whether the principal can also be held responsible for a tort of the agent.

B. <u>Agent's Liability for the Agent's Tort</u>. An agent will always be responsible for torts that the agent commits. This is true even when other parties, such as the principal, are found to also be liable for the agent's tort.

C. <u>Principal's Liability for Agent's Tort</u>. Because agents often have little money, a lawsuit by an injured third party against an agent is often pointless.

1. *Negligence--Scope of Authority Is the General Test.* If the agent was acting within the **scope of authority** when the tort was committed, the principal will usually be held liable. This rule is used in cases of negligence or fraud. Where an employee is involved, the test is often stated as "scope of employment." The concepts are the same regardless of the terminology used. Whether an action took place within the scope of authority is based on all the facts and circumstances in the situation. There are several related doctrines used to determine if conduct is within the scope of authority.

   a. Frolic and Detour. A principal is not liable for torts committed by the agent while on a **frolic and detour**. The agent is on a frolic and detour when he has abandoned the duties of the agency, even if only temporarily. Running a personal errand or stopping at a bar for a drink are situations that might be a frolic and detour.

   b. Coming and Going Rule. Principals and Employers are generally not liable for torts committed by employees and agents on their way to and from work, even if an employer-owned car is used. The **coming and going rule** exists because the employer cannot control the distance from work (and the amount of risk) that an employee lives.

   c. Dual-Purpose Mission. Where an agent is acting partly for the principal and partly for himself, he is said to be on a **dual purpose mission**. Running personal errands while also making sales calls is an example. Most states hold that the principal is liable for agent torts while on a dual-purpose mission.

   d. Failure to Follow Instructions. The principal cannot avoid liability solely because the agent was not following the principal's instructions. For example, if a pizza store owner instructed its drivers to always obey all traffic laws, the owner could not avoid liability because the driver was speeding when the injury occurred. The test is simply whether the driver was on a pizza delivery run when the injury occurred. This gives the principal incentive to not merely set the set the rules, but to also ensure that the drivers follow them. **Exam tip #7.**

2. *Intentional Torts--Two Rules.* The scope of authority rule is not used for intentional torts. Principal liability for the intentional tort of an agent is determined using one of two different rules, depending on the state.

   a. Motivation Test. Under the **motivation test**, the principal is liable if the agent committing the intentional tort was motivated by the principal's best interests, including situations where the agent's evaluation of the employer's best interests is misguided.

   b. Work-Related Test. Under the **work-related test**, the principal is liable if the intentional tort occurred in a work-related time or space.

   c. Examples. If a hardware store employee injures a customer in a dispute over returning merchandise, the employer will be liable under either test. The employee's motivation was to not refund the employer's money (in the employer's interest) and the tort occurred at the workplace. If an acquaintance of the employee came to the store and the employee injured the acquaintance in a dispute over a football game the previous day, the employer would not be liable in states applying the motivation test, but would be liable in states applying the work-related test. **Exam tip #8.**

EXAM TIPS

1. Be sure to know that the agent does not need capacity and that the principal does. Do not confuse an adult acting as a minor's agent (which is invalid) with the common situation of an adult acting as a cosigner. As a cosigner, the adult becomes liable on the contract and is not acting as the minor's agent in doing so.
2. Tort liability of an employer for the torts of a worker depends on if the worker is an employee or an independent contractor. Contract liability of the employer depends on if the worker is an agent. There are some situations, explained later, where an employer can have contract liability for actions by someone who is not an agent at the time of contracting. This is by ratifying the unauthorized act.
3. Be sure to not confuse the definitions of implied and apparent authority. And be sure to know that only statements made by the **principal**, or other actions of the principal, can create apparent authority. An agent's conduct or statements cannot create apparent authority.
4. Remember that the duty of loyalty is not breached where the agent discloses the situation and the principal consents. The specific violations of the duty of loyalty are easily confused. Be sure to understand the differences and be able to determine which applies in a fact situation.
5. Many of the duties of either party can be modified by agreement. For example, the parties might agree that the principal will not reimburse the agent for expenses.
6. With contract liability, the principal is always liable, so long as there was authority for the contract. Another way to state the rule for agent liability is that the agent can be held liable in any case with less than full disclosure of both the existence and identity of the principal.
7. Remember that the agent who commits a tort is always liable for that tort. Most important for the CPA exam are the scope of authority rule and the effect of a frolic and detour. Because whether an agent was on a frolic and detour depends on all the surrounding circumstances, the facts in any CPA exam questions are usually quite clear.
8. For agency questions, it is often helpful to draw a diagram if the question involves three parties. Use the diagram to keep track or who has done what to whom, or owes something to someone, etc. In questions involving liability of the agent or principal to a third party, be sure to apply the correct rule. Candidates often try to analyze a tort liability question using the contract liability rules and vice versa. Multiple choice questions can be especially tricky with the answer choices mixing up contract, tort, duty, and authority concepts.

KEY CONCEPTS LIKELY TO BE TESTED ON THE CPA EXAM

1. Whether a worker is an independent contractor or an employee.
2. The different types of authority, including the ability to determine which exists in a fact situation, especially ones distinguishing between implied and apparent authority.
3. Duties of principals and agents to one another.
4. Contract liability of an agent in a fact situation.
5. Tort liability of a principal in a fact situation, especially for negligence and especially involving a possible frolic and detour.

KEY TERMS

Principal	Duty of Notification	Duty to Cooperate
Agent	Duty of Loyalty	Fully Disclosed Principal
Consensual	Dual Agency	Partially Disclosed Principal
Independent Contractor	Usurp an Opportunity	Undisclosed Principal
Express Authority	Self-Dealing	Scope of Authority
General Power of Attorney	Duty of Obedience	Frolic and Detour
Special Power of Attorney	Duty of Accountability	Coming and Going Rule
Attorney-in-Fact	Duty of Compensation	Dual-Purpose Mission
Implied Authority	Duty of Reimbursement	Motivation Test
Incidental Authority	Duty of Indemnification	Work-Related Test
Apparent Authority	Misuse of Confidential Information	
Agency by Ratification	Duty to Provide Safe Working Conditions	
Duty of Performance		

MULTIPLE CHOICE QUESTIONS

1.   **Law Nov 94 #16**

Which of the following actions requires an agent for a corporation to have a written agency agreement?
A. Purchasing office supplies for the principal's business.
B. Purchasing an interest in undeveloped land for the principal.
C. Hiring an independent general contractor to renovate the principal's office building.
D. Retaining an attorney to collect a business debt owed the principal.

2.   **Law Nov 93 #11**

Noll gives Carr a written power of attorney. Which of the following statements is correct regarding this power of attorney?
A. It must be signed by both Noll and Carr.
B. It must be for a definite period of time.
C. It may continue in existence after Noll's death.
D. It may limit Carr's authority to specific transactions.

3.   **Law Nov 93 #14**

Which of the following rights will a third party be entitled to after validly contracting with an agent representing an undisclosed principal?
A. Disclosure of the principal by the agent.
B. Ratification of the contract by the principal.
C. Performance of the contract by the agent.
D. Election to void the contract after disclosure of the principal.

4.   **Law Nov 91 #12**

When an agent acts for an undisclosed principal, the principal will **not** be liable to third parties if the
A. Principal ratifies a contract entered into by the agent.
B. Agent acts within an implied grant of authority.
C. Agent acts outside the grant of actual authority.
D. Principal seeks to conceal the agency relationship.

5.   Law May 92 #6

A principal and agent relationship requires a

A. Written agreement.
B. Power of Attorney.
C. Meeting of the minds and consent to act.
D. Specified consideration.

6.   Law Nov 91 #11

Forming an agent relationship requires that

A. The agreement between the principal and agent be supported by consideration.
B. The principal and agent **not** be minors.
C. Both the principal and agent consent to the agency.
D. The agent's authority be limited to the express grant of authority in the agency agreement.

7.   Law Nov 94 #17

Bolt Corp. dismissed Ace as its general sales agent and notified all of Ace's known customers by letter. Young Corp., a retail outlet located outside of Ace's previously assigned sales territory, had never dealt with Ace. Young knew of Ace as a result of various business contacts. After his dismissal, Ace sold Young goods, to be delivered by Bolt, and received from Young a cash deposit for 20% of the purchase price. It was not unusual for an agent in Ace's previous position to receive cash deposits. In an action by Young against Bolt on the sales contract, Young will

A. Lose, because Ace lacked any implied authority to make the contract.
B. Lose, because Ace lacked express authority to make the contract.
C. Win, because Bolt's notice was inadequate to terminate Ace's apparent authority.
D. Win, because a principal is an insurer of an agent's acts.

8.   Law May 92 #8

Long Corp. is a real estate developer and regularly engages real estate brokers to act on its behalf in acquiring parcels of land. The brokers are authorized to enter into such contracts, but are instructed to do so in their own names without disclosing Long's identity or Long's relationship to the transaction. If a broker enters into a contract with a seller on Long's behalf,

A. Long will **not** be liable for any negligent acts committed by the broker while acting on Long's behalf.
B. The broker will have the same actual authority as if Long's identity had been disclosed.
C. The broker will **not** be personally bound by the contract because the broker has express authority to act.
D. Long will be bound by the contract because of the broker's apparent authority.

9.   Law May 89 #13

Simmons, an agent for Jensen, has the express authority to sell Jensen's goods. Simmons also has the express authority to grant discounts of up to 5% of list price. Simmons sold Hemple goods with a list price of $1,000 and granted Hemple a 10% discount. Hemple had not previously dealt with either Simmons or Jensen. Which of the following courses of action may Jensen properly take?

A. Seek to void the sale to Hemple.
B. Seek recovery of $50 from Hemple only.
C. Seek recovery of $50 from Simmons only.
D. Seek recovery of $50 from either Hemple or Simmons.

ESSAY QUESTION (Estimated time -- 15 to 20 minutes)

Law Nov 90 #3

Prime Cars, Inc. buys and sells used automobiles. Occasionally Prime has its salespeople purchase used cars from third parties without disclosing that the salesperson is in fact buying for Prime's used car inventory. Prime's management believes better prices can be negotiated using this procedure. One of Prime's salespeople, Peterson, entered into a contract with Hallow in accordance with instructions from Prime's sales manager. The car was to be delivered one week later. After entering into the contract with Hallow, and while driving back to Prime's place of business, Peterson was involved in an automobile accident with another vehicle. Peterson's negligence, and the resulting collision, injured Mathews, the driver of the other car involved in the accident.

Prime terminated Peterson's employment because of the accident. Following Prime's general business practices, Prime published an advertisement in several trade journals that gave notice that Peterson was no longer employed by Prime. Shortly thereafter, Peterson approached one of Prime's competitors, Bagley Autos, Inc., and contracted to sell Bagley several used cars in Prime's inventory. Bagley's sales manager, who frequently purchased cars out of Prime's inventory from Peterson, paid 25% of the total price to Peterson, with the balance to be paid ten days later when the cars were to be delivered. Bagley's sales manager was unaware of Peterson's termination. Prime refused to deliver the cars to Bagley or to repay Bagley's down payment, which Prime never received from Peterson.

Prime also refused to go through with the contract entered into by Peterson with Hallow. Mathews sued both Peterson with Hallow. Mathews sued both Peterson and Prime for the injuries sustained in the automobile accident. Bagley sued Prime for failing to deliver the cars or return the down payment paid to Peterson.

Required:

Answer each of the following questions, setting forth the reasons for your conclusions.

a. What rights does Hallow have against Prime or Peterson?

b. Will Mathews prevail in the lawsuit against Prime and Peterson?

c. Will Bagley prevail in its lawsuit against Prime?

EXPLANATIONS TO MULTIPLE CHOICE QUESTIONS

1. B is the correct answer. An agency arrangement is required to be in writing if the contract for which the agency is created is required to be in writing. Because a contract for the purchase of land must be in writing, so must the related agency arrangement. Choice C is incorrect because although the contract relates to land, it is a services contract and need not be in writing.

2. D is the correct answer. A general power of attorney grants broad powers, but a principal can also execute a special power of attorney granting limited powers. Choice A is incorrect because only the principal must sign. Choice C is incorrect because a power of attorney ceases at death.

3. C is the correct answer. An agent contracting for an undisclosed principal is liable on any contracts entered into. Choice A is incorrect because the agent is not obligated to disclose the principal. Choice B is incorrect because so long as the contract is within the agent's authority, the principal is always liable on contracts made by the agent, thus ratification is meaningless here. The facts of the question state that the contract was validly entered into. Choice D is incorrect because a third party cannot void a contract merely because it was entered into by an agent.

4. C is the correct answer. This question deals with contract authority although it does not explicitly state so. The principal **would** have tort liability to third parties so long as the agent was within the scope of the agency, which is a broader concept than actual authority. For contract liability, the principal is always liable on contracts entered into by the agent unless the agent acts beyond the scope of the authority or has acted without any authority. Choice A is incorrect because ratification makes the principal liable on an unauthorized contract, but will not end the agent's liability.

5. C is the correct answer. An agency arrangement is consensual, meaning that both parties must want to be in it. Choice A is incorrect because most agencies need not be in writing. Choice D is incorrect because an agency does not need consideration to be valid. Without consideration, the rights of the principal and agent against one another are limited, but the agency remains a valid agency arrangement.

6. C is the correct answer. An agency arrangement requires the consent of both parties. Choice B is incorrect because a minor can act as an agent. The principal cannot be a minor. Choice D is incorrect because authority can arise in several ways other than by express authority. Implied and apparent authority are a couple of examples.

7. C is the correct answer. While employed, Ace had express authority from the terms of his employment and perhaps apparent authority because of the position given to him by the principal, Bolt. Upon his termination, the express authority ended immediately. But he continued to have lingering apparent authority after his termination. Bolt should have published a notice in trade journals or other appropriate places to terminate this apparent authority. Note that the reasons given in answer choices A and B are correct statements (Ace had neither express not implied authority), although the conclusion that Young loses is incorrect.

8. B is the correct answer. The actual, or express, authority of an agent depends on the terms of the agency agreement between the principal and the agent. Those terms are unaffected by whether or not the principal is disclosed. Choice A is incorrect because Long will have tort liability for any torts of the agent committed within the scope of the agency; this is true whether or not the agent ever enters into a contract on behalf of the principal. Choice C is incorrect because the liability of the broker does not depend on the type of authority, but on the degree of disclosure. Choice D is incorrect because it is impossible to have apparent authority where the identity of the principal is not disclosed, because the apparent authority must come from words or acts of the principal to the third party, and would make the principal's identity known.

9. C is the correct answer. A principal is bound by the contract entered into by its agent so long as any one of the types of authority is present. Here there was no express authority for the 10 percent discount. Implied authority might exist if there were a history of Jensen accepting discounts larger than 5 percent, but that is not the case here. There is apparent authority because Jensen, the principal, has indirectly told the world that Simmons has authority to make reasonable and customary discounts by virtue of his position as an agent of Jensen. Because a 10 percent discount is reasonable, there is apparent authority, and that authority means that Jensen is bound to honor the contract. Jensen cannot recover from Hemple, the customer, but Jensen can recover from Simmons for violating the agent's duty of obedience.

UNOFFICIAL AICPA ANSWER TO ESSAY QUESTION

Law Nov 90 #3

a. Peterson was acting for an undisclosed principal (Prime) with regard to the contract with Hallow. Peterson was acting with actual authority; therefore, Prime is liable to Hallow. Peterson is also liable to Hallow because agents acting on behalf of undisclosed principals are liable to the third parties on the contracts they enter into with such third parties on behalf of the principal. Hallow, however, cannot collect damages from both Peterson and Prime and must make an election between them.

b. At the time of the accident, Peterson was acting within the scope of employment because the conduct engaged in (that is, entering into a contract with Hallow) was authorized by Prime. Prime, therefore, will be liable to Mathews because the accident occurred within the scope of Peterson's employment.

Peterson will also be liable to Mathews because all persons are liable for their own negligence.

c. Peterson's actual authority to enter into contracts on Prime's behalf ceased on termination of employment by Prime. Peterson, however, continued to have apparent authority to bind Prime because:
*   Peterson was acting ostensibly within the scope of authority as evidenced by past transactions with Bagley.
*   Bagley was unaware of Peterson's termination.

The trade journal announcement was not effective notice to terminate Peterson's apparent authority in relation to Bagley because:
*   Prime was obligated to give actual notice to Bagley that Peterson was no longer employed;
*   Actual notice is required because of Bagley's past contact with Peterson while Peterson was employed by Prime.

Author's Note:
The answer to part **a.** refers to making an election. This means that Hallow would be able to collect from only one or the other. A better explanation of the situation is that Hallow could not collect more than the amount of the loss. It is possible that Hallow would collect a portion of his loss from each.

Note also the use of the term "actual authority" which is the same as express authority.

CHAPTER 19
PARTNERSHIPS AND LIMITED LIABILITY COMPANIES

OVERVIEW

This chapter covers the partnership form of business organization. If a business with more than one owner does not select another business form, it is a partnership. Much of partnership law is based on agency law because every partner is an agent of every other partner. The **Uniform Partnership Act (UPA)**, which has been adopted in nearly every state is the source of partnership law in those states and is tested on the CPA exam. In addition to general partnerships, this chapter covers limited partnerships and limited liability companies. The main issues in this area include formation and operation of the entity, the rights and duties of the partners or members with respect to each other and the business entity, and partners' rights and duties with respect to third parties.

OUTLINE

I. **General Partnership Formation.**
   A. <u>Uniform Partnership Act</u>. The Uniform Partnership Act is a uniform law which nearly every state has adopted. Like the UCC, the UPA can be viewed as a "default" statue, meaning that its provisions apply only if the partnership agreement does not address the issue. Thus, the partnership agreement can modify most provisions of the UPA.
   B. <u>Entity Theory</u>. The UPA has adopted an entity theory, meaning that the partnership can be sued or hold property in its own name. Even though treated as a separate legal entity, a partnership is not a separate tax entity, nor does the entity treatment eliminate the personal liability of partners for the debts of a partnership.
   C. <u>Every Partner Is an Agent</u>. In a partnership, every partner is an agent for the partnership and for every other partner. Thus, much of partnership law is based on the law of agency.
   D. <u>Partnership Definition</u>. Under the UPA, there are four requirements in order for a partnership to exist:
      1. *An Association of Two or More Persons*. The term "person" includes corporations, limited liability companies, and other partnerships.
      2. *Carrying on a Business*. This usually means that there must be a series of transactions, rather than a single transaction. Merely owning a piece of property held for investment purposes would not qualify as operating a business, but if it is operated as rental property, in most instances, there would be a business being carried on.
      3. *As Co-Owners*. The persons in the business must act as owners. This includes receiving a share of the profits, and, in most cases, having the power to manage the business.
      4. *For Profit*. The partnership must have a profit motive, although actual profitability is not required. Two individuals buying a home where both live in the home and share expenses would usually not meet this requirement.
   A court will examine all the facts and circumstances to see if all four of the above requirements are met.

E. <u>Not Required for a Partnership</u>. The following are not required for a partnership to exist.
   1. *Express Intent*. Intent is necessary to form a partnership, but that intent can be implied from the conduct of the parties. The partnership can exist without the knowledge of the partners. For example, if two friends started painting houses together and shared the profits, they would have formed a partnership. This is true even if they never expressly intended to form a partnership, and would be true even if they had never heard of the concept of a partnership. The intent would be implied from the conduct of operating the business together, sharing the profits, etc.
   2. *Written Agreement*. A written partnership agreement is not necessary, although it is highly desirable. An express oral agreement is not needed either. The agreement can be implied from the parties' conduct.
   3. *Formal Filing*. There are no formal filing requirements for forming a partnership. So long as the four requirements above are met, a partnership exists.

F. <u>Partnership Name</u>. A partnership can operate in the names of the partners, or under a fictitious business name. Any **fictitious business name** (a name where the identity of the partners is not indicated in the name) must be filed with the appropriate state agency and an advertisement placed in a newspaper of general circulation giving notice of the name.

G. <u>Partnership Capital</u>. Assets invested by the partners become capital which cannot be withdrawn without the consent of the other partners. Loans and the value of services are not considered capital. When cash or other assets are transferred to a partnership, the transferring partner should clearly indicate whether they are to be treated as capital contributions or loans.

H. <u>Partnership Duration</u>.
   1. *Partnership for a Term*. A **partnership for a term** is a partnership of fixed duration, such as 10 years or until completion of a project.
   2. *Partnership at Will*. A **partnership at will** is a partnership without a specified term. Such a partnership will terminate upon the death or withdrawal of a partner.

I. <u>Partnership Agreement</u>. A partnership agreement can be oral or written, express or implied. An agreement for a partnership which cannot be completed within a year, or for a partnership to deal in real estate, must be in writing. Even when not required, a written agreement is preferred and can include the following terms:
   1. *Firm Name*.
   2. *Partners' Names and Addresses, and the Partnership's Principal Office*.
   3. *The Nature of the Partnership's Business*.
   4. *The Duration of the Partnership*.
   5. *Partners' Capital Contributions*.
   6. *Profit and Loss Allocations to the Partners, Including Any Salaries Allocated*.
   7. *Duties of the Partners Regarding the Management of the Partnership*.
   8. *Terms for the Admission or Withdrawal of Partners*.
   9. *Terms for Continuation of the Partnership Upon the Death of a Partner, Withdrawal of a Partner, or Other Events Causing Dissolution*.

J. <u>Partnership by Estoppel</u>. Where one person has falsely claimed that another is her partner, the one who made the false claim will be **estopped**, or prevented, from denying the existence of the partnership and will be treated as a partner of the person claimed to be a partner and will therefore be liable for the actions of the person falsely said to be a partner.

II. Rights of Partners.

A. <u>Participate in Management</u>. Partners have a right to participate in management unless the partnership agreement places the management power is a single partner, or in a few partners, often called a management committee.

1. *Majority Vote Needed for Most Matters.* For most matters, a majority vote of the partners is needed unless the partnership agreement provides otherwise.

2. *Tie Vote Equals Defeat.* The matter being voted on is defeated in a tie vote, absent a provision to the contrary in the partnership agreement.

3. *Unanimous Vote Needed.* The following matters need a unanimous vote of the partners:
   a. Assignment of Partnership Property for the Benefit of Creditors.
   b. Disposal of Partnership Goodwill.
   c. Actions That Would Make It Impossible to Carry On the Partnership Business.
   d. Submission of a Partnership Claim or Liability to Arbitration.
   e. Admission of a New Partner.
   f. Actions in Contravention of the Partnership Agreement.
   g. Actions Changing the Nature of the Business.
   These unanimous consent rules can be changed by the partnership agreement.

4. *One Partner, One Vote.* Each partner gets one vote, regardless of the amount of capital contributed, unless otherwise agreed.

B. <u>Right to Share in Profits and Losses</u>. All partners are entitled to share in the profits and losses of the partnership.

1. *Share Equally, Unless Otherwise Agreed.* Partners share profits and losses equally if the partnership agreement is silent on the issue. This is true regardless of the amounts of capital invested or the amounts of time devoted to the partnership.

2. *Losses Follow Profits.* If the agreement specifies the allocation of profits but is silent about losses, losses are allocated in the same way as profits.

3. *Profits Do Not Follow Losses.* Where only the allocation of losses is specified, the loss allocation is ignored for profit allocation purposes and profits are divided equally.

C. <u>No Right to Compensation</u>. Unless specifically provided, no partner is entitled to compensation for time and efforts devoted to the partnership, other than through the allocation of profits and losses. **Exam tip #1.**

D. <u>Right of Indemnification</u>. The right of **indemnification** is also known as the right of reimbursement and is a partner's right to recover partnership expenses and costs which have been paid on behalf of the partnership.

E. <u>Right to Return of Advances and Capital</u>. A partner has a right to the **return of advances**, but only after all debts to creditors other than partners have been paid. After all partners' advances have been paid, partners are entitled to the **return of capital balances**.

F. <u>Right to Information</u>. A partner has an absolute **right to information** about partnership matters, including an absolute right to inspect and copy all partnership books and records.

G. <u>Right to an Accounting</u>. In an **action for an accounting**, a partner requests a court to review the partnership and relevant transactions of the partners in order to award each partner the proper share of partnership assets. For example, if one of three partners collected rent and disbursed expenses in connection with partnership rental property, either of the other partners could file an action for an accounting to determine the amounts owed to each partner.

III.   Duties Among Partners.

    A. <u>Duty of Loyalty</u>. A partner's **duty of loyalty** is similar to an agent's duty of loyalty and is a general duty act in the partnership's best interest in all matters related to the business of the partnership. Many of the common ways this duty can be breached are also similar. The following situations violate the duty of loyalty, but are not a violation if the partnership has been notified and consents to the situation.

        1. *Self-Dealing*. A partner cannot simultaneously be on both sides of a transaction, one on her own behalf and the other as partner for the partnership. This is **self-dealing**. Thus a partner could not sell her own land to the partnership, unless the fact that she had an interest in the land was disclosed to the partnership prior to the sale.

        2. *Usurping on Opportunity*. When a partner locates an opportunity (such as a piece of land for purchase) for the partnership, the partner cannot **usurp the opportunity** by taking it for himself, unless he first offers it to the partnership.

        3. *Competing With the Partnership*. A partner cannot **compete with the partnership** by attempting to do the same on his own behalf as he is doing for the partnership. A CPA breaches this duty by soliciting or doing accounting work for someone who is not a client of the firm, and keeping the revenues rather than turning them over to the partnership. This duty is breached even if the partner is not successful in acquiring the client.

        4. *Secret Profits*. A partner is not entitled to keep any **secret profits** connected with partnership business. An example would be a rebate on a partnership purchase.

        5. *Breach of Confidentiality*. A partner has a duty to not disclose confidential partnership information.

        6. *Misuse of Property*. A partner has a duty to not use partnership property for personal use.

    B. <u>Duty of Obedience</u>. A partner has a duty to follow the terms of the partnership agreement and to follow operating decisions of the partnership. Where the agreement provides for a managing committee, a partner is obligated to follow the decisions of the committee.

    C. <u>Duty of Care</u>. A partner has a duty to exercise reasonable care in the transacting of partnership business. Failure to exercise the appropriate level of care is negligence and results in liability for the partner. A partner is not liable for honest errors in business judgment so long as the partner exercised due care in making the decision. This is often called the **business judgment rule** which also applies to actions of corporate officers and directors.

    D. <u>Duty to Inform</u>. A partner has a duty to inform the partnership about matters relevant to the partnership's business. Even if a partner does not inform the partnership, the partner's knowledge is imputed to the partnership. For example, if a tax client informs a CPA that she will be leaving town three weeks before the tax filing deadline (and thus need to have her tax return completed by that time), knowledge of that fact is imputed to all partners and the partnership, even if the one partner does not actually inform the other partners or the partnership.

IV.   Property Rights of the Partnership and Partners.

    A. <u>Partnership Property</u>. Property contributed to a partnership and all property acquired by the partnership is **partnership property**. Such property is subject to attachment and execution by partnership creditors.

    B. <u>Tenancy in Partnership</u>. A partner owns property as a **tenant in partnership** with the other partners. A deceased partner's share of partnership property goes to the other partners.

C. <u>Interest in the Partnership</u>. The deceased partner's interest in the partnership passes according to the terms of the deceased partner's will. Thus, the beneficiary will own an interest in the partnership, but will not have a direct interest in the property owned by the partnership.

D. <u>Assignment of Partnership Interest</u>. A partner may **assign her partnership interest** to a third party, which can be either a full or partial assignment. The assignment of a partnership interest does not make the assignee a partner and does not give the assignee many of the rights of a partner. Such an assignment merely gives the assignee the right to receive the assignor's share of partnership profits. For example, if Mary, a partner in a CPA firm, assigned her partnership interest to her brother, Mary would continue to be a partner and function within the partnership exactly as before, but Mary's share of partnership profits would now belong to her brother because of the assignment. An assignment would also give to the assignee any of the assignor's rights in the event that the partnership is liquidated. **Exam tip #2.**

E. <u>Charging Order</u>. A **charging order** is a court-ordered assignment of a partner's partnership interest, generally to satisfy a judgment or other debt. The judgment creditor's position is similar to that of other assignees of a partnership interest.

V. **Partner Liability to Third Parties.**
   A. <u>Contract Liability--Joint Liability</u>. So long as there was authority of some type (express, implied, emergency, or apparent) for a partner entering into a contract on behalf of the partnership, the partnership is liable and the partners have **joint liability**. This means that a third party must name the partnership and all partners as defendants. Any partner who pays more than that partner's share, can seek indemnification from the partnership or the other partners.

   B. <u>Tort Liability--Joint and Several Liability</u>. Partners have **joint and several liability** for the torts of a partner committed within the scope of partnership business, or otherwise with the authority of the partners. With joint and several liability, a plaintiff can sue any one partner and recover the entire amount from that one partner. **Exam tip #3.**

   C. <u>Right to Recover from Wrongful Partner</u>. Any party (the partnership or a partner) who has paid out an amount can recover from the partner, if any, who was at fault in causing the loss. If that partner cannot pay, the other partners must bear the loss.

   D. <u>Incoming Partners</u>. Incoming partners have unlimited liability only for actions occurring after their admission to the partnership. Incoming partners have liability to the extent of their capital investment for actions and debts arising prior to their admission to the partnership.

   E. <u>Partners Cannot Eliminate Liability</u>. An agreement among partners that they will not be liable for the actions of each other is ineffective with respect to third parties. Only if the third party is also a party to the agreement will the partners' unlimited liability be affected. Third parties' rights cannot be compromised by an agreement to which they are not a party.

VI. **Termination of Partnerships.**
   A. <u>Steps in Termination</u>. There are three main steps in the termination of a partnership.
   1. *Dissolution.* The step which signals the end of the partnership's existence and begins the process to end the partnership is **dissolution**. Once dissolution has occurred, partnership actions are focused on ending the partnership.

2. *Winding Up.* The process of **winding up** involves completing the business of the partnership, selling the assets of the partnership, and distributing the cash or other assets. Assets are distributed to parties in the following order:
   a. Creditors Who Are Not Partners.
   b. Partner Creditors. These are loans or advances made by a partner to the partnership.
   c. Partners' Capital Balance.
   d. Any Remaining Assets to the Partners as Profits.
3. *Negative Capital Balance.* If the above results in a negative capital balance for a partner, that partner must reimburse the partnership. If the partner cannot do so or does not do so for any reason, the amount not paid back must be absorbed by the remaining partners in their relative loss-sharing ratios. For example, Amy, Bob, and Carl shared profits and losses 25 percent, 50 percent, and 25 percent respectively. If the winding up process resulted in a negative capital balance of $6,000 for Cal, then Amy and Bob would absorb any amount that Cal did not pay back. If Cal paid none of it back, Amy would absorb $2,000 ($6,000 x 25%/ (25% + 50%)) and Bob would absorb $4,000 ($6,000 x 50%/ (25% + 50%)). **Exam tip #4.**
4. *Termination.* **Termination** occurs when the last assets are distributed. At that point the legal existence of the partnership comes to an end.

B. <u>Dissolution by Acts of the Partners</u>. Partnerships are based on consent, thus a partner is always able to dissolve a partnership, even if doing so is contrary to the partnership agreement. The following acts of the partners dissolve a partnership:
   1. *Stated Time Period or Purpose Is Completed.* A partnership for a fixed period of time or to accomplish a particular goal will be dissolved upon reaching that point. This is considered an act of the parties because the parties originally set the terms of the partnership.
   2. *Withdrawal of Partner.* Any withdrawal of a partner will dissolve a partnership. If the withdrawal is contrary to the partnership agreement, is a **wrongful dissolution** which entitles the remaining parties to recover any damages caused by the wrongful dissolution from the party wrongfully dissolving. For example, if a partnership was formed for a five-year term for the purpose of buying investment property, a withdrawal by a partner during the third year would result in a wrongful dissolution. Although wrongfully caused, the partnership would nonetheless be dissolved, but any loss incurred due to the premature dissolution could be recovered from the wrongfully dissolving party. **Exam tip #5.**
   3. *Expulsion of a Partner.*
   4. *Admission of a Partner.* The old partnership is dissolved and a new one formed upon the new partner's admission.
   5. *Mutual Agreement of the Partners.* The partners may unanimously agree to dissolve the partnership.

C. <u>Dissolution by Operation of Law</u>. Certain events result in automatic dissolution of a partnership.
   1. *Death of a Partner.* A partner's death always results in the dissolution of a partnership.
   2. *Continuation Agreement.* Partnership agreements often include a **continuation agreement** providing for the automatic "continuation" of a partnership with the remaining partners in the event that a partner dies or withdraws from the partnership. In reality, a continuation agreement results in the termination of the old partnership and the automatic formation of a new one. **Exam tip #6.**

      3. *Bankruptcy of Any Partner or the Partnership.* Bankruptcy, but not mere insolvency, dissolves a partnership because the bankrupt partner's legal obligation to pay his debts is changed by the bankruptcy discharge.

      4. *Illegality.* A partnership is dissolved if the partnership's business becomes illegal. For example, a partnership to operate a casino would be dissolved if it became illegal in that state to operate a casino.

  D. Judicial Decree. A court can order dissolution, with the more common reasons including:

      1. *A Partner Is Adjudicated Insane or Is Shown to Be of Unsound Mind.*

      2. *A Partner Becomes Incapable of Performing Her Duties.*

      3. *A Partner Engages in Improper Conduct That Compromises the Ability to Perform His Partnership Duties.*

      4. *A Partner Repeatedly Violates the Partnership Agreement.*

      5. *The Partnership Can Be Carried On Only at a Loss.*

  E. Notice of Dissolution.

      1. *To Partners.* Notice of a dissolution must be given to all partners. Any contract entered into by a partner who has not been given notice of dissolution will be binding on the partnership.

      2. *To Parties Who Have Dealt With the Partnership.* Parties who have actually dealt with the partnership should be given notice to avoid liability based on apparent authority. The notice eliminates possible claims that there was lingering apparent authority.

      3. *To Parties With Knowledge of the Partnership.* Parties who know of the partnership must be given actual or constructive (publication in a newspaper of general distribution) notice to avoid liability based on apparent authority.

VII.   Limited Partnerships.

  A. Generally. A **limited partnership** is a partnership where some partners, the limited partners, have limited liability. Limited partnerships operate as general partnerships in many respects, but contain some differences.

  B. Revised Uniform Limited Partnership Act. The **Revised Uniform Limited Partnership Act (RULPA)** covers limited partnerships in the states that have adopted it.

  C. Partner Requirements. A limited partnership must have at least one **general partner** and at least one **limited partner.** Any general partners have unlimited personal liability just as the partners in a general partnership.

  D. Filing Required. A limited partnership must execute a **certificate of limited partnership** and file it with the secretary of state in the appropriate state.

  E. Corporation Can Be General Partner. The RULPA permits a corporation to be the general partner in a limited partnership.

  F. New Partners. New partners admitted must be approved by all of the partners. This requirement cannot be waived with respect to new general partners, but the partnership agreement can waive it with respect to new limited partners.

  G. Profit and Loss Sharing. Unless otherwise specified, profits and losses are shared in accordance with capital contribution, but limited partnership agreements usually do provide for a specified sharing of profits and losses. A limited partner cannot lose more than the amount invested.

H. <u>Limited Partner's Loss of Limited Liability</u>. A limited partner can lose his limited liability protection if he becomes involved in the management of the partnership. In such a case, the partner will be treated as a general partner with respect to liability. Such a limited partner will have unlimited liability. **Exam tip #7.**

I. <u>Partner as Both Limited and General Partner</u>. A partner can simultaneously be both a limited and general partner. This might occur where a general partner purchases limited partnership interests to increase her share of profits. Such a partner has unlimited personal liability by virtue of the general partner status.

J. <u>Limited Liability Partnerships</u>. Many states now recognize **limited liability partnerships** where all partners have limited liability. Many states limit their use to certain professionals, such as CPAs and attorneys.

VIII. Limited Liability Companies.

A. <u>Generally</u>. **Limited Liability Companies (LLCs)** were first recognized in the late 1980s and provide limited liability for all owners while allowing the possibility of taxation as a partnership. The same result can be achieved with an S Corporation, but S Corporation status was not possible for many corporations. Initially, a limited liability company required careful structuring to ensure that it would be taxed as a partnership. Today, an LLC will be taxed as a partnership unless it desires to be taxed as a corporation.

B. <u>Source of Law</u>. Most states have passed statutes authorizing limited liability companies. Much of the law governing LLCs is based on partnership law, except that the law relative to the liability of the owners to third parties is based on corporate law. For example, the laws of the management of an LLC and transfer of owners' interests are similar to partnership provisions.

C. <u>Filing Required</u>. An LLC is required to file **articles of organization** with the secretary of state's office in the appropriate state.

D. <u>Members</u>. The owners of an LLC are called members.

EXAM TIPS

1. A partner is always entitled to the allocated share of profits and losses, but not to a salary or other payment based on time devoted to the partnership unless the partnership agreement specifically provides for it.

2. The effect of assigning a partnership interest is heavily tested. Be sure to know that it does not make the assignee a partner, nor does it entitle the assignee to take part in managing the partnership.

3. In practice, the distinction in these two types of liability is not important because plaintiffs usually sue all partners and the partnership, which would be sufficient under either type of liability.

4. Candidates must be prepared to calculate the distribution of assets. This process is somewhat similar to that in a bankruptcy. An additional complication is the handling of negative capital balances. Whenever an amount is given as available for distribution, pay close attention to whether any amounts have already been paid. For example, a question could state that $80,000 is available before creditors are paid, or it could be the amount remaining after creditors were paid.

5. Partners always have the **power** to dissolve, but have the **right** to do so only if it is proper. A partner's dissolution is usually proper unless it is prevented by the partnership agreement.

6. Be sure to know that with a continuation agreement the old partnership is terminated and a new one is formed.
7. A limited partner's loss of limited liability is heavily tested on the CPA exam. Pay close attention for facts indicating a limited partner's involvement in managing the partnership.

KEY CONCEPTS LIKELY TO BE TESTED ON THE CPA EXAM

1. Requirements to form a partnership.
2. Liability of a partner for partnership obligations, both in concept and as computed in a fact situation.
3. Rights of partners and rights of assignees of a partnership interest.
4. How a partnership can be dissolved.
5. Distribution of partnership assets upon dissolution.
6. Limited partnership requirements, and the treatment of limited partners as general partners.

KEY TERMS

Uniform Partnership Act	Secret Profits	Termination
Fictitious Business Name	Business Judgment Rule	Wrongful Dissolution
Partnership for a Term	Partnership Property	Continuation Agreement
Partnership at Will	Tenancy in Partnership	Limited Partnership
Partnership by Estoppel	Charging Order	General Partner
Indemnification	Joint Liability	Limited Partner
Right to Return of Advances	Joint and Several Liability	Limited Liability Partnership
Right to Return of Capital	Dissolution	Limited Liability Company
Right to Information	Winding Up	Articles of Organization
Action for an Accounting	Competing With the Partnership	
Duty of Loyalty	Assignment of Partnership Interest	
Self-Dealing	Revised Uniform Limited Partnership Act	
Usurp an Opportunity	Certificate of Limited Partnership	

MULTIPLE CHOICE QUESTIONS

1.   Law Nov 91 #14
A general partnership must
A. Pay federal income tax.
B. Have two or more partners.
C. Have written articles of partnership
D. Provide for apportionment of liability for partnership debts.

2.   Author
If a partner wants a court to determine that partner's share of partnership assets, the partner should seek
A. A charging order.
B. An indemnification.
C. An accounting.
D. A dissolution.

3.   Law R 97 #2

Which of the following statements is correct regarding the apparent authority of a partner to bind the partnership in dealing with third parties? The apparent authority

A. Must be derived from the express powers and purposes contained in the partnership agreement.
B. Will be effectively limited by a formal resolution of the partners of which third parties are unaware.
C. May allow a partner to bind the partnership to representations made in connection with the sale of goods.
D. Would permit a partner to submit a claim against the partnership to arbitration.

4.   Law May 89 #16

Kroll, Inc., a partner in the JKL Partnership, assigns its interest in the partnership to Trell, who is not made a partner. After the assignment, Trell asserts the rights to

I. Receive Kroll's share of JKL's profits and
II. Inspect JKL's books and records.

Trell is correct as to which of the rights?

A. I only.
B. II only.
C. I and II.
D. Neither I nor II.

5.   Law Nov 91 #16

In a general partnership, a partner's interest in specific partnership property is

A. Transferable to the partner's individual creditors.
B. Subject to a partner's liability for alimony.
C. Transferable to the partner's estate upon death.
D. Subject to a surviving partner's right of survivorship.

6.   Law Nov 95 #18

Which of the following statements is correct regarding the division of profits in a general partnership when the agreement only provides that losses be divided equally among the partners? Profits are to be divided

A. Based on the partners' ratio of contribution to the partnership.
B. Based on the partners' participation in day to day management.
C. Equally among the partners.
D. Proportionately among the partners.

7.   Law Nov 95 #20

Park and Graham entered into a written partnership agreement to operate a retail store. Their agreement was silent as to the duration of the partnership. Park wishes to dissolve the partnership. Which of the following statements is correct?

A. Park may dissolve the partnership at any time
B. Unless Graham consents to a dissolution, Park must apply to a court and obtain a decree ordering the dissolution.
C. Park may **not** dissolve the partnership.
D. Park may dissolve the partnership only after notice of the proposed dissolution is given to all partnership creditors.

8.   Law May 92 #11

Which of the following statements is correct with respect to a limited partnership?

A. A limited partner may **not** be an unsecured creditor of the limited partnership.
B. A general partner may **not** also be a limited partner at the same time.
C. A general partner may be a secured creditor of the limited partnership.
D. A limited partnership can be formed with limited liability for all partners.

9.   Law Nov 89 #6

Gillie, Taft, and Dall are partners in an architectural firm. The partnership agreement is silent about the payment of salaries and the division of profits and losses. Gillie works full-time in the firm, and Taft and Dall each work half-time. Taft invested $120,000 in the firm, and Gillie and Dall invested $60,000 each. Dall is responsible for bringing in 50% of the business, and Gillie and Taft 25% each. How should profits of $120,000 for the year be divided up?

A. Gillie $60,000, Taft $30,000, Dall $30,000.
B. Gillie $40,000, Taft $40,000, Dall $40,000.
C. Gillie $30,000, Taft $60,000, Dall $30,000.
D. Gillie $30,000, Taft $30,000, Dall $60,000.

10.   Law May 93 #14

Locke and Vorst were general partners in a kitchen equipment business. On behalf of the partnership, Locke contracted to purchase 15 stoves from Gage. Unknown to Gage, Locke was not authorized by the partnership agreement to make such contracts. Vorst refused to allow the partnership to accept delivery of the stoves and Gage sought to enforce the contract. Gage will

A. Lose, because Locke's action was **not** authorized by the partnership agreement.
B. Lose, because Locke was **not** an agent of the partnership.
C. Win, because Locke had express authority to bind the partnership.
D. Win, because Locke had apparent authority to bind the partnership.

ESSAY QUESTION (Estimated time -- 15 to 20 minutes)

Law Nov 90 #4

Smith, Edwards, and Weil formed Sterling Properties Limited Partnership to engage in the business of buying, selling and managing real estate. Smith and Edwards were general partners. Weil was a limited partner entitled to 50% of all profits.

Within a few months of Sterling's formation, it became apparent to Weil that Smith's and Edwards' inexperience was likely to result in financial disaster for the partnership. Therefore, Weil became more involved in day-to-day management decisions. Weil met with prospective buyers and sellers of properties; assisted in negotiating partnership loans with its various lenders; and took an active role in dealing with personnel problems. Things continued to deteriorate for

Sterling, and the partners began blaming each other for the partnership's problems.

Finally, Smith could no longer deal with the situation, and withdrew from the partnership. Edwards reminded Smith that the Sterling partnership agreement specifically prohibited withdrawal by a general partner without the consent of all the other partners. Smith advised Edwards and Weil that she would take no part in any further partnership undertaking and would not be responsible for partnership debts occurred after this withdrawal.

With Sterling on the verge of collapse, the following situations have occurred:

• Weil demanded the right to inspect and copy the partnership's books and records and Edwards refused to allow Weil to do

[continued on next page]

so, claiming that Weil's status as a limited partner precludes that right.

- Anchor Bank, which made a loan to the partnership prior to Smith's withdrawal, is suing Sterling and each partner individually, including Smith, because the loan is in default. Weil denied any liability based on his limited partner status. Smith denies liability based on her withdrawal.

- Edwards sued Smith for withdrawing from the partnership and is uncertain about the effect of her withdrawal on the partnership.

- Weil wants to assign his partnership interest to Fred Alberts, who wants to become a substitute limited partner. Weil is uncertain about his right to assign this interest to Alberts and, further, the right of Alberts to become a substitute limited partner. Edwards contends that Edwards' consent is necessary for the assignment or the substitution of Alberts as a limited partner and that without this consent any such assignment would cause a dissolution of the partnership. The Sterling partnership agreement and certificate are silent in this regard.

Required:

Answer the following questions, setting forth reasons for the conclusions stated.

a. Is Weil entitled to inspect and copy the books and records of the partnership?

b. Are Weil and/or Smith liable to Anchor Bank?

c. Will Edwards prevail in the lawsuit against Smith for withdrawing from the partnership?

d. What is the legal implication to the partnership of Smith's withdrawal?

e. Can Weil assign his partnership interest to Alberts?

f. Can Edwards prevent the assignment to Alberts or the substitution of Alberts as a limited partner?

g. What rights does Alberts have as assignee of Weil's partnership interest?

h. What effect does an assignment have on the partnership?

EXPLANATIONS TO MULTIPLE CHOICE QUESTIONS

1. B is the correct answer. There must be at least two partners in a partnership. Choice C is incorrect because an agreement can be oral or can be implied from the conduct of the parties. Choice D is incorrect because this is not required. Furthermore, even with such an agreement, it will not eliminate the personal liability of the partners for partnership debts.

2. C is the correct answer. An accounting determines the individual claims of the partners to partnership assets and profits.

3. C is the correct answer. Apparent authority is based on a claim or appearance of authority made by the principal. In a partnership, all partners are agents of the partnership and the other partners. Thus, the other partners and partnership also function as principals. By making a person a partner, the partnership and other partners are holding the partner out as an agent, thereby creating apparent authority.

4. A is the correct answer. When a partnership interest is assigned, the assignee receives the right to the assignor's share of profits as well as the assignor's rights in the event of a liquidation. The assignee does not become a partner and does not acquire the other rights of a partner.

5. D is the correct answer. Specific partnership property is owned by the partners as a tenancy in partnership which has a right of survivorship. Thus, the remaining partners will own it. Choices A, B, and C are incorrect because in each case only the partner's partnership interest could be transferred, but not the partner's share in individual partnership property.

6. C is the correct answer. When a partnership specifies the allocation of profits, but not losses, any losses are divided in the same way as profits. But the converse is not true. Where the partnership agreement specifies the allocation of losses, but not profits, the allocation of losses does not affect profit allocation, and any profits are divided equally. Note that this question was set up so that if you erroneously thought that you would allocate profits in the same way as losses, you would get the correct answer. It is a rare CPA exam question where incorrect reasoning will nonetheless lead you to the correct answer. Furthermore, answer choice D can be quickly eliminated because it states that profits are to be divided "proportionately" without saying in proportion to what they are divided.

7. A is the correct answer. Note the logical relationship of answer choices A and C. It is highly unlikely that neither is correct, thus the question can quickly be narrowed down to A and C, which improves the chance of correctly answering the question. Choice A would be true even if the partnership agreement provided that Park could not withdraw. In such a case, Park would have the power to withdraw, but not the right to do so. Without a fixed duration, Park has both here.

8. C is the correct answer. Choice A is incorrect because a limited partner can simultaneously be an unsecured creditor. Choice B is incorrect because a limited partner can also simultaneously be a general partner.

9. B is the correct answer. When a partnership agreement is silent as to the division of partnership profits, they are divided equally. There is no right, unless specifically provided in the partnership agreement, to an additional share of profit based on time worked, capital invested, or income generated.

10. D is the correct answer. By virtue of being a partner, Gage has apparent authority to bind the partnership on matters of partnership business. Choice A is incorrect because Gage's position will create the apparent authority, and this apparent authority will not be affected by the terms of the partnership agreement which are not known to third parties.

UNOFFICIAL AICPA ANSWER TO ESSAY QUESTION

Law May 90 #4

a. Weil is entitled to inspect and copy Sterling's books and records. A limited partner such as Weil has the right to have the partnership books kept at the principal place of business of the partnership and to inspect and copy them at all times.

b. Generally, limited partners are not liable to partnership creditors except to the extent of their capital contributions. In Weil's case, however, he will probably be liable to Anchor Bank in the same manner as Sterling's general partners because he has taken part in the control of the business of the partnership and, therefore, has lost his limited liability. Smith, as a general partner, would also be personally liable to Anchor because liability was incurred prior to withdrawal.

c. Edwards will likely prevail in his lawsuit against Smith for withdrawing because the partnership agreement specifically prohibits a withdrawal by a general partner without the consent of the other partners. Therefore, Smith has breached the partnership agreement and will be liable to Edwards for any damages resulting from Smith's withdrawal.

d. The withdrawal (retirement) of a general partner dissolves the partnership unless the remaining general partners continue the business of the partnership under a right to do so provided in the limited partnership certificate, or unless all partners consent. Therefore, it is possible that Smith's withdrawal will result in Sterling's dissolution.

e. Weil is free to assign his limited partnership interest to Alberts in the absence of any prohibitions in the Sterling partnership agreement or certificate.

f. Alberts, however, cannot be a substitute limited partner without the consent of the remaining general partner, Edwards.

g. Therefore, Alberts, as an assignee of Weil's limited partnership interest, may not exercise any rights of a partner. Alberts is entitled only to any distributions from Sterling to which Weil would have been entitled.

h. Finally, the assignment by Weil of his partnership interest does not create a dissolution of the partnership.

Author's Note:
   Notice that pronoun references are rarely used in this answer. Rather than use the terms "he" and "she," the answer uses the partner's name, even in instances where it might sound a little awkward. This approach leaves no doubt in the grader's mind which partner is being referred to. In situations with multiple parties, it is probably a good idea to avoid the use of pronouns whenever possible. This will help avoid ambiguous references.

CHAPTER 20
THE NATURE, FORMATION, AND FINANCING OF CORPORATIONS

OVERVIEW

Corporations are covered in this chapter and the next two. Corporations are the traditional form of business organization providing limited liability for the owners. Unlike partnerships, which can be formed without the partners even being aware of it, there are a number of specific steps which must be completed in order for a corporation to come into existence. Once created, a corporation is a separate entity from its owners. This chapter examines the general characteristics of corporations, the types of corporations, the steps necessary for their formation, and the rights of shareholders.

OUTLINE

I. **The Nature or Corporations.**
   A. Created Under Statutory Authority. A **corporation** can be created only if there is a statute authorizing its creation. Such statutes exist in every state.
   B. Public and Private Corporation. Private corporations can have as few as one shareholder or as many as millions. Public corporation are owned by governmental units or may be a governmental unit itself. Do not confuse a public corporation with a "publicly held" private corporation, such as General Motors, which has millions of shareholders. The term "publicly held" is a general descriptive term which is often shortened to "public." Thus, private corporations with many shareholders are sometimes called public corporations even though they are actually private corporations which are publicly held.
   C. Separate Entity. A corporation is a separate legal entity for most purposes. Thus, it can sue and be sued in its own name, own property, enter into contracts, be punished for criminal behavior (generally through fines, since it is impossible to put a corporation in prison), and must pay its own taxes.
   D. Corporate Characteristics.
      1. *Limited Liability.* The owners of a corporation are liable only to the extent of their investment in the corporation, which is described as **limited liability**.
      2. *Free Transferability of Shares.* Shares are **freely transferable**, with certain exceptions under the securities laws. Shareholders may agree among themselves to restrict the transferability of shares.
      3. *Perpetual Existence.* Corporations have a **perpetual existence** apart from the lives of their owners, and exist forever unless there is a stated duration in the articles of incorporation.
      4. *Centralized Management.* A corporation has a **centralized management** vested in a **board of directors**, which selects **officers**. The officers and the board of directors constitute the management of the corporation. **Exam tip #1.**
   E. Revised Model Business Corporation Act. The **Revised Model Business Corporation Act (RMBCA)** was issued in 1984 as a revision of the Model Business Corporation Act. It is tested on the CPA exam and is state law in the states that have passed it.

F. <u>Federal Laws Affecting Corporations</u>. There is no general federal law governing the formation and operation of corporations, although there are many other federal statutes which affect corporations in various ways. This chapter addresses the law governing the formation of corporations.

II. Classification of Corporations.

A. <u>Based on the Place of Incorporation</u>.
1. *Domestic Corporation.* A corporation is a **domestic corporation** in the state of its incorporation.
2. *Foreign Corporation.* A corporation is a **foreign corporation** in any state other than its state of incorporation.
3. *Alien Corporation.* An **alien corporation** is one that is incorporated in another nation, and in most instances, is treated as a foreign corporation. **Exam tip #2.**
4. *Incorporate in Only One State.* A corporation can incorporate in only one state.
5. *Certificate of Authority.* Many states require foreign and alien corporations to obtain a certificate of authority to do business in the state.

B. <u>Based on Profit Motivation</u>.
1. *Profit Corporation.* A **profit corporation** is operated for profit with the goal of generating profits for the shareholders.
2. *Nonprofit Corporation.* A **nonprofit corporation** (also known as not-for-profit) does not have the earning of profits as a goal. It is acceptable for a nonprofit corporation to earn a profit, but the corporation cannot distribute any of those profits to its members, directors, or officers.

C. <u>Based on the Number of Shareholders</u>.
1. *Publicly Held Corporation.* A **publicly held corporation** is owned by many shareholders, with the shares of many such corporations traded on organized securities markets.
2. *Closely Held Corporation.* A **closely held corporation** is owned by a few shareholders, who, in many cases, are relatives or friends. The stockholders often participate in management. These are descriptive terms without clear limits on shareholder numbers.

D. <u>Professional Corporations</u>. A **professional corporation** is formed by certain professionals, such as doctors, lawyers, or CPAs. Some states impose personal liability on members for the professional malpractice of other professionals in the corporation.

E. <u>S Corporations</u>. S Corporation status affects only the corporation's tax status. In all other respects, S Corporation status is irrelevant and S Corporations are treated as other corporations.

III. Promoters' Activities.

A. <u>Generally</u>. **Promoters** are the persons who form a corporation. Promoters often enter into contracts on behalf of the yet-to-be-formed corporation.

B. <u>Role as Agent</u>. The promoter often acts as an agent of the corporation. The promoter's role is somewhat different than that of most agents because a promoter acts as agent for a principal that does not yet exist. Thus the promoter has no authority and must rely on the corporation to later ratify or adopt the contract.

C. <u>Contract Liability of Corporation</u>. The corporation becomes liable on promoters' contracts only if the board of directors chooses to **adopt**, or ratify, the contract.

D. <u>Contract Liability of Promoter</u>. A promoter has contingent liability on contracts entered into on behalf of the corporation, even if the corporation is identified by name. This is because the corporation is not yet in existence. The promoter will be liable on the contract in any of the following circumstances:
   1. *The Corporation Is Not Formed.*
   2. *The Corporation Is Formed, But Does Not Adopt the Contract.*
   3. *The Corporation Is Formed, Adopts the Contract, But Does Not Perform.*

   Thus, any set of events short of adoption and full performance by the corporation will subject the promoter to liability on the contract. **Exam tip #3.**

E. <u>Novation Will Release the Promoter</u>. The promoter will be released if the corporation, promoter, and third party enter into a three-party agreement in which the promoter is released and the corporation agrees to be bound.

F. <u>Automatic Release Upon Adoption</u>. The promoter and third party can agree and include a term in the contract when it is originally negotiated that the promoter will be released automatically upon the adoption of the contract by the corporation.

G. <u>Subscription Agreement</u>. In a **stock subscription agreement**, a party agrees to purchase shares of a corporation once it is formed. If breached by the purchaser, the corporation can either sue to collect the amount due or rescind the agreement and sell the shares to another party.

IV.   **Incorporation Procedures.**
A. <u>State Law Determines Procedures</u>. Incorporation procedures differ somewhat from state to state.

B. <u>Purpose</u>. A corporation must state a purpose, but today, most corporations are formed for "any lawful purpose."

C. <u>State of Incorporation</u>. Any states can be chosen, but smaller corporations usually incorporate where they will be doing most of their business, whereas larger corporations often choose a state, such as Delaware, whose laws are favorable for internal operations of the corporation.

D. <u>Incorporators</u>. **Incorporators** sign the articles of incorporation and often become shareholders, officers, or directors of the corporation.

E. <u>Articles of Incorporation</u>. The RMBCA requires relatively few items to be included in the **articles of incorporation** compared with earlier statutes. Other items can be placed in the bylaws; this is advantageous because the bylaws are easier to amend. The articles must include:
   1. *The Name of the Corporation.*
   2. *The Number of Shares the Corporation Is Authorized to Issue.*
   3. *The Name of the Initial Registered Agent.*
   4. *The Name and Address of Each Incorporator.*

   Other provisions, such as the corporation's duration or other items which would be included in the bylaws, may be included in the articles. **Exam tip #4.**

F. <u>Filing</u>. The corporation comes into existence upon the filing of the articles of incorporation. In most states, the filing is at the office or the secretary of state. Under the RMBCA, the filing is conclusive proof of the corporation's existence.

G. <u>Issuance of Certificate</u>. After filing, a certificate of incorporation will be issued.

H. <u>Amendment of Articles</u>. The articles can be amended if the amendment is:
   1. *Recommended for Adoption by the Board of Directors*, and
   2. *Approved by a Vote of the Shareholders.*

I.   Amendment Not Affecting Rights of Shares. An amendment that does not affect the rights attached to shares can be approved by a resolution of the board only. **Exam tip #5.**

J.   Registered Agent. The **registered office** is the location where service or process is served to the **registered agent,** who is the party designated to receive service of process. The registered agent can be an individual or another corporation, and is the party to whom any legal notice or summons should be sent.

K.   Bylaws. The **bylaws** govern the internal management structure of the corporation and are more detailed than the articles of incorporation.
   1. *Initial Adoption.* The bylaws can be initially adopted by either the incorporators or the initial directors.
   2. *Filing Not Required.* There is no filing requirement for the bylaws.
   3. *Typical Provisions.* The bylaws can contain any provision that does not conflict with the law or with the articles of incorporation. Typical provisions would address:
       a. Time and Place of the Annual Shareholders' Meeting.
       b. How Special Shareholders' Meetings Are Called.
       c. Time and Place of Monthly Board of Directors' Meetings.
       d. Quorum and Voting Requirements.
       e. Corporate Officers and Their Duties.
       f. Committees of the Board of Directors.
       g. Location of Corporate Records.
       h. Shareholders' Inspection Rights of Corporate Records.
   4. *Amendment.* The board of directors can amend the bylaws, but the shareholders always have an absolute right to amend them, including overriding any board of directors amendment.

L.   Organizational Meeting.   After the articles are filed, the initial directors must hold an **organizational meeting** where bylaws are adopted, officers are elected, and any other business is conducted. The adoption of promoters' contracts and the formation of committees of the board of directors are frequently accomplished at the organizational meeting.

V. Equity Financing of Corporations.

A.   Common Stock. The basic ownership of a corporation is represented by **common stock.** The **common stockholders** (or **shareholders**) are the parties who own the common stock. All corporations must issue common stock.
   1. *Right to Vote.* Each share of common stock usually entitles the holder to one vote. It is possible to issue more than one type of common stock, and the voting rights can differ. It is possible to issue common stock that has no voting rights. The stockholders vote directly on important matters such as mergers or amendments to the articles of incorporation.
   2. *Election of Directors.* The common stockholders elect the board of directors.
   3. *Dividends.* The common stockholders have the right to receive dividends, but **only** if the board of directors declares them. A dividend payment is a distribution of a portion of the corporation's earnings, but it is not an expense. Corporate net income is not affected by paying a dividend.
   4. *Residual Claim.* In the event of liquidation, the common stockholders are entitled to the residual assets of the corporation after all creditors have been satisfied and after preferred stockholders' claims have been satisfied.

5. *Indirect Governance.* The common stockholders do not vote directly on most corporate matters. The common shareholders elect the board of directors, and the board of directors then votes on most matters.

6. *Par Value of Shares.* **Par value** of stock historically was the minimum amount a corporation could receive when initially issuing shares of common stock. It has nothing to do with market value. Corporations usually set the par value so low that the concept has come to have little meaning. The RMBCA has eliminated the concept of par value of common stock. Par value does have accounting significance.

B. Preferred Stock. Corporations can also issue **preferred stock**, although they are not required to do so. Corporations can issue preferred stock with a variety of characteristics:

1. *Preferences.* Preferred stock gets its name from the preferences that the preferred shareholders receive. The preferred shareholders receive their dividends ahead of the common shareholders, and, in a liquidation, receive payment for their shares ahead of the common shareholders.

2. *Preferred Is Not Better.* Preferred stock is not better than common stock, but simply receives certain payments ahead of the common shareholders. For example, even though the preferred shareholders have the first right to dividends, the common shareholders might receive far larger dividends relative to their investment.

3. *No Right to Vote.* Preferred stock usually has no voting rights.

4. *Fixed Dividend.* Most preferred stock is entitled to a **fixed dividend** if dividends are declared. This is often stated as a fixed amount, such as $5.30 per share, or as a percentage of par value, such as 7 percent. The stated dividend is the amount per year, thus a shareholder would receive on fourth of that amount in each payment if dividends are paid four times a year.

5. *No Right to Dividends.* Even though the dividend amount is stated, and even though the preferred stockholders receive dividends ahead of the common stockholders, the preferred stockholders have no right to dividends unless the board of directors declares them.

6. *Characteristics of Debt.* In concept, preferred stock has some characteristics of common stock (for example, no right to dividends) and some characteristics of debt (for example, a fixed return and no right to vote). For the CPA exam, preferred stock is a type of equity.

7. *Optional Characteristics.* Preferred stock represents a contract between the corporation and the shareholder. As with most contracts, there can be a variety of provisions, with the possible varieties of preferred stock being limited only by the imagination of the parties. Characteristics often seen include:

   a. Cumulative. With **cumulative preferred stock**, the preferred shareholders are entitled to receive any unpaid prior years' dividends in addition to the current year dividend before common shareholders receive any dividends. For example, assume that a corporation paid its full preferred dividend in 1998, but did not pay any dividends in 1999 or 2000. In 2001, owners of cumulative preferred stock would be entitled to receive their dividends for 1999, 2000, and 2001 before the common shareholders could receive a dividend. In the same circumstances, owners of **noncumulative preferred stock** would be entitled to only the 2001 dividend ahead of the common shareholders.

b. Participating. Preferred shareholders are entitled to receive only the fixed dividend amount associated with their stock. If the preferred stock is **participating**, it is possible that the preferred shareholders will receive additional dividend amounts if the total dividend declared is large enough. This would usually result if the corporation is very profitable. Participating preferred stock will specify the mathematical formula under which these additional profits are shared.

c. Convertible. **Convertible preferred stock** can be exchanged, at the shareholder's option, for a specified amount of common stock. Because common stock market value is usually more volatile than that of preferred stock, conversion is usually favorable when the company is very profitable. Once converted to common stock, the shareholder does not have the option to convert back to preferred.

d. Callable. **Callable**, or **redeemable**, preferred stock gives the corporation the right to repurchase it, at the corporation's option, from the shareholder at a predetermined price.

Preferred stock can have none of these characteristics or any combination of them. Preferred stock can also have other characteristics not listed here. **Exam tip #6.**

C. Number of Shares. There are three important numbers relative to shares of stock:

1. *Shares Authorized.* The number of shares **authorized** is the maximum number that the corporation can legally issue, and is stated in the articles of incorporation. Because the articles must be amended to issue additional shares, corporations often set this number very high.

2. *Shares Issued.* The number of shares **issued** is the number that the corporation has sold to shareholders, whether they are currently in the hands of a shareholder or the corporation has reacquired them as **treasury stock**. Treasury stock is the corporation's own stock which it has reacquired from shareholders and gets its name from the fact that it is considered to be held in the corporate treasury.

3. *Shares Outstanding.* The number of shares **outstanding** is the number of shares which are currently in the hands of shareholders. Thus, the mathematical difference in the number of shares issued and the number outstanding is the number of shares of treasury stock.

D. Stock Options and Warrants.

1. *Stock Option.* A **stock option** is a right to buy a share of stock at a stated price. The value of a stock option comes from the possibility of buying the stock below its market value. Stock options can contain expiration dates and other restrictions on their exercise.

2. *Stock Warrant.* A **stock warrant** is a stock option evidenced by a certificate.

E. Debt Securities. Corporations also finance their operations by incurring debt. Large corporations often borrow money directly from investors and issue securities to the investor/lender to evidence the debt.

1. *Debenture.* A **debenture** is a long-term unsecured debt instrument. Repayment is based on the corporation's general debt-paying ability.

2. *Bond.* A **bond** is a long-term secured debt instrument. Repayment is based on the corporation's general debt-paying ability, but the collateral is available to satisfy the obligation in the event of default.

The terms of a debt security are often contained in an **indenture agreement**. The terms might include limits on incurring additional debt or the right to convert the debt into preferred or common stock.

VI.   Corporate Powers.

    A. Express Powers. Corporations have express powers from the following sources:

       1. *The U.S. Constitution.*

       2. *State Constitutions.*

       3. *Federal Statutes.*

       4. *State Statutes.*

       5. *The Articles of Incorporation.*

       6. *The Bylaws.*

       7. *Resolutions of the Board of Directors.*

    B. Implied Powers. A corporation has implied powers to accomplish its purposes. These include the power to open bank accounts, purchase insurance, and pay its employees.

    C. Ultra Vires Acts. An **ultra vires act** is an act beyond the power of a corporation. This is seldom a problem for a corporation whose purpose is "any lawful purpose." But a corporation formed to operate in the retail food industry would be committing an ultra vires act if it purchased a hotel. Thre are several remedies available if an ultra vires act is committed.

       1. *Shareholder Suit.* The shareholders can sue the corporation to get an injunction preventing the ultra vires act.

       2. *Corporation Suit.* The corporation can sue the officer or director responsible for the ultra vires act for any resulting damages.

       3. *Attorney General.* The attorney general of the state of incorporation can sue to either enjoin (prevent) the act or dissolve the corporation.

EXAM TIPS

1. Candidates must know the general structure of corporate governance, especially the distinct roles of the board of directors and officers, and their relationship to one another. Shareholders elect board members, and the board elects the officers. Shareholders do **not** elect the officers.

2. Be sure to know these definitions, especially that a foreign corporation is **not** a corporation based in another nation.

3. Contract liability for agents is discussed in Chapter 18 of this Guide. Be sure to understand how promoter liability differs from the general rules for agents.

4. It is important to know exactly what is required to be included in the articles, and thus also know what is not required to be included.

5. Be sure to know that the general rule is that shareholder approval is needed to amend the articles of incorporation. The board cannot do it unilaterally. Apply this general rule unless the question specifically states that the amendment does not affect the rights attached to shares.

6. The special characteristics are present only if specifically provided for. Thus, holders of preferred stock which does not state that it is participating are not entitled to receive any dividends beyond the stated dividend.

KEY CONCEPTS LIKELY TO BE TESTED ON THE CPA EXAM

1. Items required to be included in the articles of incorporation.
2. The rights and powers of the shareholders and the board of directors.
3. The rights specific to common or preferred stock.
4. The optional characteristics that can be present in preferred stock.
5. The characteristics and rights associated with dividends.
6. General corporate characteristics.

KEY TERMS

Corporation
Limited Liability
Free Transferability
Perpetual Existence
Centralized Management
Board of Directors
Officers
Domestic Corporation
Foreign Corporation
Alien Corporation
Profit Corporation
Nonprofit Corporation
Publicly Held Corporation
Closely held Corporation
Professional Corporation
Revised Model Business Corporation Act

Promoter
Adoption of a Contract
Stock Subscription Agreement
Incorporator
Articles of Incorporation
Registered Office
Registered Agent
Bylaws
Organizational Meeting
Common Stock
Shareholder
Par Value
Preferred Stock
Fixed Dividend
Cumulative Preferred Stock

Noncumulative Preferred Stock
Participating Preferred Stock
Convertible Preferred Stock
Callable Preferred Stock
Redeemable Preferred Stock
Shares Authorized
Shares Issued
Treasury Stock
Shares Outstanding
Stock Option
Stock Warrant
Debenture
Bond
Indenture Agreement
Ultra Vires Act

MULTIPLE CHOICE QUESTIONS

1.   Law Nov 95 #21
Which of the following facts is(are) generally included in a corporation's articles of incorporation?

	Name of registered agent	Number of authorized shares
A.	Yes	Yes
B.	Yes	No
C.	No	Yes
D.	No	No

2.   Law Nov 95 #22
Which of the following statements best describes an advantage of the corporate form of doing business?
A. Day to day management is strictly the responsibility of the directors.
B. Ownership is contractually restricted and is **not** transferable.
C. The operation of the business may continue indefinitely.
D. The business is free from state regulation.

3.   Law May 91 #4

Which of the following statements is correct with respect to the differences and similarities between a corporation and a limited partnership?

A. Stockholders may be entitled to vote on corporate matters, but limited partners are prohibited from voting on any partnership matters.

B. Stock of a corporation may be subject to the registration requirements of the federal securities laws but limited partnerhsip interests are automatically exempt from those requirements.

C. Directors owe fiduciary duties to the corporation and limited partners owe such duties to the partnership.

D. A corporation and a limited partnership may be created only under a state statute and each must file a copy of its organization document with the proper governmental body.

4.   Law May 90 #7

Absent a specific provision in its articles of incorporation, a corporation's board of directors has the power to do all of the following, **except**

A. Repeal the bylaws.

B. Declare dividends.

C. Fix compensation of directors.

D. Amend the articles of incorporation.

5.   Law May 94 #11

Under the Revised Model Business Corporation Act, which of the following must be contained in a corporation's articles of incorporation?

A. Quorum voting requirements.

B. Names of stockholders.

C. Provisions for issuance of par and non-par shares.

D. The number of shares the corporation is authorized to issue.

6.   Law May 92 #19

Price owns 2,000 shares of Universal Corp.'s $10 cumulative preferred stock. During its first year of operations, cash dividends of $5 per share were declared on the preferred stock but were never paid. In the second year, dividends on the preferred stock were neither declared nor paid. If Universal is dissolved, which of the following statements is correct?

A. Universal will be liable to Price as an unsecured creditor for $10,000.

B. Universal will be liable to Price as an unsecured creditor for $20,000.

C. Price will have priority over the claims of Universal's bond owners.

D. Price will have priority over the claims of Universal's unsecured judgment creditors.

7.   Law May 90 #9

Johns owns 400 shares of Abco Corp. cumulative preferred stock. In the absence of any specific contrary provision in Abco's articles of incorporation, which of the following statements is correct?

A. Johns is entitled to convert the 400 shares of preferred stock to a like number of shares of common stock.

B. If Abco declares a cash dividend on its preferred stock, Johns becomes an unsecured creditor of Abco.

C. If Abco declares a dividend on its common stock, Johns will be entitled to participate with the common stock shareholders in any dividend distribution after preferred dividends are paid.

D. John will be entitled to vote if dividend payments are in arrears.

8.   Law Nov 95 #24
Carr Corp. declared a 7% stock dividend on
its common stock. The dividend
A. Must be registered with the SEC pursuant
   to the Securities Act of 1933.
B. Is includable in the gross income of the
   recipient taxpayers in the year of receipt.
C. Has **no** effect on Carr's earnings and
   profits for federal income tax purposes.
D. Requires a vote of Carr's stockholders.

9.   Law May 92 #17
Unless prohibited by the organization
documents, a stockholder in a publicly held
corporation and the owner of a limited
partnership interest both have the right to
A. Ownership of the business' assets.
B. Control management of the business.
C. Assign their interest in the business.
D. An investment that has perpetual life.

ESSAY QUESTION (Estimated time -- 15 to 20 minutes)

Law Nov 90 #5

On May 12, 1987, West purchased 6% of
Ace Corp.'s outstanding $3 Cumulative
preferred stock and 7% of Ace's outstanding
common stock. These are the only two
classes of stock authorized by Ace's charter.
Both classes of stock are traded on a national
stock exchange. Ace uses the calendar year
for financial reporting purposes. During 1987
and 1988, Ace neither declared dividends nor
recorded dividends in arrears as a liability on
its books. West was disturbed about this and,
on February 8, 1989, sent a written demand to
examine Ace's books and records to
determine Ace's financial condition. Ace has
refused to permit West to examine its books
and records.

On May 8, 1989, West lost the stock
certificate representing the shares of preferred
stock. On May 9, 1989, West notified Ace of
the lost stock certificate and requested that
Ace issue a new stock certificate. West
offered to file an indemnity bond with Ace
and to fulfill any reasonable requests made by
Ace. Although Ace has no knowledge that

any other party has acquired the lost stock
certificate, Ace refused to issue a new stock
certificate or accept the indemnity bond.

As a result of the foregoing, West has
made the following assertions:

- Ace should have recorded the dividends in
  arrears for 1987 and 1988 as a liability
  that, in effect, would treat West as a
  general creditor to the extent ot the
  dividends in arrears.

- West is entitled to examine Ace's books
  and records.

- West is entitled to receive a new stock
  certificate to replace the lost stock
  certificate.

Required: In separate paragraphs, discuss
West's assertions. Indicate whether such
assertions are correct and the reason therefor.
Do **not** consider securities laws.

EXPLANATIONS TO MULTIPLE CHOICE QUESTIONS

1. A is the correct answer. Under the Revised Model Business Corporation Act, both the name of the registered agent and the and the number of authorized shares must be included in a corporation's articles of incorporation.

2. C is the correct answer. Choice A is incorrect because the officers are primarily responsible for the day-to-day management of the corporation. The directors share this responsibility, but it is not true that the directors are the only persons responsible. Choice B is incorrect because shares of stock are freely transferable unless the stockholders enter into an agreement to restrict the transferability. Choice D is incorrect because a corporation is subject to considerable state regulation, beginning with the requirement that articles of incorporation be filed to create the corporation.

3. D is the correct answer. Generally, any form of business organization with limited liability for any of its owners requires a filing of the appropriate document. Choice A is incorrect because there are certain matters, generally those outside the day-to-day operations, on which limited partners are entitled to vote. Choice B is incorrect because most limited partnership interests are classified as securities and might be required to be registered. Choice D is incorrect because limited partners owe no fiduciary duties to the partnership.

4. D is the correct answer. Amendment of the articles of incorporation generally requires the approval of the shareholders. Choice C is incorrect because the directors are authorized to set their own compensation. Although this might appear to be a conflict of interest, the fact that the shareholders can vote to remove a director or directors operates as an incentive for the directors to not pay themselves an excessive amount.

5. D is the correct answer. Choice B is incorrect because it is the incorporators, not the shareholders, whose names must appear in the articles.

6. A is the correct answer. Even when preferred stock is cumulative, dividends become a liability of the corporation only if they are declared by the board of directors. In this question, only a portion of one year's dividends had been declared, thus Price has a claim to only the $10,000 that has been declared. For this amount, he is an unsecured creditor. Price will have a claim to the other $10,000 of the first year's dividends, and the second year's dividends, but those claims will be as a preferred shareholder and not as an unsecured creditor. Choice D is incorrect because Price will have equal priority with other unsecured creditors for the amount that has been declared.

7. B is the correct answer. Choice B correctly states the rule that Johns would become a creditor only upon the declaration of a dividend. Choice A is incorrect because preferred stock is convertible only if the preferred stock so states. Likewise, choice C is incorrect because preferred stock is participating only if it so states.

8. C is the correct answer. Note that this question refers to a stock dividend, which is a distribution of additional shares to current shareholders. In any question on any section of the CPA exam which addresses dividends, be alert to whether the dividend is a cash or stock dividend. Choice D is incorrect because the board of directors, not the shareholders, votes to declare dividends of any kind. Note that choice C would be true even if the question concerned a cash dividend. For cash dividends, choice B would also be true.

9. C is the correct answer. Most property rights are assignable, including ownership interests in any type of business. Choice A is incorrect because shareholders and limited partners have an ownership interest in the business, but do not have a direct ownership interest in the individual assets of the business.

UNOFFICIAL AICPA ANSWER TO ESSAY QUESTION

Law Nov 89 #5

West's assertion that Ace should have recorded the dividends in arrears for 1987 and 1988 as a liability is incorrect. A shareholder of cumulative preferred stock is entitled to receive all dividend arrearages plus any dividends for the current year before any dividends may be distributed to the shareholders of common stock. However, preferred stock represents a contribution of capital, not a debt of the corporation, and until a dividend is declared, a shareholder of cumulative preferred stock is not a creditor of the corporation. Thus, Ace was correct in not classifying the dividend arrearages as a liability because a dividend was not declared by Ace's board of directors. Ace should disclose the dividend arrearages in notes to its financial statements.

West's assertion that West is entitled to examine Ace's books and records is correct. A shareholder, upon proper written demand, is entitled to examine, at reasonable times, the books and records of the corporation, so long as the examination is for a proper purpose (in good faith). If the corporation refuses to permit the examination, the shareholder may obtain a court order compelling access to the books and records.

West's assertion that West is entitled to receive a new stock certificate to replace the lost stock certificate is correct. Because the subject matter in this case is a stock certificate of a corporation, the UCC Investment Securities Article applies. Under that article, the stock certificate of Ace is classified as a certificated security because it is one of a class of Ace's shares that is represented as an instrument in West's name and is traded on a national securities exchange. If the owner of a certificated security claims that the security has been lost, the issuer shall issue a new certificated security, or, at the option of the issuer, an equivalent uncertificated security in place of the original security if the owner makes a request before the issuer has notice that the security has been acquired by a bona fide purchaser; files a sufficient indemnity bond with the issuer; and satisfies any other reasonable requirements imposed by the issuer. Based on the facts of this case, West is entitled to receive a new stock certificate because West requested that a new stock certificate be issued before Ace had notice the lost certificate was acquired by any other party' offered to file an indemnity bond with Ace; and offered to cooperate with any reasonable requests made by Ace.

CHAPTER 21
RIGHTS, DUTIES, AND LIABILITY OF CORPORATE DIRECTORS, OFFICERS, AND SHAREHOLDERS

OVERVIEW

This chapter addresses the rights and duties of the directors, officers, and shareholders of a corporation. It includes coverage of some of the internal operations of a corporation, such as stockholders' meetings, voting requirements, and dividend declaration.

OUTLINE

I. **Rights of Shareholders.**
  A. <u>Shareholder Meetings</u>.
    1. *Annual Meeting.* The **annual meeting** must be held within 15 months of the prior annual meeting or 6 months of year end, whichever is sooner. If the meeting is not held, a shareholder can petition the courts for an order that it be held. Directors are elected at the annual meeting, and other actions are taken as needed.
    2. *Special Shareholders' Meetings.* A **special shareholders' meeting** can be called by any of the following:
      a. The Board of Directors.
      b. Shareholders Owning at Least 10 Percent of the Voting Shares.
      c. Anyone Else Authorized in the Articles of Incorporation.
    3. *Notice.* Notice of all meetings, annual or special, must be given between 10 and 50 days in advance of the meeting. For special meetings, the notice must state the purpose, and only matters identified in the notice can be discussed at the special meeting.
    4. *Written Consent.* Any action that could be taken at a shareholders' meeting can be accomplished by all shareholders signing a **written consent** to the action. This is obviously more practical in a closely held corporation. **Exam tip #1.**
  B. <u>Proxies</u>. A shareholder can appoint someone else as her **proxy** (a type of agent) to vote her shares. The proxy can be directed how to vote, or directed to vote as the proxy sees fit. Proxy arrangements are usually revocable. A proxy must be in writing.
  C. <u>Voting Requirements</u>.
    1. *One Share, One Vote.* Each share of common stock usually is entitled to one vote. The Revised Model Business Corporation Act (RMBCA) allows corporations to grant greater or lesser voting rights in connection with stock, including having some nonvoting stock. There can be different classes of stock with different voting rights, but there must be at least one class of stock that does have voting rights.
    2. *Record Date.* A **record date** will be determined for each meeting. The party who owns the stock on the record date is the party entitled to vote those shares.
    3. *Quorum.* Unless otherwise stated in the articles, a majority of the shares entitled to vote must be represented (directly or by proxy) at the meeting for a **quorum** to exist.

4. *Majority Is Based on Shares Present.* If a quorum is present, a majority of the shares present will pass an item.

5. *Director Elections.* When electing directors, a shareholder is entitled to cast one vote for each share owned for each seat to be filled. For example, a shareholder owning 1,000 shares at a meeting where five director positions were being filled would have 5,000 votes to cast. There are two possible rules for how such a shareholder could cast those 5,000 votes:

   a. Straight Voting. Under **straight voting,** the shareholder could cast no more than 1,000 votes for any one candidate or seat on the board.

   b. Cumulative Voting. Under **cumulative voting,** the shareholder could allocate the votes in any manner desired, including casting all 5,000 votes for one candidate. Cumulative voting can allow certain minority shareholders to be assured of electing at least one person to the board. By voting for each director position separately under straight voting, a 45 percent shareholder would have no assurance of choosing even one director. The ability to aggregate votes would assure at least some representation on the board of directors. **Exam tip #2.**

6. *Supramajority Voting Requirement.* The articles or bylaws can impose a **supramajority** voting requirement for some or all matters. The vote to institute such a requirement must meet the same requirement. Thus, to impose a 75 percent supramajority requirement would require passage by at least 75 percent.

7. *Voting Agreements.* Other than by granting a proxy, there are a couple of ways that a shareholder can limit his right to vote.

   a. Voting Trust. With a **voting trust,** the shares are transferred to a trustee who then has the right to vote them. The voting trust can be at the direction of the shareholders or at the trustee's discretion.

   b. Voting Agreement. A **voting agreement** is a contract among two or more shareholders to vote according to the terms of the contract. A party to such an agreement can be ordered by the court to vote in accordance with the agreement.

D. Transfer of Shares. Shares of stock are normally freely transferable.

   1. *Lost Shares.* A corporation is required to issue a replacement certificate if a shareholder posts an indemnity bond to protect the corporation against any loss from issuing the replacement certificate.

   2. *Restrictions on Transfer.* Shareholders often agree to restrict the transferability of their stock. This is often done in closely held corporations to prevent a shareholder from selling the share to an "outsider." Many provisions can appear in these agreements, often in combination with one another. Common provisions include:

      a. Mandatory Sale and Purchase. This provision would force a shareholder to sell shares to the corporation or other shareholders upon some event, such as the death of the shareholder or the shareholder's ceasing active involvement in the business.

      b. Right of First Refusal. A **right of first refusal** gives the corporation and/or other shareholders the right to buy shares from a shareholder who proposes selling them. The corporation or other shareholders would have the right to purchase the shares on the same terms as the shareholder's proposed sale. If not exercised, the shares could be sold under the terms proposed.

E. Preemptive Rights. The **preemptive right** is shareholder's right to maintain her percentage ownership in the corporation. The shareholder has a right of first refusal any time the corporation issues additional shares. Thus, a shareholder who currently owns 16 percent of the stock would have the first right to purchase 16 percent of the shares in any new offering. This right must be granted in the articles in order to exist, but it is very common.

F. Right of Inspection. A shareholder's **right of inspection** is limited.
1. *Absolute Right to Inspect Certain Items.* A shareholder has an absolute right to inspect shareholder lists, the articles of incorporation, the bylaws, and the minutes of shareholders' meetings within the past three years.
2. *Limited Right to Inspect Other Items.* A shareholder's right to inspect other records, such as tax returns or minutes of meetings of the board of directors, is limited. The shareholder must demonstrate a proper corporate purpose. Reviewing records to determine how to vote is a proper purpose, but acquiring information for the shareholder to use in the shareholder's business is not.
3. *Appointing an Agent to Perform the Inspection.* A shareholder can appoint an agent, such as an attorney, to do the actual inspection on the shareholder's behalf. **Exam tip #3.**

G. Derivative Lawsuits. If a shareholder believes that the board of directors has a valid claim against another party, but is not bringing the suit for some reason, the shareholder can file a **derivative lawsuit** on behalf of the corporation. Any recovery in the lawsuit belongs to the corporation. In order to bring such a suit, the shareholder must:
1. *Have Been a Shareholder at the Time of the Act Complained of,*
2. *Fairly and Adequately Represent the Interests of the Corporation,* and
3. *Make a Written Demand That the Corporation Take Adequate Action.*

If the corporation rejects the demand, or 90 days pass without response, the suit can be filed. The suit will be dismissed if a majority of the outside directors or a court-ordered panel determines that it is not in the best interest of the corporation. For example, a suit against a supplier might do significant harm to an important business relationship. The shareholder can recover reasonable costs, including attorneys' fees, if the suit is successful. **Exam tip #4.**

II. Rights of Directors.
A. Generally. The directors' role is to oversee the operation of the corporation, and thus directors can make decisions regarding capital structure, can select and terminate officers, etc. There are certain actions requiring shareholder approval that also require a **resolution** of the board recommending that the shareholders approve the item.
B. Inside and Outside Directors. An **inside director** is also an officer of the corporation, whereas an **outside director** is one who is not also an officer. Most boards are composed of both inside and outside directors.
C. Qualifications for Board Members. There are no special qualification to be a board member unless the articles of incorporation set them.
D. Number of Directors. The RMBCA allows as few as one director, although some states require at least three.
E. Term of Office. Board members' terms usually extend until the next annual shareholders' meeting.

F. Staggered Terms Possible if Nine or More Directors. The RMBCA allows corporations which have 9 or more directors to set staggered terms on a two-year or three-year cycle. Thus a corporation with 12 directors could set three-year terms with four positions elected in each year. The number of positions elected each year must be as equal as possible.

G. Vacancies. A vacancy occurring on the board can be filled by the shareholders or the remaining directors. Note that because the shareholders can remove a director at any time with or without cause, there is minimal risk of the remaining board members electing a director contrary to the shareholders' interests. The shareholders could immediately vote to remove any new board member selected by the board.

H. Removal of Board Member. Any or all board members can be removed by a majority shareholder vote, with or without cause, unless the articles require cause for removal.

I. Board of Directors Meetings.
   1. *Regular Meetings.* Regular meetings are held as determined in the bylaws and do not require notice.
   2. *Special Meetings.* Special meetings can be held as the bylaws provide and require at least two days' notice unless this is waived.
   3. *Written Consent.* The board can take action without a meeting if all members sign written consent to the action.
   4. *Quorum.* A majority of the board constitutes a quorum unless the articles provide otherwise. So long as a quorum is present, a majority vote of the members present will result in approval of the item.
   5. *Proxies Not Allowed.* Board members cannot vote by proxy.

J. Director Compensation. Directors can be compensated, and can usually set their own compensation.

K. Directors' Absolute Inspection Right. Directors, unlike shareholders, have an absolute right to inspect corporate books and records. The right cannot be eliminated in the articles or bylaws, or by any other means.

L. Right to Declare Dividends. The directors have discretion to declare dividends, so long as certain requirements are met. The shareholder who owns stock on the **record date**, which is usually a few weeks before the payment date, is entitled to receive the dividend for that share of stock. In order to be legal, payment of a cash dividend must meet the following requirements:
   1. *The Corporation Must Be Solvent After Payment.* This generally requires that the corporation be able to pay its debts as they come due and that the payment not cause liabilities to exceed assets.
   2. *The Payment Must Come From Retained Earnings.* This is sometimes referred to as the surplus. Some states allow transfers from other accounts into retained earnings for purposes of dividend payment.
   3. *The Payment Must Not Violate Any Other Limitation.* The dividend payment cannot violate any other restriction in the articles, bylaws, or violate any restriction imposed by a resolution of the board.

If these requirements are met, the dividend can be declared, and at that point becomes a liability of the corporation. The shareholders then become unsecured creditors of the corporation.

III.   **Rights of Officers.**
   A.   Generally. The **officers** are elected by the board and hired by the corporation to perform broad management duties for the corporation. Most corporations have, at a minimum, a president, one or more vice presidents, a secretary, and a treasurer.
   B.   Agency Authority. Officers are frequently given express agency authority, and might have apparent authority by virtue of their position. Officers are not liable on contracts so long as their signature indicates their agent capacity. This results in a fully disclosed principal (the corporation), thus the agent (the officer) does not have contract liability.
   C.   Officer Removal. Unless an employment contract provides otherwise, officers are removable at the discretion of the board of directors. An officer removed in violation of an employment contract can recover damages from the corporation.

IV.   **Liability of Officers and Directors.**
   A.   Generally. Both directors and officers have fiduciary duties to the corporation. The duties are essentially the same for each.
   B.   Duty of Obedience. Officers and directors have a **duty of obedience**. This means that they must comply with laws affecting the corporation and with the articles, bylaws, and resolutions of the board. An officer would violate this duty by not complying with a board resolution or policy.
   C.   Duty of Care. The **duty of care** requires that directors and officers carry out their duties with reasonable care. This requires that they carry out their duties:
      1.   *In Good Faith,*
      2.   *With Reasonable Care in the Circumstances,* and
      3.   *Reasonably Believed to Be in the Corporation's Best Interests.*
   D.   Business Judgment Rule. The **business judgment rule** is a defense available to a director or officer against a claim of violating the duty of care. This rule provides that a director or officer will not be liable for honest errors in business judgment if the decision was made with care. Thus, the officer or director will not be liable for a carefully made decision that later turns out to not have been a good one. The focus is on the actions undertaken (whether other alternatives were considered, or any needed analysis was performed, etc.) at the time the decision was made, and not on the course of events following the decision. **Exam tip #5.**
   E.   Reliance on Others. Officers and directors cannot investigate every matter themselves, and thus are allowed to rely on the reports and opinions of:
      1.   *Officers and Employees.*
      2.   *Lawyers, Accountants, and Other Professionals.*
      3.   *Committees of the Board of Directors on Which the Officer or Director Does Not Serve.*
      In all cases, the person relying on the information must reasonably believe that the person providing the information is reliable and competent in providing it.
   F.   Duty of Loyalty. A director or officer's **duty of loyalty** is similar to an agent's or partner's duty of loyalty and is a general duty to act in the corporation's best interest in all matters related to the business of the corporation. Many of the common ways that this duty can be breached are also similar. The following situations violate the duty of loyalty, but are not a violation if the corporation has been notified and consents to the situation.

1. *Self-Dealing.* A director or officer cannot simultaneously be on both sides of a transaction, one on her own behalf and the other as agent for the corporation. This is **self-dealing**. Thus, a director or officer could not sell her own land to the corporation, unless the fact that she had an interest in the land was disclosed to the corporation. Such a contract is valid if approved by majority of the disinterested directors or if it is fair to the corporation.

2. *Usurping a Corporate Opportunity.* When a director or officer locates an opportunity (such as a piece of land for purchase) for the corporation, the director or officer cannot **usurp the opportunity** by taking it for herself, unless she first offers it to the corporation.

3. *Competing With the Corporation.* A director or officer cannot **compete with the corporation** by attempting to do the same on his own behalf as he is doing for the corporation. A director of a corporation operating a hotel breaches this duty by operating a second hotel competing with that of the corporation for which he is a director. **Exam tip #6.**

4. *Secret Profits.* A director or officer is not entitled to keep any **secret profits** connected with any of these breaches of the duty of loyalty.

G. Indemnification of Directors and Officers. Corporations can **indemnify** (not recover from them for losses they cause, and reimburse them for any losses they incur) directors and officers or can purchase insurance coverage to cover such losses. This is a proper expenditure of corporate resources because without such protection, many potential directors and officers would be unwilling to serve.

V. Liability of Shareholders.

A. Generally. Shareholders generally have personal liability only for the amount of their investment in the corporation. Stated differently, this means that the worst that could happen to a shareholder is that the stock becomes worthless. The primary exception follows:

B. Piercing the Corporate Veil. In certain situations the courts will disregard the corporate entity, or **pierce the corporate veil**. This means that the imaginary "veil" protecting the shareholder from creditors of the corporation will be ignored, causing the shareholder to lose the limited liability protection that a corporation usually provides. Courts will pierce the corporate veil in any situation they deem appropriate, but there are two primary situations:

1. *Thin Capitalization.* When a corporation has inadequate capital for its purposes, the corporation is said to be **thinly capitalized**, and the corporate veil will be pierced. For example, where the sole shareholder of a corporation holds title (as an individual) to the major operating assets used by the business and leases them to the corporation, there might be almost no corporate assets. If the assets actually owned by the corporation are really insufficient for that type of business, a court might pierce the corporate veil.

2. *Failure to Follow Corporate Formalities.* The **failure to follow corporate formalities** can consist of several failures. The failure to maintain corporate finances separate from those of the shareholders would result in the veil being pierced. Likewise, a failure to hold shareholder and board of director meetings could result in the veil being pierced.

C. No Shareholder Fiduciary Duty. Shareholders generally do not have a fiduciary duty to the corporation. Thus a Coca Cola shareholder does not violate the duty by drinking Pepsi products. Some states have started imposing a fiduciary duty on controlling shareholders who engage in certain actions which are oppressive with respect to minority shareholders, but shareholders generally have no fiduciary duties to the corporation.

EXAM TIPS

1. Be sure to know the requirements for both types of meetings. An essay question might describe a situation and the candidate would need to determine if the meeting was properly called and noticed, or if an action undertaken at the meeting was valid. Voting requirements can also be a part of such a question. Because there is no board of directors' annual meeting, any reference to an annual meeting is a reference to the annual shareholders' meeting.
2. The word "cumulative" when used in reference to voting for directors is wholly unrelated to its use in describing preferred stock's priority rights in connection with unpaid dividends from prior years.
3. Note the distinction between a shareholder's limited right of inspection and a partner's unlimited right of inspection. Because a partner has unlimited personal liability, the partner's right to inspect is unlimited. With a shareholder, the personal liability is limited, as is the right of inspection.
4. A derivative suit is filed by a shareholder **on behalf of** a corporation, **not against** a corporation. The goal of a shareholder filing a derivative suit is to protect the value of her investment by allowing the corporation to recover the amount in the suit.
5. The business judgment rule is very important. The officer or director will be liable based on whether the decision or action was carefully considered when it was undertaken, not on whether, with the benefit of hindsight, it turned out to be a good decision. In fact situation questions on this issue, look for information about how the officer or director researched a decision before making the decision.
6. It is possible for a director to be involved with a competing business, whether on the board or otherwise, but the director must disclose the situation and be very careful not to compete unfairly or to allow the use of confidential information, etc.

KEY CONCEPTS LIKELY TO BE TESTED ON THE CPA EXAM

1. The various rights of shareholders, and whether they have been violated in a specific situation. An essay question might present a number of actions requiring the candidate to analyze whether any shareholder rights have been violated.
2. The requirements for shareholder meetings.
3. The limited inspection right of corporate books and records for shareholders and the absolute inspection right for directors and officers.
4. Requirements and effects of derivative suits.
5. The structure and procedures of the board of directors.
6. Directors' and officers' duties and breaches of those duties.
7. Dividend requirements.
8. Issues surrounding piercing the corporate veil.

KEY TERMS

Annual Shareholders' Meeting	Voting Agreement	Duty of Care
Special Shareholders' Meeting	Right of First Refusal	Business Judgment Rule
Written Consent	Preemptive Right	Duty of Loyalty
Proxy	Right of Inspection	Self-Dealing
Record Date	Derivative Lawsuit	Usurp an Opportunity
Quorum	Board Resolution	Compete With the Corporation
Straight Voting	Inside Director	Secret Profits
Cumulative Voting	Outside Director	Indemnification
Supramajority	Officer	Pierce the Corporate Veil
Voting Trust	Duty of Obedience	Thin Capitalization
Failure to Follow Corporate Formalities		

MULTIPLE CHOICE QUESTIONS

1.   **Law R98 #4**

For what purpose will a stockholder of a publicly held corporation be permitted to file a stockholders' derivative suit in the name of the corporation?

A. To compel payment of a properly declared dividend.

B. To enforce a right to inspect corporate records.

C. To compel dissolution of the corporation.

D. To recover damages from corporate management for an *ultra vires* management act.

2.   **Law Nov 95 #23**

To which of the following rights is a stockholder of a public corporation entitled?

A. The right to have annual dividends declared and paid.

B. The right to vote for the election of officers.

C. The right to a reasonable inspection of corporate records.

D. The right to have the corporation issue a new class of stock.

3.   **Law R96 #12**

Under the Revised Model Business Corporation Act, a corporate director is authorized to

A. Rely on information provided by the appropriate corporate officer.

B. Serve on the board of directors of a competing business.

C. Sell control of the corporation.

D. Profit from insider information.

4.   **Law May 94 #12**

Under the Revised Model Business Corporation Act, which of the following statements is correct regarding corporate officers of a public corporation?

A. An officer may not simultaneously serve as a director.

B. A corporation may be authorized to indemnify its officers for liability incurred in a suit by stockholders.

C. Stockholders always have the right to elect a corporation's officers.

D. An officer of a corporation is required to own at least one share of the corporation's stock.

5.   **Law Nov 93 #20**

The corporate veil is most likely to be pierced and the shareholders held personally liable if

A. The corporation has elected S corporation status under the Internal Revenue Code.

B. The shareholders have commingled their personal funds with those of the corporation.

C. An ultra vires act has been committed.

D. A partnership incorporates its business solely to limit the liability of its partners.

6.   **Law Nov 92 #2**

A stockholder's right to inspect books and records of a corporation will be properly denied if the stockholder

A. Wants to use corporate stockholder records for a personal business.

B. Employs an agent to inspect the books and records.

C. Intends to commence a stockholder's derivative suit.

D. Is investigating management misconduct.

7.   **Law May 91 #6**

The limited liability of a stockholder in a closely held corporation may be challenged successfully if the stockholder

A. Undercapitalized the corporation when it was formed.

B. Formed the corporation solely to have limited personal liability.

C. Sold property to the corporation

D. Was a corporate officer, director, or employee.

8.   **Law Nov 90 #15**

Knox, president of Quick Corp., contracted with Tine Office Supplies, Inc. to supply Quick's stationery on customary terms and at a cost less than that charged by any other supplier. Knox later informed Quick's board of directors that Knox was a majority stockholder in Tine. Quick's contract with Tine is

A. Void because of Knox's self-dealing.

B. Void because the disclosure was made after execution of the contract.

C. Valid because of Knox's full disclosure.

D. Valid because the contract is fair to Quick.

9.   **Law May 74 #41**

After proper incorporation of Bryan, it was decided to purchase a plant site. Shephard, a newly elected director, has owned a desirable site for many years. He purchased the property for $60,000, and its present fair value is $100,000. What would be the result if Shephard offered the property to Bryan for $100,000 in an arm's-length transaction with full disclosure at a meeting of the seven directors of the corporation?

A. The sale would be proper only upon requisite approval by the appropriate number of directors and at no more than Shephard's cost.

B. The sale would be void under the self-dealing rule.

C. The sale would be proper and Shephard would not have to account for his profit if the sale was approved by a disinterested majority of the directors.

D. The sale would not be proper, if sold for the present fair value of the property, without the approval of all of the directors.

OTHER OBJECTIVE FORMAT QUESTION (Estimated time -- 10 to 15 minutes)

Law R96 #1

Question Number 1 consists of 6 items. Select the **best** answer for each item. Use a No. 2 pencil to blacken the appropriate ovals on the *Objective Answer Sheet* to indicate your answers. **Answer all items.** Your grade will be based on the total number of correct answers.

Drain Corp. has two classes of stock: 100,000 shares of authorized, issued, and outstanding voting common stock; and 10,000 shares of authorized, issued and outstanding nonvoting 5% cumulative, nonparticipating preferred stock with a face value of $100 per share. In 1994, Drain's officers and directors intentionally allowed pollutants to be discharged by Drain's processing plant. These actions resulted in Drain having to pay penalties. Solely as a result of the penalties, no dividends were declared for the years ended December 31, 1994 and December 31, 1995. The total amount Drain paid in penalties was $1,000,000. In 1995, Drain was able to recover the full amount of the penalties from an insurance company that had issued Drain a business liability policy. Drain's directors refused to use this money to declare a dividend and decided to hold the $1,000,000 in a special fund to pay future bonuses to officers and directors.

Required:
Items 1 through 6 refer to the above fact pattern. For each item, select the correct answer that completes the statement and blacken the corresponding oval on the *Objective Answer Sheet*. An answer may be selected once, more than once, or not at all.

1. The actions by Drain's officers and directors in allowing pollutants to be discharged generally would be considered a violation of the
2. A stockholder's derivative suit, if successful, probably would result in the officers and directors being
3. A stockholder's derivative suit, if successful, probably would result in the $1,000,000 being considered
4. If the $1,000,000 was distributed to the shareholders in 1995, the distribution would be characterized as a
5. If the $1,000,000 was distributed in 1995, each share of 5% cumulative preferred stock would receive
6. If the $1,000,000 was distributed in 1995, each share of voting common stock would receive

A. Available for distribution as a dividend.
B. Fiduciary duty to prevent losses.
C. Cash dividend.
D. Fiduciary duty of care.
E. Fiduciary duty of loyalty.
F. Illegal dividend.
G. Immune form liability.
H. Liable for abuse of discretion.
I. Liable to the corporation for $1,000,000.
J. Property dividend.
K. Stock dividend.
L. Surplus or earnings held for expansion.
M. $ 5.00.
N. $ 9.00.
O. $10.00.
P. $18.00.

ESSAY QUESTION (Estimated time -- 15 to 20 minutes)

Law Nov 91 #2

Frost, Glen, and Bradley own 50%, 40%, and 10%, respectively, of the authorized and issued voting common stock of Xeon Corp. They had a written stockholders' agreement that provided they would vote for each other as directors of the corporation.

At the initial stockholders' meeting, Frost, Glen, Bradley, and three others were elected to a six-person board of directors. The board elected Frost as president of the corporation, Glen as secretary, and Bradley as vice president. Frost and Glen were given two-year contracts with annual salaries of $50,000. Bradley was given a two-year contract for $10,000 per year.

At the end of its first year of operation, Xeon was in financial difficulty. Bradley disagreed with the way Frost and Glen were running the business.

At the annual stockholders' meeting, a new board of directors was elected. Bradley was excluded because Frost and Glen did not vote for Bradley. Without cause, the new board fired Bradley as vice president even though 12 months remained on Bradley's contract.

Despite the corporation's financial difficulties, the new board, relying on the assurances of Frost and Glen and based on fraudulent documentation provided by Frost and Glen, declared and paid a $200,000 dividend. Payment of the dividend caused the corporation to become insolvent.

- Bradley sued Frost and Glen to compel them to follow the written stockholders' agreement and reelect Bradley to the board.

- Bradley sued the corporation to be reinstated as an officer of the corporation, and for breach of the employment contract.

- Bradley sued each member of the board for declaring and paying an unlawful dividend, and demanded its repayment to the corporation.

Required:

State whether Bradley would be successful in each of the above suits and give the reasons for your conclusions.

EXPLANATIONS TO MULTIPLE CHOICE QUESTIONS

1. D is the correct answer. A derivative suit is a suit brought by a shareholder with the goal of recovering an amount for the corporation. Management would be liable to the corporation for any damages resulting from an ultra vires act. Choices A and B are incorrect because they describe suits against the corporation rather than on its behalf.

2. C is the correct answer. Choice A is incorrect because the payment of dividends is at the discretion of the board of directors. Shareholders have a right to dividends only if the board declares them. Choice B is incorrect because the shareholders elect the directors, but the directors elect the officers. Note that the word "public" is used in the sense of a publicly held corporation, not in the sense of a corporation owned by a government entity.

3. A is the correct answer. Because directors cannot personally investigate or study every matter themselves, they are allowed to rely on information provided by corporate officers if it is reasonable to do so. Choice B is incorrect because serving on a competing board would usually violate the duty of loyalty.

4. B is the correct answer. The ability to indemnify directors and officers for liability incurred in shareholder suits removes some of the risk of being a director or officer, and is considered a proper expenditure of corporate funds.

5. B is the correct answer. Choice A is incorrect because S status affects only the corporation's taxation. Otherwise, the corporation is treated like any other. In fact, the office of the secretary of state would not even know if a corporation had elected S status on its tax return. Choice C is incorrect because an ultra vires act occurs when a corporation acts beyond its powers. The act might be enjoined, or the responsible party sued for damages, but the veil would not be pierced solely because the act was ultra vires.

6. A is the correct answer. Choices C and D are incorrect because they both represent legitimate reasons to inspect the books and records.

7. A is the correct answer. Undercapitalization is one of the two primary reasons that courts will pierce the corporate veil. Choice B is incorrect because it is completely proper to form a corporation solely to have limited liability.

8. D is the correct answer. Because the contract is fair to the corporation, it is valid. Choice C is incorrect because the full disclosure would be a reason to allow the contract only if the disclosure was made prior to the contract's formation. Choice B is incorrect because the full disclosure is not needed where the contract is fair to the corporation.

9. C is the correct answer. If a majority of the disinterested directors approves the sale, the contract is valid and the selling director would not violate the duty of loyalty. Choice A is incorrect because selling the land above cost is acceptable so long as either a majority of the disinterested directors approve the transaction or the transaction is fair to the corporation. Choice D is incorrect because unanimous approval is not needed.

EXPLANATION TO OTHER OBJECTIVE FORMAT QUESTION

1. E is the correct answer. When the pollutants were intentionally discharged, the officers and directors were intentionally acting against the corporation's best interests and thus violated the duty of loyalty. Choice D is incorrect because the discharge was not caused by carelessness. If carelessness had led to the discharge, choice D would have been the correct answer.

2. H is the correct answer. It was an abuse of discretion to allow the discharge of the pollutants. Choice I is incorrect because of the recovery of the $1,000,000 from the insurance company.

3. A is the correct answer. Because the facts state that the payment of the fine was the sole reason that dividends were not paid, all the legal requirements for a dividend must have been otherwise met.

4. C is the correct answer. Because the $1,000,000 would be considered to be available for distribution as a dividend, if the $1,000,000 were distributed to the shareholders, it would be a cash dividend.

5. O is the correct answer. The preferred stock is entitled to an annual dividend of $5.00 per share, calculated by multiplying the 5% rate by the face value per share of $100.00. Because the stock is cumulative, preferred shareholders would be entitled to the 1994 and 1995 dividends before common shareholders could receive any dividends. Note that this question does not explicitly tell you that the preferred shareholders received a dividend in 1993. Because there is no answer choice greater than $10.00 which is a multiple of $5.00, choice O must be the correct choice.

6. N is the correct answer. The preferred shareholders would receive the first $10.00 per share for 10,000 shares, or $100,000 in total. Because the preferred stock is nonparticipating, the common shareholders would receive all amounts beyond the first $100,000. That would make $900,000 available to be divided among 100,000 shares, or $9.00 per share.

UNOFFICIAL AICPA ANSWER TO ESSAY QUESTION

Law Nov 91 #2

Bradley would be successful in the suit against Frost and Glen for failing to vote Bradley to the board of directors. The stockholders have the right to elect the directors of a corporation. The stockholders have the right to agree among themselves on how they will vote. Therefore, the voting provision of the stockholders' agreement between Bradley, Frost, and Glen is enforceable.

Bradley would be unsuccessful in attempting to be reinstated as vice president. A corporation's board oversees the operations of the business, which includes hiring officers and, at its discretion, dismissing officers with or without cause. Bradley would be successful in collecting some damages for the breach of the employment contract because there was not demonstrated cause for Bradley's dismissal.

Bradley would be successful in having Frost and Glen held personally liable of the corporation for declaring and paying the dividend because payment of a dividend that threatens a corporation's solvency is unlawful. Ordinarily, directors who approve such a dividend would be personally liable for its repayment to the corporation. However, the directors, other than Frost and Glen, in relying on the assurances and information supplied by Frost and Glen, as corporate officers, are protected by the business judgment rule. Therefore, only Frost and Glen would be held personally liable.

Author's Note:

Note from the second paragraph of the answer that Bradley's claim for damages exists because of his fixed term employment contract. If Bradley had no employment contract, he would not be able to collect damages regardless of the reason for his dismissal.

CHAPTER 22
MERGERS, ACQUISITIONS, AND TERMINATION OF CORPORATIONS

OVERVIEW

This is the last chapter covering corporations. The outline for this chapter is much shorter than most because much of the material in the textbook chapter has been tested only lightly on the CPA exam. The material on corporate combinations, however, is tested quite heavily.

OUTLINE

I. **Proxies.**
   A. <u>Generally</u>. A **proxy** is a written document which assigns a shareholder's right to vote to another person, often a director or officer of the corporation. For many large corporations, the solicitation of proxies is the only practical way to ensure a quorum at the annual shareholders' meeting.
   B. <u>Source of Law</u>. Section 14(a) of the Securities Exchange Act allows the Securities and Exchange Commission (the SEC) to regulate proxies and the solicitation of proxies. Companies who are required to file reports under the Securities Exchange Act of 1934 are subject to the proxy solicitation rules of Section 14(a).
   C. <u>Proxy Solicitations</u>. The management of corporations often solicits proxies from shareholders.
      1. *Annual Report.* An annual report with audited financial statements must be sent to shareholders prior to any meeting where proxies are being solicited for the election of directors.
      2. *Proxy Statement.* Management, and any other party soliciting proxies, must prepare a proxy statement that describes the matter for which the proxy is being solicited, who is soliciting the proxy, and any other pertinent information.
      3. *Filing With the SEC.* The proxy and proxy statement must be filed with the SEC at least 10 days before it is sent out. If the SEC determines that additional disclosures are needed, the proxy mailing can be delayed.
   D. <u>Proxy Contests</u>. A **proxy contest** occurs when an opposing faction also seeks shareholders' proxies. Management must either provide a shareholder list to the dissenting group or mail the proxy materials of the dissenting group along with those of management.
   E. <u>Shareholder Proposals</u>. Shareholders have the right to have **shareholder proposals** sent to shareholders along with the proxy solicitation materials. Shareholder proposals must relate to the corporation's business and the matter must be a policy matter. They cannot relate to day-to-day operations nor to the payment of dividends.

II. **Types of Corporate Combinations.**
   A. <u>Generally</u>. Corporations can combine using several different methods.
   B. <u>Mergers</u>. In a **merger**, one corporation is absorbed into another. The **merged corporation** ceases to exist and becomes part of the **surviving corporation**.
      1. *Rights Acquired.* The surviving corporation gains the rights, privileges, and powers of the merged corporation.

2. *Obligations Assumed.* The surviving corporation also assumes the duties, obligations, and liabilities of the merged corporation.

3. *Property Transferred.* Property of the merged corporation automatically becomes the property of the surviving corporation.

4. *Merged Corporation Shares Are Surrendered.* The shareholders of the merged corporation relinquish their shares in exchange for shares of the surviving corporation or other consideration provided for in the merger agreement.

C. Consolidations. In a **consolidation**, two corporations combine to form a new corporation. Both of the prior corporations cease to exist.

1. *New Corporation Takes the Place of Both Prior Corporations.* In a consolidation, the new corporation acquires the rights, assumes the obligations, and receives the property of the original corporations much as the surviving corporation does in a merger.

2. *Seldom Used Today.* Consolidations seldom occur today because of the advantages, tax and otherwise, when one of the corporations survive.

D. Share Exchange. A **share exchange** occurs when one corporation acquires all the shares of another corporation.

1. *Retain Separate Legal Existence.* After a share exchange, the **parent corporation** will own all the shares of the **subsidiary corporation**, but the subsidiary will still exist separately.

2. *Holding Companies.* Share exchanges are often used to create holding companies.

III. **Required Approvals for Combinations.**

A. Requirements. An ordinary merger or share exchange requires the approval of:
1. *The Boards of Directors of Both Corporations*, and
2. *The Shareholders of Both Corporations.*

B. Supramajority Requirement. The articles of incorporation or the bylaws can require a **supramajority** vote, such as 75 percent, for these approvals.

C. 20 Percent or Smaller Increase in Shares. The approval of the surviving corporation's shareholders is not needed if the number of voting shares of the surviving corporation increases by less than 20 percent. This occurs when a large corporation acquires a much smaller one, and from the large corporation's standpoint, is not sufficiently significant to require shareholder approval. **Exam tip #1.**

D. Short-Form Merger. A simplified merger can be followed in some mergers:

1. *90 Percent or More Ownership Prior to Merger.* The short-form merger requires that the parent corporation own 90 percent of the subsidiary corporation prior to the merger.

2. *Only Board of Parent Must Approve.* The only approval needed is that of the board of directors of the parent corporation. The approval of the subsidiary's board and shareholders is not needed because the parent corporation would determine the outcome of such votes by virtue of their 90 percent or greater ownership of the subsidiary's stock. The parent's shareholder's approval is not needed because the increase in ownership is not significant enough to require shareholder approval. **Exam tip #2.**

E. Sale or Lease of Substantially All Assets. If a corporation sells, leases, or otherwise disposes of all or substantially all of its assets, the disposal must be approved by:
1. *The Board of Directors.*
2. *The Shareholders.*

IV.   **Dissenting Shareholder's Appraisal Rights.**
    A. <u>General Purpose</u>. The **dissenting shareholder appraisal right** allows a shareholder who opposes a transaction to receive the fair value of her shares rather than be forced to go along with the transaction. The rights apply even when the transaction has received all needed approvals.
    B. <u>Applicable Transactions</u>. The appraisal right exists for regular mergers, short-form mergers, and for share exchanges.
    C. <u>Notice to Shareholders</u>. The corporation must notify shareholders of the appraisal right prior to the applicable vote.
    D. <u>Requirements</u>. A shareholder obtains appraisal rights only if the shareholder:
        1. *Delivers Written Notice.* The shareholder must deliver written notice to the corporation of his intent to demand payment for his shares. This must be done prior to the vote.
        2. *Not Vote in Favor.* The shareholder must not vote in favor of the action. Thus, a shareholder who delivered the notice, but then decided to vote in favor of the action, would lose her appraisal right.
    E. <u>Payment to Shareholder</u>. Once the action is taken, the corporation must pay the shareholder the fair value of the shares.
    F. <u>Dispute Over Value</u>. If the shareholder is dissatisfied, the corporation must petition the court to determine the shares' value.

V. **Tender Offers.**
    A. <u>Generally</u>. A **tender offer** occurs when the board of the **target corporation** does not approve a merger or acquisition. The acquiring corporation (the **bidder**) can then make an offer (to purchase shares) directly to the shareholders of the target corporation.
    B. <u>Filing Requirement</u>. The bidder must file a statement with the SEC disclosing past dealings with the target, the source of the bidder's funds, the bidder's plans concerning the target, and copies of the bidder's financial statements.
    C. <u>Statement of Target's Management</u>. The management of the target must give a statement, with reasons, to the shareholders recommending whether or not to accept the tender offer or stating that management has no opinion.

VI.   **Dissolution of Corporations.**
    A. <u>Voluntary Dissolution</u>. A voluntary dissolution requires approval of the board of directors and the shareholders.
    B. <u>Administrative Dissolution</u>. The secretary of state can obtain **administrative dissolution** if the corporation:
        1. *Failed to File an Annual Report.*
        2. *Failed for 60 Days to Maintain a Registered Agent in the State.*
        3. *Failed for 60 Days to Notify the Secretary of State of a Change of Its Registered Agent.*
        4. *Failed to Pay Its Franchise Fee.*
        5. *Reached the End of a Period of Duration Stated in the Articles.*
    Failure to cure any of the above within 60 days of being given notice will give the secretary of state the power to issue a **certificate of dissolution**.

C. <u>Judicial Dissolution</u>. Courts are reluctant to order the dissolution of a corporation, but will do so in a few circumstances.

    1. *Attorney General.* The attorney general can request judicial dissolution if the corporation procured its articles of incorporation by fraud or has exceeded its legal authority. Acts of the corporation exceeding its legal authority are known as ultra vires acts.

    2. *Creditors' Petition.* A creditor or creditors can request a judicial dissolution if execution of a valid judgment was unsuccessful (meaning that the court could not attach sufficient assets to satisfy the judgment) or the corporation has admitted in writing that the creditor's claim (or claims) is due and owing.

4. <u>Winding Up, Liquidation, and Termination</u>. Upon dissolution, a corporation must cease business other than as necessary to **wind up and liquidate** its business affairs. Assets are sold, and the proceeds are used to pay creditors in the following order:

    1. *Liquidation Expenses and Creditors.*

    2. *Preferred Shareholders.*

    3. *Common Shareholders.*

Once the assets have been distributed, **termination** occurs and the corporation ceases to exist.

EXAM TIPS

1. When the surviving corporation's shares increase by 20 percent or less, the approval of both boards and of the shareholders of the acquired corporation are required, thus only one approval is eliminated.

2. Notice that with a short-form merger, three approvals are eliminated. Be sure to not confuse the requirements where the **parent's** shares increase by 20 percent with the short-form requirements which are based on the parent's ownership of the subsidiary's shares prior to the merger.

KEY CONCEPTS LIKELY TO BE TESTED ON THE CPA EXAM

1. The general characteristics of the different kinds of corporate combinations.
2. The approvals needed for business combinations, especially short-form mergers.
3. The requirements and effects of the dissenting shareholder appraisal right.

KEY TERMS

Proxy	Share Exchange	Bidder
Proxy Contest	Parent Corporation	Administrative Dissolution
Shareholder Proposal	Subsidiary Corporation	Certificate of Dissolution
Merger	Supramajority	Winding Up
Merged Corporation	Tender Offer	Liquidation
Surviving Corporation	Target Corporation	Termination
Consolidation	Dissenting Shareholder Appraisal Right	

MULTIPLE CHOICE QUESTIONS

1.   Law Nov 94 #25
A parent corporation owned more than 90%
of each class of the outstanding stock issued
by a subsidiary corporation and decided to
merge that subsidiary into itself. Under the
Revised Model Business Corporation Act,
which of the following actions must be taken?
A. The subsidiary corporations's board of
   directors must pass a merger resolution.
B. The subsidiary corporation's dissenting
   stockholders must be given an appraisal
   remedy.
C. The parent corporation's stockholders
   must approve the merger.
D. The parent corporation's dissenting
   stockholders must be given an appraisal
   remedy.

2.   Law May 91 #42
Which of the following statements is correct
regarding the proxy solicitation requirements
of Section 14(a) of the Securities Exchange
Act of 1934?
A. A corporation does **not** have to file proxy
   revocation solicitations with the SEC if it
   is a reporting company under the
   Securities Exchange Act of 1934.
B. Current unaudited financial statements
   must be sent to each stockholder with
   every proxy solicitation.
C. A corporation must file its proxy
   statements with the SEC if it is a reporting
   company under the Securities Exchange
   Act of 1934.
D. In a proxy solicitation by management
   relating the election of officers, all
   stockholder proposals must be included in
   the proxy statement.

3.   Law R97 #3
Which of the following actions may be taken
by a corporation's board of directors without
stockholder approval?
A. Purchasing substantially all of the assets
   of another corporation.
B. Selling substantially all of the
   corporation's assets.
C. Dissolving the corporation.
D. Amending the articles of incorporation.

4.   Law Nov 95 #25
Which of the following statements is a general
requirement for the merger of two
corporations?
A. The merger plan must be approved
   unanimously by the stockholders of both
   corporations.
B. The merger plan must be approved
   unanimously by the boards of both
   corporations.
C. The absorbed corporation must amend its
   articles of incorporation.
D. The stockholders of both corporations
   must be given due notice of a special
   meeting, including a copy or summary of
   the merger plan.

5.   Law May 94 #14
Under the Revised Model Business
Corporation Act, a merger of two public
corporations usually requires all of the
following **except**
A. A formal plan of merger.
B. An affirmative vote by the holders of a
   majority of each corporation's voting
   shares.
C. Receipt of voting stock by all shareholders
   of the original corporations.
D. Approval by the board of directors of each
   corporation.

6.   Law May 92 #20

Which of the following actions may a corporation take without its stockholders' consent?

A. Consolidate with one or more corporations.
B. Merge with one or more corporations.
C. Dissolve voluntarily.
D. Purchase 55% of another corporation's stock.

7.   Law Nov 92 #3

Which of the following must take place for a corporation to be voluntarily dissolved?

A. Passage by the board of directors of a resolution to dissolve.
B. Approval by the officers of a resolution to dissolve.
C. Amendment of the certificate of incorporation.
D. Unanimous vote of the shareholders.

ESSAY QUESTION (Estimate time -- 15 to 25 minutes)

Law May 93 #3

Edwards, a director and 10% stockholder in National Corp., is dissatisfied with the way National's officers, particularly Olsen, the president, have been operating the corporation. Edwards has made many suggestions that have been rejected by the board of directors, and has made several unsuccessful attempts to have Olsen removed as president.

National and Grand Corp. had been negotiating a merger that Edwards has adamantly opposed. Edwards has blamed Olsen for initiating the negotiation and has urged the board to fire Olsen. National's board refused to fire Olsen. In an attempt to defeat the merger, Edwards approached Jenkins, the president of Queen Corp., and contracted for Queen to purchase several of National's assets. Jenkins knew Edwards was a National director, but had never done business with National. When National learned of the contract, it notified Queen that the contract was invalid.

Edwards, filed an objection to the merger before the stockholders' meeting called to consider the merger proposal was held. At the meeting, Edwards voted against the merger proposal.

Despite Edwards' efforts, the merger was approved by both corporations. Edwards then orally demanded that National purchase Edwards' stock, citing the dissenters' rights provision of the corporation's by-laws, which reflects the Model Business Corporation Act.

National's board has claimed National does not have to purchase Edwards' stock.

As a result of the above:

- Edwards initiated a minority stockholder's action to have Olsen removed as president and to force National to purchase Edwards' stock.
- Queen sued National to enforce the contract and/or collect damages.
- Queen sued Edwards to collect damages.

Required:

Answer the following questions and give the reasons for your answers.

a. Will Edwards be successful in a lawsuit to have Olsen removed as president?

b. Will Edwards be successful in a lawsuit to have National purchase the stock?

c. 1. Will Queen be successful in a lawsuit against National?

2. Will Queen be successful in a lawsuit against Edwards.

EXPLANATIONS TO MULTIPLE CHOICE QUESTIONS

1. B is the correct answer. It is the acquired corporation's shareholders who have the appraisal remedy, and it applies to all mergers, including short-form merger.

2. C is the correct answer. Choice D is incorrect because only proper proposals must be included.

3. A is the correct answer. Purchasing all the assets of another corporation could be a relatively insignificant transaction where a large corporation bought the assets of a small corporation.

4. D is the correct answer. Choices A and B are incorrect because the a majority (or supramajority) is all that is required; a unanimity requirement would give each individual shareholder veto power.

5. C is the correct answer. Shareholders of the merged corporation can receive non-stock consideration.

6. D is the correct answer. The purchase could be insignificant to the acquiring corporation.

7. A is the correct answer. Choice B is incorrect because the directors and shareholders must approve the resolution; the officers are not part of the approval process.

UNOFFICIAL AICPA ANSWER TO ESSAY QUESTION

Law May 93 #3

a. Edwards will not win the suit to have Olsen removed as president. The right to hire and fire officers is held by the board of directors. Individual stockholders, regardless of the size of their holding, have no vote in the selection of officers. Individual stockholders may exert influence in this area by voting for directors at the annual stockholders' meeting.

b. Edwards will lose the suit to have National purchase the stock. A stockholder who dissents from a merger may require the corporation to purchase his or her shares if the statutory requirements are met and would be entitled to the fair value of stock (appraisal remedy). To compel the purchase, Edwards would have had to file an objection to the merger before the stockholders' meeting at which the merger proposal was considered, vote against the merger proposal, and make a written demand that the corporation purchase the stock at an appraised price. Edwards will lose because the first two requirements were met but Edwards failed to make a written demand that the corporation purchase the stock.

c. 1. Queen will lose its suit against national to enforce the contract, even though Edwards was a National director. Jenkins may have assumed that Edwards was acting as National's agent, but Edwards had no authority to contract with Queen. A director has a fiduciary duty to the stockholders of a corporation, but unless expressly authorized by the board of directors or the officers of the corporation, has no authority to contract on behalf of the corporation. There is no implied agency authority merely by being a director.

   2. Queen will win its suit against Edwards because Edwards had no authority to act for National. Edwards will be personally liable for Queen's damages.

CHAPTER 23
SECURITIES REGULATION AND INVESTOR PROTECTION

OVERVIEW

This chapter covers the federal securities laws. These laws originated in the 1930s in response to the stock market crash of 1929 and the great depression that followed. The purpose of the securities laws is to give investors full information so that they can make decisions with the relevant facts available. The securities laws are not designed to rate investments or protect investors from losing money. They are designed to ensure that complete and accurate information is provided to the marketplace. In general, the securities laws impose certain registration and disclosure requirements when securities are offered to the public. In addition, there are ongoing reporting requirements for certain companies based on their size and whether their securities are traded on a national exchange. Equally important in this area on the CPA exam, candidates must understand the numerous exceptions to the registration requirements. Lastly, candidates must know the requirements under each act for imposing liability for misstatements and omissions. These requirements differ greatly for the two primary acts.

OUTLINE

I. **The Securities and Exchange Commission.**
   A. <u>Creation</u>. The **Securities and Exchange Commission** (the **SEC**) is a federal agency which was created as part of the Securities Exchange Act of 1934. There are five commissioners who are presidential appointees.
   B. <u>Responsibilities</u>. The SEC has the following responsibilities:
      1. *Adopting Rules and Regulations Under the Securities Statutes.* Many of these rules are interpretations of the statutes.
      2. *Enforcing the Securities Laws.* The SEC can both investigate suspected violations and bring civil enforcement actions. The SEC makes criminal enforcement recommendations to the Department of Justice.
      3. *Regulating Securities Brokers and Advisors.* This includes registration of brokers and advisors as well as bringing enforcement actions against alleged violators.

II. **Securities.**
   A. <u>Generally</u>. The securities laws apply only to **securities**, of which there are several types.
   B. <u>Stocks, Bonds, etc.</u> Common stock, preferred stock, stock options, stock warrants, bonds, and debentures are the most common types of securities.
   C. <u>Other Named Instruments and Interests</u>. The securities acts specifically identify other specific types of interests as securities. Examples include interests in oil and gas, mineral rights, and limited partnership interests.
   D. <u>Other Investment Contracts With Profits Expected From the Efforts of Others</u>. Any other investment contract where the investor plays a passive role, that is, does not put in any effort (time, management, etc.) toward the success of the investment, is a security.
   E. <u>Partnership Is Not a Security</u>. A general partnership interest is not a security because the partner has the right, even if not exercised, to take part in the partnership's management.

III.   The Securities Act of 1933.

A.   <u>General Purpose and Requirements</u>. The **Securities Act of 1933** (the **1933 Act**) requires that public offerings of securities be registered with the SEC and that certain information be disclosed to purchasers of the securities. These requirements are designed to ensure that securities purchasers have adequate information available to evaluate the potential investment. They are not designed to ensure safety of the investment, nor do they result in the SEC either "rating" or "approving" investments. Offerings through the mail or using a facility of interstate commerce are covered under the 1933 Act.

B.   <u>Registration Statement</u>. The **registration statement** is the document which must be filed with the SEC. The registration statement must contain audited financial statements including a balance sheet dated within 90 days of filing, and income statements for the preceding five years, if the issuer has been in business that long. The registration statement must also contain descriptions of:

1.   *The Securities Offered for Sale*.

2.   *The Registrant's Business*. The registrant is also known as the issuer.

3.   *The Management of the Registrant*. This includes compensation, benefits, stock options, and any material transactions with the registrant.

4.   *Pending Litigation*.

5.   *Planned Use of the Offering's Proceeds*.

6.   *Government Regulation*. This would include a description of how the business is regulated and how those regulations might affect the business and its profitability.

7.   *The Degree of Competition in the Industry*.

8.   *Risk Factors*.

The registration statement is effective 20 days after it is filed, assuming that the SEC has not notified the registrant that more information is needed. A new 20-day period begins any time an amended statement is filed (including one filed to provide additional information requested by the SEC). Once effective, the registrant can issue the covered securities. **Exam tip #1.**

C.   <u>Shelf Registration</u>. Large companies that frequently issue securities can submit a **shelf registration**. It is a registration valid for multiple securities issues and must be kept up to date.

D   <u>Prospectus</u>. The **prospectus** is the disclosure document which must be given to a prospective investor in order to evaluate the merits of the investment. It includes much of the same information as the registration statement, and must be filed with the SEC along with the registration statement. **Exam tip #2.**

E.   <u>Permissible Issuer Activities</u>. During the various periods in the registration process, the issuer is limited in its activities associated with the securities.

1.   *Prefiling Period*. The **prefiling period** includes all the time prior to the filing of the registration statement, and includes the time that the issuer plans and prepares the registration statement and prospectus. During this period, the issuer:

a.   Cannot Sell the Securities.

b.   Cannot Offer to Sell the Securities.

c.   Cannot Condition the Market. An issuer cannot **condition the market** by making announcements, claims, or issuing press releases in order to make an investment in the issuer sound attractive. Items that would normally be newsworthy, such as major discoveries or changes in officers, can be announced.

2. *Waiting Period.* The **waiting period** is the period between the filing and the expiration of the 20-day period during which the SEC can object and require additional information. During the waiting period, the issuer can:
   a. Make Oral Offers to Sell.
   b. Distribute a Preliminary Prospectus. A **preliminary prospectus** is also called a "red herring" due to the red stamp on its cover indicating that it is not final, and includes most of the disclosures of the final prospectus, except for price.
   c. Issue a Summary Prospectus. A **summary prospectus** summarizes the major provisions contained in the prospectus.
   d. Place Tombstone Advertisements. A **tombstone ad** is an advertisement which merely lists the terms of the securities offered. Such ads frequently appear in the financial newspapers.
3. *Posteffective Period.* The **posteffective period** begins once the registration becomes effective. During the posteffective period, the issuer can:
   a. Close Sales of the Securities.
   b. Solicit New Offers and Sales. **Exam tip #3.**

F. Final Prospectus Must Be Given to Investor. A final prospectus must be given to the investor by the time of confirming the sale or sending the security to the investor.

G. Regulation A: Simplified Offering. Issuers may use a simplified registration process under **Regulation A** for offerings of up to $5 million in a 12-month period. Issuers must file an **offering statement** with the SEC and give investors an **offering circular**. These contain fewer disclosures than are required in a registration statement and prospectus. **Exam tip #4.**

H. Exempt Securities. Certain types of securities are exempt from registration, either because of their type or because they are regulated in other ways. Exempt securities include:
   1. *Any Government-Issued Securities.*
   2. *Short-Term Notes or Drafts With a Nine-Month or Shorter Maturity.*
   3. *Securities Issued by Nonprofit Entities.*
   4. *Securities Issued by Financial Institutions.*
   5. *Securities Issued by Common Carriers.*
   6. *Insurance and Annuity Contracts Issued by Insurance Companies.*
   7. *Stock Dividends and Stock Splits.*
   8. *Securities Issued in Exchange in a Corporate Reorganization.*

I. Accredited Investors. Certain exempt transaction rules contain provisions based on whether some or all of the investors are **accredited investors**. Generally, an accredited investor is one who is experienced in investing or is wealthy, and thus in less need of the protections of the securities laws. They are better able to prevent a loss and/or more able to bear a loss. Any of the following are accredited investors:
   1. *Natural Persons With a Net Worth of at Least $1 million.*
   2. *Natural Persons Earning $200,000 Per Year.* The person must have earned $200,000 for each of the two previous years and reasonably expect to earn $200,000 in the current year.
   3. *Any Corporation, Trust, or Partnership With Assets of $5 Million or More.*
   4. *Insiders of Issuers.* This would include officers, directors, or partners of an issuer.
   5. *Institutional Investors.* Examples include pension plans and universities.

J. Exempt Transactions. These exemptions are based on how the security is transferred rather than the security type.

1. *Nonissuers.* A nonissuer, such as a typical investor selling shares of stock, is not subject to the securities laws.

2. *Intrastate Offerings.* An **intrastate offering** is an offering within a single state and is exempt if all of the following requirements are met:

   a. Issuer Is a Resident. The issuer must be a resident of the state for which the exemption is claimed, which, for a corporation, is the state of incorporation.

   b. Issuer Does Business in the State. The issuer must derive 80 percent of its revenues from within the state and use 80 percent of the proceeds from the offering within the state.

   c. Purchasers Must Be Residents. All purchasers must be residents of the state for which the exemption is claimed.

3. *Regulation D: Small Offerings.* There are three rules under **Regulation D** allowing small offerings to be made without registration. These rules have various combinations of limits on the number and type of investors and on the dollar amount issued. **Exam tip #5.**

   a. Rule 504. Under **Rule 504**, also known as the **small offering** exemption, there is a limit of $1 million, but there is no limit on the number or type of investors. There are no requirements to provide any information to the investors.

   b. Rule 505. Under **Rule 505**, there is a $5 million limit. The securities can be sold to no more than 35 **nonaccredited investors**, but there is no limit on the number of accredited investors. If the only investors are accredited investors, there is no requirement to provide any information to them. But if there are any unaccredited investors, then all investors, including the accredited ones, must be given an annual report including an audited balance, and other financial statements if available.

   c. Rule 506. Under **Rule 506**, there is no dollar limit on the amount of securities issued. Rule 506 is also known as the **private placement** exemption. The requirements are generally the same as under Rule 505 with one important difference. If there are any accredited investors, each must be sophisticated, meaning experienced and knowledgeable in financial matters. This requirement can also be met if an unsophisticated accredited investor is represented by someone with the necessary knowledge and experience.

K. Resale Restrictions. Because issuers could avoid the limits on exempt transactions by issuing securities to a limited number of investors who immediately resell to a larger number, securities issued under certain exemptions are **restricted securities**, which means that they cannot be resold for a specified period of time.

1. *Requirements.* An issuer of exempt securities must:

   a. Obtain an Affidavit From the Purchaser Agreeing to Not Resell,

   b. Mark the Securities as Restricted, and

   c. Notify the Transfer Agent to Not Record a Prohibited Transfer.

2. *Time Limits of Resale Restrictions.*

   a. Intrastate Offerings: Nine Months.

   b. Rule 504: No Restriction.

   c. Rule 505 and 506: Two Years.

   The two-year restrictions are lifted gradually, with all restrictions lifted by the third year.

L. 15-Day Notice to the SEC. The SEC must be notified of the exempt offering within 15 days of the sale of the first security under the exemption.

M. Integration of Exempt Offerings. The SEC can **integrate offerings** occurring close together for eligibility requirements. For example, a $600,000 and a $700,000 offering occurring a month later might be considered a single offering of $1.3 million, and thus could not qualify under Rule 504 even though each separate offering does qualify. Generally, there is a "safe harbor" rule that offerings occurring more than six months apart will not be integrated.

N. Criminal Liability. Under Section 24 of the Act, any person who willfully violates the Act or any related rules is subject to punishment of up to five years' imprisonment.

O. Private Actions Under Section 11. **Section 11** of the 1933 Act imposes civil liability on all persons associated with the issuance of covered securities for any material misstatements or omissions in the information provided to investors. Thus, CPAs and attorneys, in addition to the issuer, can be held liable under Section 11.

1. *Elements of a Section 11 Case.* The plaintiff in a Section 11 case has very little to prove:
    a. There Is a Material Misstatement or Omission, and
    b. The Plaintiff Suffered Damages.
    The plaintiff initially does not need to prove negligence or intent. The damages are generally the amount that the security has declined in value.

2. *Due Diligence Defense.* The **due diligence defense** is a broad defense that generally proves the absence of negligence. For the defense to apply, the defendant must prove that the defendant had reasonable grounds to believe and did believe that the statements were true and were free of any errors and omissions. **Exam tip #6.**

3. *Lack of Causation.* If the defendant can prove that the misstatement did not cause the loss, the defendant is not liable. This can be proven by showing that a misstatement was immaterial or that the plaintiff knew that the statement was incorrect when the securities were purchased.

IV. **The Securities Exchange Act of 1934.**

A. General Purpose and Requirements. The Securities Act of 1933 provides no protections to persons who purchase securities after their initial issuance. The **Securities Exchange Act of 1934 (the 1934 Act)** has the goal of making complete and accurate information available to traders on the securities markets. The 1934 Act also contains provisions on trading of securities by insiders.

B. Covered Companies. Companies are subject to the reporting requirements of the 1934 Act if any of the following three requirements is met:
    1. *Assets of More Than $5 Million and at Least 500 Shareholders,*
    2. *The Company's Equity Securities Are Traded on a National Exchange,* or
    3. *The Company Made a Registered Offering Under the 1933 Act.*

C. Continuous Reporting Requirements. Covered companies must file the following reports:
    1. *Annual Report: Form 10-Q.* The annual report must include financial statements, but financial statements comprise only a portion of the report.
    2. *Quarterly Report: Form 10-K.*
    3. *Monthly Report: Form 10-Q.* This report, also known as a current report, must be filed only if a significant event occurs, such as a merger. It is due in the month following the event.

D. <u>Private Actions Under Section 10(b)</u>. Under **Section 10(b)** and the related **Rule 10b-5**, conduct directed at avoiding the requirements and intent of the securities laws is prohibited.

1. *Requirements of a Section 10(b) Action*. Rule 10b-5 provides that a plaintiff must prove that
   a. The Conduct of the Defendant Was Fraudulent,
   b. It Resulted in a Material Misstatement or Omission,
   c. The Misstatement or Omission Was Made With Knowledge of Its Falsity,
   d. It Was Made in Connection With the Sale or Purchase of a Security,
   e. It Involved Interstate Commerce,
   f. The Misstatement Was Relied Upon, and
   g. Damages Resulted.

   The most tested requirement is that of scienter. The interstate commerce requirement is easily met in most cases. Damages are usually measured by the drop in the security's value.

2. *Scienter*. The **scienter** requirement means that the defendant knew of the omission or misstatement when the information (usually the financial statements) was issued. Scienter also exists if the defendant made the statement with a reckless disregard for the truth. The scienter, or knowledge, requirement is heavily tested on the CPA exam.

3. *Comparison With Section 11 of the 1933 Act*. It is much harder to prove a Rule 10b-5 case. Under Section 11 of the 1933 Act, the plaintiff does not even need to prove negligence. Under Rule 10b-5 of the 1934 Act, even proof of negligence is not sufficient. The plaintiff must go beyond proof of negligence and prove intent.

4. *Due Diligence Is Not Applicable*. If a plaintiff has proven scienter, it would not be possible for the due diligence defense to apply. The due diligence defense applies only to Section 11 actions. **Exam tip #7.**

E. <u>Insider Trading</u>. The 1934 Act prohibits **insider trading**. Insider trading allows the insider to take unfair advantage of the inside information when trading with the general investing public. The insider trading rules are contained in Rule 10b-5.

1. *Insiders*. **Insiders** are defined as:
   a. Officers, Directors, and All Employees,
   b Lawyers, Accountants, Consultants, and Others Hired Temporarily, and
   c. Others Who Owe a Fiduciary Duty to the Company.

2. *Statutory Requirement*. An insider with material nonpublic information must:
   a. Refrain From Trading in the Company's Securities or
   b. Disclose the Information to the Party on the Other Side of the Transaction.

3. *Tipper-Tippee Liability*. A **tipper** is one who provides nonpublic information to a **tippee**.
   a. Tippers. Tippers are liable for their own profits as well as profits made by their tippees, and by any remote tippees (tippees further removed who received information through the original tippee).
   b. Tippees. Tippees are liable for their profits if they knew or should have known that they were given nonpublic information. If this test is met, the tippee is also liable for the profits of any remote tippees (the immediate and remote tippees of the original tippee).

4. *Penalties for Violation*. The SEC can impose fines and seek criminal penalties for insider trading violations. In addition, the other party to the transaction can recover damages or obtain rescission of the transaction.

F. <u>Short-Swing Profits</u>. The **short-swing profits** rule under Section 16(a) of the 1934 Act requires that certain profits made by insiders trading in a corporation's stock belong to the corporation. This is based partly on the premise that the insiders (officers and directors) should devote their time to managing the corporation and not to making short-term profits from trading in the corporation's stock.

1. *Definition of Insider*. For Section 16(a), purposes an insider is an executive officer, a director, or a 10-percent shareholder. **Exam tip #8.**

2. *Reporting Companies Only*. The short-swing profits rule is applicable only to companies subject to the reporting requirements of the 1934 Act.

3. *All Transactions Must Be Reported*. All transactions by insiders in the corporation's stock must be reported to the SEC, even those not subject to the short-swing profits rule.

4. *Six-Month Period*. The rule applies only to purchases and sales made within six months of one another.

5. *Intent or Possession of Inside Information Need Not Be Shown*. Insiders are liable for short-swing profits without a showing that they possessed inside information and without regard to intent.

6. *Any Purchase and Sale Can Be Matched*. In calculating the amount of short-swing profits, the SEC can match any purchase and sale within six months of one another, even if there was not an actual profit made in the particular sale.

7. *Example*. Assume that an insider acquired a large quantity of stock in a corporation in 1997 at a cost of $100 per share. In January, 2001, she sold 600 shares for $80, and in April of the same year purchased 500 shares for $70. The April purchase at $70 per share would be matched with the January sale at $80 resulting in short-swing profits of $10 per share. The applicable number of shares is 500 because that is the number of shares for which there was both a purchase and sale within six months. Note that the insider is liable for short-swing profits even though none of the shares purchased in April could have been part of the January sale. Also note that the price paid in 1997 is irrelevant for the short-swing profits rule because it was not within six months of the sale.

8. *Profits Belong to the Corporation*. The corporation can bring an action to recover short-swing profits from the insider.

EXAM TIPS

1. Many persons claim that the disclosures required in a registration statement (and prospectus) are so broad that no one would buy the securities if they were all read with care. In order to ensure that all risks are disclosed, the tenor of a registration statement is to disclose even those risks which have almost no chance of coming to pass.

2. Candidates must know the difference between the registration statement and the prospectus. The registration statement is filed with the SEC. It is seldom seen by potential investors. The prospectus is given to potential investors, but it must also be filed with the SEC. This is because the SEC determines if the disclosures to investors contained in the prospectus are adequate.

3. Note that the focus of these rules is what is permissible. These are not required activities.

4. Regulation A is **not** an exemption from registration, but a simplified registration process.

5. The rules under Regulation D are confusing and heavily tested. Candidates must know them in detail. For example, the sophistication requirement applies only under rule 506 and applies only to the accredited investors. Note that generally the higher the dollar limit of a particular rule, the greater the restrictions on the types of investors. The antifraud provisions of the 1933 Act apply to these exempt transactions.

6. Candidates must know and understand the elements of a Section 11 case and the defenses. Note that although the plaintiff does not need to prove negligence initially, under the due diligence defense the defendant will be able to avoid liability by essentially proving the absence of negligence.

7. Candidates must also know the elements of a Rule 10b-5 action. Furthermore, candidates must know the differences in a Section 11 case under the 1933 Act and a Rule 10b-5 case under the 1934 Act.

8. Note that the definition of "insider" is different under the short-swing profits rule than under the general Rule 10b-5 insider trading rules.

KEY CONCEPTS LIKELY TO BE TESTED ON THE CPA EXAM

1. Which securities are covered by the securities acts, and which types of securities are exempt.
2. The role of the registration statement and prospectus, and the purpose of providing investors with a prospectus.
3. Permissible activities at different stages of the securities registration process.
4. Regulation A and Regulation D, especially the specific requirements of Rules 504, 505, and 506.
5. Section 11 liability under the 1933 Act, the requirements of a case, and the due diligence defense.
6. The reporting requirements under the 1934 Act, including the requirements to be subject to reporting and the types of reports required.
7. Rule 10b-5 liability under the 1934 Act, and how it differs from 1933 Act Section 11 liability.
8. Insider trading rules.

KEY TERMS

Securities	Offering Statement	Integration of Offerings
Securities Act of 1933	Offering Circular	Section 11
Registration Statement	Accredited Investor	Due Diligence Defense
Prospectus	Intrastate Offering	Securities Exchange Act of 1934
Prefiling Period	Regulation D	Section 10(b)
Condition the Market	Rule 504	Rule 10b-5
Waiting Period	Small Offering	Scienter
Preliminary Prospectus	Rule 505	Insider Trading
Summary Prospectus	Nonaccredited Investor	Insider
Tombstone Ad	Rule 506	Tipper
Posteffective Period	Private Placement	Tippee
Regulation A	Restricted Securities	Short-Swing Profits
Securities and Exchange Commission		

MULTIPLE CHOICE QUESTIONS

1.   Law Nov 94 #41
Under the Securities Act of 1933, which of the following statements most accurately reflects how securities registration affects an investor?
A. The investor is provided with information on the stockholders of the offering corporation.
B. The investor is provided with information on the principal purposes for which the offering proceeds will be used.
C. The investor is guaranteed by the SEC that the facts contained in the registration statement are accurate.
D. The investor is assured by the SEC against loss resulting from purchasing the security.

2.   Law May 94 #33
A tombstone advertisement
A. May be substituted for the prospectus under certain circumstances.
B. May contain an offer to sell securities.
C. Notifies prospective investors that a previously-offered security has been withdrawn from the market and is therefore effectively "dead."
D. Makes known the availability of a prospectus.

3.   Law May 93 #35
Regulation D of the Securities Act of 1933
A. Restricts the number of purchasers of an offering to 35.
B. Permits an exempt offering to be sold to both accredited and nonaccredited investors.
C. Is limited to offers and sales of common stock that do **not** exceed $1.5 million.
D. Is exclusively available to small business corporations as defined by Regulation D.

4.   Law May 94 #34
Which of the following factors, by itself, requires a corporation to comply with the reporting requirements of the Securities Exchange Act of 1934?
A. Six hundred employees.
B. Shares listed on a national securities exchange.
C. Total assets of $2 million.
D. Four hundred holders of equity securities.

5.   Law May 94 #37
Which of the following transactions will be exempt from the full registration requirements of the Securities Act of 1933?
A. All intrastate offerings.
B. All offerings made under Regulation A.
C. Any resale of a security purchased under a Regulation D offering.
D. Any stockbroker transaction.

6.   Law May 93 #30
Which of the following is **least** likely to be considered a security under the Securities Act of 1933?
A. Stock options.
B. Warrants.
C. General partnership interests.
D. Limited partnership interests.

7.   Law May 92 #45
For an offering to be exempt under Regulation D of the Securities Act of 1933, Rules 504, 505, and 506 each require that
A. There be a maximum of 35 unaccredited investors.
B. All purchasers receive the issuer's financial information.
C. The SEC be notified within 10 days of the first sale.
D. The offering be made without general advertising.

OTHER OBJECTIVE FORMAT QUESTION (Estimated time -- 10 to 15 minutes)

Law Nov 95 #3(b)

b. Items 1 through 5 are based on the following:

Coffee Corp., a publicly-held corporation, wants to make an $8,000,000 exempt offering of its shares as a private placement offering under Regulation D, Rule 506, of the Securities Act of 1933. Coffee has more than 500 shareholders and assets in excess of $1 billion, and has its shares listed on a national securities exchange.

Required:

Items 1 through 5 relate to the application of the Securities Act of 1933 and the Securities Exchange Act of 1934 to Coffee Corp. and the offering. For each item, select from List II whether only statement I is correct, whether only statement II is correct, whether both statements I and II are correct, or whether neither statement I nor II is correct. Blacken the corresponding oval on the *Objective Answer Sheet*.

List II
A. I only.
B. II only.
C. Both I and II.
D. Neither I nor II.

1. I.   Coffee Corp. may make the Regulation D, Rule 506, exempt offering.
   II. Coffee Corp., because it is required to report under the Securities Exchange Act of 1934, may **not** make an exempt offering.

2. I.   Shares sold under a Regulation D, Rule 506, exempt offering may only be purchased by accredited investors.
   II. Shares sold under a Regulation D, Rule 506, exempt offering may be purchased by any number of investors provided there are **no** more than 35 non-accredited investors.

3. I.   An exempt offering under Regulation D, Rule 506, must **not** be for more than $10,000,000.
   II. An exempt offering under Regulation D, Rule 506, has **no** dollar limit.

4. I.   Regulation D, Rule 506, requires that all investors in the exempt offering be notified that for nine months after the last sale, **no** resale be made to a nonresident.
   II. Regulation D, Rule 506, requires that the issuer exercise reasonable care to assure that purchasers of the exempt offering are buying for investment and are **not** underwriters.

5. I.   The SEC must be notified by Coffee Corp. within 5 days of the first sale of the exempt offering securities.
   II. Coffee Corp. Must include an SEC notification of the first sale of the exempt offering securities in Coffee's next filed Quarterly Report (Form 10-Q).

ESSAY QUESTION (Estimated time -- 15 to 25 minutes)

Law May 95 #5

Perry, a staff accountant with Orlean Associates, CPAs, reviewed the following transactions engaged in by Orlean's two clients: World Corp. and Unity Corp.

WORLD CORP.

During 1994, World Corp. made a $4,000,000 offering of its stock. The offering was sold to 50 nonaccredited investors and 150 accredited investors. There was a general advertising in the offering. All purchasers were provided with material information concerning World Corp. The offering was completely sold by the end of 1994. The SEC was notified 30 days after the first sale of the offering.

World did not register the offering and contends that the offering and any subsequent resale of the securities are completely exempt from registration under Regulation D, Rule 505, of the Securities Act of 1933.

UNITY CORP.

Unity Corp. has 750 equity stockholders and assets in excess of $100,000,000.

Unity's stock is traded on a national stock exchange. Unity contends that it is not a covered corporation and is not required to comply with the reporting provisions of the Securities Exchange Act of 1934.

Required:

a. 1. State whether World is correct in its contention that the offering is exempt from registration under Regulation D, Rule 505, of the Securities Act of 1933. Give the reasons(s) for your conclusion.

2. State whether World is correct in its contention that on subsequent resale the securities are completely exempt from registration. Give the reason(s) for your conclusion.

b. 1. State whether Unity is correct in its contention that it is not a covered corporation and is not required to comply with the reporting requirements of the Securities Exchange Act of 1934 and give the reasons(s) for your conclusion.

2. Identify and describe two principal reports a covered corporation must file with the SEC.

EXPLANATIONS TO MULTIPLE CHOICE QUESTIONS

1. B is the correct answer. The primary purpose of the Securities Act of 1933 is to provide full disclosure of all relevant information to potential purchasers of securities. Part of that information is the use which will be made of the proceeds. Choice C is incorrect because the SEC makes no representations as to the accuracy of the information in a registration statement. There is a duty to disclose only accurate information, and to not omit material information, but the SEC does not verify or audit all the information in a registration statement. The SEC has the power to check into the accuracy of material in a registration statement, but does not routinely verify all such information. Choice D is incorrect because the securities acts are not designed to protect investors against losses where full information was provided.

2. D is the correct answer. A tombstone ad announces the details of an offering and is called a tombstone ad because it uses words only, much like a tombstone does. The tombstone ad typically states that it is not an offer, and it refers to the prospectus. Answer choice C might be a rare example of humor on the CPA exam.

3. B is the correct answer. Note that this question simply asked about Regulation D without specifying a particular rule within Regulation D. Thus, the correct answer choice must be applicable to all three of the Regulation D rules. Rule 504 does not limit investor types, and Rules 505 and 506 allow sales to both types, although there are limitations. Choice A is incorrect because the 35-investor limit applies to unaccredited investors. Even if choice A referred to accredited investors, note that it would be incorrect because there is no limit under Rule 504 on the type of investors. Candidates must thoroughly know the details of the Regulation D rules.

4. B is the correct answer. Being listed on a national securities exchange is one of the ways that a company comes under the reporting requirements of the Securities Exchange Act of 1934. Note that if choice C was more than $5 million or choice D was 500 or more, neither would be the correct answer because neither, by itself, meets the reporting requirements.

5. B is the correct answer. Regulation A does not provide a reporting exemption, but it does provides a simplified registration. This question can be tricky because of the word "exempt." However, the exemption in the question is from "full" registration, pointing out the importance of reading every word of every question carefully. Choice A is incorrect because intrastate offerings are exempt only if certain requirements are met.

6. C is the correct answer. In a general partnership, the partners manage and use their own efforts in attempting to make a profit. One characteristic of a security is earning profits solely from the efforts of others.

7. D is the correct answer. This question also seeks a requirement that applies under all three of the Regulation D rules. Choice A is incorrect because the 35 unaccredited investor limit does not apply to Rule 504.

EXPLANATION TO OTHER OBJECTIVE FORMAT QUESTION

1. A is the correct answer. Rule 506 contains no dollar limit on the amount of the offering. The second statement is not true because being subject to the reporting requirements does not prevent a company from making a private placement under Rule 506.

2. B is the correct answer. Note the logical structure of the two statements which makes it impossible for both to be true. Based solely on the structure of the statements, both could be false. Both would be false if the investor limit in the second question were 50 investors. Analyzing the logical structure of questions can sometimes help when having difficulty.

3. B is the correct answer. Again, the logical structure of the statements makes it impossible for both to be true.

4. B is the correct answer. The first statement is not true because under Rules 505 and 506 there is a two-year resale restriction. The nine-month resale restriction applies to securities sold in an intrastate offering.

5. D is the correct answer. The issuer must notify the SEC within 15 days of issuing the first exempt security but does not need to include that information in the quarterly report.

UNOFFICIAL AICPA ANSWER TO ESSAY QUESTION

Law May 95 #5.

a. 1. World is incorrect in its first contention that the offering is exempt from registration under Regulation D, Rule 505, of the Securities Act of 1933. World did not comply with the requirements of Rule 505 for the following reasons: the offering was sold to more than 35 nonaccredited investors; there was a general advertising of the offering; and the SEC was notified more than 15 days after the first sale of the offering.

2. World is also incorrect in its second contention that the securities of the offering would be completely exempt from registration if the offering were exempt. Securities originally purchased under a Regulation D limited offering exemption are restricted securities. They must be registered prior to resale unless sold subject to another exemption.

b. 1. Unity is incorrect in its contention that it is not required to comply with the reporting requirements under the Securities Exchange Act of 1934. Unity must comply because it has more than 500 stockholders and total assets in excess of $5,000,000. Alternately, Unity must comply because its shares are traded on a national securities exchange.

2. A covered corporation must file the following reports with the SEC: Quarterly Reports (10-Qs); Annual Reports (10-Ks); and Current Reports (8-Ks). These reports are intended to provide a complete, current statement of all business operations and matters affecting the value of the corporation's securities.

Author's Note:

Regarding the requirement that resales must qualify under an exemption or be registered, remember that most individual investors would qualify for the nonissuer exemption.

Notice that the last part of the question asked the candidate to "identify and describe two principal reports" which must be filed with the SEC. The unofficial answer included all three of the principal reports. If time permits, it generally can only help your score to include a little extra. Note also that although the question asked for a description, the descriptions in the unofficial answer are quite limited. You should include a more thorough description, such as the information to be included in each, and, for the current reports, when one must be filed.

CHAPTER 24
ENVIRONMENTAL PROTECTION

OVERVIEW

This chapter covers environmental law, which has only begun to be tested in recent years. Most environmental law is based on federal statutes. There are many accountants who question whether it is even appropriate for CPA exam candidates to be tested on environmental law, but the few questions that have been asked have been general in nature. The outline for this material primarily identifies the main provisions of the most important federal environmental statutes.

OUTLINE

I. The Environmental Protection Agency.
   A. Generally. The **Environmental Protection Agency** (the EPA) was created in 1970 and is the federal agency responsible for implementation and enforcement of most environmental laws.
   B. Powers. The EPA has the following powers and responsibilities.
      1. *Rule-Making Power.* The EPA has broad powers to make rules and regulations related to environmental statutes. Many environmental statutes specifically designate the EPA as responsible for making the related rules and regulations.
      2. *Adjudicative Powers.* The EPA can hold hearings of various types in connection with environmental laws.
      3. *Prosecute Violations.* The EPA can initiate court proceedings against suspected violators.

II. National Environmental Policy Act.
   A. Generally. The **National Environmental Policy Act** (NEPA) requires that the federal government consider the adverse environmental impact of any proposed federal action.
   B. Federal Action. **Federal action** is broadly defined and includes:
      1. *Proposed Federal Legislation.*
      2. *Proposed Federal Rules and Regulations.*
      3. *Proposed Federal Projects.* Examples include a federal highway project or construction of a federal office building.
      4. *Private Projects With Federal Government Involvement.* Federal action includes private actions where the federal government plays a role, such as granting an approval. For example, a privately operated ski resort that is on federal land which needs a federal permit in order to operate would be considered federal action. **Exam tip #1.**
   C. Environmental Impact Statement. NEPA requires that an **Environmental Impact Statement** (EIS) be prepared for all proposed legislation or federal action that significantly affects the quality of the human environment. The EIS must:
      1. *Describe the Affected Environment,*
      2. *Describe the Effect of the Proposed Action on the Environment,*
      3. *Identify and Discuss Alternative Actions,*
      4. *List the Resources That Would Be Committed to the Action,* and
      5. *Contain Cost-Benefit Analyses of the Proposed Action and the Alternatives.*

D. <u>Public Review and Comment</u>. There is usually a 30-day period where the public can comment on the proposed EIS.

E. <u>EPA Decision</u>. The EPA decides whether the proposed action can proceed. The EPA's decision appealable to the U.S. Court of Appeals.

F. <u>EIS Does Not Determine Outcome</u>. The purpose of the EIS is for the federal government to consider the environmental consequences of an action. It is possible for the action to proceed even if there are adverse environmental impacts so long as they have been considered in the government's decision. **Exam tip #2.**

G. <u>NEPA Is Not Applicable to State and Local Government Action</u>. NEPA applies only to action by the federal government.

III. **Other Environmental Statutes.**

A. <u>Generally</u>. Most environmental statutes are federal statutes, and these are the ones which can be tested on the CPA exam. The statute's names usually indicate what they regulate, and this might be sufficient information to answer a multiple choice question.

B. <u>Clean Air Act</u>. The **Clean Air Act** regulates several aspects of air pollution. The Clean Air Act allows states, rather than the EPA, to administer portions of the Act if they choose.

1. *Ambient Air Standards*. Under the **ambient air standards**, there are maximum levels of various pollutants which are allowable in the air of a community. The air is monitored and tested to determine compliance.

   a. Nonattainment Area. A **nonattainment area** is a region that does not meet the standards. The states and communities in nonattainment areas must institute programs to meet the standards. Automobile emission testing and subsidized public transit are examples. New stationary pollution sources might be prohibited in nonattainment areas.

   b. Attainment Area. An **attainment area** is a region that does meet the standards. Adding new stationary sources such as factories is easier in attainment areas.

2. *Stationary Sources*. The Clean Air Act sets technology and other standards for **stationary sources.**

   a. Reasonably Available Control Technology. Most existing stationary sources are required to meet this technology standard.

   b. Best Available Control Technology. Large stationary sources are required to meet this standard. States can also require existing sources to meet this standard.

3. *Mobile Standards*. The Clean Air Act sets emission standards for **mobile sources**, primarily automobiles and trucks, but includes other standards.

4. *Toxic Pollutants*. The Clean Air Act requires the EPA to establish standards for emissions of various toxic pollutants.

C. <u>Clean Water Act</u>. The **Clean Water Act** regulates water pollution in several ways.

1. *Point Sources*. There are technological standards for **point sources**, which are sources such as a factory or sewage treatment plant where the pollution enters the water at an identifiable point.

   a. Best Practical Control Technology. Existing point sources are required to meet this technological standard.

   b. Best Available Control Technology. New point sources must meet this standard, and the EPA has established timetables for existing sources to meet it.

2. *Permitting System.* All point sources are required to obtain an EPA permit to make any discharges of pollutants into water. The EPA can deny or put limitations on the permit.
3. *Nonpoint Sources.* **Nonpoint sources,** such as a field where there is pesticide runoff, are not regulated. **Exam tip #3.**
4. *Wetlands.* **Wetlands** are areas of land inundated with water. Filling or dredging wetlands requires a permit from the Army Corps of Engineers.
5. *Thermal Pollution.* The Clean Water Act controls thermal pollution, which occurs when water is discharged that is hotter than the body of water into which it is discharged.
6. *Oil Spills.* The Clean Water Act authorized the federal government to clean up oil spills within 12 miles of shore and on the continental shelf and to recover the costs from the responsible parties.

D. Safe Drinking Water Act. The **Safe Drinking Water Act** regulates the safety of the drinking water supply and prohibits the dumping of wastes into wells used for drinking water.

E. Federal Insecticide, Fungicide, and Rodenticide Act. The **Federal Insecticide, Fungicide, and Rodenticide Act** regulates these substances.
1. *Registration With the EPA.* These chemicals must be registered with the EPA before they can be sold. The EPA can:
a. Deny Registration,
b. Certify for General or Restricted Use, or
c. Set Limits on Residue on Crops.
2. *Suspension of Registration.* The EPA can suspend the registration of a chemical if it is found to pose an imminent danger or emergency.

F. Toxic Substances Control Act. The **Toxic Substances Control Act** regulates toxic substances in several ways.
1. *Testing Required By Manufacturers.* New chemicals must be tested for health and environmental effects with the results reported to the EPA before they can be marketed.
2. *EPA Can Prohibit.* The EPA can prohibit or limit the manufacture and sale of toxic substances.
3. *Labeling Requirements.* The EPA can require special labeling for toxic substances.

G. Resource Conservation and Recovery Act. The **Resource Conservation and Recovery Act** (RCRA) regulates the disposal of new hazardous wastes. **Exam tip #4.**
1. *Permit System.* Permits are required for parties who generate, treat, store, transport, or dispose of hazardous wastes.
2. *"Cradle to Grave" Tracking System.* Detailed records are required to be kept accounting for all hazardous waste from the time it is generated until its ultimate disposal. This is known as the **cradle to grave** tracking system.
3. *Broadly Defined.* The definition of hazardous waste is very broad, with the EPA able to designate additional substances determined to be hazardous.
4. *Packaging and Labeling Requirement.* Hazardous wastes must be accurately and adequately packaged and labeled before they can be shipped.
5. *Household Waste.* Hazardous household waste is regulated under RCRA.

H. <u>Comprehensive Environmental Response, Compensation, and Liability Act</u>. In order to address hazardous waste sites, the **Comprehensive Environmental Response, Compensation, and Liability Act** (CERCLA) was passed, also known as the **Superfund Act**. CERCLA addresses the management and cleanup of hazardous wastes that were generated in the past.

   1. *Hazardous Waste Sites*. CERCLA requires the EPA to identify existing hazardous waste sites and rank them according to the severity of risk that they present.
   2. *National Priority List*. The sites with the highest risk are placed on the **National Priority List**.
   3. *Taxes on Hazardous Chemicals*. CERCLA imposes taxes on certain hazardous chemicals.
   4. *Superfund*. The taxes imposed by CERCLA go into the Superfund to pay for the cleanup of hazardous waste sites.
   5. *Cleanup of Hazardous Waste Sites*. CERCLA gives the EPA the authority to clean up hazardous waste sites. The EPA can clean up either priority or nonpriority sites quickly to eliminate imminent dangers including contamination of drinking water.
   6. *Financial Liability*. The EPA can order a responsible party to clean up a site, and if it does not, the EPA can recover the cleanup cost from the responsible party. CERCLA liability is very broad. **Exam tip #5.**
      a. A Partly Responsible Party Can Be Liable for the Entire Cleanup Cost.
      b. Parties Can Have Current Responsibility for Past Actions.
      c. Very Few Defenses Are Available.
   7. *Responsible Parties*. Responsible parties under CERCLA include:
      a. The Generator of the Waste.
      b. The Transporter of the Waste to the Site.
      c. The Owner of the Site at the Time of Disposal.
      d. The Current Owner and Operator of the Site. Note that the current owner of the site can be held financially responsible for the actions of past owners. This is a primary reason why environmental audits have become so important when purchasing property.
   8. *Community Right to Know Provision*. CERCLA contains a **community right to know** provision which requires:
      a. Annual Disclosure of Toxic Emissions.
      b. Disclosure of the Presence of Certain Listed Chemicals.
      c. Immediate Notification of Spills, Accidents, and Other Emergencies.

I. <u>Nuclear Waste Policy Act</u>. The **Nuclear Waste Policy Act** requires the federal government to create a plan and select a site for the disposal of radioactive nuclear waste.

J. <u>Endangered Species Act</u>. The **Endangered Species Act** protects wildlife.
   1. *Department of Commerce*. This Act is administered by both the EPA and the Department of Commerce.
   2. *Endangered and Threatened Species*. The Secretary of the Interior can designate a species as either **endangered** or **threatened**, with endangered species receiving the higher level of protection.
   3. *Critical Habitat*. Activities or projects in critical habitat areas for these species can be prohibited or restricted.
   4. *Applicable to Private Parties*. The Endangered Species Act can prevent private parties from developing land or engaging in other activities threatening to wildlife.

K. <u>Noise Control Act</u>. The **Noise Control Act** authorizes the EPA to set noise standards on products sold in the United States. It also allows the EPA to work with other agencies on noise standards for airplanes and trucks.

EXAM TIPS

1. In connection with NEPA, be sure to know that federal action is broadly defined and that NEPA does not apply to actions by state or local governments or to actions solely by private parties.
2. Remember that NEPA requires that environmental impacts be considered, but it does not prohibit the proposed government action from going forward, even when there are significant environmental impacts.
3. Note that air pollution sources are classified as mobile or stationary, while water pollution sources are classified as point or nonpoint.
4. There are two major statutes addressing hazardous waste, CERCLA and RCRA. Be sure to know the provisions of each statute and to not confuse them. Unlike most of the environmental statutes, the names of these two statutes give little indication of what they address.
5. The CERCLA liability provisions are very broad and should be thoroughly understood.

KEY CONCEPTS LIKELY TO BE TESTED ON THE CPA EXAM

1. The powers, responsibilities, and role of the EPA.
2. The provisions of NEPA.
3. The general provisions of the other environmental protection laws, especially the Clean Air Act, the Clean Water Act, RCRA, and CERCLA.

KEY TERMS

Environmental Protection Agency	Wetlands
National Environmental Policy Act (NEPA)	Safe Drinking Water Act
Federal Action	Insecticide, Fungicide, and Rodenticide Act
Environmental Impact Statement	Toxic Substances Control Act
Clean Air Act	Resource Conservation and Recovery Act
Ambient Air Standards	Cradle to Grave Tracking System
Nonattainment Area	Superfund
Attainment Area	National Priority List
Stationary Source	Community Right to Know
Mobile Source	Nuclear Waste Policy Act
Clean Water Act	Endangered Species Act
Point Source	Threatened Species
Nonpoint Source	Noise Control Act

Comprehensive Environmental Response, Compensation, and Liability Act

MULTIPLE CHOICE QUESTIONS

1.   Law R96 #7
Under the federal Clean Air Act, which of the following statements is correct?
A. Power plants are required to eliminate all air polluting emissions.
B. Factories that emit toxic air pollutants are required to reduce emissions by installing the best available emission control technology.
C. Automobile manufacturers are required to have emission control equipment installed on previously manufactured vehicles.
D. Homeowners are required to remove all pollutants from their residences.

2.   Law May 95 #56
Under the Comprehensive Environmental Response, Compensation, and Liability Act (CERCLA), commonly known as Superfund, which of the following parties would be liable to the Environmental Protection Agency (EPA) for the expense of cleaning up a hazardous waste disposal site?

   I. The current owner or operator of the site.
   II. The person who transported the wastes to the site.
   III. The person who owned or operated the site at the time of the disposal.

A. I and II.
B. I and III.
C. II and III.
D. I, II, and III.

3.   Author
Attainment areas are applicable under the
A. Clean Water Act.
B. Clean Air Act.
C. Resource Conservation and Recovery Act.
D. Endangered Species Act.

4.   Law Nov 95 #57
Which of the following activities is(are) regulated under the Federal Water Pollution Control Act (Clean Water Act)?

	Discharge of heated water by nuclear power plants	Dredging of wetlands
A.	Yes	Yes
B.	Yes	No
C.	No	Yes
D.	No	No

5.   Author
The Community Right to Know provisions are related to
A. The right of a community to review an environmental impact statement affecting the areas in and around the community.
B. The release of toxic substances into the air of the community.
C. The "cradle to grave" record-keeping requirements of the Resource Conservation and Recovery Act.
D. The public availability of information on which areas qualify as attainment areas.

6.   Author
Which of the following is true about environmental impact statements?
A. They are a requirement under the Endangered Species Act.
B. The are required any time there is an action taken by a state government which could have an adverse environmental impact on the environment.
C. They are required to identify and discuss alternatives to the proposed action.
D. They are generally required for actions by private entities.

OTHER OBJECTIVE FORMAT QUESTION

Author

For each of the following statements, choose the appropriate item from List I and blacken the corresponding oval on the Objective Answer Sheet. An item in the list may be used once, more than once, or not at all.

List I
A. National Environmental Policy Act.
B. Clean Air Act.
C. Clean Water Act.
D. Safe Drinking Water Act.
E. Resource Conservation and Recovery Act.
F. Comprehensive Environmental Response, Compensation and Liability Act.
G. Nuclear Waste Policy Act.
H. Endangered Species Act.

1. The "cradle to grave" tracking system is found in the

2. The designation of attainment areas is required pursuant to the

3. The statute which is also known as the Superfund legislation is the

4. Mobile sources standards are a provision of the

5. A factory that discharges hot water into a stream would be subject to

6. The authority of the federal government to clean up oil spills and seek recovery from responsible parties is found in

7. Point sources of pollution are addressed under the

8. The requirement to file an environmental impact statement is found in the

9. Taxes are imposed on certain hazardous substances under the

EXPLANATIONS TO MULTIPLE CHOICE QUESTIONS

1. B is the correct answer. Choice A is incorrect because it is simply not practical for power plants to eliminate all emissions. Choice C is incorrect because automobile manufacturers are required to meet emissions standards for new cars, but are not required to install pollution control equipment on previously manufactured vehicles.

2. D is the correct answer. Under CERCLA, there is very broad liability for cleanup costs of hazardous waste sites, and all three of the listed parties could be held responsible.

3. B is the correct answer. Attainment areas are areas which meet the ambient air standards under the Clean Air Act. Such areas can more readily allow new stationary air pollution sources, such as factories, to be built.

4. A is the correct answer. Both of these are covered under the Clean Water Act. The dredging (and filling) of wetlands is jointly administered by the EPA and the Army Corps of Engineers.

5. B is the correct answer. The community right to know provisions require disclosure of the amounts of identified toxic substances released during the year.

6. C is the correct answer. Choice A is incorrect because environmental impact statements are a requirement of the National Environmental Policy Act. Choice B is incorrect because the requirement to prepare an environmental impact statement is required only of the federal government. Choice D is incorrect because private entities are generally not required to file an environmental impact statement. Where a private entity is operating under the authority of the federal government, an environmental impact statement might be required.

EXPLANATION TO OTHER OBJECTIVE FORMAT QUESTION

1. E is the correct answer. This tracking system requires a written manifest to accompany all movement and storage of hazardous waste.

2. B is the correct answer. Attainment areas relate to the ambient air standards under the Clean Air Act and are areas which meet the standards. Nonattainment areas must implement programs with the goal of becoming an attainment area.

3. F is the correct answer. The term "Superfund" refers to the fund which is used to clean up toxic waste sites where there is no responsible party willing and able to clean the site.

4. B is the correct answer. The primary mobile sources are automobiles and trucks. The concept of mobile sources relates only to sources of air pollution.

5. C is the correct answer. Hot water discharges are referred to as thermal pollution because water significantly hotter than that naturally occurring in a body of water can have just as adverse an environmental effect as other types of water pollution.

6. F is the correct answer. The Clean Water Act authorizes the federal government to clean up oil spills within 12 miles of the shore or on the continental shelf and recover costs from the responsible party.

7. C is the correct answer. Point sources are regulated under the Clean Water Act, whereas nonpoint sources of water pollution, such as a farmer's field of crops, are not regulated.

8. A is the correct answer. One of the primary provisions of the National Environmental Policy Act is the requirement to prepare an Environmental Impact Statement for proposed federal action.

9. F is the correct answer. The taxes imposed on these hazardous substances are used to provide money for the Superfund to be used to finance the cleanup of hazardous waste sites.

CHAPTER 25
EMPLOYMENT AND LABOR LAW

OVERVIEW

This is the first of two chapters covering employment law. This chapter primarily addresses federal statutes regulating labor relations and other aspects of employment law. The workers' compensation statutes, on the other hand, are state law and are similar in most states. For the most part, this material requires the memorization of various statutory provisions. A knowledge of the general purposes of the statutes will help where a question addresses a provision unfamiliar to the candidate.

OUTLINE

I. Federal Labor Statutes.
    A. <u>National Labor Relations Act</u>.
        1. *Purpose.* The **National Labor Relations Act**, also known as the **Wagner Act**, established the rights of employees to organize and bargain collectively for wages and other employment conditions.
        2. *Employer's Duty of Good Faith.* The Act places an affirmative duty on employers to bargain in good faith with unions.
        3. *Prohibitions.* An employer cannot interfere with employee attempts to unionize. Nor can employers discriminate against employees based on union membership (except when membership is required under a contract) or for reporting or testifying about the employer's violations of the Act.
    B. <u>Labor-Management Relations Act</u>.
        1. *Purpose.* The **Labor-Management Relations Act**, also known as the **Taft-Hartley Act**, imposes good faith and fair dealing requirements on unions.
        2. *Duties Imposed on Unions.* This Act imposed duties and prohibitions on unions in their dealings with employers and with their membership.
          a. Unions Cannot Charge Excessive Membership Fees.
          b. Unions Cannot Strike for Improper Reasons.
          c. Unions Cannot Charge Employers for Work Not Performed.
          d. Unions Must Allow Employers to Make Statements Against Unions Prior to Elections.
        3. *Allows Expanded Areas of Union Activities.*
        4. *Cooling-Off Period.* The Act provides a cooling off period in certain circumstances, during which a strike cannot be called.
        5. *Presidential Injunction Allowed.* The Act allows the President of the United States to seek an injunction against a strike for up to 80 days if the strike would create a national emergency.
    C. <u>Labor-Management Reporting and Disclosure Act</u>.
        1. *Purpose.* The **Labor-Management Reporting and Disclosure Act**, also known as the **Landrum-Griffen Act**, contains financial reporting requirements and establishes a number of rights of union members.

2. *Elections*. Unions must hold regularly scheduled elections for union officials conducted by secret ballot. The act establishes other rights of members in the conduct of meetings and elections.

3. *Officials Are Accountable*. Union officials are accountable for union funds and property.

4. *No Communists or Ex-Convicts in Office*. The Act prohibits Communists or ex-convicts from holding union offices. (This Act was passed in 1959 at the height of the cold war.)

5. *Legal Actions Authorized*. The Act authorizes civil and criminal actions against officials for engaging in certain unauthorized conduct.

II. Workers' Compensation Acts.

A. Generally. **Workers' compensation acts** are state law. Most of the acts have similar provisions, and the CPA exam tests on those provisions which most states have in common.

B. Purpose. The workers' compensation acts were passed in order to create a more fair and efficient means for workers to receive compensation for work-related injuries. Before these acts, workers often had to sue to be compensated for injuries with no assurance that they would recover. Two workers with similar injuries under similar circumstances might receive vastly different results at trial. Employers buy workers' compensation insurance to cover the payment of claims.

C. Administrative Board. Most states require a claim to be filed with an administrative board or commission, which rules on the legitimacy and amount of the claim.

D. Appeal to State Court. The worker can appeal this decision to the state's court system.

E. Established Limits For Recovery. Each state establishes set amounts or ranges recoverable in various circumstances. The amounts are usually less than a worker might recover if the worker could sue in a court.

F. Employment-Related Injury. Workers' compensation pays only for injuries that are caused in connection with employment.

G. Exclusive Remedy. An injured worker must use the workers' compensation system for work-related injuries and cannot file a negligence suit against the employer in an ordinary court. Workers can separately sue the employer only if the employer intentionally caused the injury.

H. Certain Defenses Not Applicable. Several common law defenses are not applicable in a workers' compensation claim. This means that the worker will collect on the claim even if the defense is present. These disallowed defenses are:

1. *Strict Liability*. The worker can recover even if the worker's own negligence or gross negligence caused the injury. Thus worker's compensation is based on the doctrine of strict liability.

2. *Contributory or Comparative Negligence*. Nor can the employer use contributory or comparative negligence of the worker to deny recovery.

3. *Negligence of a Fellow Employee*. Under the common law **fellow servant doctrine**, an employer was able to avoid liability if the injury was caused by the negligence of another employee. Under workers' compensation, the worker can recover even if a fellow employee's negligence caused the injury.

4. *Assumption of Risk*. An employee's assumption of the risk does not prevent recovery. In an ordinary negligence lawsuit, the employer would not be liable if it could prove that the employee had voluntarily assumed a risk. **Exam tip #1.**

J. <u>No Recovery for Self-Inflicted Injuries</u>. Workers do not receive compensation for self-inflicted injuries.

K. <u>No Recovery for Intoxication-Caused Injuries</u>. There is no award where the injury was caused by the intoxication of the employee.

L. <u>Third-Party Suits</u>. Workers are able to recover from third parties who cause their work-related injuries, such as a customer or the manufacturer of a piece of equipment.

    1. *Reimbursement for Workers' Compensation Benefits*. To the extent that the recovery from a third-party lawsuit covers the same injuries as workers' compensation benefits received, the recovery must be turned over to the insurance carrier who paid the benefits.

    2. *Subrogation When Worker Does Not Sue*. If the worker chooses not to sue, the workers' compensation insurance carrier is subrogated to the rights of the employee and can sue the third party.

M. <u>Benefits</u>. Amounts are usually payable for:

    1. *Medical Care*.

    2. *Disability*. These payments represent a partial wage continuation plan.

    3. *Death*. These payments are made to a surviving spouse and minor children.

N. <u>No Payment for Pain and Suffering</u>. Most workers' compensation laws do not allow payment for pain and suffering.

III. **Federal Statutes Regulating Employment.**

A. <u>Occupational Safety and Health Act</u>. The **Occupational Safety and Health Act (OSHA)** regulates safety in the workplace. The Act is administered by the **Occupational Safety and Health Administration** (also abbreviated as **OSHA**). **Exam tip #2.**

    1. *Safety Standards*. OSHA has the responsibility to develop specific safety standards and has used that authority to develop a large number of safety standards, some of which are very detailed and specific.

    2. *General Duty to Provide Safe Conditions*. In addition to meeting the specific standards, an employer has a general duty to provide safe working conditions. **Exam tip #3.**

    3. *Investigation and Inspection*. OSHA investigates complaints and inspects workplaces for safety violations.

    4. *Search Warrants*. If an employer objects to a workplace inspection, OSHA must obtain a search warrant showing probable cause that there is a violation.

    5. *Citations*. OSHA issues citations for violations. These can contain civil penalties and are reviewed by a commission whose decisions are appealable to the federal circuit court of appeals.

    6. *Whistle Blowers Are Protected*. Workers who report violations to OSHA cannot be discharged or discriminated against for doing so.

    7. *Orders to Correct Conditions*. OSHA can order employers to correct unsafe conditions.

B. <u>Fair Labor Standards Act</u>. The **Fair Labor Standards Act** regulates the working hours, conditions, and allowable ages of workers. It applies to private employers and employees affecting interstate commerce. This includes most companies.

    1. *Oppressive Child Labor Is Prohibited*. Rules under this provision include:

        a. Children Under Age 14. Children under 14 can work only as newspaper deliverers.

    b. Children of Ages 14 and 15. Children aged 14 and 15 can work limited hours in nonhazardous jobs approved by the Department of Labor.

    c. Children of Ages 16 and 17. Children aged 16 and 17 can work unlimited hours in nonhazardous jobs.

    d. Persons of Age 18 and Over. Persons aged 18 and over can work at any job whether or not it is hazardous.

2. *Minimum Wage Provisions.* Employees must be paid at least the minimum wage, which is changed periodically by Congress. There is a lower minimum wage for certain student employees working in retail or service establishments, or working on farms or in institutions of higher education. Certain apprentices can also be paid a lower wage.

3. *Overtime Provisions.* Covered workers must be paid a rate one and a half their regular rate for hours in excess of 40 worked in a week. This applies separately to each week. Thus, a worker who works 30 hours in the first week of a pay period and 55 hours in the second week would be entitled to overtime pay for the 15 overtime hours in the second week.

4. *Numerous Exclusions.* There are numerous exclusions for certain workers under the Act. For example, professional employees are subject to neither the minimum wage requirements nor the overtime pay provisions. Some workers are excluded from only one provision, others from several.

C. <u>Employee Retirement Income Security Act.</u> The **Employee Retirement Income Security Act (ERISA)** regulates pension plans for companies that choose to provide one.

1. *Pension Plans Are Not Required.* No company is required to provide a pension plan under ERISA or under any other statute. **Exam tip #4.**

2. *Purposes.* Although no company is required to provide a pension plan, ERISA was enacted to regulate the plans of those companies that do provide a plan and to:

    a. Prevent Fraud and Abuse,

    b. Provide Full Disclosure, and

    c. Ensure That Pension Payments Will Be Made.

Prior to ERISA, many plans were misleading to employees, had significant forfeiture provisions, had little or no management oversight, or were not adequately funded. ERISA provisions are directed at eliminating these problems.

3. *Specific Requirements.*

    a. Written Plan. Pensions plans must be in writing.

    b. Manager. The plan must name a manager.

    c. Investment Limitations. ERISA contains restrictions and requirements for investing plan assets, including a limitation that the plan cannot invest more than 10 percent of its assets in the securities of the sponsoring employer. This minimizes the risk to the pension plan from financial difficulties of the sponsoring employer.

    d. Vesting. An employee becomes **vested** with respect to benefits when the employee will not lose benefits if the employee ceases employment with the company. Benefits must completely vest by the fifth year after being earned, or can vest gradually over a seven-year period beginning when earned. Employee contributions vest immediately.

    e. Reporting Requirements. ERISA sets financial reporting requirements for pension plans. This allows participants to evaluate a plan's financial condition.

   f. Funding Requirements. ERISA sets minimum funding requirements, helping to ensure that promised benefits will actually be paid.

   g. Plan Insurance. ERISA established the Pension Benefit Guaranty Corporation to insure benefit payments of plans that fail.

D. Consolidated Omnibus Budget Reconciliation Act. The **Consolidated Omnibus Budget Reconciliation Act (COBRA)** provides employees the opportunity to continue their group health insurance after separation of employment or other qualifying event.

  1. *Twenty or More Employees*. COBRA applies to companies with 20 or more employees.

  2. *Qualifying Event*. COBRA provisions apply following a qualifying event, including:

   a. Separation of Employment. This applies regardless of the reason for separation.

   b. Reduction in Hours. A worker whose reduction in hours causes health care coverage eligibility to end is covered under COBRA.

   c. Death. Survivors of a deceased employee can continue the coverage.

   d. Divorce. The divorced spouse and children can continue coverage.

  3. *Insured Party Must Pay*. COBRA does not require the coverage to be provided at no cost. The person must pay the applicable group rate under the plan, and may be charged a slightly higher amount to cover the additional costs of administration.

  4. *Coverage Period*. In most cases of separation, the coverage is available for 18 months, but in cases of death or divorce, the period is 36 months.

  5. *Notice to Employee*. Within 14 days of the qualifying event, the employee (or survivors) must be given a notice of the eligibility for coverage, the cost, place of payment, etc.

E. Immigration Reform and Control Act. The **Immigration Reform and Control Act** prohibits employers from hiring illegal immigrants. Employers must inspect documents to verify the employee's status and complete an **INS Form I-9b** for each employee.

F. Federal Unemployment Tax Act. The **Federal Unemployment Tax Act (FUTA)** sets up a system for collecting tax to be used for the payment of unemployment benefits to persons who are temporarily unemployed.

  1. *Programs Are Run by the States*. Although the system was established by a federal statute, each state runs its own program and sets the rules such as the level of benefits and the eligibility requirements.

  2. *Employer Pays the Tax*. The tax is paid by the employer only. The rate is 6.2 percent of the first $7,000 of wages per year for each covered employee. This rate can be lowered due to credits for state unemployment taxes paid or when the employer experiences a lower than average number of claims made by former employees.

  3. *Participation Requirements*. Employers are required to participate if they meet either of the following requirements:

   a. Quarterly Payroll of at Least $1,500.

   b. Employment of at Least One Person for One Day a Week for 20 Weeks in a Year.

  4. *Business Expense*. Payments made by the employer for unemployment tax are deductible by the employer as an ordinary business expense.

G. Social Security. The **Social Security** system provides retirement and death benefits to certain employees and dependents. The amount of the benefits is limited, but benefits are available in a variety of situations.

1. *Types of Benefits*. Social Security benefits include the following:
   a. Retirement Benefits.
   b. Survivors' Benefits. These are paid to the survivors of covered deceased workers.
   c. Disability Benefits.
   d. Medicare. Medicare pays medical and hospitalization benefits.

2. *Taxation*. Social Security taxes are paid equally by the employer and the employee and have two components. The rate is 6.2 percent of gross wages for the Social Security portion and 1.45 percent for the Medicare portion. Both the employer and employee pay tax at the stated rates. The Social Security portion is paid on wages only up to a ceiling amount. This base amount increases by several thousand dollars each year and is $72,600 for 1999. The Medicare portion is paid on all wages.

3. *Employer Must Withhold*. The employer must withhold the employee's portion and remit both portions to the Internal Revenue Service.

4. *Self-Employed Persons*. The law essentially treats self-employed persons as both employer and employee, thus a self-employed person must pay both halves.
   a. Based on Net Earnings. Self-employed persons pay the taxes on their net earnings from self employment. **Exam tip #5.**
   b. Single Income Limit. The income limit on the Social Security portion of the tax applicable to an employee also applies to a self-employed person. A person with both wages and self-employment income pays the tax first on wages. If the limit has not been reached, she would pay self-employment tax from that point until the limit has been reached.
   c. Example. If John had $40,000 of wages and $50,000 of net self-employment income, he would pay the Social Security portion of the tax on his $40,000 of wages, and only on the portion of the self-employment income until the limit were reached. In 1999, with the $72,600 limit, he would pay the tax on only $32,600 of the self-employment income. All gross wages and net self-employment income is subject to the Medicare portion of the tax.

5. *Not a Savings Plan*. The amounts paid by an employee are not kept in a separate account. Benefits are paid from taxes collected currently. Records of the amounts paid by an employee are maintained in order to determine benefit levels, but they do not represent amounts kept in an individual account for the employee.

6. *Benefits Depend on Earnings Record*. The amount of benefits payable depends on the earnings record of the employee or the employee's spouse. In the case of divorce, a former spouse can use the earnings of the former spouse in determining benefit levels so long as the marriage lasted at least 10 years. Doing so does not affect the benefits received by the former spouse.

EXAM TIPS

1. It is important to understand the general scheme and purpose of workers' compensation. Injured workers can more easily recover with workers' compensation than without it, but the amount recovered will be less than in a regular court system. Covered workers are required to use the workers' compensation claims system, thus the worker does not have the option to sue in a regular court.
2. When reading a question that uses the abbreviation "OSHA," pay attention to whether it refers to the statute or the agency.
3. This general requirement to maintain a safe workplace means that an employer might be liable for a safety violation even though no specific safety standard is violated.
4. Be sure to know that no employer is required to provide a pension plan, but if an employer does provide one, it must comply with the many provisions of ERISA.
5. Note that the tax for an employee is based on **gross** wages while that of a self-employed person is based on **net** self-employment income.

KEY CONCEPTS LIKELY TO BE TESTED ON THE CPA EXAM

1. Workers' compensation provisions.
2. The requirements of the Occupational Safety and Health Act and the powers of the Occupational Safety and Health Administration.
3. The Employee Retirement Income Security Act, including the concept of vesting and the fact that no company is required to provide a pension plan.
4. The Federal Unemployment Tax Act, including the fact that the tax is paid only by the employer.
5. The Social Security System, including how the tax is paid, the benefits that are provided, and the fact that it is not an individual savings system.

KEY TERMS

National Labor Relations Act
Wagner Act
Labor-Management Relations Act
Taft-Hartley Act
Landrum-Griffen Act
Workers' Compensation
Fellow Servant Doctrine
Occupational Safety and Health Act
Occupational Safety and Health Administration

Labor-Management Reporting and Disclosure Act
Fair Labor Standards Act
Employee Retirement Income Security Act
Vesting of Benefits
Consolidated Omnibus Budget Reconciliation Act
Immigration Reform and Control Act
INS Form I-9b
Federal Unemployment Tax Act
Social Security

MULTIPLE CHOICE QUESTIONS

1.   Law May 89 #37
Under the Federal Insurance Contributions Act (FICA) and the Social Security Act (SSA),
A. Persons who are self-employed are **not** required to make FICA contributions.
B. Employees who participate in private retirement plans are **not** required to make FICA contributions.
C. Death benefits are payable to an employee's survivors only if the employee dies before reaching the age of retirement.
D. The receipt of earned income by a person who is also receiving social security retirement benefits may result in a reduction of such benefits.

2.   Law Nov 95 #34
Generally, which of the following statements concerning workers' compensation laws is correct?
A. The amount of damages is based on comparative negligence.
B. Employers are strictly liable without regard to whether or **not** they are at fault.
C. Workers' compensation benefits are **not** available if the employee is negligent.
D. Workers' compensation awards are payable for life.

3.   Law Nov 93 #36
Which one of the following statements concerning workers' compensation laws is generally correct?
A. Employers are strictly liable without regard to whether or **not** they are at fault.
B. Workers' compensation benefits are **not** available if the employee is negligent.
C. Workers' compensation awards are **not** reviewable by the courts.
D. The amount of damages recoverable is based on comparative negligence.

4.   Law May 95 #39
When verifying a client's compliance with statutes governing employees' wages and hours, an auditor should check the client's personnel records against relevant provisions of which of the following statutes?
A. National Labor Relations Act.
B. Fair Labor Standards Act.
C. Taft-Hartley Act.
D. Americans With Disabilities Act.

5.   Law May 95 #40
Under the provisions of the Employee Retirement Income Security Act of 1974 (ERISA), which of the following statements is correct?
A. Employees are entitled to have an employer established pension plan.
B. Employers are prevented from unduly delaying an employee's participation in a pension plan.
C. Employers are prevented from managing retirement plans.
D. Employees are entitled to make investment decisions.

6.   Law Nov 91 #34
Workers' Compensation laws provide for all of the following benefits **except**
A. Burial expenses.
B. Full pay during disability.
C. The cost of prosthetic devices.
D. Monthly payments to surviving dependent children.

7.   Law May 91 #36
Social security benefits may include all of the following **except**
A. Payments to divorced spouses.
B. Payments to disabled children.
C. Medicare payments.
D. Medicaid payments.

8.   Law May 94 #27

Which of the following statements is correct regarding the scope and provisions of the Occupational Safety and Health Act (OSHA)?

A. OSHA requires employers to provide employees a workplace free from risk.
B. OSHA prohibits an employer from discharging an employee for revealing OSHA violations.
C. OSHA may inspect a workplace at any time regardless of employer objection.
D. OSHA preempts state regulation of workplace safety.

9.   Law May 95 #37

Under which of the following conditions is an on-site inspection of a workplace by an investigator from the Occupational Safety and Health Administration (OSHA) permissible?

A. Only if OSHA obtains a search warrant after showing probable cause.
B. Only if the inspection is conducted after working hours.
C. At the request of employees.
D. After OSHA provides the employer with at least 24 hours notice of the prospective inspection.

ESSAY QUESTION (Estimated time -- 6 to 8 minutes)

Law Nov 88 #3

Maple owns 75% of the common stock of Salam Exterminating, Inc. Maple is not an officer or employee of the corporation, and does not serve on its board of directors. Salam is in the business of providing exterminating services to residential and commercial customers.

Dodd performed exterminating services on behalf of Salam. Dodd suffered permanent injuries as a result of inhaling one of the chemicals used by Salam. This occurred after Dodd sprayed the chemical in a restaurant that Salam regularly services. Dodd was under the supervision of one of Salam's district managers and was trained by Salam to perform exterminating services following certain procedures, which he did. Later that day several patrons who ate at the restaurant also suffered permanent injuries as a result of inhaling the chemical. The chemical was manufactured by Ace Chemical Corp. and sold and delivered to Salam in a closed container. It was not altered by Salam. It has now been determined that the chemical was defectively manufactured and the injuries suffered by Dodd and the restaurant patrons were a direct result of the defect.

Salam has complied with an applicable compulsory workers' compensation statute by obtaining an insurance policy form Spear Insurance Co.

As a result of the foregoing, the following actions have been commenced:

- Dodd sued Spear to recover workers' compensation benefits.
- Dodd sued Salam based on negligence in training him.

Required:

Discuss the merits of the actions commenced by Dodd, indicating the likely outcomes and your reasons therefor.

EXPLANATIONS TO MULTIPLE CHOICE QUESTIONS

1. D is the correct answer. Earned income will not reduce benefits for taxpayers over the age of 70. Choice A is incorrect because self-employed persons make their contributions through self-employment tax.

2. B is the correct answer. Choices A and C are incorrect because the negligence of the employee does not reduce or prevent a workers' compensation award.

3. A is the correct answer. Although the employer is considered liable, the award is paid by the workers' compensation carrier. Choice C is incorrect because an award is appealable.

4. B is the correct answer. The Fair Labor Standards Act regulates working hours and wages.

5. B is the correct answer. The correct answer choice refers to the vesting requirements under ERISA. Choice C is incorrect because the employer can be the required designated plan manager.

6. B is the correct answer. Disability payments are based on a portion of the employee's regular pay.

7. D is the correct answer. Medicaid is a state-run program separate from Social Security.

8. B is the correct answer. Choice A is incorrect because it is impossible to eliminate all risk. Choice C is incorrect because OSHA must obtain a search warrant if the employer objects to an inspection.

9. C is the correct answer. Choice A is incorrect because a search warrant is required only if the employer objects to the inspection. Choice B is incorrect because the inspection can be conducted during working hours.

UNOFFICIAL AICPA ANSWER TO ESSAY QUESTION

Law Nov 88 #3

Dodd is entitled to recover workers' compensation benefits from Spear because Dodd was an employee of Salam, the injury was accidental, and the injury occurred out of and in the course of his employement with Salam. Based on the facts of this case, Dodd would be considered an employee and not an independent contractor because Salam had control over the details of Dodd's work by training Dodd to perform the services in a specified manner and Dodd was subject to Salam's supervision.

Dodd will be unsuccessful in his action against Salam based on negligence in training him because Dodd is an employee of Salam and Salam has complied with the applicable compulsory workers' compensation statute by obtaining workers' compensation insurance. Under workers' compensation, an employee who receives workers' compensation benefits cannot successfully maintain an action for negligence against his employer seeking additional compensation. Therefore, whether Salam was negligent in training Dodd is irrelevant.

CHAPTER 26
EQUAL OPPORTUNITY IN EMPLOYMENT

OVERVIEW

This chapter covers the federal statutes passed in order to eliminate discrimination in employment on several bases. The movement against employment discrimination began in the 1960s, with additional statutes passed into the 1990s. The CPA exam has tested this topic in a general manner, with a general knowledge of the statutory provisions being adequate to correctly answer most questions.

OUTLINE

I. **Title VII of the Civil Rights Act of 1964.**
   A. Generally. The **Civil Rights Act of 1964** prohibits discrimination in a number of areas, one of which is employment. **Title VII** is the portion covering discrimination in employment.
   B. Protected Classes. Discrimination is prohibited on the following bases:
      1. *Race.*
      2. *Color.*
      3. *Religion.*
      4. *Sex.*
      5. *National Origin.* **Exam tip #1.**
   C. Parties Subject to Title VII.
      1. *Employers With 15 or More Employees for at Least 20 Weeks in the Current or Preceding Year.*
      2. *All Employment Agencies.*
      3. *Labor Unions With 15 or More Members.*
      4. *State and Local Governments and Their Agencies.*
      5. *Employees in Most Federal Government Employment.*
   D. Prohibited Discrimination. Title VII is violated if any of the protected categories is a factor in an employment decision even if it is not the only factor. It is illegal to discriminate in any of the following:
      1. *Hiring.*
      2. *Firing.*
      3. *Promotion or Demotion.*
      4. *Compensation.*
      5. *Training and Apprenticeship Opportunities.*
      6. *Work Rules.*
      7. *Any Other "Term, Condition, or Privilege" of Employment.*
   E. Forms of Actions. A Title VII case can be brought in either of the following forms:
      1. *Disparate Treatment.* **Disparate treatment** discrimination occurs when an individual is treated less favorably than others on the basis of race, color, religion, sex, or national origin. The plaintiff has a claim if membership in the protected class was a factor in the unfavorable decision, even if not the only factor.

2. *Disparate Impact.* **Disparate impact** discrimination occurs when an employer discriminates against an entire protected class. Disparate impact discrimination can occur when rules or policies which appear to be neutral on their face have a discriminatory impact. For example, if an airline adopted a rule that flight attendants could be no taller than five feet, six inches, the rule would have a disparate impact on male applicants even though the rule was applied in the same manner to men and women.

E. Equal Employment Opportunity Commission. The **Equal Employment Opportunity Commission (EEOC)** is a federal agency responsible for enforcing most federal antidiscrimination laws. A party must first file a Title VII complaint with the EEOC, which the EEOC will review. The EEOC might choose to sue the employer on the complainant's behalf; otherwise the EEOC will issue the complainant a **right to sue letter** which allows the complainant to file the suit in a regular court.

F. Remedies. Plaintiffs can recover up to two years back pay and attorneys' fees. There are caps on the allowable recovery based on the number of employees in a company. The caps range from $50,000 for small companies to $300,000 for those with more than 500 employees. The courts can also grant various equitable remedies including reinstatement or the granting of fictional seniority.

G. Pregnancy Discrimination Act. The **Pregnancy Discrimination Act** is an amendment to Title VII which prohibits discrimination on the basis of pregnancy, childbirth, or related conditions. Basing a decision on a woman's childbearing status or plans is a violation.

H. Sexual Harassment. Because Title VII prohibits discrimination in any conditions of employment, **sexual harassment** is considered sex discrimination. Such conduct is more offensive to one gender (usually, but not always, women) than the other, thus creating different working conditions based on gender. There are two general types of sexual harassment.

1. *Quid Pro Quo.* **Quid pro quo** sexual harassment usually involves a sexual favor in exchange for something else, such as a job or promotion.

2. *Hostile Work Environment.* **Hostile work environment** sexual harassment is much more subjective and involves circumstances that make the workplace uncomfortable for members of one gender or another. The display of lewd photographs, frequent telling of offensive jokes, or employees repeatedly making unwanted sexual advances can all create a hostile work environment. The employer has a duty to take reasonable steps to prevent a hostile work environment, and should usually include an effective system to handle sexual harassment complaints.

I. Defenses to a Title VII Action. There are three primary defenses to a Title VII action.

1. *Merit.* Merit, such as typing ability, or the level of sales generated, can be used as a criteria. Merit can be used for hiring decisions as well as promotion decisions.

2. *Seniority.* A seniority system generally can be used to determine pay, promotion, or other conditions of employment for existing employees.

3. *Bona Fide Occupational Qualification.* A **bona fide occupational qualification** is any discrimination based on membership in a protected class that is job-related and a business necessity. Thus a church can hire a pastor based on membership in the religion of the church. This defense can never apply to race or color. **Exam tip #2.**

II. Equal Pay Act of 1963.

A. Generally. The **Equal Pay Act** prohibits disparate pay based on gender for jobs that require equal skill, equal effort, or equal responsibility, or that have similar working conditions.

B. Parties Protected By the Act. All private sector employees and employees of state and local government are covered by the Act. Federal employees are not covered.

B. Determination of Whether Jobs Are Equal. The court determines if two jobs are equal or similar, which is often a difficult task. If they are considered to be equal, the employer cannot pay different amounts based on gender.

C. Remedies. Successful plaintiffs can recover back pay and liquidated damages. The employer must raise the pay of the plaintiff, and cannot lower other wages to equalize them.

D. Acceptable Criteria. The Equal Pay Act identifies four criteria allowing a difference in pay:
1. *Seniority.*
2. *Merit.*
3. *Quantity or Quality of Production.*
4. *Any Factor Other Than Sex.* **Exam tip #3.**

III.   Age Discrimination in Employment Act of 1967.

A. Generally. The **Age Discrimination in Employment Act** protects certain persons against discrimination based on their age.

B. Parties Subject to the Act. The Act applies to:
1. *Nonfederal Employers With at Least 20 Nonseasonal Employees,*
2. *Labor Unions With at Least 25 Members,*
3. *All Employment Agencies.*
4. *Certain Employees of State and Local Governments.*
5. *Employees of Certain Sectors of the Federal Government.*

C. Protects Workers Age 40 and Over. The Act protects all workers of age 40 and over, and provides no protection to workers under age 40. This effectively prohibits most mandatory retirement age policies. Discrimination against those in their forties in favor of those in theirs fifties would be illegal. **Exam tip #4.**

D. Exceptions. Mandatory retirement ages are allowable in certain professions, such as for airline pilots. Employees can always be forced to retire if they are no longer able to perform the functions of their job.

E. Remedies. Successful plaintiffs can recover back pay, attorneys' fees, and equitable relief such as hiring, reinstatement, or promotion.

IV.   Americans With Disabilities Act of 1990.

A. Generally. The **Americans With Disabilities Act (ADA)** protects discrimination based on an individual's disabilities. In addition to employment, the ADA places duties on providers of public transportation, telecommunications, and public accommodations. The ADA contains many vague and general provisions which must be interpreted by the courts.

B. Parties Subject to the ADA Employment Provisions. The employment provisions of the ADA apply to companies with 15 or more employees. These provisions do not apply to the federal government, to corporations owned by the federal government, or to qualified tax-exempt private clubs.

C. Prohibited Discrimination. Qualified individuals with disabilities cannot be discriminated against in job application procedures, hiring, compensation, training, promotion, or termination.

D. Reasonable Accommodation. An employer is required to make **reasonable accommodations** in order to enable a qualified disabled person to perform a job. For example, the employer might be required to purchase special computer equipment for a visually-impaired employee. The type and cost of what is considered to be a reasonable accommodation is decided on a case by case basis. Thus, an expenditure that might be considered reasonable (and thus required) for a large employer might not be required of a small employer.

E. Definition of Disability. A person is considered disabled if he has:

   1. *A Physical or Mental Impairment That Limits a Major Life Activity,*
   2. *A Record of Such an Impairment,* or
   3. *Is Regarded as Having Such an Impairment.*

   This is a broad definition which covers numerous conditions such as epilepsy, cancer, infection with HIV, mental retardation, to name a few. Past alcohol and drug abusers are covered, but current abusers are not. **Exam tip #5.**

F. Interview Inquiries. Employers are prohibited from asking about disabilities during interviewing or in any other inquiry prior to making a job offer. A medical exam can be required after an offer has been extended so long as they are required of all employees.

G. Remedies. The procedures under the ADA are similar to those under Title VII. Plaintiffs can recover back pay and attorneys' fees. They can also obtain equitable relief such as hiring, reinstatement, promotion, or an order that the employer provide an accommodation.

V. Family and Medical Leave Act of 1993.

A. Generally. The **Family and Medical Leave Act** gives workers the right to unpaid time off from work for certain illnesses or medical emergencies. **Exam tip #6.**

B. Parties Subject to the Act. The Act applies to companies of 50 or more employees as well as federal, state, and local governments.

C. Eligible Employees. Employees must have been employed at least one year and have worked at least 1,250 hours in the preceding 12-month period to qualify.

D. Up to 12 Weeks Unpaid Leave. An eligible employee can take up to 12 weeks leave without pay each year. The leave does not need to be taken all at once.

E. Purposes of Leave. The following reasons justify leave:

   1. *Birth, and Care of, a Child.*
   2. *Placement of a Child for Adoption or Foster Care.*
   3. *Serious Health Condition Causing an Inability of the Employee to Perform the Job.*
   4. *Care for a Spouse, Child, or Parent With a Serious Health Problem.*

F. Protections. Upon returning, the employee must be returned to the same or a similar position with equivalent pay. The employee is not entitled to accrue seniority while on leave.

G. Exceptions. The employer need not return the employee to the same or a similar position if:

   1. *The Employee Is Among the Highest-Paid 10 Percent of That Employer's Employees,* or
   2. *Restoring the Employee Would Cause Substantial and Grievous Injury to the Employer.*

EXAM TIPS

1. Be sure to know which categories are protected under Title VII. Note that sexual preference is not a protected category.
2. These defenses might be present in a factual situation question. Candidates must be prepared to recognize their existence.
3. Note that these defenses are slightly different than those under Title VII. Be sure you know the differences. Also, remember that the Equal Pay Act protects against gender-based discrimination only.
4. In a sense, because only workers aged 40 and over are covered, the Age Discrimination in Employment Act, itself, discriminates. Any type of age discrimination against persons 40 and over is prohibited, and all age discrimination against those under 40 is allowable.
5. The definition of a disability is very broad. Courts continue to determine which situations and conditions qualify and which do not.
6. Be sure to know that the leave required under the Family and Medical Leave Act is unpaid.

KEY CONCEPTS LIKELY TO BE TESTED ON THE CPA EXAM

1. The types of discrimination prohibited by each act.
2. The remedies available under each of the acts.
3. Any defenses to a claim brought under each of the acts.
4. Which employers must comply with each act.
5. The parties protected under each act.

KEY TERMS

Civil Rights Act of 1964
Title VII
Disparate Treatment
Disparate Impact
Equal Employment Opportunity Commission
Right to Sue Letter
Pregnancy Discrimination Act
Sexual Harassment

Quid Pro Quo
Hostile Work Environment
Bona Fide Occupational Qualification
Equal Pay Act
Age Discrimination in Employment Act
Americans With Disabilities Act
Reasonable Accommodation
Family and Medical Leave Act

MULTIPLE CHOICE QUESTIONS

1.   Law Nov 95 #36

Which of the following Acts prohibit(s) an employer from discriminating among employees based on sex?

	Equal Pay Act	*Title VII of the Civil Rights Act*
A.	Yes	Yes
B.	Yes	No
C.	No	Yes
D.	No	No

2.   Law May 95 #38

Under the provisions of the Americans With Disabilities Act of 1990, in which of the following areas is a disabled person protected from discrimination?

	Public transportation	*Privately operated public accommodations*
A.	Yes	Yes
B.	Yes	No
C.	No	Yes
D.	No	No

3.   Law Nov 94 #38

Under the Federal Age Discrimination in Employment Act, which of the following practices would be prohibited?

	Compulsory retirement of employees below the age of 65	*Termination of employees between the ages of 65 and 70 for cause*
A.	Yes	Yes
B.	Yes	No
C.	No	Yes
D.	No	No

4.   Law May 94 #28

Under Title VII of the 1964 Civil Rights Act, which of the following forms of discrimination is **not** prohibited?
A. Sex.
B. Age.
C. Race.
D. Religion.

5.   Author

Which of the following is true about the Family and Medical Leave Act?
A. Covered employees are entitled to receive up to 12 weeks of leave with pay per year.
B. Covered employees are entitled to accrue seniority while on leave.
C. Leave is available for the placement of a child for adoption.
D. Leave is available for the care of a grandchild with a serious health problem.

6.   Author

Which of the following statements is true about the Americans With Disabilities Act?
A. A potential employer is required to ask applicants about any disabilities so that the employer will be able to provide any necessary accommodations.
B. An employee who is regarded as having a disability is not protected unless the employee has an actual disability.
C. One employer might be required to provide a particular accommodation even though another employer might not be required to provide the same accommodation.
D. Past alcohol abuse is not protected under the ADA.

7.   Law R96 #14
Under the federal Age Discrimination in Employment Act, which of the following practices is prohibited?
A. Termination of employees between the ages of 65 and 70 for cause.
B. Mandatory retirement of any employee.
C. Unintentional age discrimination.
D. Termination of employees as part of a rational business decision.

8.   Law Nov 95 #35
Under the Age Discrimination in Employment Act, which of the following remedies is (are) available to a covered employee?

	Early retirement	*Back pay*
A.	Yes	Yes
B.	Yes	No
C.	No	Yes
D.	No	No

OTHER OBJECTIVE FORMAT QUESTION

Author

For each of the following statements, choose the appropriate item or items from List I and blacken the corresponding oval on the objective answer sheet. An item in the list may be used once, more than once, or not at all. Each question can have more than one answer.

List I
A. Civil Rights Act of 1964 (Title VII)
B. Equal Pay Act.
C. Age Discrimination in Employment Act.
D. Americans With Disabilities Act.
E. Family and Medical Leave Act.
F. The statement applies to none of the acts listed above.

1. Employers are required to provide paid leave in connection with the birth of a child of the employee.

2. Discrimination on the basis of the state of residence is prohibited.

3. Discrimination on the basis of past alcohol abuse is prohibited.

4. No federal government employees are subject to the Act.

5. An employee is entitled to recover back pay based on improper discrimination.

6. An employee must work for the employer for more than one year in order to be protected by the Act.

7. A private sector employer with 40 employees is covered by the Act.

8. The Pregnancy Discrimination Act is an amendment to this Act.

ANSWERS TO MULTIPLE CHOICE QUESTIONS

1. A is the correct answer. Gender is the only basis of protection under the Equal Pay Act.

2. A is the correct answer. Protection under the ADA extends beyond employment discrimination.

3. B is the correct answer. Termination of employees for cause is always permissible.

4. B is the correct answer. Discrimination based on age is covered under a different act. Notice that the candidate must know which discrimination basis is protected by which statute.

5. C is the correct answer. Choice A is incorrect because the required available leave is without pay.

6. C is the correct answer. What amounts to a reasonable accommodation will depend on the circumstances, such as financial resources, of each employer. Choice A is incorrect because the potential employer is prohibited from asking these questions during the interview process. The employer can learn of this information after the employee has been offered a job. Choice B is incorrect because merely being regarded as having an impairment qualifies one for protection.

7. C is the correct answer. Age discrimination, as well as other types of discrimination, is a violation whether or not the discrimination was intentional. Choice B is incorrect because mandatory retirement is acceptable in some circumstances, such as with airline pilots.

8. C is the correct answer.

EXPLANATION TO OTHER OBJECTIVE FORMAT QUESTION

1. Choice F is correct. The leave required under the Family and Medical Leave Act is unpaid.

2. Choice F is correct. No statute provides protection on the basis of the state of residence.

3. Choice D is correct. The Americans With Disabilities Act provides protection based on past alcohol abuse. Protection is not provided for current alcohol abuse.

4. Choices B and D are correct. Both the Equal Pay Act and the Americans With Disabilities Act specifically exempt the federal government from coverage.

5. Choices A, B, C, and D are correct. Back pay is recoverable under all four of these acts.

6. Choice E is correct. The Family and Medical Leave Act requires that leave be provided only if the employee has been employed for more than a year and has worked at least 1,250 hours in the preceding 12-month period. The other antidiscrimination statutes protect persons from discrimination even if they are not yet employed.

7. Choices A, B, C, and D are correct. Only employers with 50 or more employees are covered under the Family and Medical Leave Act. The other acts all have limits less than 40.

8. Choice A is correct. The Family and Medical Leave Act is an amendment to Title VII of the Civil Rights Act of 1964.

CHAPTER 27
PERSONAL PROPERTY AND BAILMENTS

OVERVIEW

This chapter addresses personal property and the related topics of bailments, documents of title, and computer technology rights. A bailment exists when personal property is in the possession of someone other than the owner. Documents of title determine who has ownership of personal property which is in the hands of a common carrier or public warehouse. They give directions to the party holding the goods, and operate in many ways like negotiable instruments. The last part of this chapter relates to a specific type of personal property, computer technology rights, which has recently begun to be tested on the CPA exam. A portion of the material in this last section is based on material in Chapter 5 of *Contemporary Business Law*.

OUTLINE

I. The Nature of Personal Property.
   A. Property Classification. All property can be classified as real or personal property.
      1. *Real Property.* **Real property** includes land and the property permanently attached to it. This would include buildings and trees. Note that it is possible to remove many of the items considered permanently attached. A tree can be cut down, and a building can be demolished and removed.
      2. *Personal Property.* **Personal property** includes all property that is not real property. Property, including personal property, can be further classified. **Exam tip #1.**
         a. Tangible Personal Property. **Tangible personal property** is property that is physically defined, or can be touched.
         b. Intangible Personal Property. **Intangible personal property** is property that cannot be reduced to physical form. It includes stock in a corporation, bonds, patents, copyrights, and contract rights. **Exam tip #2.**
   B. Character Can Change. Property can change from one classification to the other. A tree is real property while growing, becomes personal property when cut down and cut into lumber, becomes real property again if the lumber is used in building a house, and would become personal property if the house became a pile of rubble in a tornado.
   C. Fixtures. A **fixture** is an item of property which was previously personal property but has become attached to real property in such a way that it has become part of the real property. Many factors are considered in whether an item has become a fixture. **Exam tip #3.**
      1. *Intent of the Party Who Attached the Property.* This is often the most important factor. This often depends on the person who attached the item. For example, a shelf attached by a landlord to a wall is more likely intended to become part of the real property than an identical shelf attached by a tenant.
      2. *Method of Attachment.* The more permanent the form of attachment, the more likely the item will be considered a fixture. This test is often applied by determining whether the building would be damaged by the item's removal. The more damage that would result, the more likely the item is a fixture.

3. *Purpose or Use of Personal Property.* The more that the item is designed or used specifically for the particular building, the more likely that it is a fixture.

4. *Examples.* A central air conditioning unit is usually a fixture, while a window unit is not. A window unit that is mounted through a hole in the building's wall could either be fixture or not, depending on the analysis of these factors.

5. *Implications.* A sale of real property includes all fixtures unless specifically excluded. Parties to a contract for the sale of real property should specify whether any items that might be considered fixtures are part of the sale. Fixtures can be an issue when a will leaves all real property to one party and all personal property to another. It can also be an issue with property tax where the assessment is based on the value of the real property.

II. Acquiring Ownership in Personal Property.

A. Capture. Property can be acquired by **capturing** or **taking possession** of it. This applies to unowned property such as wild animals, and was far more common in the early days of the nation. This can occur today while legally hunting or fishing.

B. Purchase. As part of the **purchase** transaction, ownership is transferred to the purchaser.

C. Production. **Production** of property results in ownership of the finished product.

D. Gift. A **gift** is a voluntary transfer of property without consideration from a **donor** to a **donee**. There are three requirements for a valid completed gift:

1. *Donative Intent.* The donor must have intended to make the gift. The **donative intent** can be inferred from the language or circumstances surrounding the gift.

2. *Delivery.* There must be **delivery** for the gift to be valid. Where there is not **physical delivery**, this requirement can be met by **constructive**, or **symbolic, delivery**. For example, where the gift is a bicycle which is locked to a rack, delivery of the key to the lock is constructive delivery of the bicycle.

3. *Acceptance.* Acceptance is usually presumed, but the gift is not effective if the donee does not want the gift. **Exam tip #4.**

E. Gifts *Inter Vivos* and *Causa Mortis*. An **inter vivos** gift is one made during life without the contemplation of death. A **gift** *causa mortis* is a gift made in contemplation of death. The gift is conditional on the donor dying, thus if the donor survives, the donor can recover the gift. If the donor dies, and the three requirements for a valid gift are met, the gift is valid. If there is a valid gift *cause mortis*, it takes precedence over any provision in a will purporting to dispose of the property. This is because the property no longer belonged to the decedent at the time of death.

F. Will or Inheritance. Property can be acquired by **will** or by **inheritance** under the state's intestate succession laws for decedents dying without a will.

G. Accession. **Accession** is an increase in property such as the offspring of live animals or an improvement to personal property.

H. Confusion. Where fungible goods (items such as wheat or oil which are interchangeable) are commingled, one has a right to a pro rata share of the commingled goods. This can result in acquiring ownership to goods that were previously owned by another.

I. Divorce. Property can be acquired as part of a divorce decree.

III.   Mislaid, Lost, and Abandoned Property.

A. <u>Mislaid Property</u>. **Mislaid property** is property which was intentionally placed somewhere, but which the owner has forgotten. The owner of the premises, and not the finder, is entitled to possess it. This is based on the assumption that the owner is likely to remember it and return to the premises to seek its return.

B. <u>Lost Property</u>. **Lost property** is property which somehow accidentally came to be in the place where it is found. It might have fallen or been dropped off a truck. Lost property was never intentionally placed in the location where it was found. The finder of lost property is entitled to keep it and has title against everyone except the true owner.

C. <u>Abandoned Property</u>. The finder of **abandoned property** acquires title against the entire world, including the party who abandoned the property.

D. <u>Estray Statutes</u>. **Estray statutes** provide that if the finder of property takes certain steps, such as turning it over to the appropriate agency, the finder will obtain good title if the original owner does not claim it within a certain period of time. Such statutes encourage the finder to turn over property to the authorities because good title, even against the original owner, can eventually be obtained.

IV.   Bailments.

A. <u>Generally</u>. A **bailment** is an arrangement where personal property is in the possession of someone other than its owner. The owner of the property is the **bailor** who gives possession to the **bailee**. A borrowed lawn mower, the use of a rental car, or a car at a repair shop are all examples of bailments.

B. <u>Requirements</u>. Three elements are necessary for a bailment.

   1. *Personal Property.* Only personal property can be the subject of a bailment. It can be either tangible or intangible.

   2. *Delivery of Possession.* Delivery of possession requires that
      a. The Bailee Have Exclusive Possession.
      b. The Bailee Knowingly Accept the Property.

   3. *Bailment Agreement.* There must be an agreement, but it can be either express or implied. The bailment can be for a fixed term, which terminates at the end of the term, or can be at will, which can be terminated at any time by either party. **Exam tip #5.**

C. <u>Duty of Care</u>. Traditionally, bailments were classified in three categories based on which party derived benefit from the bailment. This determined the bailee's duty of care.

   1. *Sole Benefit of the Bailor -- Slight Care.* This arises where the bailee cares for the bailed property as a favor for the bailor. For example, a friend agrees to store a bike for the winter for his neighbor who has no garage. The bailee is receiving no benefit from the bailment and therefore owes only a **duty of slight care.**

   2. *Sole Benefit of Bailee -- Utmost Care.* This arises where the bailor lends the bailed property to the bailee as a favor for the bailee. For example, a neighbor borrowing a lawnmower to cut his lawn results in a bailment for the sole benefit of the bailee. The bailee is receiving the sole benefit of using the bailor's property and thus owes a **duty of utmost**, or **great, care.**

3. *Mutual Benefit -- Reasonable Care.* Where a bailment is for the benefit of both parties, the bailee owes a **duty of ordinary**, or **reasonable**, **care**. Most bailments involving a payment are mutual benefit bailments. A customer's computer at a repair shop and a rental car arrangement are both examples of mutual benefit bailments.

4. *Modern Trend -- Reasonable Care in All Cases.* The modern trend in many states is to impose a duty of reasonable care in light of all the facts and circumstances, with the type of bailment being one of the facts and circumstances.

D. Bailee's Duty to Return Goods. These duties to care for the bailed goods exist because the bailee's basic duty is a **duty to return the bailed goods** in accordance with the contract.

E. Bailee's Rights. A bailee has rights according to the terms of the bailment contract. The bailee usually has the right to exclusive possession of the bailed goods. The bailee also might have the right to use the bailed property, and might be entitled to compensation for work done or services provided.

F. Bailor's Duties. A bailor can have the following duties, depending upon the bailment agreement's terms:
1. *Duty to Pay Any Agreed Upon Compensation.*
2. *Not Interfere With the Bailee's Possession.*
3. *Notify the Bailee of Defects or Conditions in the Bailed Property That Could Cause Injury.*

G. Common Carriers. A **common carrier** is a party who offers transportation services to the general public and is a type of special bailee.
1. *Parties.* The parties in a common carrier bailment are
   a. Shipper. The **shipper** is the party whose goods are being transported. The shipper is the bailor and is also known as the **consignor. Exam tip #6.**
   b. Common Carrier. The transportation company is the common carrier, who is the bailee. The common carrier is also known as the **consignee.**
2. *Strict Liability.* A common carrier has a **duty of strict liability** to return or deliver the goods in the same condition as they were received. This is an even higher duty than the duty of utmost care.
3. *Exceptions to Strict Liability.* A common carrier is not responsible for losses caused by:
   a. Acts of God. Earthquakes or floods are examples.
   b. Acts of a Public Enemy.
   c. Government Orders.
   d. Acts of the Shipper. Improperly packing the goods is the most common example.
   e. The Inherent Nature of the Goods. Perishability is an example.
4. *Limitation of Liability Is Acceptable.* A common carrier is permitted to limit liability to a specified dollar amount in the contract.

H. Warehouses. Public warehouses store goods for a fee, and thus are considered to be in bailments for mutual benefit. They owe a duty of reasonable care, but can limit their liability to a specified dollar amount in the bailment contract.

I. Innkeepers. Under common law, innkeepers were strictly liable for losses to the property of guests. Almost all states have passed statutes to override the common law rule and limit the liability of innkeepers for the property of guests.

V. Documents of Title.

A. <u>Generally</u>. **Documents of title** are used to transfer title to goods which are in the hands of a common carrier or public warehouse. In such circumstances, the identity of the bailor can change while the goods are in the hands of the warehouse or common carrier. Documents of title provide a convenient way to transfer title to goods when the goods are in someone else's possession, and allow warehouses and common carriers to know who is entitled to receive goods. There are two primary types of documents of title. Negotiable instruments can be used to conveniently transfer money which is located somewhere else (in a bank) while documents of title can be used to conveniently transfer title to goods which are located in a warehouse or in the hands of a common carrier.

B. <u>Warehouse Receipts</u>.

1. *Definition*. A **warehouse receipt** is a written document issued by a person who is in the business of storing goods for hire. The warehouse receipt then serves as proof of who is entitled to receive the goods from the warehouse.

2. *Form and Requirements*. A warehouse receipt need not be in any particular form, but must include the following:

a. The Location of the Goods.

b. The Date of Issue.

c. The Consecutive Number of the Receipt.

d. A Statement of To Whom the Goods Are To Be Delivered. They can be deliverable (1) to bearer, (2) to a specified person or his order, or (3) to a specified person. If deliverable only to a specified person as in this third alternative, the warehouse receipt is nonnegotiable. It is nonetheless a warehouse receipt.

e. The Rate of Storage and Handling Charges.

f. The Signature of the Warehouseman or Agent.

g. A Description of the Goods or the Packages Containing Them.

h. If the Warehouseman Has Any Ownership Interest in the Goods, a Statement Describing it.

I. A Description of Any Advances Made by the Warehouseman for Which the Warehouseman Claims a Lien or Security Interest.

The warehouseman is liable for any loss caused by the omission of these terms. The warehouse receipt can contain any other terms not contrary to the warehouseman's duty to deliver the goods or the Uniform Commercial Code.

3. *Warehouseman's Lien*. A warehouseman acquires a lien for the necessary expenses incurred in storing and handling the goods.

C. <u>Bills of Lading</u>.

1. *Definition*. A **bill of lading** is a written document issued by a common carrier when goods are received for shipping and gives delivery instructions for the goods.

2. *Form and Requirements*. A bill of lading must include the following:

a. A Description of the Goods or the Packages Containing Them.

b. The Destination to Which the Goods Are Being Shipped.

c. The Identity of the Party From Whom the Goods Were Received.

d. The Identity of the Person To Whom, or To Whose Order, the Goods Will Be Delivered.

D. <u>Negotiability</u>. There is only one special requirement of a document of title in order for it to be negotiable. It must state that the goods are deliverable "to bearer" or to "the order of a named person" on demand or at a specified time. Some examples:
1. *"To Bearer."* Negotiable.
2. *"To Jane Doe or Her Order."* Negotiable.
3. *"To the Order of Jane Doe."* Negotiable.
4. *"To Jane Doe."* Nonnegotiable. This does not contain the required words.

E. <u>Negotiation</u>. **Negotiation** of a document of title is similar to that for a negotiable instrument.
1. *Bearer Paper.* If the document is payable to bearer or the last endorsement is a blank endorsement, negotiation merely requires delivery.
2. *Order Paper.* If the document is payable to the order of a specific person, or the last endorsement names a specific person, negotiation requires endorsement and delivery.
3. *Nonnegotiable Documents.* Nonnegotiable documents cannot be negotiated. They can be transferred, but such a transfer is an **assignment**. The assignee can receive no greater rights than the assignor.

F. <u>Due Negotiation</u>. A document of title is **duly negotiated** when it is negotiated to a holder who takes it
1. *In Good Faith,*
2. *In the Ordinary Course of Business,*
3. *Without Notice of a Defense,* and
4. *By Paying Value.* Unlike with becoming a holder in due course of a negotiable instrument, taking a document of title in settlement of a preexisting obligation does not meet the "paying value" requirement.

The concept of due negotiation is similar to that of becoming a holder in due course of a negotiable instrument. The party meeting these requirements is a **holder by due negotiation**.

G. <u>Rights Acquired by a Holder By Due Negotiation</u>.
1. *Title to the Document.*
2. *Title to the Goods.*
3. *All Rights Accruing Under the Law of Agency or Estoppel.*
4. *Right to the Issuer's Obligation With Respect to the Goods.* This is usually either the delivery of the goods or their storage.

H. <u>Real and Personal Defenses</u>. A holder by due negotiation has a right to the goods free of any personal defenses, but is subject to real defenses, just as a holder in due course.

I. <u>Stolen Goods</u>. Where a document of title is issued for stolen goods, even a holder by due negotiation must surrender the goods to the true owner from whom the goods were stolen.

J. <u>Assignment</u>. If the requirements of due negotiation are not met, or if the document transferred is nonnegotiable, the transferee is merely an assignee, and acquires no greater rights to the instrument and goods than those of the transferor.

K. <u>Transfer Warranties</u>. The transferor of a document of title makes the following warranties:
1. *The Document is Genuine,*
2. *The Transferor Has No Knowledge of Any Fact That Would Impair Its Validity or Worth,* and
3. *The Negotiation or Transfer Is Rightful and Effective With Respect to Both the Document and the Related Goods.*

V. Computer Technology Rights.

  A. Generally. The law with respect to computer technology rights is based on traditional intellectual property law supplemented with recent federal statutes. Intellectual property law, other than the law of trade secrets, is generally federal law. **Exam tip #7.**

  B. Trade Secrets. A **trade secret** is any formula, pattern, design, compilation of data, customer list or, other business secret which gives the business an advantage over its competitors.

   1. *Obligation to Protect.* The owner of a trade secret has a duty to take all reasonable precautions to prevent its discovery by others. Hiring of security guards and limiting access to facilities are examples. Methods applicable to computer software include:

      a. Licensing and Prohibiting Copying.

      b. Selling of Software in Object Code.

      c. Confidentiality (Nondisclosure) Agreements.

   2. *Protection for Improper Discovery.* Trades secrets are generally protected only from improper discovery. Discovery by disassembling a product is acceptable.

   3. *Remedies.* A successful plaintiff who has had a trade secret stolen can recover:

      a. Profits of the Defendant From the Secret,

      b. Damages, and

      c. Injunctive Relief. This might be an order prohibiting the defendant from using or selling the secret.

  C. Patents. **Patents** are protected rights with respect to machines, processes, compositions of matter, improvements to existing machines, processes or compositions of matter, designs, and genetically engineered plants and animals.

   1. *Ideas Not Patentable.* A mere idea cannot be patented.

   2. *Requirements.* A patent must be:

      a. Novel,

      b. Useful, and

      C. Nonobvious.

   3. *Twenty-Year Protection.* A patent is protected for 20 years, except for design patents, which are protected for 14 years. A design patent relates to appearance rather than function.

   4. *Computer Programs.* Recently, computer programs have been found to be patentable. Previously they were thought to be unpatentable ideas, although usually copyrightable.

   5. *Public Use Doctrine.* If the item has been in use by the public for more than one year before the patent is applied for, the patent will be denied.

   6. *Remedies.* A successful plaintiff in a patent infringement suit can recover damages, obtain an order to destroy the infringing items, and obtain injunctive relief.

  D. Copyrights. **Copyrights** protect original creative works. Any original work is protected. Protection is automatic, thus the copyright notice is no longer required in order to obtain protection.

   1. *Writing.* Copyright law protects "writings," but that term has been broadly interpreted to include almost any form of creative work.

   2. *Period of Protection.*

      a. Individuals. A copyright of an individual lasts until 50 years after the author's death.

      b. Corporations. A copyright of a corporation lasts until 100 years after creation or 75 years after publication, whichever is shorter.

3. *Fair Use Doctrine.* Limited use of copyrighted material is allowable. For example, portions of a work can be copied and distributed for teaching and other purposes.

4. *Computer Programs.* Computer programs can generally be copyrighted.

5. *Remedies.* A successful plaintiff in a copyright infringement suit can recover damages, including lost profits, and can obtain injunctive relief.

E. Trademarks. **Trademarks** protect a party's name, packaging, distinctive graphics and help prevent consumers from being confused about the origin of a good. Service marks are similar to trademarks but relate to services.

1. *Distinctive.* Marks must be distinctive in order to be protected, such as "Exxon."

2. *Secondary Meaning.* An ordinary word can receive protection if it has acquired a secondary meaning, such as "Mustang" has for Ford Motor Co.

3. *No Protection for Ordinary Words.* Absent obtaining a secondary meaning, ordinary words like "shoes" or "milk" cannot be protected.

4. *Period of Protection.* A trademark is protected for 10 years, and can be renewed for an unlimited number of 10-year periods.

5. *Lost Protection If Mark Becomes Generic.* When a trademark becomes used as a generic term, the trademark protection can be lost. For example, kerosene was once a trademarked product name, but the term is now generic.

6. *Remedies.* A plaintiff must prove that the infringer's similar mark was likely to cause confusion, mistake, or deception among the public as to the origin of goods or services. A successful plaintiff can recover damages, including lost profits. A plaintiff can also obtain an order to destroy any infringing goods and can obtain injunctive relief.

F. Computer Software Copyright Act. The **Computer Software Copyright Act** specifically includes computer programs among the copyrightable items and broadly defines a computer program to be "a set of statements or instructions to be used directly or indirectly in a computer in order to bring about a certain result."

G. Semiconductor Chip Protection Act of 1984. The **Semiconductor Chip Protection Act** expands protections for the hardware components of a computer. Computer chips cannot be disassembled in order to copy them, but disassembly is permitted if the purpose is to create a chip of a new design. This modifies trade secret law applicable to chips. The Act also protects the **mask**, or original software program, used in creating a computer chip.

EXAM TIPS

1. Note that personal property is defined in the negative as everything that is <u>not</u> real property.

2. Note that items such as stock certificates and airline tickets are intangible property. Even though there is a physical form of the certificate or ticket which can be touched, those forms simply represent the actual property. The actual property is the fractional ownership of the corporation or the contract right to passage on a future airline flight.

3. Fixtures are heavily tested on the exam, especially the factors in determining if an item has become a fixture.

4. Do not confuse the requirements for a valid completed gift with the contract law principle that a court will not enforce a promise to make a gift. A promise to make a gift will not be enforced, but if all three requirements for a valid completed gift have been met, the court will not undo the gift, and the donee will be entitled to keep the item. If there has been a promise to make a gift but all the requirements for a completed gift have not been met, the court will not enforce the gift, and the property will remain the property of the donor.

5. Many candidates have never heard the term "bailment" prior to studying for the CPA exam. Candidates should know the requirements of a bailment and realize the large number of circumstances where bailments exist.

6. Note that the person who sends the goods is the shipper. The shipper is not the transportation company.

7. Testing of computer technology rights is new to the CPA exam, thus it is unclear what areas the examiners will focus on.

KEY CONCEPTS LIKELY TO BE TESTED ON THE CPA EXAM

1. Identification of property type, such as real or personal, tangible or intangible.
2. Fixtures, including the factors in determining if an item is a fixture.
3. Bailment requirements and duties.
4. The strict liability of a common carrier and the exceptions to strict liability.
5. General characteristics and types of documents of title.
6. The requirements to duly negotiate a document of title.

KEY TERMS

Real Property	Inheritance	Shipper
Personal Property	Accession	Consignor
Tangible Property	Mislaid Property	Consignee
Intangible Property	Lost Property	Duty of Strict Liability
Fixture	Abandoned Property	Document of Title
Capture of Property	Estray Statutes	Warehouse Receipt
Purchase of Property	Bailment	Bill of Lading
Production of Property	Bailor	Assignment
Gift	Bailee	Due Negotiation
Donor	Duty of Slight Care	Trade Secret
Donee	Duty of Great Care	Patent
Donative Intent	Duty of Reasonable Care	Copyright
Physical Delivery	Duty to Return Goods	Trademark
Constructive Delivery	Common Carrier	Computer Chip Mask
Inter Vivos Gift	Computer Software Copyright Act	
Gift *Causa Mortis*	Semiconductor Chip Protection Act	
Will		

MULTIPLE CHOICE QUESTIONS

1.   Law R96 #9
Which of the following rights is(are) considered intangible personal property?

	An easement	A contract right
A.	Yes	Yes
B.	Yes	No
C.	No	Yes
D.	No	No

2.   Law Nov 95 #56
Which of the following factors help determine whether an item of personal property is a fixture?

I. Degree of the item's attachment to the property.
II. Intent of the person who had the item installed.

A. I only.
B. II only.
C. Both I and II.
D. Neither I nor II.

3.   Law May 94 #60
Which of the following requirements must be met to create a bailment?

I. Delivery of personal property to the intended bailee.
II. Possession by the intended bailee.
III. An absolute duty on the intended bailee to return or dispose of the property according to the bailor's directions.

A. I and II only.
B. I and III only.
C. II and III only.
D. I, II, and III.

4.   Law Nov 95 #58
Which of the following methods of obtaining personal property will give the recipient ownership of the property?

	Lease	Finding abandoned property
A.	Yes	Yes
B.	Yes	No
C.	No	Yes
D.	No	No

5.   Law Nov 95 #59
A common carrier bailee generally would avoid liability for loss of goods entrusted to its care if the goods are
A. Stolen by an unknown person.
B. Negligently destroyed by an employee.
C. Destroyed by the derailment of the train carrying them due to railroad employee negligence.
D. Improperly packed by the party shipping them.

6.   Law May 95 #55
Which of the following factors help determine whether an item of personal property has become a fixture?

	Manner of affixation	Value of the item	Intent of the annexor
A.	Yes	Yes	Yes
B.	Yes	Yes	No
C.	Yes	No	Yes
D.	No	Yes	Yes

7.   Law May 95 #57
Which of the following items is tangible personal property?
A. Share of stock.
B. Trademark.
C. Promissory note.
D. Oil painting.

8.   Author

Ed is very ill and does not expect to survive his illness. He says to his grandson, "I want you to have my toy train set from my childhood. I have told your grandmother to get it out of the attic for you. You can go pick it up this afternoon." The grandson did not pick up the train before Ed died. Which of the following is true?

A. The grandson will get the train set because this is a valid gift *causa mortis*.
B. The grandson will get the train set because this is a valid *inter vivos* gift.
C. The grandson will not get the train set because there was not a valid completed gift.
D. The grandson will not get the train because the courts do not enforce gifts.

9.   Law May 95 #58

Which of the following standards of liability best characterizes the obligation of a common carrier in a bailment relationship.

A. Reasonable care.
B. Gross negligence.
C. Shared liability.
D. Strict liability.

10.   Law R97 # 5

Under the Documents of Title Article of the UCC, which of the following terms must be contained in a warehouse receipt?

I. A statement indicating whether the goods received will be delivered to the bearer, to a specified person, or to a specified person or his/her order.
II. The location of the warehouse where the goods are stored.

A. I only.
B. II only.
C. Both I and II.
D. Neither I nor II.

11.   Law R97 #15

Under the Documents of Title Article of the UCC, a negotiable document of title is "duly negotiated" when it is negotiated to

A. Any holder by endorsement.
B. Any holder by delivery.
C. A holder who takes the document in payment of a money obligation.
D. A holder who takes the document for value, in good faith, and without notice of any defense or claim to it.

12.   Law R96 #15

Under the Documents of Title Article of the UCC, which of the following statements is(are) correct regarding a common carrier's duty to deliver goods subject to a negotiable, bearer bill of lading?

I. The carrier may deliver the goods to any party designated by the holder of the bill of lading.
II. A carrier who, without court order, delivers goods to a party claiming the goods under a missing negotiable bill of lading is liable to any person injured by the misdelivery.

A. I only.
B. II only.
C. Both I and II.
D. Neither I nor II.

13.   Author

Which of the following is true about trademark protection?

A. A trademark is protected only for a statutory period of time, after which there can be no further protection.
B. Once protected, trademark protection cannot be lost.
C. Ordinary words can be protected if they acquire a secondary meaning.
D. Trademark protection lasts 20 years.

OTHER OBJECTIVE FORMAT QUESTION

Author

Each of the following statements presents a situation that could involve one or more of the areas of law identified in List I. For each of the statements, choose the appropriate item or items from List I and blacken the corresponding oval or ovals on the objective answer sheet. An item in the list may be used once, more than once, or not at all.

List I
A. Trade Secrets Law
B. Patent Law
C. Copyright Law
D. Trademark Law
E. Computer Software Copyright Act
F. Semiconductor Chip Protection Act

1. A small startup computer firm is disclosing none of its work to anyone, and has not filed for any sort of federal protections.

2. A software developer has just completed a new computer program and wants to prevent it from being copied.

3. Computer component manufacturer has invented a new type of disk drive that accesses data more quickly than current models.

4. A computer chip manufacturer has developed a new processing chip.

5. A computer software firm has developed software for a new operating system which it calls "doors" because the firm believes this new system opens doors to new software applications and wants to protect the name.

6. A computer hardware manufacturer has introduced a new shape design for a monitor which is different from existing monitors, although it functions no differently than existing models.

EXPLANATIONS TO MULTIPLE CHOICE QUESTIONS

1. C is the correct answer. An easement is a right to use land, a type of real property.

2. C is the correct answer. These are the two most important factors in whether an item is a fixture.

3. D is the correct answer. All three of the statements are true about a bailment. The question asks for "requirements," but the third item is actually more of a result than a requirement.

4. C is the correct answer. Finding abandoned property will give title to the finder. A lease transfers possession and certain rights of use, but it does not transfer ownership.

5. D is the correct answer. A common carrier is not responsible for improper packing by the shipper. A common carrier has a strict liability duty to deliver the goods as called for, and is liable for losses caused by the events described in the incorrect answer choices.

6. C is the correct answer. The value of the item is irrelevant in determining if it is a fixture.

7. D is the correct answer. Even though a stock certificate and a promissory note have a physical existence, each is a mere representation of the related intangible property right.

8. C is the correct answer. There was no completed gift because there was no delivery. Choice D is incorrect because a court will not enforce a **promise** to make a gift, but if the three requirements of a completed gift have been met, a court will enforce the right of the donee to keep the item. Because this would have been a gift *causa mortis*, even if the gift had been completed, Ed could have revoked it if he survived his illness.

9. D is the correct answer. There are only a few exceptions to this duty of strict liability.

10. C is the correct answer. Both items are among those that must be included in a warehouse receipt.

11. D is the correct answer. The requirements to become a holder by due negotiation are similar to those to become a holder in due course. The rights acquired are also similar.

12. C is the correct answer. A common carrier has a duty of strict liability to deliver the goods as called for in the bill of lading. The common carrier takes a risk of violating that duty by delivering goods to a party without the bill of lading.

13. C is the correct answer. Ordinary words are generally not protected, but if they acquire a secondary meaning in connection with a product or service, they can be protected.

EXPLANATION TO OTHER OBJECTIVE FORMAT QUESTION

1. Choices A and C are correct. This firm would be protected by trade secret law, and by copyright law, if applicable, because copyright protection is automatic.

2. Choices A, B, C, D, and E are correct. Some computer programs are now patentable.

3. Choices A and B are correct. This is a mechanical device and could be patentable. Note that filing a patent would require disclosure and would eliminate much of the trade secret protection.

4. Choices A, B, C, D, E, and F are correct. Depending on the circumstances and the aspects of the chip which the manufacturer wants to protect, any of these areas of law might be relevant.

5. Choice D is correct. A trademark will be granted if the word "doors" has acquired a secondary meaning in connection with the product.

6. Choice B is correct. A patent, valid for 14 years, can be obtained for a new product design.

CHAPTER 28
REAL PROPERTY AND LANDLORD-TENANT RELATIONSHIP

OVERVIEW

This chapter focuses on real property law, including the law relating to landlords and tenants. Real property law is primarily state law, and can differ from state to state. Because real property is unmoveable, there is less need for uniformity among the states. The CPA exam generally tests on those aspects of real property law which do not differ greatly among states. In some cases, however, the candidate must know the different laws. For example, candidates should know all three kinds of deed recording statutes. Real property questions, especially essay questions, often combine real property law concepts with insurance concepts. Insurance is covered in the next chapter.

OUTLINE

I. **The Nature of Real Property.**
   A. Definition. **Real property** consists of land and the items permanently attached to the land. This includes buildings, timber and other plants, as well as fixtures which have become part of a building. In addition, mineral rights, air rights, water rights, and easements are real property.
   B. Fixtures. A **fixture** is an article which has become attached to real property and has become part of the real property. Fixtures are discussed in detail in the previous chapter.

II. **Estates in Land.**
   A. Generally. Because land lasts forever and for other historical reasons, the ownership of land can be divided up in numerous ways, including divisions by time and by right.
   B. Fee Simple Absolute. **Fee simple absolute** represents the most complete form of ownership possible. It is what most people think of when they think of the rights associated with ownership. Among other rights, the owner of a fee simple absolute interest can make any legal use of the land, can rent it to others, can sell it, and can transfer it by a provision in a will.
   C. Fee Simple Defeasible. **Fee simple defeasible** is an interest which gives as complete ownership as fee simple absolute, except that there is a condition that might result in the holder losing the land. It can be thought of as total ownership with a "string" attached. There are two types of fee simple defeasible interests.
      1. Fee Simple Determinable. Under a **fee simple determinable** interest, the property is automatically taken away from the owner if the condition is violated. For example, if Fred received a piece of land but the deed said it belonged to Fred "so long as he did not operate a restaurant on the land," Fred would have a fee simple determinable interest. If Fred opened a restaurant, he would automatically lose ownership of the land.
      2. Fee Simple Subject to a Condition Subsequent. With a **fee simple subject to a condition subsequent** interest, the owner of the land does not automatically lose it upon violation of the condition. The prior owner or other party entitled to take the land upon the violation of the condition must take affirmative steps to get the land. Thus, if Fred opened the restaurant but the prior owner did not reclaim the land, Fred would not lose ownership.

      3.   <u>Where Used</u>. Candidates often wonder why anyone would ever buy real property with such restrictions. Land is seldom purchased with these restrictions, but land transferred by donation to charitable organizations or land transferred by the terms of a will is often restricted. For example, a farmer might transfer land to his oldest son so long as he farmed it, and if he ceased to farm, the land might then go to one of the son's siblings.

  D. <u>Life Estate</u>. A **life estate** entitles the holder to occupy and use the land for the remainder of that person's life. The right ends at death, so there is nothing to transfer in a will. A life estate can be sold, but the interest will terminate upon the transferor's, and not the transferee's, death. Thus, if Mary holds a life estate, she can sell that to Randy. Randy's ownership of the land will last until Mary's death. If Randy dies first, his heirs will hold the life estate until Mary's death. Such a life estate measured by someone else's life is a life estate ***pour autre vie***, which means for another's life.

  E. <u>Remainders and Reversions</u>. A **remainder** or **reversion** is the interest which follows any interest other than fee simple absolute.

      1.   *Remainder*. The interest is called a remainder when it is held by someone other than the prior owner. Thus, if Ann transferred land to Amy for Amy's life, with the land then going to Wyatt, Amy would have a life estate and Wyatt would have a remainder.

      2.   *Reversion*. The interest is called a reversion when it is held by the prior owner. Thus, if Ann transferred the land to Eric for his life, but did not specify what would happen to the land after Eric's death, it would revert back to Ann (or her estate if she died before Eric). Ann would also hold a reversion if she had stated that it would revert to her. **Exam tip #1.**

III.   **Concurrent Ownership.**

  A. <u>Generally</u>. It is possible for more than one party to simultaneously own real property. This is known as **co-ownership** or **concurrent** ownership. There are several ways that property can be owned by more than one party. **Exam tip #2.**

  B. <u>Joint Tenancy</u>. With **joint tenancy**, the co-owners have a **right of survivorship**. Under the right of survivorship, when one co-owner dies, the other co-owner(s) will automatically acquire the share of the deceased co-owner. The deceased co-owner's share never becomes part of the deceased co-owner's estate, thus any will provision regarding the property is irrelevant.

      1.   *Joint Tenancy Is Disfavored*. Because most co-owners want their share of property to pass according to their will rather than go to the other joint tenants, courts will treat an ambiguous deed as creating a tenancy in common. For example, a deed which stated that property was deeded to Mary and Alice as "joint tenants in common" is ambiguous, but would be treated as a tenancy in common.

      2.   *The Four Required Unities*. To be valid, the creation of a joint tenancy requires that there exist **four unities**. These are:

         a. Unity of Title. The parties must have acquired the interests in the same deed.

         b. Unity of Time. The parties must have acquired the interests at the same time.

         c. Unity of Interest. The parties must have identical interests. This means that they must be of the same duration, and of the same fractional interest. Three joint tenants must each have a one-third interest.

         d. Unity of Possession. The parties must have equal rights to possess the property.

3. *Transfer of One of the Interests Destroys Joint Tenancy.* When one joint tenant sells her interest to another party, the purchaser of that interest becomes a tenant in common with the other original owners. The original joint tenants remain joint tenants with respect to each other. For example, Ann, Bob, and Charlie were joint tenants in a piece of property. If Charlie sold his interest to Danielle, Danielle would become a tenant in common. This is because Danielle does not meet the four required unities; she did not acquire her interest at the same time as Ann and Bob. Ann and Bob remain joint tenants with respect to each other. Danielle would be a joint tenant if Ann, Bob, and Charlie together conveyed a deed to Ann, Bob, and Danielle.

C. Tenancy in Common. **Tenancy in common** is the basic form of co-ownership. If the language in a deed creating co-ownership is ambiguous, it will be treated as a tenancy in common. There is no right of survivorship for interests held as tenants in common. Upon death, these interests pass according to the terms of a will, rather than automatically to the co-owners.

1. *Unequal Interests Allowed.* There is no requirement that tenants in common have equal interests.

2. *Equal Right to Possession.* All tenants in common have an equal right to possession of the property. This applies even if the fractional interests held are unequal. A one-third interest tenant in common has the same right to possession as a two-thirds interest tenant in common.

D. Tenancy by the Entirety. **Tenancy by the entirety** can be thought of as a special type of joint tenancy.

1. *Husband and Wife Only.* To hold property as tenants by the entirety, the parties must be husband and wife.

2. *Unilateral Sale of an Interest Is Void.* The distinguishing feature of a tenancy by the entirety is that neither party can sell a half interest without the consent of the other party. This requires that the nonselling party's signature also be on the deed. Any party, including each spouse of a married couple, holding property as either joint tenants or tenants in common can always sell one interest without the knowledge or consent of the other co-owners. With tenancy by the entirety, an attempted transfer by the husband would be void and therefore invalid unless the wife joined in the conveyance.

E. Examples.

1. *Joint Tenancy.* If Amy, Billy, and Carla owned property as joint tenants, but Amy died, Billy and Carla would each own one-half as joint tenants. Any provision in Amy's will would not have an effect on the outcome. If Billy then died, Carla would acquire full ownership.

2. *Tenancy in Common.* If Adam, Bonnie, and Chuck owned property as tenants in common, but Adam died, Bonnie's and Chuck's ownership interests would be unchanged. There would be a new owner of Adam's interest based on the terms of Adam's will, or based on the intestacy statute if Adam did not have a will. (An intestacy statute determines who inherits the property of someone dying without a will.)

3. *Both Types of Interests Present.* Assume that Andy, Beth, and Connie owned property as joint tenants, but then Connie sold her interest to Dave. At this point Andy and Beth would be joint tenants with respect to each other and tenants in common with Dave. If Dave died, his interest would pass according to his will or the intestacy statute. If Andy or Beth died, the survivor would acquire the other's one-third interest. Thus, if Beth were the first of the owners to die, Andy would own two-thirds as a tenant in common with Dave. **Exam tip #3.**

F. <u>Community Property</u>. Nine states have **community property** laws under which all property acquired during the marriage is considered to be owned equally by each spouse. Property owned separately at the start of the marriage, and any property acquired by one spouse by gift or inheritance, remains separate property.

G. <u>Cooperative</u>. With a **cooperative**, generally found in the larger cities, the unit residents own shares in a corporation which owns the building. The ownership in the corporation entitles the shareholder to occupy a particular unit.

H. <u>Condominium</u>. In a **condominium**, the units are owned individually and the common areas are owned as tenants in common.

IV. **Transfer of Ownership in Real Property.**

A. <u>Generally</u>. Real property can be transferred in many ways, but generally must be evidenced by a writing in order to comply with the Statute of Frauds. A transfer of real property is often called a **conveyance** of real property and is accomplished be executing and delivering a deed.

B. <u>Sale</u>. A real estate sale is the most common way that real property is transferred. The sale transaction is usually conducted in two steps. A **real estate sales contract** is signed which sets the terms of the sale. This is followed by a **closing** or **settlement** a month or two later at which the purchase price is paid (usually with borrowed funds that are advanced at the closing) and the seller conveys the property to the buyer by executing and delivering a deed. **Exam tip #4.**

C. <u>Tax Sale</u>. A governmental unit may sell property at a **tax sale** if the owner has failed to pay the property taxes due on the property. There might be a **redemption period** following the sale during which the owner can pay past taxes and expenses of the sale to reclaim the property.

D. <u>Gift, Will, or Inheritance</u>. Property can be acquired by gift or by will. If the owner dies without a will, it will pass by inheritance according to the state's intestacy statute.

E. <u>Adverse Possession</u>. Property can be acquired by possessing it and meeting certain other requirements. This is known as **adverse possession** and is sometimes informally referred to as obtaining squatter's rights. If the requirements are met, the adverse possessor acquires good title to the property. Adverse possession requires that the possession be:

1. *For the Statutory Period of Time.* Each state sets its own requirement, but most are between 10 and 20 years.

2. *Open, Visible, and Notorious.* The possessor will not meet the requirements by secretly possessing the land.

3. *Actual and Exclusive.* The means that the possessor must physically use the land as an owner would use it and exclude others from it as an owner would.

4. *Continuous and Peaceful.* The required statutory period must be met without interruption. This does not mean that the possessor can never leave. The possessor merely must use the land as an owner would without interruption. Thus, the possessor could take vacations without violating the continuity requirement. The peaceful requirement means that the owner cannot use force, such as a gun, to stay on the land and exclude the owner.

5. *Hostile and Adverse.* This means that the occupancy must be without the permission of the owner. As used here, "hostile" means contrary to the permission of the owner. Intent is <u>not</u> required. Thus, adverse possession can occur accidentally, such as when a fence is unknowingly placed beyond the property line, or intentionally, such as when a party occupies land in hopes of obtaining ownership to it. **Exam tip #5.**

V. Deeds.
A. <u>Generally</u>. A deed is a written document by which ownership of real property is transferred. The transferor is the **grantor** and the transferee is the **grantee**. The deed is prepared by the seller or the seller's attorney. A deed is proof that property was conveyed to the grantee on a certain date. A deed is not proof of current ownership because the original grantee might have subsequently conveyed the property to another party. **Exam tip #6.**
B. <u>Requirements for Deeds</u>. A valid deed must meet a number of requirements.
   1. *Writing*. The Statute of Frauds requires deeds to be in writing.
   2. *Identification of the Parties*.
   3. *Signature of the Grantor*.
   4. *Description of the Property*. The description must be adequate to identify the property with certainty.
   5. *Recital of Consideration*. A deed must state that there was consideration for the conveyance.
   6. *Words of Conveyance*. A deed must contain words indicating that the interest in property is being conveyed from the grantor to the grantee.
   7. *Description of the Interest Conveyed*. For example, fee simple absolute or a life estate.
   8. *Acknowledgment*. The acknowledgment is the witnessing by a notary of the signing of the deed.
   9. *Delivery*.
   10. *Acceptance*. The deed must be accepted by the grantee.
C. <u>Not Required</u>. A deed does not require:
   1. *Signature of the Grantee*. The deed requires only the signature of the party who is conveying away the property.
   2. *Purchase Price*. To be valid as a deed, the purchase price need not be stated. Note, however, that many states now require the purchase price to be stated in a deed. The purpose of this is to help determine the fair value of the property for property tax purposes. **Exam tip #7.**
   3. *Filing*. A deed is valid between grantor and grantee without filing.
D. <u>Types of Deeds</u>. There are several types of deeds.
   1. *General Warranty Deed*. A **general warranty deed** provides the greatest level of assurance from the grantor to the grantee. The grantor of a general warranty deed makes the following covenants:
      a. The Grantor Owns the Property.
      b. The Grantor Has the Right to Convey the Property.
      c. The Property Is Free From Encumbrances Not Disclosed in the Deed.
      d. The Grantee Will Have Quiet Enjoyment of the Property. This means that no one will assert a valid claim of ownership against the grantee.
      e. The Grantor Will Defend the Grantee's Title Against Legitimate Claims.
      f. The Grantor Will Take Reasonable Steps to Perfect an Imperfect Title.
      The grantor has an obligation to comply with any of these covenants, even if the problem relates to the period of time prior to when the grantor owned the property.
   2. *Special Warranty Deed*. The grantor of a **special warranty deed** makes promises only in connection with the time that the grantor owned the property. The grantor warrants that:
      a. The Grantor Has Not Previously Conveyed the Property to Another Party.
      b. The Grantor Has Caused No Encumbrances to Be Placed on the Property.

3. *Quitclaim Deed*. A **quitclaim** deed makes no warranties. The grantor essentially is saying to the grantee that the grantor "quits claiming" any interest in the property. The grantor does not make any claim of ownership. Nothing is promised in a quitclaim deed. Quitclaim deeds are sometimes used in divorce when one spouse quitclaims the house in favor of the other property, or in boundary disputes which have been settled. The party giving up claim to the disputed strip of land will quitclaim it in favor of the other party.

VI.   **Recording Statutes.**

A. Generally. Because land lasts forever, there is always the possibility that someone might assert a false ownership claim to the land originating a hundred years or more in the past. Recording statutes are designed to provide a permanent legal record of ownership in order to prevent such claims and to prevent honest mistakes.

B. Deed Is Valid Without Recording. A deed is valid as between the grantor and grantee without recording. Thus, the grantee's possession of a deed from the grantor will entitle the grantee to the property in a dispute with the grantor over ownership. Recording the deed protects the grantee from later conveyances of the same property by the grantor to other grantees.

C. The Recording System. The recording system provides a complete record of all property transactions in a jurisdiction, usually the county. Thus, the complete ownership history of a parcel of real property is available. Normally, the records are kept at the office of the county clerk and recorder. A deed is **recorded** in most states by filing the deed at this office.

D. Notice to the World. The recording of a deed gives notice to the world of conveyance of property. Once the deed is recorded, all possible grantees are treated as having knowledge of it. This puts a duty on any purchaser of real property to search the real estate records prior to paying for and accepting a deed. The search ensures that the grantor truly owns the property and has the right to convey it.

E. Two Kinds of Notice. There are two kinds of notice of a conveyance.

1. *Constructive Notice*. **Constructive notice** exists due to the filing of the deed.

2. *Actual Notice*. **Actual notice** exists when an individual has actual knowledge of a conveyance.

F. First Deed Is Recorded. When a grantee immediately records her deed, if the grantor later executes a second deed purporting to convey the same property to a second grantee, the second grantee will have no claim to the property because the second grantee will be considered to have notice of the earlier conveyance.

G. First Deed Is Not Recorded. A more difficult issue arises when a second deed follows an earlier deed which has not been recorded. The first grantee always keeps the property if the first deed was recorded, but if it was not recorded, there are three different types of laws which could apply. Each state uses one of these recording statutes.

1. *Notice Statute*. Under a **notice statute**, the second grantee gets the property if the second grantee had no notice of the first deed. Thus, if the second grantee did not have actual knowledge of the first deed, the first grantee will not get the property and can only sue the grantor for damages.

2. *Notice-Race Statute.* Under a **notice-race statute**, the second grantee gets the property if the second grantee had no notice of the first deed <u>and</u> records that deed before the first grantee records. Unlike under the notice statute, the second grantor must file first in addition to being without knowledge of the earlier conveyance. If the second grantee fails to meet both requirements, the first grantee gets the property.

3. *Race Statute.* Under a **race statute**, the rule is simple. The first grantee to record gets to keep the property. Notice, or lack of notice, is irrelevant.

Most CPA exam questions in this area involve an unrecorded first conveyance. **Exam tip #8.**

H. Title Insurance. **Title insurance** insures against recorded title defects. It does not insure against unrecorded title defects. Title insurance policies often contain exceptions which are not covered. The insurance only covers the purchaser of the policy, thus a subsequent purchaser of the real property is not covered and would need to purchase his own policy.

I. Easements. An **easement** is a nonpossessory interest in real property. A positive easement grants a positive right to use another's land, such as a right of access. In a negative easement, a landowner agrees to limit the use of his own land, such as agreeing to not build an otherwise legal structure which would block the view of a neighbor.

VII. Landlord-Tenant Relationship.

A. Nonfreehold Estate. A **landlord-tenant relationship** results in the tenant acquiring a **nonfreehold estate**, meaning that the tenant has a right of possession, but not title.

B. Leases. The agreement between the landlord and tenant is called a **lease**, with the landlord as **lessor** and the tenant as **lessee**.

C. Lease Requirements. Leases must be in writing if the lease term is greater than one year. The lease must contain a description of the leased premises and other essential terms such as the identification of the parties. A lease need not specify the due date for the payment of rent because the court can imply a reasonable term if it is omitted.

D. Types of Tenancies. There are four types of tenancies. The type generally depends on whether there is a stated duration and when rent is due.

1. *Tenancy for Years.* Any fixed term lease, whether for one month or 50 years, is a **tenancy for years**. A tenancy for years expires automatically at the end of the lease term with no notice required.

2. *Periodic Tenancy.* A **periodic tenancy** exists when a lease specifies the interval at which rent is due, but does not specify the length of the lease term. Such leases can be terminated by either party by giving adequate notice. At common law, the required notice was one period, thus a month-to-month tenancy required one month notice. Most states have passed statutes specifying the notice requirement.

3. *Tenancy at Will.* A **tenancy at will** can be terminated at any time by either party. No notice was required under common law, but most states have set minimum notice periods for tenancies at will.

4. *Tenancy at Sufferance.* A **tenancy at sufferance** is created when a tenant retains possession of property following the termination of another type of tenancy or a life estate. This actually is a trespassing situation, but the tenant is responsible for rent for the time the property is occupied. The landlord can evict a tenant at sufferance.

E. <u>Landlord's Duties</u>. A landlord's duties can arise from the lease, can be imposed by statute, or can be implied by law.

1. *Duty to Deliver Possession.* The landlord has a duty to deliver exclusive possession to the tenant unless the lease provides otherwise. This means that a landlord does not have the right to enter the leased premises unless the lease provides for it.

2. *Covenant of Quiet Enjoyment.* There is an **implied covenant of quiet enjoyment** in all leases. It is violated if the landlord, or anyone acting with the landlord's consent, interferes with the tenant's use and enjoyment of the property.

3. *Constructive Eviction.* If the landlord physically prevents the tenant from being able to use the premises, for example by not providing running water, it results in **constructive eviction**. The constructive evicted tenant can either retain possession of the property and sue for damages or treat the lease as terminated, move out, and cease paying rent.

4. *Duty to Maintain the Premises.* Under common law, the tenant was responsible to repair and maintain the leased premises. Today, many states have imposed certain duties on landlords to maintain and keep leased premises in good repair. Even where there is no such statute, the lease often places this duty on the landlord.

5. *Warranty of Habitability.* Many states impose a **warranty of habitability** on residential leases. In these jurisdictions, the landlord is required to keep the premises at some minimal level of suitability for human habitation.

F. <u>Tenant's Duties</u>. A tenant has certain duties as well.

1. *Duty to Pay Rent.* The tenant has a duty to pay the rent in the amount and at the time and place as stated in the lease. Nonpayment entitles the landlord to bring an eviction action or sue for the payment of rent, or both.

2. *Duty to Not Improperly Use the Leased Premises.* The tenant has a duty to not use the premises in any illegal manner or in any manner prohibited by the lease. If the lease imposes no restrictions, the tenant can use the premises for any lawful purpose.

3. *Duty to Not Commit Waste.* The tenant has a **duty to not commit waste** to the leased premises. Waste is any substantial and permanent damage beyond normal wear and tear.

4. *Duty to Not Disturb Other Tenants.* This duty extends to other tenants in the same building and is violated by excessive noise, odors, etc.

VIII. **Transfer of Rights Under a Lease.**

A. <u>Transfer of Landlord's Rights</u>.

1. *Assignment of Right to Collect Rent.* A landlord can assign the right to collect rent to another party without selling the property. Upon proper notice, the tenant is then obligated to make rent payments to the landlord's assignee.

2. *Sale of Property.* A sale by the landlord of the leased premises usually transfers the right to collect rent to buyer. The buyer is obligated to honor the terms of an existing lease.

B. <u>Transfer of Tenant's Rights</u>. A tenant can assign his rights through either an **assignment** or a **sublease**.

1. *Assignment.* In an **assignment**, all rights of the tenant under the lease are transferred to the assignee. The assignee becomes directly liable to the landlord, but the original tenant also remains liable if the assignee does not perform. The landlord can sue either the original tenant or the assignee to recover rent.

2. *Novation.* If, as part of the assignment, the landlord releases the original tenant, the parties have entered into a **novation**. The landlord can sue only the assignee for performance.
3. *Sublease.* A **sublease** is characterized by the tenant assigning less than all of the rights under the lease, such as a sublease for two months while the tenant will be overseas, after which the tenant will return to the leased premises. The original tenant is the **sublessor** and the temporary tenant is the **sublessee**. The original landlord is not a party to a sublease and cannot enforce payment of rent against the sublessee. The sublessee is subject to any rules or restrictions contained in the original lease. **Exam tip #9.**

IX. **Mortgages.**
   A. Terminology. A **mortgage** is a security interest in real property which allows a creditor to sell the property and use the proceeds to satisfy the debt. The related loan is separate from the mortgage. In everyday language, the related loan is almost universally called a "mortgage" in statements such as "I am going to get a mortgage to buy a home." This statement incorrectly refers to the loan as the mortgage. This would be correctly stated by saying, "I am going to get a loan to buy a home, but the lender will require me to give a mortgage in order to get the loan." The homeowner is the **mortgagor** who gives the mortgage (the right of repossession and sale to satisfy the debt) to the lender who is the **mortgagee**. **Exam tip #10.**
   B. Requirements for Mortgages. Because a mortgage is considered to be a conveyance of an interest in real property, the requirements are similar to those for deeds.
      1. *Writing.*
      2. *Identification of the Parties.*
      3. *Signature of the Mortgagor.* The mortgagor is also the grantor.
      4. *Description of the Property.*
      5. *Words of Conveyance.*
      6. *Acknowledgment.*
      7. *Delivery.*
      8. *Acceptance.*
   C. Recording of Mortgages. Because a mortgage is an interest in real property, mortgages are recorded in the real estate records just as deeds are. The priority rules discussed above for the recording of deeds also apply where an owner grants two or more mortgages on the same property. The rules apply where both mortgages and deeds are involved.
   D. Two-Party Mortgage Transaction. In a two-party mortgage transaction, the borrower, who is the mortgagor, gives a mortgage to the lender who is the mortgagee. In the event of default, the mortgagee may go to court to file a foreclosure action. The property will be sold and the proceeds used to satisfy the debt.
   E. Three-Party Deed of Trust Transaction. In a three-party **deed of trust** transaction, the borrower conveys a deed of trust to a third party who is known as the **trustee**, often a public official. The trustee will hold this deed until one of two events occurs:
      1. *Underlying Debt Is Satisfied.* If the underlying debt is satisfied, the deed of trust becomes null and void. The borrower will then own the property free of this encumbrance.

2. *Default.* Upon default, the trustee will sell the property under a **power of sale**. This is generally done without going through the courts, and is thus much faster.

In substance, the rights of the borrower and lender are the same, except relating to foreclosure, under either the traditional mortgage or deed of trust transaction.

F. Sale of Property Before Satisfaction of a Mortgage. When property is sold that has a valid mortgage against it, there are several possible courses of action.

1. *Due on Sale Clause.* Many loan agreements today contain a **due on sale clause** requiring the full balance to be paid if the ownership interest in the property changes. At the closing, a portion of the buyer's funds (usually including some funds borrowed separately by the buyer) are used to pay off the seller's loan, at which point the seller's lender (the original mortgagee) releases, or cancels, the mortgage. **Exam tip #11.**

2. *Assumption of Mortgage.* If the buyer **assumes the mortgage**, the buyer agrees to become liable on the debt. The seller also remains liable on the debt if the buyer defaults.

3. *Subject to the Mortgage.* If the buyer takes the property **subject to the mortgage**, the buyer is not obligated to pay the underlying loan. The buyer, however, must continue to pay the underlying loan to keep the property, because if the loan is not paid, the mortgagee can foreclose. The seller remains liable on the debt.

4. *Novation.* A **novation** occurs if the buyer, seller, and mortgagee enter into a three-party agreement where the buyer assumes the obligations of the underlying debt and the seller is released from all liability. **Exam tip #12.**

G. Assignment by Mortgagee. A mortgagee is free to assign the mortgage to another party. This usually occurs in connection with an assignment of the right to collect payments on the underlying loan. This occurs frequently, with homeowners often being notified that their "mortgage has been sold." Actually, in this situation, the rights under both the mortgage and the underlying note have been sold.

H. Foreclosure. **Foreclosure** is the process, after default, in which the mortgagee obtains a court order for the property to be sold in order to satisfy the underlying debt. The property is sold at a judicial sale, with any excess proceeds (amounts exceeding the debt and the cost of the foreclosure) paid to the defaulting borrower after any other encumbrances are satisfied.

I. Deficiency. If property is foreclosed and the proceeds of sale are not sufficient to satisfy the debt and related costs, the mortgagee can obtain a **deficiency judgment** for the difference and will be an unsecured creditor to that extent.

J. Power of Sale. Under a **power of sale**, the mortgagee is able to sell the property without a court order. This power usually exists in deed of trust transaction, but in most states it can also be given by the mortgagor to the mortgagee in a two-party mortgage transaction. The power exists only if stated in the mortgage.

K. Redemption. The **right of redemption** gives the mortgagor the right, after default, to fully pay the debt and thereby keep the property. The specifics for redemption differ from state to state, but generally there are two types of redemption rights. To redeem, the mortgagor must fully pay the amount due, including interest and any late fees, as well as any expenses that have been incurred by the mortgagee in the foreclosure process.

1. *Equitable Right of Redemption.* The **equitable right of redemption** exists under both foreclosure and power of sale. The right begins once the foreclosure process or sale process has begun and ends once the sale takes place.

2. *Statutory Right of Redemption*. The **statutory right of redemption** exists only in connection with a judicial sale. The statutory right of redemption exists after the sale has taken place. The redemption period is between six months and one year in most states which have one. The purchaser at the court sale does not receive a deed until the statutory redemption period has expired.

L. <u>Installment Land Contract</u>. An **installment land contract** is a contract which does not involve a mortgage. The buyer and seller enter into a contract with the seller not conveying a deed until the buyer has fully paid the purchase price. An installment land contract is often called a **contract for deed**.

EXAM TIPS

1. The described estates in land are only the most common types. They have not been heavily tested in recent years.
2. The types of co-ownership are heavily tested, especially questions of who owns property following a transfer, by sale or death, of one of the co-owner's shares.
3. In factual situations, remember that one co-owner can simultaneously be a tenant in common and joint tenant. It is often helpful to draw a diagram. Remember that a conveyance of a fractional interest without the knowledge or consent of the other parties is valid except in a tenancy by the entirety.
4. Be sure to understand the two steps (contract formation, and the closing) of most real property transactions and that the property is transferred to the buyer only by the execution and delivery of a valid deed.
5. Although the adverse possessor obtains ownership by meeting the adverse possession requirements, the possessor usually must go to court to get a court declaration that the requirements have been met, thus establishing the ownership.
6. It is important to understand that a deed merely proves that the described property was transferred from the grantor to the grantee on the specified date. Because each time property is sold, a new deed is prepared and the old one is not destroyed, possession of a deed is not proof of current ownership. A deed operates a little like a receipt for merchandise. Bob's possession of a receipt from 1998 for the purchase of a bicycle proves only that he acquired it on that date, but does not prove that he currently owns it. He might have sold it since then, but retained the receipt.
7. Be sure to know what is required, as well as what is not required for a deed to be valid. For purposes of the CPA exam, the purchase price need not be stated in a deed.
8. The types of recording statutes and their application are heavily tested. They can be summarized as follows:
   Notice: The second grantee gets the property if the second grantee had no notice, actual or constructive, of the earlier conveyance to the earlier grantee.
   Notice-Race: The first innocent (no notice, actual or constructive, of earlier conveyances) grantee to record gets the property.
   Race: The first party to record gets the property.
9. With leases, be sure to know the types of tenancies and the differences in assignments and subleases.
10. Be sure to understand mortgage terminology and correctly use it in any essay question.

11. Since the early 1980s, most mortgage loan arrangements include a due on sale clause, thus greatly reducing the number of mortgage assumptions and novations.
12. In everyday discussions, the word "assumption" is often used to describe a situation that is actually a novation. Be sure to know for the CPA exam that the seller is not released from liability for the debt in an assumption. The seller is released only in a novation.

KEY CONCEPTS LIKELY TO BE TESTED ON THE CPA EXAM

1. Concepts and applications of the different kinds of concurrent ownership.
2. The types of deeds and requirements for a deed to be valid.
3. Recording statutes and their application to a factual situation.
4. The types of leaseholds, as well as assignments and subleases.
5. Mortgage terminology and requirements.
6. The different ways that property with an existing mortgage can be transferred.

KEY TERMS

Real Property
Fixture
Fee Simple Absolute
Fee Simple Defeasible
Fee Simple Determinable
Life Estate
Pour Autre Vie
Remainder
Reversion
Co-ownership
Joint Tenancy
Right of Survivorship
Four Unities
Tenancy in Common
Tenancy by the Entirety
Community Property
Cooperative
Condominium
Conveyance
Real Estate Sales Contract
Real Estate Closing
Real Estate Settlement
Tax Sale
Redemption Period
Adverse Possession

Grantor
Grantee
General Warranty Deed
Special Warranty Deed
Quitclaim Deed
Recording of a Deed
Constructive Notice
Actual Notice
Notice Statute
Notice-Race Statute
Race Statute
Title Insurance
Easement
Landlord Tenant Relationship
Nonfreehold Estate
Lessor
Lessee
Tenancy for Years
Periodic Tenancy
Tenancy at Will
Tenancy at Sufferance
Constructive Eviction
Warranty of Habitability
Fee Simple Subject to a Condition Subsequent
Implied Covenant of Quiet Enjoyment

Duty to Not Commit Waste
Assignment of a Lease
Novation of a Lease
Sublease
Sublessor
Sublessee
Mortgage
Mortgagor
Mortgagee
Deed of Trust
Trustee
Power of Sale
Due on Sale Clause
Assumption of a Mortgage
Taking Subject to a Mortgage
Novation of a Mortgage
Assignment by a Mortgagee
Foreclosure
Deficiency Judgment
Equitable Right of Redemption
Statutory Right of Redemption
Installment Land Contract
Contract for Deed

MULTIPLE CHOICE QUESTIONS

1.   Law Nov 95 #55
Rich purchased property from Sklar for
$200,000. Rich obtained a $150,000 loan
from Marsh Bank to finance the purchase,
executing a promissory note and a mortgage.
By recording the mortgage, Marsh protects its
A. Rights against Rich under the promissory
    note.
B. Rights against the claims of subsequent
    bona fide purchasers for value.
C. Priority against a previously filed real
    estate tax lien on the property.
D. Priority against all parties having earlier
    claims to the property.

2.   Law May 95 #53
For a deed to be effective between a purchaser
and seller of real estate, one of the conditions
is that the deed must
A. Be recorded within the permissible
    statutory time limits.
B. Be delivered by the seller with an intent to
    transfer title.
C. Contain the actual sales price.
D. Contain the signatures of the seller and
    purchaser.

3.   Law May 94 #56
Court, Fell, and Miles own a parcel of land as
joint tenants with right of survivorship.
Court's interest was sold to Plank. As a result
of the sale from Court to Plank,
A. Fell, Miles, and Plank each own one-third
    of the land as joint tenants.
B. Fell and Miles each own one-third of the
    land as tenants in common.
C. Plank owns one-third of the land as a
    tenant in common.
D. Plank owns one-third of the land as a joint
    tenant.

4.   Law May 90 #55
On February 2, Mazo deeded a warehouse to
Parko for $450,000. Parko did not record the
deed. On February 12, Mazo deeded the same
warehouse to Nexis for $430,000. Nexis was
aware of the prior conveyance to Parko.
Nexis recorded its deed before Parko
recorded. Who would prevail under the
following recording statutes?

	Notice statute	Race statute	Race-Notice statute
A.	Nexis	Parko	Parko
B.	Parko	Nexis	Parko
C.	Parko	Nexis	Nexis
D.	Parko	Parko	Nexis

5.   Law May 94 #58
Which of the following conditions must be
met to have an enforceable mortgage?
A. An accurate description of the property
    must be included in the mortgage.
B. A negotiable promissory note must
    accompany the mortgage.
C. Present consideration must be given in
    exchange for the mortgage.
D. The amount of the debt and the interest
    rate must be stated in the mortgage.

6.   Law Nov 91#54
A purchaser who obtains real estate title
insurance will
A. Have coverage for the title exceptions
    listed in the policy.
B. Be insured against all defects of record
    other than those excepted in the policy.
C. Have coverage for title defects that result
    from events that happen after the effective
    date of the policy.
D. Be entitled to transfer the policy to
    subsequent owners.

7.   Law May 95 #52
Which of the following provisions must be
included in a residential lease agreement?
A. A description of the leased premises.
B. The due date for payment of rent.
C. A requirement that the tenant have public
   liability insurance.
D. A requirement that the landlord will
   perform all structural repairs to the
   property.

8.   Law Nov 92 #53
Which of the following forms of tenancy will
be created if a tenant stays in possession of
the leased premises without the landlord's
consent, after the tenant's one-year written
lease expires?
A. Tenancy at will.
B. Tenancy for years.
C. Tenancy from period to period.
D. Tenancy at sufferance.

ESSAY QUESTION (Estimated time -- 15 to 20 minutes)

Law Nov 89 #3

On March 2, 1988, Ash, Bale, and Rangel
purchased an office building from Park Corp.
as joint tenants with right of survivorship.
There was an outstanding note and mortgage
on the building, which they assumed. The
note and mortgage named Park as the
mortgagor (borrower) and Vista Bank as the
mortgagee (lender). Vista has consented to
the assumption.

Wein, Inc., a tenant in the office building,
had entered into a 10-year lease dated May 8,
1985. The lease was silent regarding Wein's
right to sublet. The lease provided for Wein
to take occupancy on June 1, 1985, and that
the monthly rent would be $5,000 for the
entire 10-year term. On March 10, 1989,
Wein informed Ash, Bale, and Rangel that it
had agreed to sublet its office space to Nord
Corp. On March 17, 1989, Ash, Bale, and
Rangel notified Wein of their refusal to
consent to the sublet. The following
assertions have been made:

- The sublet from Wein to Nord is void
  because Ash, Bale, and Rangel did not
  consent.

- If the sublet is not void, Ash, Bale, and
  Rangel have the right to hold either Wein
  or Nord liable for payment of the rent.

On April 4, 1989, Ash transferred his
interest in the building to his spouse.

Required: Answer the following, setting
forth reasons for any conclusions stated.

a. *For this item only*, assume that Ash,
Bale, and Rangel default on the mortgage
note, that Vista forecloses, and a deficiency
results. Discuss the personal liability of Ash,
Bale, and Rangel to Vista and the personal
liability of Park to Vista.

b. Discuss the assertions as to the sublet,
indicating whether such assertions are correct
and the reasons therefor.

c. *For this item only*, assume that Ash
and Rangel died on April 20, 1989. Discuss
the ownership interest(s) in the office building
as of April 5, 1989, and April 21, 1989.

EXPLANATIONS TO MULTIPLE CHOICE QUESTIONS

1. B is the correct answer. The recording of the mortgage protects against most later claims to the property, including those by a bona fide purchaser for value. The recording gives constructive notice of the mortgage interest. Choice A is incorrect because recording has no effect on the rights and duties of the mortgagor and mortgagee with respect to each other.

2. B is the correct answer. Delivery and an intent to transfer title are both required for a deed to be effective. Choice A is incorrect because as with a mortgage, recording has no effect on the validity of the deed or on the rights of the grantor and grantee with respect to each other. Choice C is incorrect because the inclusion of the sales price is not necessary for a deed. Choice D is incorrect because only the seller's signature is necessary. This question illustrates the importance of knowing both the required items and the items not required.

3. C is the correct answer. The sale of Court's interest destroys the joint tenancy with respect to that particular interest because the four required unities for a joint tenancy are no longer met. The purchaser of that interest, Plank, will be become a tenant in common. Note that Fell and Miles will continue to be joint tenants with respect to each other and tenants in common with Plank.

4. B is the correct answer. Under notice statutes and race-notice statutes the second grantee obtains the property only if the second grantee was unaware of the earlier conveyance and, in this question, the second grantee, Nexis, did know about the earlier conveyance. Thus Nexis would not get the property under either a notice or race-notice statute. Under a race statute, sometimes called a "pure race" statute, the notice is irrelevant and Nexis obtains the property merely by being the first to file.

5. A is the correct answer. Choice B is incorrect because the note need not accompany the mortgage, nor is any note required to be negotiable. Choice C is incorrect because a mortgage can be given to secure a preexisting debt.

6. B is the correct answer. Title insurance insures only against those defects that appear in the public records, and only up to the date of the policy. Title insurance policies are not transferable to subsequent owners of the property.

7. A is the correct answer. Choice B is incorrect because a reasonable time for payment of rent can be implied if one is not specified. Choice D is incorrect because many leases do place a repair obligation on the landlord, but this is not required. Absent such a provision, the tenant is usually liable for repairs to the property.

8. D is the correct answer. A tenant at sufferance is a holdover tenant who has wrongfully refused to vacate the premises following the termination of another type of tenancy. The tenant is a trespasser, and the landlord can either evict the tenant from the premises or hold the tenant responsible for the payment of rent.

UNOFFICIAL AICPA ANSWER TO ESSAY QUESTION

Law May 89 #3

a. Ash, Bale, and Rangel will be personally liable to Vista for the deficiency resulting from the foreclosure sale because they became the principal debtors when they assumed the mortgage. Park will remain liable for the deficiency. Although Vista consented to the assumption of the mortgage by Ash, Bale, and Rangel, such assumption does not relieve Park from its obligation to Vista unless Park obtains a release from Vista or there is a novation.

b. The assertion that the sublet from Wein to Nord is void because Ash, Bale, and Rangel must consent to the sublet is incorrect. Unless the lease provides otherwise, a tenant may sublet the premises without the landlord's consent. Since the lease was silent regarding Wein's right to sublet, Wein may sublet Nord without the consent of Ash, Bale, and Rangel.

The assertion that if the sublet was not void Ash, Bale, and Rangel have the right to hold either Wein or Nord liable for payment of rent is incorrect. In a sublease, the sublessee/subtenant (Nord) has no obligation to pay rent to the landlord (Ash, Bale, and Rangel).

The subtenant (Nord) is liable to the tenant (Wein), but the tenant (Wein) remains solely liable to the landlord (Ash, Bale, and Rangel) for the rent stipulated in the lease.

c. Ash's inter vivos transfer of his 1/3 interest in the office building to his spouse on April 4, 1989 resulted in his spouse obtaining a 1/3 interest in the office building as a tenant in common. Ash's wife did not become a joint tenant with Bale and Rangel because the transfer of a joint tenant's interest to an outside party destroys the joint tenancy nature of the particular interest transferred. Bale and Rangel will remain as joint tenants with each other.

As of April 21, 1989, the office building was owned by Ash's spouse who had a 1/3 interest as tenant in common and Bale who had a 2/3 interest as tenant in common.

Ash's death On April 20, 1989 will have no effect on the ownership of the office building because Ash had already transferred all of his interest to his wife on April 4, 1989.

Rangel's death on April 20, 1989 resulted in his interest being acquired by Bale because of the right of survivorship feature in a joint tenancy. Because there are no surviving joint tenants, Bale will become a tenant common who owns 2/3 of the office building. Ash's spouse will not acquire any additional interest due to Rangel's death because she was a tenant in common with Rangel.

Author's Note:

Note that in part **(b.)** of the answer the names of the parties are placed in parentheses after their role. This can help make your answer more clear to the examiners.

This answer used "1/3" and "2/3" to refer to the ownership percentage. In an essay it would be better to spell out the fractions, such as one-third, etc.

Lastly, in the last paragraph, the answer states that Bale "owns 2/3 of the office building." A better way to state this is that Bale would "have a two-thirds interest in the office building." This would more clearly indicate to the examiners the candidate's knowledge that a fractional interest in property is a fractional interest in the whole property.

CHAPTER 29
INSURANCE, WILLS, AND TRUSTS

OVERVIEW

The first topic in this chapter, insurance, is often tested in conjunction with real property law, which is covered in the previous chapter. The remainder of this last chapter addresses wills, trusts, and estates. The material on insurance and trusts has been tested more heavily in recent years than the material on wills and estates.

OUTLINE

I. **Insurance.**
   A. <u>Generally</u>. The CPA exam questions on insurance have primarily focused in two areas. The first is insurable interest and the second is coinsurance.
   B. <u>Insurable Interest</u>. In order to recover under an insurance policy, the insured must have an **insurable interest**. Without an insurable interest, the insurance contract is considered to be a gambling contract, and therefore an illegal contract as being against public policy. Generally speaking, a party has an insurable interest if damage to the property could result in a loss to that party.
   C. <u>Insurable Interest in Property Insurance</u>.
      1. *Ownership of Property*. For property insurance, ownership creates an insurable interest.
      2. *Other Insurable Interests in Property*. Mortgagees, tenants, and lienholders have an insurable interest in the related property. In addition, the purchaser of property under an executory purchase and sale contract has an insurable interest in the property to be purchased. Note that the purchaser acquires an insurable interest upon the contract formation even though the purchaser will not own the property until the deed is conveyed at closing. The purchaser has a insurable interest because the purchaser might incur a loss if the property is destroyed, even if the destruction occurs prior to closing.
      3. *Insurable Interest Must Exist at the Time of Loss*. For property insurance, the insurable interest must exist at the time of the loss in order to be recoverable. Thus, if Hanna had failed to cancel a car insurance policy after selling the covered vehicle, she would no longer have an insurable interest if the car was damaged when it was no longer hers.
   D. <u>Insurable Interest in Life Insurance</u>.
      1. *Close Family Relationship*. Close relatives, such as spouses, parents, children, and siblings have an insurable interest in each other's lives.
      2. *Economic Benefit*. A party who receives an economic benefit from the continued life of another has an insurable interest in that person's life. Thus, corporations have a insurable interest in the continued life of officers and key executives, and often purchase "key person" life insurance policies on these individuals. With remote family relatives, such as aunts, uncles, or cousins, an insurable interest exists if the relative is a source of support.
      3. *Insurable Interest Must Exist at the Time of Policy Issuance*. With life insurance, the insurable interest must exist when the policy is issued, but need not exist when the loss occurs. **Exam tip #1.**

E. <u>Coinsurance</u>. A **coinsurance clause** requires that the insured obtain property insurance for a minimum percentage of the property's value. For example, an 80 percent coinsurance clause would require that the insured purchase coverage for at least 80 percent of the property's value. If this requirement is not met, the insured will be considered to be a **coinsurer** and would thus not be able to collect the full loss amount. The insured will bear a proportionate share of the loss.

1. *Coinsurance Formula.* The CPA exam often tests on the formula used to determine the amount of insurance recovery. The formula is as follows:

$$\frac{\text{(Face Amount of the Policy) x (Amount of Loss)}}{\text{(Coinsurance Percentage) x (Fair Market Value of Property)}} = \begin{array}{l}\text{Amount of} \\ \text{Recovery}\end{array}$$

The formula can be used to calculate the recovery from a single policy or from multiple policies. Using the amount of only one policy as the "face amount of the policy" will give the recovery for that policy, and combining amounts for multiple policies will give the total amount to be recovered.

2. *Two Constraints.* The amount calculated by the formula must be checked against two amounts. The recovery cannot be greater than either of these amounts even if the calculated amount is greater. The recovery cannot be greater than:
   a. The Face Amount of the Policy or
   b. The Amount of the Loss.

3. *Example.* Assume that a building is covered by a $250,000 policy when the building is worth $200,000 and is totally destroyed. The policy has an 80%-coinsurance provision. Applying the formula:

$$\frac{(\$250,000) \text{ x } (\$200,000)}{(80\,\%) \text{ x } (\$200,000)} = \$312,500$$

The computed amount, $312,500, must be compared to the face amount of the policy and the amount of the loss. The recovery cannot be greater than either of these amounts. Here, the policy amount is $250,000 and the loss is $200,000, thus the recovery would be limited to $200,000. **Exam tip #2.**

F. <u>Pro Rata Clause</u>. Insurance policies often have a **pro rata clause** which limits the amount recoverable under each individual policy.

1. *Basic Concept.* The recovery from each company is based on the proportion of that company's policy amount compared to that of all policies on the property.

2. *Example.* Assume in the example above that there were two insurance policies, one with Alpha Insurance company for $100,000 and one with Beta Insurance Company for $150,000. The total amount recoverable would be $200,000 as computed above. The individual recoveries would be:
   Alpha: ($100,000/($100,000 + $150,000)) x $200,000 = $80,000.
   Beta: ($150,000/($100,000 + $150,000)) x $200,000 = $120,000.
   These amounts would be the total recoverable from each company even if one of the companies did not pay for some reason. In other words, if Beta did not pay, the insured could nonetheless recover only $80,000 from Alpha.

G. Deductible Clause. Many property and liability insurance policies contain a **deductible** clause which means that the insurance company pays on a loss only to the extent that the loss exceeds the deductible amount.

H. Duties of the Insured. The insured has a duty to pay premiums when they are due, to promptly notify the insurer of insured events, and to cooperate with the insurer in the investigation of claims.

I. Duties of the Insurer. The insurer has a duty to pay legitimate claims up to the policy limit, and is liable for damages and penalties for not doing so. In addition, the insurer has a duty to defend any lawsuit involving an insured event.

J. Subrogation. **Subrogation** occurs when an insurance company pays its insured for a loss caused by a third party. For example, if the insurance company pays for damages from a fire intentionally caused by Mark, the insurance company is subrogated to the rights of the insured. Prior to payment of the claim, the owner of the building could have sued Mark, but once the insured's insurance company pays the claim, the insurance company "steps into the insured's shoes" with respect to the ability to sue and recover from Mark.

K. Incontestability Clause for Life Insurance. Most states require that the policy cannot be contested (for false information on an application) after a specified time has passed. Once the **incontestability clause** becomes effective, the policy can be canceled for nonpayment of premiums, but not due to information contained in the application or omitted from it.

II. Wills and Estates.

A. Generally. A **will** is a declaration of how a person wants her property distributed at death, and might also indicate her wish for the care and guardianship of any surviving minor children. The person who makes the will is the **testator**. The person is called a **testatrix** if she is female, although the term "testator" is often used today to refer to persons of both genders. When the testator dies, an **estate** is formed by operation of law into which all (with some exceptions) of the testator's property is placed. An estate is essentially a trust with the purpose of distributing the decedent's assets.

B. Requirements for a Valid Will. Wills and estates are governed by state law which differs somewhat from state to state, but in most states the following is required.

1. *Testamentary Capacity.* The testator must have **testamentary capacity** by being of legal age and sound mind when the will is made. This means that the testator must know of the extent of her property and the "natural objects of her bounty," including their relationship to her. This standard is fairly easy to meet.

2. *Writing.* Generally, a will must be in writing, though no particular form is needed. There are some exceptions explained below.

3. *Signature of the Testator.* All states require that a will have the testator's signature, with most states requiring that the signature appear at the end of the will.

4. *Attestation.* A will must be witnessed by mentally competent witnesses, two or three in most states. The **attestation clause** contains the witnesses signatures and usually follows the testator's signature.

C. Codicils. A **codicil** is used to change a will. Because a will cannot be changed by striking out a provision, a codicil, which is a separate document, must be used and must follow the same formalities as a will. It must refer to the will that it is changing.

D. <u>Revoking a Will</u>. An entire will may be revoked in a number of ways.
   1. *Subsequent Will.* A **subsequent will** can revoke a prior will, either expressly in the later will or by implication. Where there is no express revocation of the earlier will, the two wills are read together, but when inconsistent, the terms of the second will are controlling.
   2. *Physical Destruction.* Any intentional act of destruction, such as tearing or burning, revokes a will.
   3. *Operation of Law.* Certain changes in the testator's circumstances, such as a divorce, can revoke a will in whole or in part. A divorce usually revokes only the dispositions to the former spouse.
   4. *Birth of Child Does Not Revoke.* Birth of a child does not revoke a will, but can change the distribution for certain dispositions. For example, a provision leaving property equally to the testator's children will be divided among one additional child following the birth of a child. Otherwise, the will is not revoked.
E. <u>Simultaneous Deaths</u>. Where persons who would receive property from each other, such as a husband and wife, die at the same time or in circumstances where it cannot be determined who died first, each party's property is distributed as if the other had died first. These **simultaneous death** statutes can also provide that persons dying within a certain period of time of one another will be treated as dying simultaneously.
F. <u>Types of Testamentary Gifts</u>.
   1. *Real or Personal Property.*
      a. Devise. A **devise** is a gift of real property in a will.
      b. Legacy. A **legacy**, or **bequest**, is a gift of personal property in a will.
   2. *Specific Gift.* A **specific gift** is a gift of a particular item, such as the testator's 1999 Toyota Camry or his Rolex watch.
   3. *General Gift.* A gift which does not specify its source is a **general gift**. Most common is a gift of a specified amount of cash.
   4. *Demonstrative Gift.* A **demonstrative gift** is one to be satisfied from a specific source, but if that source is insufficient, out of the general funds of the estate. For example, the testator might make a gift of $10,000 from her savings account, but also stating that if the account balance is insufficient, then it should be paid from the estate's general assets.
   5. *Residuary Gift.* A **residuary gift** is a gift of the remainder of the estate and would include all assets not otherwise provided for.
G. <u>Renunciation</u>. A person who is to receive property by will or under the intestacy statute can **renounce** the property, and often does so if there are associated debts or liabilities which are greater than the value of the property.
H. <u>Ademption</u>. Where a testator has made a specific gift, **ademption** occurs if the testator no longer owns the property at death. The beneficiary receives nothing.
I. <u>Abatement</u>. The doctrine of **abatement** is applied where the estate is not large enough to pay all the gifts in the will. In some ways, abatement is similar to the distribution of a bankruptcy estate in that amounts at one level are fully paid before amounts at the next level receive anything. Of course, a will involves promises of gifts, rather than legal claims, but the distribution principles are similar. **Exam tip #3.**
   1. *General Gifts Are Paid Before Residuary Gifts.* If there are sufficient assets to pay all general gifts, they will be fully paid before any residuary gifts are paid.

2. *Proportionate Reductions If Insufficient Assets for All General Gifts.* When there are insufficient assets for all general gifts, the gifts to all beneficiaries will be reduced proportionately. For example, if there are two general bequests, one of $200,000 and one of $400,000 in an estate with only $400,000 in assets, then each beneficiary will receive $400,000/$600,000, or two thirds, of the respective bequest. The amounts paid here would be $133,333 and $266,667, respectively. Any residuary beneficiaries would receive nothing here, and would not receive anything unless the general beneficiaries were fully satisfied.

J. Per Stirpes and Per Capita Distribution. When property is left to **lineal descendants**, the distribution can be made in one of two ways. Assume that a decedent had three children, each of whom had three children. Further assume that the oldest of the decedent's children had predeceased the decedent, and that all nine grandchildren are still living.

1. *Per Stirpes Distribution.* Under *per stirpes* distribution, the property is divided at each generation, and where a member of the generation has predeceased the decedent, the predeceased person's share is divided among that person's descendants. Thus, in the example above, the two younger children of the decedent would each receive one-third, and the three children of the oldest child (who predeceased the decedent) would each take one third of the deceased oldest child's one-third share, or one-ninth of the estate.

2. *Per Capita Distribution.* Under *per capita* distribution, the property is divided equally among all living descendants. Thus, in this example, each of the two living children and each of the nine grandchildren would receive one-eleventh of the estate. **Exam tip #4.**

K. Void and Lapsed Gifts. **Void gifts** and **lapsed gifts** are ineffective, with the difference based on when they became ineffective.

1. *Void Gifts.* A void gift is one that was ineffective when the will was executed. A void gift can occur if the beneficiary was already dead or otherwise incapable of taking a gift at the time the will was executed. Any gift which is against public policy or is in violation of property law is also a void gift.

2. *Lapsed Gifts.* A lapsed gift occurs when a gift was valid at the time the will was executed, but fails due to subsequent events. The most common situations of lapsed gifts are:
   a. Beneficiary Predeceases the Decedent. The gift will fail if the beneficiary predeceases the decedent. The will might provide for an alternate disposition.
   b. Beneficiary Renounces the Gift.
   c. Condition Is Not Met for a Conditional Gift. For example, a bequest to "Bill, if he is married on the date of my death," will lapse if Bill is not married when the decedent dies.

L. Anti-Lapse Statutes. All states have various forms of **anti-lapse** statutes which attempt to pass property as the decedent would have intended. Thus, a probate court might order that a gift go to the descendant of the beneficiary even if the will did not explicitly direct that it do so.

M. Special Types of Wills. There are several special types of wills.

1. *Holographic Wills.* A **holographic will** is one that is handwritten and signed by the testator. Many states recognize them even though they are not witnessed.

2. *Noncupative Wills.* A **noncupative will**, also known as a **dying declaration**, is an oral will made in front of witnesses. They are generally valid only if made during the decedent's final illness.

3. *Joint Wills*. A **joint will** is a single document with more than one testator. They are sometimes valid with respect to one testator but invalid with respect to the other(s).

4. *Reciprocal Wills*. **Reciprocal wills**, or **mutual wills**, are two separate wills where the testators leave property to one another, and agree to the further disposition of the property when the last of them dies. They are contractual in nature, and the last survivor cannot change the disposition of the property to be contrary to the earlier agreement.

N. Intestate Succession. A person dying without a will is said to die **intestate**. Every state has an **intestacy statute** to provide for the disposition of property of intestate decedents.

   1. *Heirs*. A person receiving property under an intestacy statute is an **heir**. Note that persons receiving property under the terms of a will are not heirs, even though they are often referred to as heirs in everyday language. **Exam tip #5.**

   2. *Order of Distribution*. Most intestacy statutes provide for property to be distributed in the following order:
      a. Spouse.
      b. Children.
      c. Other Lineal Heirs. These include grandchildren, parents, and siblings.
      d. Collateral Heirs. These include aunts, uncles, nieces, and nephews.
      e. Other Next of Kin. These include cousins.

   3. *Escheat*. If there are no heirs to take the property, the property **escheats** to the state.

   4. *Partial Intestacy*. It is possible for a decedent's will to provide for the distribution of some, but not all, of the decedent's property. In this circumstance, the intestacy statute will apply only to the property not disposed of in the will.

   5. *In-laws Do Not Recover*. Most intestacy statutes provide for distribution of property only to blood relatives.

O. Probate. **Probate** is the court process by which a will is proven to be valid and the assets of the estate distributed. A **personal representative** is appointed by the probate court. This person is called an **executor** if named in the will and an **administrator** if no one is named in the will or the decedent dies intestate. The personal representative is a fiduciary with respect to the estate and is responsible for the gathering of the decedent's assets and ultimately for their distribution to the beneficiaries. The personal representative might need to sell certain assets of the estate, but can do so only as authorized by the will or the probate court. Probate court proceedings, including the wills probated, are public.

III. Trusts.

A. Generally. A **trust** is a legal arrangement where one person (the **settlor** or **trustor**) transfers legal title to a **trustee** for the benefit of one or more **beneficiaries**. The property held in trust is the **trust corpus** or **trust res**. The title, which was previously held fully by the settlor, is split, with the trustee acquiring legal title and beneficiaries acquiring equitable (or beneficial) title.

B. Multiple Roles Possible. It is possible for the same person to simultaneously operate in more than one of these roles.

   1. *Settlor as Trustee*. It is possible for the settlor to name herself as trustee.

   2. *Settlor as Beneficiary*. It is also possible for the settlor to name himself as beneficiary.

3. *Trustee Cannot Be Beneficiary.* The trustee cannot be the beneficiary because both the legal and equitable title would be vested in the same person, meaning that there would be no trust. If the beneficiary is but one of multiple beneficiaries, that beneficiary can serve as trustee because the equitable and legal title would not be in the exact same names.

C. <u>Types of Beneficiaries.</u> Persons entitled to receive income from a trust are known as **income beneficiaries.** Anyone who is entitled, at trust termination, to receive the trust corpus, or a portion of it, is a **remainderman.** Either of these can be an individual person, any number of persons, or an identified class, such as the settlor's grandchildren.

D. <u>Express Trusts.</u> An **express trust** is a trust voluntarily created by the settlor. They are usually created with a written **trust instrument** or **trust agreement.** A trust which takes effect during the settlor's life is an **inter vivos trust** whereas one created pursuant to a will to take effect at death is a **testamentary trust.** Note that whether inter vivos or testamentary depends on when the trust takes effect, not when it is set up. Creation of a valid express trust requires:

1. *Intention to Create a Trust.* The intent can be based on the terms of the agreement or based on the fact that the settlor has delivered the trust corpus to the trustee.

2. *Trust Property.* There must be existing trust property of some sort, which can be either a present or a future interest.

3. *Trustee.* For inter vivos trusts, the trustee must be identified because the property must be conveyed to the trustee. For a testamentary trust, the probate court can appoint a trustee if one is not named in the will or if a named trustee is unwilling or unable to serve.

4. *Beneficiary.* There must be at least one identified beneficiary for any trust except a charitable trust.

5. *Valid Trust Purpose.* A trust purpose is not valid if it is against public policy or requires illegal conduct to carry it out.

E. <u>No Perpetual Trusts.</u> The **Rule Against Perpetuities** does not allow any trust to last longer than the life of a living person (at trust creation) plus 21 years.

F. <u>Trustee Removal.</u> A trustee can be removed if it would be detrimental to the trust to not do so. Common reasons for removal include a breach of trust, lack of capacity (such as the trustee becoming insane), conflict of interest, or hostility between the trustee and the beneficiaries.

G. <u>Implied Trusts.</u> **Implied trusts** are imposed by law in one of two situations.

1. *Constructive Trusts.* A **constructive trust** is imposed by law to prevent unjust enrichment, fraud, or injustice. A constructive trust often occurs where the trustee of the constructive trust has wrongfully obtained title to the trust property.

2. *Resulting Trusts.* A **resulting trust** is based on the conduct of the parties and occurs where, as part of a transaction, one party has paid for and has legal title to the property of another. A resulting trust can also come about where an express trust fails and the trustee is holding trust property. The settlor is usually considered to be the beneficiary of a resulting trust.

H. <u>Charitable Trusts.</u> A **charitable trust** is one established for the benefit of society in general or for a segment of society. There are several issues specific to charitable trusts.

1. *Purpose Must Be Charitable.* Acceptable purposes including helping persons living in poverty, health promotion, the promotion of religion or education, and support of museums.

2. *Cannot Benefit Specific Individuals.* A charitable trust cannot benefit specific individuals, regardless of how deserving or needy they are. Designation of the beneficiaries by a group characteristic, such as those suffering from a particular disease, is acceptable.

3. *Cy Pres*. Under the doctrine of **cy pres**, if the purpose of a trust has been accomplished or has become impractical, a court will direct that the trust assets be applied to a trust with a purpose as close as possible to that of the original trust. For example, a court might order the assets of a trust formed to support an art museum to be transferred to a similar trust supporting a history museum if the art museum closes.

I. Spendthrift Trusts. A **spendthrift trust** is established in order to provide certain protections for the assets in the trust.

1. *Beyond the Reach of the Beneficiaries' Creditors*. The assets in a spendthrift trust cannot be reached by the beneficiaries' creditors except for amounts which have been paid out and are in the hands of beneficiaries. Certain creditors, such as the government or persons providing necessaries to the beneficiaries, can reach the trust assets.

2. *Beneficiaries Cannot Access Trust Corpus*. The beneficiaries have access to the trust corpus only as provided in the trust agreement. These trusts can be used to protect an imprudent beneficiary from squandering the assets as might occur if the assets were within the direct control of the beneficiary.

3. *Assets Are Not Protected If Settlor Is Beneficiary*. A settlor cannot protect his own assets from his creditors by placing them into a spendthrift trust. **Exam tip #6.**

J. Totten Trusts. A **Totten trust** applies to a bank account opened by a settlor who deposits funds in trust for a beneficiary. The account would typically be in the name of "John Doe in trust for Billy Doe." This is a revocable trust because the settlor can withdraw funds at any time and use them for any purpose; they need not be used for the benefit of the beneficiary. Any funds in the account at the settlor's death irrevocably become the property of the beneficiary.

K. Trust Termination. Most trusts are **irrevocable**, meaning that the settlor cannot later decide to recover assets from the trust or otherwise modify the terms of a trust. If the settlor reserves the right to withdraw assets or otherwise change the terms of the trust, it is a **revocable** trust. A settlor can terminate a revocable trust in accordance with any power of revocation reserved in the trust agreement. Otherwise, trusts terminate according to the trust agreement, which might be at a specific date, or upon the happening of a specified event, such as a beneficiary reaching a certain age. Perpetual trusts are not allowed, except for charitable trusts. **Exam tip #7.**

L. Trustee's Duties.

1. *Fiduciary Duty*. A trustee has a general **fiduciary duty** to the beneficiaries with respect to the trust assets.

2. *Duty of Loyalty*. The **duty of loyalty** requires that the trustee act in the trust's best interests and that the trustee keep personal assets separate from those of the trust.

3. *Duty of Care*. The trustee has a **duty of care** to act as a reasonable person in carrying out the trust. This can require the trustee to properly account and keep records relative to trust transactions, defend any lawsuits brought against the trust, and exercise reasonable judgment in making investment decisions involving trust assets.

4. *Duty to Carry Out the Terms of the Trust*.

M. Trustee's Rights and Powers. A trustee's powers can be express, or they can be implied as needed to carry out the purposes of the trust.

1. *Unanimous Consent for Joint Trustees*. Where there are multiple trustees, unanimous consent is needed for actions to be taken.

2. *Express Powers in Trust Agreement.* A trust agreement will often grant express powers to the trustee, such as the power to invest trust assets in a specified way or at the trustee's discretion.

3. *Implied Power to Sell Trust Property.* If not expressly granted, the trustee often has implied power to sell property, especially personal property.

4. *Implied Power to Lease Trust Property.* If not expressly granted, the trustee usually has implied power to lease trust property to others.

5. *Implied Power to Incur Expenses; Right to Reimbursement.* The trustee has implied powers to incur reasonable expenses in connection with the administration of trust assets and has a right to reimbursement for those expenses.

6. *No Implied Power to Borrow.* There is generally no implied power to borrow against trust assets or to pledge them as collateral.

N. Trustee Liability.

1. *Beneficiaries.* The beneficiaries are entitled to recover damages from the trustee for any breach of the fiduciary duty.

2. *Third Parties.* A trustee has personal liability to third parties for contracts entered into on behalf of the trust, but is entitled to indemnification from the trust if the trustee suffers a loss from a contract properly entered into.

O. Allocation Between Corpus and Income. Because the income beneficiaries and remaindermen of a trust are often different persons, the allocation of items between trust corpus (principal) and income is crucial. Allocation is an issue for income received, for the proceeds of a sale of trust assets, and for expenses paid. **Exam tip #8.**

1. *Receipts Allocated to Trust Income.* These items will be allocated to trust income, and therefore would belong to the income beneficiaries.
   a. Rent Received.
   b. Royalties Received.
   c. Interest Received.
   d. Cash Dividends Received.

2. *Receipts Allocated to Trust Corpus.*
   a. Proceeds From the Sale of Trust Assets. This applies to the full amount of the proceeds including any gain.
   b. Stock Dividends and Stock Splits.
   c. Amounts Received From a Corporate Liquidation.
   d. Mutual Fund Distributions.

3. *Expenses Chargeable to, or Paid Out of, Income.*
   a. Regular Administrative Expenses.
   b. Ordinary Repairs and Maintenance.
   c. Interest Payments, Including the Interest Portion of Loan Payments.
   d. Insurance Premiums.
   e. Regular Property Taxes.
   f. Legal Fees Related to Protecting the Income Interest.

4. *Expenses Paid Out of Principal.*
   a. Principal Portions of Loan Payments.
   b. Capital Improvements (Permanent) to Trust Property.
   c. Special Property Tax Assessments.
   d. Expenses Related to the Sale of Trust Property.
   e. Legal Fees Related to Protecting Trust Corpus.
5. *Items Allocated.*
   a. Trustee Fees. Any trustee fees are allocated based on the relative amounts of time spent by the trustee on income and corpus matters.
   b. Annuities. Annuity payments are partly a return of investment and partly an income component. They are allocated accordingly.

EXAM TIPS

1. The requirements for insurable interest are heavily tested. Be sure to remember that the insurable interest must exist at the time of the loss for property insurance and at the time of policy issuance for life insurance.
2. Candidates should memorize the coinsurance formula. When working coinsurance problems, candidates should check whether the question seeks the recovery from one insurance company or all of them. Lastly, candidates should compare the calculated amount to the two constraints.
3. Ademption and abatement can exist simultaneously or separate from each other. Be sure to understand how each works and to not confuse them.
4. The term "per capita" means per head, thus each lineal descendant receives the same amount.
5. The legal meaning of "heir" is an example of the precise nature of many terms related to wills. The distinction between a devise and bequest is another.
6. These various trust characteristics are not all mutually exclusive. For example, an express trust might also be a testamentary spendthrift trust.
7. Beneficiaries generally cannot terminate a trust, even if all of the beneficiaries agree. This would often go against the intent of the settlor, especially in the case of a spendthrift trust.
8. The allocation of items to trust corpus or income is heavily tested.

KEY CONCEPTS LIKELY TO BE TESTED ON THE CPA EXAM

1. The definition of insurable interest, what constitutes an insurable interest, and when the insurable interest must exist.
2. Coinsurance computations, for total recovery or for the recovery from one company.
3. Requirements for a valid will.   .
4. Distributions under a will, including per stirpes and per capita distributions, as well intestate distributions.
5. The requirements for the creation of a trust, and requirements for the various kinds of trusts.
7. Trustee rights and duties.
8. The proper allocation of trust receipts and disbursements to corpus or income.

KEY TERMS

Insurable Interest
Coinsurance Clause
Coinsurer
Pro Rata Clause
Deductible
Subrogation
Incontestability Clause
Will
Testator
Testatrix
Estate
Testamentary Capacity
Attestation Clause
Codicil
Subsequent Will
Simultaneous Death Statute
Devise
Legacy
Bequest
Specific Gift
General Gift
Demonstrative Gift
Residuary Gift
Renunciation of a Gift

Ademption
Abatement
Lineal Descendants
Per Stirpes
Per Capita
Void Gift
Lapsed Gift
Anti-Lapse Statute
Holographic Will
Nuncupative Will
Dying Declaration
Joint Will
Reciprocal Wills
Mutual Wills
Intestate
Intestacy Statute
Heir
Escheat
Probate
Personal Representative
Executor
Administrator
Trust
Settlor

Trustor
Trustee
Beneficiary
Trust Corpus
Trust Res
Income Beneficiary
Remainderman
Express Trust
Trust Instrument
Trust Agreement
Inter Vivos Trust
Testamentary Trust
Implied Trust
Constructive Trust
Resulting Trust
Charitable Trust
Cy Pres
Spendthrift Trust
Totten Trust
Irrevocable Trust
Revocable Trust
Fiduciary Duty
Duty of Loyalty
Duty of Care

MULTIPLE CHOICE QUESTIONS

1.   Law Nov 90 #19
Which of the following expenditures resulting from a trust's ownership of commercial real estate would be allocated to the trust's principal?
A. Sidewalk assessments.
B. Building management fees.
C. Real estate taxes.
D. Electrical repairs.

2.   Law May 94 #20
Which of the following events will terminate an irrevocable spendthrift trust established for a period of five years?
A. Grantor dies.
B. Income beneficiaries die.
C. Grantor decides to terminate the trust.
D. Income beneficiaries agree to the trust's termination.

Items 3 and 4 are based on the following:

In 1988, Pod bought a building for $220,000. At that time, Pod purchased a $150,000 fire insurance policy with Owners Insurance Co. and a $50,000 fire insurance policy with Group Insurance Corp. Each policy contained a standard 80% co-insurance clause. In 1992, when the building had a fair market value of $250,000, it was damaged in a fire.

3.   Law May 93 #59
How much would Pod recover from Owners if the fire caused $180,000 in damage?
A. $ 90,000.
B. $120,000.
C. $135,000.
D. $150,000.

4.   Law May 93 #60
How much would Pod recover from Owners and Group if the fire totally destroyed the building?
A. $160,000.
B. $200,000.
C. $220,000.
D. $250,000.

5.   Law Nov 92 #57
Daly tried to collect on a property insurance policy covering a house that was damaged by fire. The insurer denied recovery, alleging that Daly had no insurable interest in the house. In which of the following situations will the insurer prevail?
A. The house belongs to a corporation of which Daly is a 50% stockholder.
B. Daly is **not** the owner of the house but a long-term lessee.
C. The house is held in trust for Daly's mother and, on her death, will pass to Daly.
D. Daly gave an unsecured loan to the owner of the house to improve the house.

6.   Law R97 #9
Generally, which of the following parties would have the first priority to receive the estate of a person who dies without a will?
A. The state.
B. A child of the deceased.
C. A parent of the deceased.
D. A sibling of the deceased.

7.   Law R96 #4
Which of the following investments generally will be a violation of a trustee's fiduciary duty to the trust?
A. Secured first mortgages on land.
B. High interest unsecured loans.
C. Tax-exempt municipal bonds.
D. Guaranteed savings certificates.

8.   Law May 94 #15
Which of the following is **not** necessary to create an express trust?
A. A successor trustee.
B. A trust corpus.
C. A beneficiary.
D. A valid trust purpose.

9.   Law Nov 92 #6
Cox transferred assets into a trust under which Smart is entitled to receive the income for life. After Smart's death, the remaining assets are to be given to Mix. In 1991, the trust received rent of $1,000, stock dividends of $6,000, interest on certificates of deposit of $3,000, municipal bond interest of $4,000, and proceeds of $7,000 from the sale of bonds. Both Smart and Mix are still alive. What amount of the 1991 receipts should be allocated to trust principal?
A. $ 7,000.
B. $ 8,000.
C. $13,000.
D. $15,000.

OTHER OBJECTIVE FORMAT QUESTION

Law Nov 95 #2(b)

b. Items 1 through 5 are based on the following:

Under the provisions of Glenn's testamentary trust, after payment of all administrative expenses and taxes, the entire residuary estate was to be paid to Strong and Lake as trustees. The trustees were authorized to invest the trust assets, and directed to distribute income annually to Glenn's children for their lives, then distribute the principal to Glenn's grandchildren, per capita. The trustees were also authorized to make such principal payments to the income beneficiaries that the trustees determined to be reasonable for the beneficiaries' welfare. Glenn died in 1992. On Glenn's death there were two surviving children, aged 21 and 30, and one two-year-old grandchild.

On June 15, 1995, the trustees made the following distributions from the trust:

- Paid the 1992, 1993, and 1994 trust income to Glenn's children. This amount included the proceeds from the sale of stock received by the trust as a stock dividend.
- Made a $10,000 principal payment for medical school tuition to one of Glenn's children.
- Made a $5,000 principal payment to Glenn's grandchild.

Required:

Items 1 through 5 relate to the above fact pattern. For each item, select from List II whether only statement I is correct, whether only statement II is correct, whether both statements I and II are correct, or whether neither statement I nor II is correct. Blacken the corresponding oval on the *Objective Answer Sheet.*

List II
A. I only.
B. II only.
C. Both I and II.
D. Neither I nor II.

1. I. Glenn's trust was valid because it did **not** violate the rule against perpetuities.
    II. Glenn's trust was valid even thought it permitted the trustees to make principal payments to income beneficiaries.

2. I. Glenn's trust would be terminated if both of Glenn's children were to die.
    II. Glenn's trust would be terminated because of the acts of the trustees.

3. I. Strong and Lake violated their fiduciary duties by making any distributions of principal.
    II. Strong and Lake violated their fiduciary duties by failing to distribute the trust income annually.

4. I. Generally, stock dividends are considered income and should be distributed.
    II. Generally, stock dividends should be allocated to principal and remain as part of the trust.

5. I. The $10,000 principal payment was an abuse of the trustee's authority.
    II. The $5,000 principal payment was valid because of its payment to a non-income beneficiary.

ESSAY QUESTION (Estimated time -- 15 to 25 minutes)

Law Nov 94 #4

On January 1, 1993, Stone prepared an *inter vivos* spendthrift trust. Stone wanted to provide financial security for several close relatives during their lives, with the remainder payable to several charities. Stone funded the trust by transferring stocks, bonds, and a commercial building to the trust. Queen Bank was named as Trustee. The trust was to use the calendar year as its accounting period. The trust instrument contained no provision for the allocation of receipts and disbursements to principal and income.

The following transactions involving trust property occurred in 1993:

- The trust sold stock it owned for $50,000. The cost basis of the stock was $10,000. $40,000 was allocated to income and $10,000 to principal.

- The trust received a stock dividend of 500 shares of $10 par value common stock selling, at the time, for $50 per share. $20,000 was allocated to income and $5,000 to principal.

- The trust received bond interest of $18,000, which was allocated to income. The interest was paid and received semiannually on May 1 and November 1.

- The trust made mortgage amortization payments of $40,000 on the mortgage on the commercial building. The entire amount was allocated to principal.

On December 31, 1993, all the income beneficiaries and the charities joined in a petition to have the court allow the trust to be terminated and all trust funds distributed.

Required:

a. State the requirements to establish a valid *inter vivos* spendthrift trust and determine whether the Stone trust meets those requirements.

b. State whether the allocations made in the four transactions were correct and, if not, state the proper allocation to be made under the majority rule. Disregard any tax effect of each transaction.

c. State whether the trust will be terminated by the court and give the reasons for your conclusion.

EXPLANATIONS TO MULTIPLE CHOICE QUESTIONS

1. A is the correct answer. Sidewalk assessments would be chargeable to principle because the assessment theoretically increases the value of the property by having the sidewalks in the vicinity. Note that this question asks for the amount "allocated to" principal even though these are expenditures, and would actually be deducted from principal.

2. B is the correct answer. If the income beneficiaries die, the there is no purpose to keeping the trust assets in the trust, thus they must be distributed to any remaindermen.

3. C is the correct answer. This question tests the coinsurance formula which states that the: Recovery = ((Policy Face Amount)x(Loss Amount))/((Coinsurance %)x(FMV of the Property)). Recovery = (($150,000)x($180,000))/((80%)x($250,000)) = $135,000. This must be checked against the two constraints of the policy amount, $150,000, and the amount of the loss, $180,000. The calculated amount is less than both constraints, thus the calculated amount is the amount of the recovery. Note that this question sought the recovery from only one company, thus the face amount of that policy only is used in the formula.

4. B is the correct answer. Using the same formula as in the prior question results in: Recovery = (($200,000)x($250,000))/((80%)x($250,000)) = $250,000. This must then be checked against the two constraints of the policy amount, $200,000, and the amount of the loss, $250,000. Because the combined policy amount is only $200,000, the recovery is limited to that amount even though the formula results in a calculation of $250,000.

5. D is the correct answer. As an unsecured creditor of the owner of the house, Daly would not have a sufficiently direct interest in the house to have an insurable interest. The incorrect answer choices all represent persons who could suffer a direct financial loss if the house were damaged or destroyed.

6. B is the correct answer. Under the intestacy laws of most states, the spouse has the top priority to take assets of the deceased. Children generally have the second priority. Thus, of the parties listed, a child would have top priority.

7. B is the correct answer. The critical factor is that these loans are unsecured. With trusts, principal preservation is more important than high returns, unless the trust agreement provides otherwise.

8. A is the correct answer. It is not necessary to name a successor trustee because one can be named by the court should it become necessary. The incorrect answer choices all identify items required for the creation of a valid trust.

9. C is the correct answer. Stock dividends are allocated to principal. Furthermore, the proceeds from the sale of a trust asset are allocated to principal, including the amount representing any gain on the sale. Do not erroneously allocate any of a gain on the sale of assets to income.

EXPLANATION TO OTHER OBJECTIVE FORMAT QUESTION

1. C is the correct answer. The rule against perpetuities says that a trust cannot last longer than a current living person plus 21 years. The trust will terminate upon the death of Glenn's children who are current living persons at the time the trust is created. It is possible to put all kinds of provisions into a trust, including the discretion to make principal payments to income beneficiaries.

2. A is the correct answer. The trust provided for the distribution of principal to the grandchildren at the end of the lives of Glenn's children. The trustee's acts cannot terminate the trust, although certain improper acts of the trustees might result in their removal as trustees.

3. B is the correct answer. There was no violation of the fiduciary duty for the distributions of principal because the trust agreement specifically gave that power to the trustees. The trustees violated the trust agreement by not distributing income annually, and thereby breached their fiduciary duties.

4. B is the correct answer. Stock dividends are considered principal because the shareholder (in this case, the trust) has received nothing other than additional stock certificates. The trust would own the same percentage of the same corporation after the stock dividend as before. Notice that logic alone dictates that the two statements cannot both be correct.

5. D is the correct answer. The first statement is incorrect because the trust agreement allows discretionary principal distributions to the income beneficiaries. The second statement is incorrect because the remainderman will receive the principal upon the termination of the trust, but there is no express or implied power to distribute any principal to a remainderman prior to the trust's termination.

UNOFFICIAL AICPA ANSWER TO ESSAY QUESTION

Law Nov 94 #4

a. The requirements to establish a valid *inter vivos* spendthrift trust are as follows:

- Grantor
- Trust Res
- Intent to create a trust
- Lawful purpose
- Trustee and separate beneficiaries

Stone created a valid spendthrift trust. As grantor, Stone transferred stocks, bonds, and real estate (res) to the trust with a present intent to create the trust for the express lawful purpose of providing income for life to close relatives with the remainder left to charity. Stone designated Queen Bank as Trustee.

b.
- Incorrect. The entire proceeds from the sale of the stock should be allocated to principal.
- Incorrect. The entire amount of the stock dividend should be allocated to principal.
- Incorrect. One-third of the semiannual payment of bond interest received on May 1 had already accrued when the trust was created on January 1, 1993. Therefore, $3,000 should be allocated to principal and $15,000 to income.
- Correct/Incorrect. All mortgage payments representing a repayment of a mortgage debt should be allocated to principal. However, if any portion of the payment includes interest on the mortgage, that amount should be allocated to income.

c. The petition to have the trust terminated and distributed will fail. Even though all beneficiaries and remaindermen joined in the petition, termination of the trust, while any of the income beneficiaries is alive, would defeat the intent of the grantor in establishing a spendthrift trust.